8/6/82

237

COLLECTANEA HISTORICA

ESSAYS IN MEMORY OF STUART RIGOLD

(Photo. C.F. Stell)

STUART EBORALL RIGOLD,

1919-80

(Frontispiece

COLLECTANEA HISTORICA

ESSAYS IN MEMORY OF STUART RIGOLD

M.A., F.S.A., F.R.Hist.S., F.R.N.S., F.R.S.A.

Edited by
ALEC DETSICAS

KENT ARCHAEOLOGICAL SOCIETY
MAIDSTONE
1981

Produced by Alan Sutton Publishing Limited, Gloucester
Printed in Great Britain by
Page Brothers (Norwich) Limited.

Papers marked with an asterisk are published with the aid of a grant from the Department of the Environment.

ISBN 0 906746 02 7

CONTENTS

v

LIST OF CONTRIBUTORS

P. BENNETT, B.A., Deputy Director, Canterbury Archaeological Trust.

G.T.M. BERESFORD, F.S.A.,

T.F.C. BLAGG, M.A., Lecturer in Archaeology, School of Continuing Education, University of Kent at Canterbury.

W.J. BLAIR, M.A., Fellow and Praelector in Modern History, The Queen's College, Oxford.

S.A. BUTCHER, B.A., F.S.A., Principal Inspector of Ancient Monuments and Public Buildings, Department of the Environment.

J.G. COAD, M.A., F.S.A., Inspector of Ancient Monuments and Public Buildings, Department of the Environment.

C.R. COUNCER, F.S.A., Vice-President, Kent Archaeological Society.

A.P. DETSICAS, B.A., M.A., F.S.A., F.S.A.Scot., Honorary Editor, Kent Archaeological Society.

J. GEDDES, M.A., Ph.D., Inspector of Ancient Monuments and Public Buildings, Department of the Environment.

E.A. GEE, M.A., D.Phil., Hon. Dr. (York), F.S.A., F.R.Hist.S., formerly Investigator, Royal Commission on Historical Monuments (England).

R. GILYARD-BEER, O.B.E., M.A., F.S.A., formerly Assistant Chief Inspector of Ancient Monuments and Public Buildings, Department of the Environment.

H. GORDON SLADE, T.D., F.S.A.Scot., Directorate of Ancient Monuments and Public Buildings, Department of the Environment.

K.W.E. GRAVETT, M.Sc. (Eng.), F.S.A., Member of Council, Kent Archaeological Society.

L.R.A. GROVE, B.A., F.S.A., F.M.A., formerly Curator of Maidstone Museum and Art Gallery, Vice-President, Kent Archaeological Society.

M. HORTON, B.A.

F. JENKINS, M.A., Ph.D., F.S.A., Member of Council, Kent Archaeological Society.

R.F. JESSUP, F.S.A., Vice-President, Kent Archaeological Society.

J.S. JOHNSON, M.A., D.Phil., F.S.A., Inspector of Ancient Monuments and Public Buildings, Department of the Environment.

J.P.C. KENT, B.A., Ph.D., F.S.A., Deputy Keeper, Department of Coins and Medals, The British Museum.

J.K. KNIGHT, B.A., F.S.A., Inspector of Ancient Monuments and Public Buildings, Department of the Environment.

L. LEWIS, M.A., V-P.S.A.

C.P. MISCAMPBELL, M.A.

B.M. MORLEY, M.Sc., Inspector of Ancient Monuments and Public Buildings, Department of the Environment.

E.W. PARKIN, Member of Council, Kent Archaeological Society.

B.J. PHILP, A.C.I.S., M.B.I.M., F.A.A.I., Director, Kent Archaeological Rescue Unit.

D.F. RENN, B.A., Ph.D., F.S.A., F.I.A., F.S.S., Government Actuary's Department.

D. SHERLOCK, B.A., F.S.A., Inspector of Ancient Monuments and Public Buildings, Department of the Environment.

P. SMITH, B.A., F.S.A., Secretary, The Royal Commission on Ancient and Historical Monuments in Wales.

M. SPARKS, M.A.

T.W.T. TATTON-BROWN, B.A., Director, Canterbury Archaeological Trust.

A.J. TAYLOR, C.B.E., M.A., D.Litt., Dr. h.c. (Caen), F.B.A., Hon. V-P.S.A., F.R. Hist.S., formerly Chief Inspector of Ancient Monuments and Public Buildings, Department of the Environment.

P.J. TESTER, F.S.A., Member of Council, Kent Archaeological Society.

M.W. THOMPSON, M.A., Ph.D., F.S.A., Principal Inspector of Ancient Monuments and Public Buildings, Welsh Office.

J.C. THORN, Inspectorate of Ancient Monuments and Public Buildings, Department of the Environment.

J.J. WEST, M.A., B.Phil., Inspector of Ancient Monuments and Public Buildings, Department of the Environment.

C.J. YOUNG, M.A., D.Phil., F.S.A., Principal Inspector of Ancient Monuments and Public Buildings, Department of the Environment.

LIST OF FIGURES

LIST OF PLATES

Frontispiece   Stuart Eborall Rigold, 1919–1980.

ABBREVIATIONS AND REFERENCES

Antiq. Journ.	*The Antiquaries Journal*, Society of Antiquaries of London.
Arch. Camb.	*Archaeologia Cambrensis*, Cambrian Archaeological Association.
Arch. Cant.	*Archaeologia Cantiana*, Kent Archaeological Society, Maidstone.
BAR	*British Archaeological Reports*, Oxford.
Cal.	*Calendar of Letters and Papers, Henry VIII*, H.M.S.O., London.
CChR	*Calendar of Charter Rolls, Henry III, 1226-57*, London 1905.
CClR	*Calendar of Close Rolls, Henry III, 1259-61*, London 1934.
	Calendar of Close Rolls, Henry III, 1264-68, London 1937.
CIL	*Corpus Inscriptionum latinarum*, Mommsen *et al.* (Eds.), Berlin.
CPR	*Calendar of Patent Rolls, Edward I, 1281-92*, London 1893.
	Calendar of Patent Rolls, Edward II, 1317-21, London 1903.
	Calendar of Patent Rolls, Henry III, 1232-47, London 1906.
	Calendar of Patent Rolls, Henry III, 1258-66, London 1910.
	Calendar of Patent Rolls, Henry III, 1266-72, London 1913.
E.C.M.W.	*The early Christian Monuments of Wales*, V.E. Nash-Williams (Ed.), Cardiff 1950.
E.Y.C. 1947	*Early Yorkshire Charters, York Arch. Soc.*, vii (1947).
E.Y.C. 1963	*Early Yorkshire Charters, York Arch. Soc.*, xi (1963).
I.C.G.	*Inscriptions chrétiennes de la Gaule antérieures au VIIIe Siècle*, E. Le Blant (Ed.), i, Provinces gallicanes, Paris 1856; ii, Les sept Provinces, Paris 1865.
J.B.A.A.	*The Journal of the British Archaeological Association*, London.
KAR	*Kent Archaeological Review*
MBS Portfolio	*Portfolio of the Monumental Brass Society*, 1894- in progress, Monumental Brass Society, London
Med. Arch.	*Medieval Archaeology*, London.
M.G.H.	*Monumenta Germaniae historica*, Berlin.
M.P.L. Watts 31.8	Manchester Public Library: photograph by J. Watts, 1900.
M.P.L. Watts 31.11	Manchester Public Library: photograph by J. Watts, 1901.
N.R.	*Nouveau Recueil des Inscriptions chrétiennes de la Gaule antérieures au VIIIe Siècle*, E. Le Blant (Ed.), Paris 1892.
Pipe Rolls	Pipe Roll Society Publications.
Post-med. Arch.	*Post-medieval Archaeology*, London.
P.R.O.	Public Record Office, London.
P.R.O. C.133/63 (32)	Public Record Office: Inquisition *post mortem* following the death of Robert Burnell.
P.R.O. Works/14/568	Public Record Office: Office of Works file on the guardianship of Acton Burnell Castle.
PSAS	*Proceedings of the Society of Antiquaries of Scotland*, Edinburgh.
R.C.H.M.	The Royal Commission on Historical Monuments, London.

RH   *Rotuli Hundredorum*, London 1818.

RIB   R.G. Collingwood and R.P. Wright (Eds.), *The Roman Inscriptions of Britain. I: Inscriptions on Stone,* Oxford 1965.

S.C.L. 1834   S.C.L., *A brief historical and descriptive Account of Maidstone and its Environs.* 1834.

Sx. Arch. Coll.   *Sussex Archaeological Collections*, Sussex Archaeological Society, Lewes.

Sy. Arch. Coll.   *Surrey Archaeological Collections*, Surrey Archaeological Society, Guildford.

V & A   Victoria and Albert Museum, London.

VCH   *The Victoria County History*, London.

Y.A.S. 1891   Coucher, *Book of Selby I, York Arch. Soc.*, Record Series, x (1891).

(i) *Ancient authors*

Avitus of Vienne   *Letters*, Migne (Ed.), *Patrologia latina*, lix (1847).

Constantius of Lyon   *Vita Germani*, Levison (Ed.), *M.G.H. Scriptores rerum merovingiorum*, vii (1920), 247-83; Hoare (Ed.), 283-320, 1954.

Gervase   Chronicle of Gervase, *Gervasii Monachi cantuariensis Opera historica*, Rolls Series 1, Stubbs (Ed.), 536-7.

Gervase 1930   *Of the Burning and Repair of the Church of Canterbury Cathedral in 1174*, C. Cotton (Ed.), Friends of Canterbury Cathedral, Canterbury 1930.

Hydatius   *Chronicle*, Mommsen (Ed.) *M.G.H. Chronica minora*, ii, 1-36, Berlin 1894.

Orosius   *Historia adversus Paganos*, Migne (Ed.), *Patrologia latina*, xxxi, Paris 1846.

Prosper of Aquitaine   *Chronicle*, Mommsen (Ed.) *M.G.H. Auctores antiquissimi*, ix (*Chronica minora*, i), 464-85.

Sidonius Apollinaris   *Letters*, W.B. Anderson (Ed. and trans.), London 1965.

Sulpicius Severus   *Chronicle, Corpus Scriptorum ecclesiasticorum latinorum*, i, Vienna 1866.

Victricius of Rouen   *De Laude sanctorum*, Migne (Ed.), *Patrologia latina*, xx, Paris 1845.

Vita Columbani   Jonas, *Vita Columbani*, Levison (Ed.), *M.G.H. Scriptores rerum merovingiorum*, iv, 64-108.

Vita Filiberti   *Vita Filiberti Abbatis gemeticensis et heriensis*, Levison (Ed.), *M.G.H. Scriptores rerum merovingiorum*, v, 568-606.

Vita Germani   See Constantius of Lyon.

Vita Lupi   Krusch (Ed.), *Scriptores rerum merovingiorum*, vii, 295-302.

Vita Martini   See Sulpicius Severus.

(ii) *Modern Works*

Adhémar 1974   J. Adhémar, 'Les Tombeaux de la Collection Gaignières', *Gazette des Beaux-Arts,* July-September 1974.

Alcock 1966   N.W. Alcock, 'Medieval Buildings in Bishop's Clyst', *Trans. Devon Assoc.*, xcviii (1966).

Alcock 1967   L. Alcock, 'Excavations at Deganwy Castle, Caernarvonshire 1961-66', *Arch. Journ.*, cxxiv (1967), 190-201.

Alcock 1973   N.W. Alcock, *A Catalogue of Cruck Buildings*, London 1973.

Almqvist 1975   B. Almqvist, *The Stones explore Britain*, London 1975.

Altschul 1965   M. Altschul, *A baronial Family in medieval England: the Clares 1217-1314*, Baltimore 1965.

Andersen 1977   K.B. Andersen, *African traditional Architecture*, London 1977.

André 1900   J. Lewis André, 'Halnaker House', *Sx. Arch. Coll.*, xliii (1900), 201-13.

Archibald 1968	E.H.H. Archibald, *The wooden Fighting Ship in the Royal Navy*, Blandford 1968.
Atkinson 1947	T.D. Atkinson, *Local Style in English Architecture*, London 1947.
Aubert 1947	M. Aubert, *L'Architecture cistercienne en France*, Paris 1947.
Audin and Burnard 1959a	A. Audin and Y. Burnard, 'Alla Ricerca della Trace di Christianesimo sulle Tombe di Lione prima della Pace della Chiesa', *Rivista di Archeologia cristiana*, xxxv (1959), 51-70.
Audin and Burnard 1959b	A. Audin and Y. Burnard, 'Chronologie des Épitaphes romaines de Lyon', *Révue des Études anciennes*, lxi (1959), 320-52.
B. 1892	J.A.S.B., 'Acton Burnell: its Lords, Church and Castle', *Salop Notes and Queries*, i (1892), 104-6.
Babut 1913	C. Babut, in Gwynn 1913, cclxvii-cclxxv.
Badham 1979	S. Badham, *Brasses from the North-East*, London 1979.
Badham 1980	S. Badham, 'A lost bronze Effigy of 1279 from York Minster', *Antiq. Journ.*, lx (1980), 59-65.
Badham, Blair and Emmerson 1976	S. Badham, J. Blair and R. Emmerson, *Specimens of Lettering from English monumental Brasses*, London 1976.
Barton and Holden 1977	K.J. Barton and E.W. Holden, 'Excavations at Bramber Castle, Sussex, 1966-67', *Arch. Journ.*, cxxxiv (1977), 74-5.
Bateson 1891	M. Bateson (Ed.), 'Archbishop Warham's Visitation of 1511', *English Historical Review*, vi (1891), 18-35.
Battely 1711	J. Battely, *Antiquitates rutupinae*, Oxford 1711.
Bayley and Butcher 1981	J. Bayley and S.A. Butcher, 'Variations in Alloy Composition of Roman Brooches', *Révue d'Archéométrie*, iii (1981), 29-36.
Beale Poste 1847	Beale Poste, *The History of the College of All Saints, Maidstone*, Maidstone 1847.
Beazeley 1898	M. Beazeley, 'The Burial Place of Archbishop William Courtenay', *Arch. Cant.*, xxiii (1898), 49-50.
Beckynton 1934	*Register of Beckynton, Somerset Record Society*, xlix (1934).
Bennett, Frere and Stow 1981	P. Bennett, S.S. Frere and S. Stow, *Excavations at Canterbury Castle*, The Archaeology of Canterbury, i, Maidstone 1981.
Benoît 1954	F. Benoît, *Sarcophages paléochrétiens d'Arles et de Marseille, Gallia*, suppl. v, Paris 1954.
Berendsen 1967	A. Berendsen *et al.*, *Tiles, a general History*, London 1967.
Beresford 1971	G. Beresford, 'Tresmorn, St. Gennys', *Cornish Archaeol.*, x (1971), 55-74.
Beresford 1975	G. Beresford, *The medieval clay-land Village: Excavations at Goltho and Barton Blount*, Society for Medieval Archaeology Monograph Series, no. 6, London 1975.
Beresford 1976	G. Beresford, 'The Excavation of the deserted medieval Village of Goltho, Lincolnshire', *Château Gaillard, Études de Castellogie médiévale*, viii, Caen 1976.
Beresford 1977a	G. Beresford, 'Excavation Note on Caldecote, Hertfordshire', *Med. Arch.*, xxii (1978), 179-80.
Beresford 1977b	G. Beresford, 'Excavation of a moated House at Wintringham in Huntingdonshire', *Arch. Journ.*, cxxxiv (1977), 194-286.
Beresford, forthcoming	G. Beresford, *Goltho, the Development of an early medieval Manor*.
Bersu and Unversagt 1961	G. Bersu and W. Unversagt, 'Le Castellum de Fanum Martis', *Gallia*, xix (1961), 159-90.

Biddle 1969a	M. Biddle, 'Wolvesey: the *Domus quasi Palatium* of Henry de Blois in Winchester', in Taylor 1969,
Biddle 1969b	M. Biddle, 'Excavations at Winchester 1968', *Antiq. Journ.*, xlix (1969), 295-329.
Biddle 1972	M. Biddle, 'Excavations at Winchester 1970', *Antiq. Journ.*, lii (1970), 93-131.
Bieler 1949	L. Bieler, 'Insular Palaeography, present State and Problems', *Scriptorium*, iii (1949), 267-94.
Bieler 1968	L. Bieler, 'The Christianisation of the insular Celts during the sub-Roman Period and its Repercussions on the Continent', *Celtica*, viii (1968), 112-25.
Blagg 1980	T.F.C. Blagg, 'Roman civil and military Architecture in the Province of Britain: Aspects of Patronage, Influence and Craft Organisation', *World Archaeology*, xii (1980), 27-42.
Blair 1922	K.G. Blair, 'Notes on the Life History of *Rhizophagus parallelocollis* Gyll', *Entomologists' monthly Magazine*, lviii (1922), 80-3.
Blair 1978	J. Blair, 'The Bushingthorpes and their Monuments', *Trans. Monumental Brass Soc.*, xii (1978), 265-70.
Blair 1980	J. Blair, 'Henry Lakenham, Marbler of London, and a Tomb Contract of 1376', *Antiq. Journ.*, lx (1980), 66-74.
Blair and Honeyman 1954	C.H. Hunter Blair and H.L. Honeyman, *Warkworth Castle*, London 1954.
B.M. 1958	British Museum, *Antiquities of Roman Britain*, London 1958.
Bird 1933	C.H. Golding Bird, 'Meopham Church; XIV and XV Century stained Glass', *Trans. Dartford District Antiquarian Soc.*, iii (1933). 30.
Bird 1934	C.H. Golding Bird, *A History of Meopham: A Kentish Village from Saxon Times*, London 1934.
Boase 1953	T.S.R. Boase, *English Art 1110-1216*, Oxford 1953.
Böhme 1972	A. Böhme, 'Die Fibeln der Kastelle Saalburg und Zugmantel', *Saalburg Jahrbuch*, xxix (1972), 5-112.
Böhme 1974	H.W. Böhme, *Germanische Grabfunde des 4 bis 5 Jahrhunderts*, Münchner Beiträge zur Vor- und Frühgeschichte, xix, Munich 1974.
Bond 1905	F. Bond, *Gothic Architecture in England*, London 1905.
Bony 1949	J. Bony, 'French Influences on the Origins of English Gothic Architecture,' 1949.
Bony 1965	J. Bony, *Origines des Piles gothiques anglaises*, Berlin 1965.
Bony 1979	J. Bony, *The English Decorated Style*, Oxford 1979.
Bord 1976	J. and C. Bord, *Mysterious Britain*, St. Albans 1976.
Brandon 1848	R. and J.A. Brandon, *Parish Churches*, London 1848.
Brandon 1903	R. and J.A. Brandon, *An Analysis of Gothic Architecture*, (London 1844-47) Rev. edn. Edinburgh 1903.
Brodribb, Hands and Walker 1971	A.C.C. Brodribb, A.R. Hands and D.R. Walker, *Excavations at Shakenoak Farm, near Wilcote, Oxfordshire*, ii, Oxford 1971.
Brown 1976	P.D.C. Brown in Jarrett 1976, 76-82.
Browne 1847	J. Browne, *The History of the Metropolitan Church of St. Peter, York*, London 1847.
Buchanan 1957	R.H. Buchanan, 'Thatch and Thatching in north-east Ireland', *Gwerin*, iii (1957), 123-42.
Buckland 1979	P.C. Buckland, 'Thorne Moors: a palaeoecological Study of a Bronze Age Site', Occasional Publication no. 8, Department of Geography, University of Birmingham 1979.

Bushe-Fox 1926	J.P. Bushe-Fox, *First Report on the Excavation of the Roman Fort at Richborough, Kent*, Reports of the Research Committee of the Society c Antiquaries of London, vi, Oxford 1926.
Bushe-Fox 1928	J.P. Bushe-Fox, *Second Report on the Excavation of the Roman Fort at Richborough, Kent*, Reports of the Research Committee of the Society of Antiquaries of London, vii, Oxford 1928.
Bushe-Fox 1932	J.P. Bushe-Fox, *Third Report on the Excavation of the Roman Fort at Richborough, Kent*, Reports of the Research Committee of the Society of Antiquaries of London, x, Oxford 1932.
Bushe-Fox 1949	J.P. Bushe-Fox, *Fourth Report on the Excavation of the Roman Fort at Richborough, Kent*, Reports of the Research Committee of the Society of Antiquaries of London, xvi, Oxford 1949.
Butcher 1977	S.A. Butcher, 'Enamels from Roman Britain' in M.R. Apted, R. Gilyard-Beer and A.D. Saunders (Eds.), *Ancient Monuments and their Interpretation*, Chichester 1977.
Butler 1959	R.F. Butler, 'Medieval Brimpsfield: Reports and Reflections', *Proc. Cotteswold Nat. Fld. Club*, xxxiii (1959), 113-22.
Carpenter 1972	D. Carpenter, 'Westminster Abbey; some Characteristics of its Sculpture', *J.B.A.A.*, xxxv (1972), 1-14.
Carr 1973	R.D. Carr, 'Excavation Note on Wallingford Castle', *Med. Arch.*, xvii (1973), 159-61.
Casey 1979	J. Casey (Ed.), *The End of Roman Britain*, BAR 71, Oxford 1979.
Cave-Browne n.d.	J. Cave-Browne, *The History of the Parish Church of All Saints, Maidstone*, Maidstone n.d.
Chadwick 1959a	N.K. Chadwick (Ed.), *Studies in early British History*, Cambridge 1959.
Chadwick 1959b	O. Chadwick, 'The Evidence of Dedications in the early History of the Welsh Church', in Chadwick 1959a, 173-88.
Challis 1978	C.E. Challis, *The Tudor Coinage*, Manchester 1978.
Cherry 1979	M. Cherry, 'The Courtenays, Earls of Devon: the Formation and Disintegration of a late medieval aristocratic Affinity', *Southern History*, i (1979), 71-97.
Clapham 1930	A.W. Clapham, *English romanesque Architecture before the Conquest*, Oxford 1930.
Clapham and Godfrey 1913	A.W. Clapham and W.G. Godfrey, *Some famous Buildings and their Story*, London 1913.
Clarijs 1970	P. Clarijs, *Een Huis vol Tegels*, Amsterdam 1970.
Clarke 1979	G. Clarke, *The Roman Cemetery at Lankhills*, Winchester Studies iii, Oxford 1979.
Clarke and Stoyel 1975	D. Clarke and A. Stoyel, *Otford in Kent*, Otford 1975.
Clay 1959	Sir C. Clay (Ed.), *York Minster Fasti, Yorks. Arch. Soc.*, Records Series, cxxiv (1959).
Clifton-Taylor 1972	A. Clifton-Taylor, *Pattern of English Building*, London 1972.
Collinge 1978	J.M. Collinge, *Navy Board Officials 1660-1832*, University of London, Institute of Historical Research, 1978.
Collingwood Bruce 1978	J. Collingwood Bruce, *Handbook to the Roman Wall*, 13th edn. C. Daniels (Ed.), Newcastle-upon-Tyne 1978.
Colvin 1963	H.M. Colvin, R.A. Brown and A.J. Taylor (Eds.), *The History of the King's Works*, vols. i and ii, London 1963.

Colvin 1973	H.M. Colvin, R.A. Brown and A.J. Taylor (Eds.), *The History of the King's Works*, vol. vi, London 1973.
Colvin 1975	H.M. Colvin, R.A. Brown and A.J. Taylor (Eds.), *The History of the King's Works*, vol. iii, London 1975.
Compton MSS.	Lord Alwyn Compton, *Manuscript Plan of Tile Pavements and Tracings of Tiles*, Library, Society of Antiquaries of London.
Connor 1970	A.B. Connor, *Monumental Brasses in Somerset*, Bath 1970.
Cotton 1939	C. Cotton, 'St. Austin's Abbey, Canterbury. Treasurers' Accounts 1468-9 and others', *Arch. Cant.*, li (1939), 66-107.
Coulson 1979	C.L.H. Coulson, 'Structural Symbolism in medieval Castle Architecture', *J.B.A.A.*, cxxxii (1979), 73-90.
Cunliffe 1968	B.W. Cunliffe (Ed.), *Fifth Report on the Excavation of the Roman Fort at Richborough, Kent*, Reports of the Research Committee of the Society of Antiquaries of London, xxiii, Oxford 1968.
Cunliffe 1980	B. Cunliffe, 'Excavations at the Roman Fort at Lympne, Kent 1976-78', *Britannia*, xi (1980), 227-88.
Curnow 1980	P.E. Curnow, 'Some Developments in military Architecture *c.* 1200. Le Coudray Salbart', in R.A. Brown (Ed.), *Proceedings of the second (Battle) Conference in 1979*, Woodbridge 1980.
Curzon and Tipping 1929	Marquis Curzon and H.A. Tipping, *Tattershall Castle*, London 1929.
Daniel 1972	G.E. Daniel, *Megaliths in History*, London 1972.
de Bouard 1975	M. de Couard, *Château Gaillard VII*, Caen 1975.
Dehaisnes 1886	C. Dehaisnes, *Documents et Extraits divers concernant l'Histoire de l' Art dans la Flandre, l'Artois et le Hainault*, Lille 1886.
Deichmann 1969	F.W. Deichmann, *Ravenna: Geschichte und Monumente*, Wiesbaden 1969.
Deichmann 1976	F.W. Deichmann, *Hauptstadt des spätantiken Abendlands*, ii, Wiesbaden 1976.
De Jonge 1971	C.H. De Jonge, *Dutch Tiles*, New York 1971.
De Knock 1976	P. De Knock, 'Tegelnummer', *Driemaandelijks heemkundig Tijschrift voor Poperinge en Omstrecken*, vi (1976).
Delatte 1959	P. Delatte, *Commentary on the Rule of St. Benedict*, 1959.
Dimier 1949	M.-A. Dimier, *Recueil de Plans d'Églises cisterciennes*, Paris 1949.
Dobson 1972	B. Dobson, 'The later Middle Ages', in G.E. Aylmer and R. Cant (Eds.), *A History of York Minster*, Oxford 1977.
Drury and Norton, forthcoming	P.J. Drury and E.C. Norton, *A Census of medieval Floor Tiles in the Counties of Essex, Suffolk and Cambridgeshire, BAR* forthcoming.
Drury and Pratt 1975	P.J. Drury and G.D. Pratt, 'A late 13th and early 14th Century Tile Factory at Danbury, Essex', *Med. Arch.*, xix (1975), 91-164.
Du Boulay 1966	F.R.H. Du Boulay, *The Lordship of Canterbury*, London 1966.
Duchesne 1910	L. Duchesne, *Fastes épiscopaux de l'ancienne Gaule*, Paris 1910.
Dufty 1970	A.R. Dufty, 'Corfe Castle', in *Inventory of the historic Monuments in Dorset: South-East*, London 1970.
Dumbreck 1958	W.V. Dumbreck, 'The Lowy of Tonbridge', *Arch. Cant.*, lxxii (1958), 138-47.
Duncan 1890	L.L. Duncan (Ed.), 'Calendar of Wills relating to the County of Kent', Lewisham Antiquarian Society, 1890.
Duncan 1895	L.L. Duncan, 'The Will of William Courtenay', *Arch. Cant.*, xxiii (1895), 55.
Duncan 1906	L.L. Duncan (Ed.), *Testamenta Cantiana: W. Kent*, Kent Archaeological Society 1906.

Duncan 1924	L.L. Duncan, *Index of Wills proven in the Rochester Consistory Court 1440-1561*, Kent Archaeological Society 1924.
Duncombe 1784	J. Duncombe, *The History and Antiquities of the two Parishes of Reculver and Herne*, London 1784.
Eames 1977	E.S. Eames, 'Medieval Floor Tiles', in J. Schofield, 'Excavations South of Edinburgh High Street 1973-4', *PSAS*, cvii (1977), 211-3.
Eames 1980	E.S. Eames, *Catalogue of medieval lead-glazed earthenware Tiles in the Department of medieval and later Antiquities, British Museum*, London 1980.
Edleston 1935	R.H. Edleston, 'Incised monumental Slabs', *63rd annual Report of the Peterborough Nat. Hist., Sc. and Arch. Soc.*, 1935.
Edwards 1912	T. Edwards, 'Dyserth Castle', *Arch. Camb.*, xii (1912), 263-94.
Edwards 1940	J.G. Edwards (Ed.), *Littere Wallie*, Cardiff 1940.
Emery 1970	A. Emery, *Dartington Hall*, Oxford 1970.
Emmerson 1978	R. Emmerson, 'Monumental Brasses: London Designs *c.* 1420-85', *J.B.A.A.*, cxxxi (1978), 50-78.
Emmerson 1980	R. Emmerson, 'St. Thomas Cantilupe's Tomb and Brass of 1287', *Bull. of the International Society for the Study of Church Monuments*, ii (1980), 41-5.
Elliott, n.d.	D.J. Elliott, *Tonbridge Castle History*, Tonbridge n.d.
Ellison, forthcoming	A.B. Ellison, Excavations at Uley, Gloucestershire.
Elmham 1858	Thomas of Elmham, 'Chronicle of the Abbey, Trinity Hall', in C. Hardwick (Ed.) *Chronicles and Memorials*, VIII Rolls Series, London 1858.
Emden 1977	A.B. Emden, *Medieval decorated Tiles in Dorset*, Chichester 1977.
Ettlinger 1973	E. Ettlinger, *Die römischen Fibeln in der Schweiz*, Bern 1973.
Evans 1904	S. Evans, 'Excavations at St. Augustine's Abbey Canterbury', *Arch. Cant.*, xxvi (1904), 1-8.
Eyton 1858	R.W. Eyton, *Antiquities of Shropshire*, vi (1858), 121-39.
Faulkner 1958	P.A. Faulkner, 'Domestic Planning from the twelfth to the fourteenth Centuries', *Arch. Journ.*, cxv (1958), 150-83.
Faulkner 1963	P.A. Faulkner, 'Castle Planning in the fourteenth Century', *Arch. Journ.*, cxx (1963), 215-35.
Ferrey 1870	E.B. Ferrey, *South Winfield Manor, Derbyshire*, London 1870.
Fowler 1903	J.T. Fowler (Ed.), *The Rites of Durham, Surtees Soc.*, cvii (1903).
Frend 1952	W.H.C. Frend, *The Donatist Church*, Oxford 1952.
Frere 1974	S.S. Frere, *Britannia: A History of Roman Britain*, London 1974.
Frere 1978	S.S. Frere, *Britannia: A History of Roman Britain*, 2nd edn., London 1978.
Fulford 1979	M. Fulford, 'Pottery Production and Trade at the end of Roman Britain', in Casey 1979, 120-32.
Geijer 1953	A. Geijer, 'En trøndersk broderiverkstad från medeltiden', *Viking* 1953.
Gibson 1695	E. Gibson (Ed.), *Camden's Britannia*, London 1695.
Giesler 1978	V. Giesler, 'Jüngerkaiserzeitliche Nietknopsforen mit Dreipunkthalterung vom Typ Leuna', *Saalburg Jahrbuch*, xxxv (1978), 5-56.
Godfrey 1929	W.H. Godfrey, 'Some medieval Hospitals of east Kent', *Arch. Journ.*, lxxxvi (1929), 99-110.
Godfrey 1942	W. Godfrey, 'La Warr Family and Halnaker House', *Sx. Arch. Coll.*, lxxxii (1942).
Goodburn and Bartholomew 1976	R. Goodburn and P. Bartholomew, *Aspects of the Notitia Dignitatum*, BAR 15S, Oxford 1976.
Graham 1952	R. Graham (Ed.), *Registrum Robert Winchelsey*, Oxford 1952.

Gray 1978   P. Gray, *St. Helen's Church, Cliffe, Kent — The Inside Story*, 1978.

Grayling 1913   F. Grayling, *Kent*, (County Churches Series), London 1913.

Green 1969-1975   C.J.S. Green, 'Interim Reports on Excavations in the Roman Cemetery at Poundbury, Dorchester', *Proc. Dorset Nat. Hist. and Arch. Soc.*, xc (1969) to xcvii (1975).

Green 1976   M. Green, *The Religions of civilian Roman Britain*, BAR 24, Oxford 1976.

Greenhill 1952   F.A. Greenhill, 'An incised Slab with Inlays from Santarém, Portugal', *Trans. Monumental Brass Soc.*, ix (1952), 39-42.

Gronemann 1959   A. Gronemann, '16th Century Floors in the Nassau Castle at Breda', *Vrien den van de Nederlands Ceramiek*, xvi (1959), 1-32.

Grosjean 1957a   P. Grosjean, 'Notes d'Hagiographie celtique 28: La seconde Visite de S. Germain d'Auxerre en Grande-Bretagne', *Analecta Bollandiana*, lxxv (1957), 174-80.

Grosjean 1957b   P. Grosjean, 'Notes d'Hagiographie celtique 29: Le dernier Voyage de S. Germain d'Auxerre', *Analecta Bollandiana*, lxxv (1957), 180-5.

Grove 1953   L.R.A. Grove, 'Medieval Objects from Kent', *Arch. Cant.*, lxvi (1953), 152.

Grove 1962   L.R.A. Grove, 'Archaeological Notes from Maidstone Museum', *Arch. Cant.*, lxxvii (1962), 205-6.

Gunstone 1964   A.J.H. Gunstone, 'The Date of the Three Shire Stones, near Batheaston', *Trans. Bristol and Glos. Arch. Soc.*, lxxxii (1964), 210.

Gwynn 1913   J. Gwynn, *Liber Ardmachanus*, Dublin 1913.

Hadingham 1975   E. Hadingham, *Circles and standing Stones*, London 1975.

Hall 1976   R.A. Hall, *The Viking Kingdom of York*, York 1976.

Hamilton-Thompson 1912   A. Hamilton-Thompson, *Military Architecture in England during the Middle Ages*, London 1912.

Hanson 1968   R.P.C. Hanson, *St. Patrick; His Origins and Career*, Oxford 1968.

Harrison 1969   A.C. Harrison, 'Excavations on the Site of St. Mary's Hospital, Strood', *Arch. Cant.*, lxxxiv (1969), 139-60.

Hartshorne 1846   C.H. Hartshorne, 'On the ancient Parliament and Castle of Acton Burnell', *Arch. Journ.*, ii (1846), 325-38.

Harvey 1969   J.H. Harvey (Ed.), *William Worcestre, Itineraries*, Oxford 1969.

Harvey 1970   J. Harvey, *The Perpendicular Style*, London 1970.

Hassall and Tomlin 1979   M.W.C. Hassall and R.O. Tomlin, 'Roman Britain in 1978', *Britannia*, x (1979), 339-56.

Hasted 1797   E. Hasted, *The History and Topography of the County of Kent*, vol. iii, 1797.

Hasted 1800   E. Hasted, *The History and Topography of the County of Kent*, vols. x and xi, 1800.

Hawkes 1968   S.C. Hawkes, 'The physical Geography of Richborough', in Cunliffe 1968, 224-31.

Hawkes 1974   S.C. Hawkes, 'Some recent Finds of late Roman Buckles', *Britannia*, v (1974), 386-93.

Hawkes and Dunning 1961   S.C. Hawkes and G.C. Dunning, 'Soldiers and Settlers in Britain, fourth to fifth Centuries', *Med. Arch.*, v (1961), 1-70.

Hayes 1972   J. Hayes, *Late Roman Pottery*, London 1972.

Henry 1967   F. Henry, *The Irish Art during the Viking Invasions*, London 1967.

Hemp 1949   W.J. Hemp, 'A reused Memorial at Hook Norton', *Trans. Monumental Brass Soc.*, viii (1949), 205-6.

Hewett 1962-3	C.A. Hewett, 'Structural Carpentry in medieval Essex', *Med. Arch.*, vi-vii (1962-3), 240-71.
Hewett 1969	C.A. Hewett, *The Development of Carpentry, 1200-1700*, London 1969.
Higham 1977	R.A. Higham, 'Excavations at Okehampton Castle, Devon. Part 1: the Motte and Keep', *Proc. Devon Arch. Soc.*, xxxv (1977), 3-42.
Higham, forthcoming	R.A. Higham, *Okehampton Castle: official Handbook*, London, forthcoming.
Hilton, n.d.	J. Hilton, *Tonbridge Castle, a short History*, Hadlow, n.d.
Hoare 1954	F.W. Hoare, *The western Fathers*, London 1954.
Hoffmann 1964	M. Hoffmann, *The warp-weighted Loom*, Oslo 1964.
Holmes 1957	G.A. Holmes, *The Estates of the higher Nobility in fourteenth-century England*, Cambridge 1957.
Hooper 1936	W. Hooper, 'The Pilgrims' Way and its supposed Pilgrim Use', *Sy. Arch. Coll.*, xliv (1936), 47-83.
Horion 1960	A. Horion, *Faunistik der mitteleuropäischen Käfer*, Uberlingen-Bodensee 1960.
Horton, forthcoming	M.C. Horton, 'The Floor Tiles', in T.W.T. Tatton-Brown, *Excavations in the Cathedral Precincts, Canterbury*, forthcoming.
Horton and Drury, forthcoming	M.C. Horton and P.J. Drury, 'Contacts across the North Sea in the medieval Floor Tile Industry', forthcoming.
Hussey 1876	R.C. Hussey, 'Documents from the Archives of Christ Church, Canterbury', *Arch. Cant.*, x (1876), 316-19.
Hussey 1911	A. Hussey, 'Chapels in Kent', *Arch. Cant.*, xxix (1911), 217-58.
Hussey 1936a	A. Hussey (Ed.), *Kent Chantries*, Kent Archaeological Society Records Branch, xii (1936).
Hussey 1936b	A. Hussey (Ed.), *Kent Obit and Lamp Rents*, Kent Archaeological Society Records Branch, xii (1936).
Hutchins 1815	J. Hutchins, *History of Dorset*, 2nd edn., London 1815.
Innocent 1971	C.F. Innocent, *English Building Construction*, Newton Abbot 1971.
Iron 1954	D. Iron, 'Excavations at Clifford Castle 1952', *Trans. Woolhope Field Club*, xxxiv (1954), 82-4.
Jaffé 1885	Jaffé, *Regesta Pontificum romanorum*, i, 1885.
Jarrett 1976	M.G. Jarrett, *Maryport, Cumbria: A Roman Fort and its Garrison*, Kendal 1976.
Jessup 1951	R. Jessup, 'Two Mounds at Nash Court, Boughton', *Arch. Cant.*, lxiv (1951), 35-8.
Jessup 1958	R. Jessup, 'Barrows and walled Cemeteries in Roman Britain', *J.B.A.A.*, xxii (1958), 1-32.
Jessup 1975	R. Jessup, *Man of many Talents: an informal Biography of James Douglas 1753-1819*, London 1975.
Jessup 1977	R. Jessup, 'The Barrow on Fawley Mount', *Antiq. Journ.*, lvii (1977), 94-5.
Jessup and Zarnecki 1953	R. Jessup and G. Zarnecki, 'The Faussett Pavilion', *Arch. Cant.*, lxvi (1953), 1-14.
Johns 1970	C.N. Johns, *Criccieth Castle: Official Handbook*, London 1970.
Johns 1971	C.N. Johns, 'The Restoration of Caerphilly Castle', *Caerphilly*, iii (1971), 20-5.
Johns 1978	C.N. Johns, *Caerphilly Castle: Official Guidebook*, London 1978.
Johnson 1963	C. Johnson, 'Ten British Species of the Genus *Rhizophagus* Herbst. (Col. Rhizophagidae)', *Proc. and Trans. Manchester Entomol. Soc.*, 1961-3, 3-9.
Johnson 1970	J.S. Johnson, 'The Date of the Construction of the Saxon Shore Fort at Richborough', *Britannia*, i (1970), 240-8.

Johnson 1980 S. Johnson, 'Excavations at Conisbrough Castle 1973-77', *Yorks. Arch. Journ.*, lii (1980), 59-88.

Johnston 1977 D.E. Johnston, *The Saxon Shore*, CBA Research Report no. 18, London 1977.

Jones 1964 A.H.M. Jones, *The later Roman Empire*, Oxford 1964.

Jones 1974 B. Jones, *Follies and Grottoes*, London 1974.

Jope 1961 E.M. Jope (Ed.), *Studies in Building History*, London 1961.

Kautzsch 1936 R. Kautzsch, *Kapitellstudien*, Berlin and Leipzig 1936.

Keller 1971 E. Keller, *Die spätrömischen Grabfunde in Südbayern*, Münchner Beiträge zur Vor- und Frühgeschichte, xiv, Munich 1971.

Kent 1964 J.P.C. Kent, 'Five Tudor Notes', *British Num. Journ.*, xxxii (1964), 161-4.

Kent 1979 J.P.C. Kent, 'The End of Roman Britain: the literary and numismatic Evidence reviewed' in Casey 1979, 15-27.

Kilburne 1659 R. Kilburne, *A Topographie or Survey of the County of Kent*, London 1659.

King 1782 E. King, 'Sequel to the Observations on ancient Castles', *Archaeologia*, vi (1782), 231-375.

King 1963 D.J.C. King, *Llanstephan Castle: Official Guidebook*, London 1963.

King 1978 D.J.C. King, 'Pembroke Castle', *Arch. Camb.*, cxxvii (1978), 75-121.

King and Perks 1956 D.J.C. King and J.C. Perks, 'Llangibby Castle', *Arch. Camb.*, cv (1956), 96-132.

Kingsford 1909 C.L. Kingsford, 'Sir Otho de Grandison 1238 (?) — 1328', *Trans. of the Royal Hist. Soc.*, iii (1909), 125-95.

Kingsford 1925 C.L. Kingsford, *Report on the Manuscripts of Lord De L'Isle and Dudley preserved at Penshurst Place*, Royal Commission on Historical Manuscripts, i (1925), 171-218.

Kirk 1949 J.R. Kirk, 'Bronzes from Woodeaton', *Oxoniensia*, xiv (1949), 1-45.

Knapp 1956 G.E.C. Knapp, 'Flemish medieval paving Tiles in Hampshire', *Proc. Hants. Field Club and Arch. Soc.*, xx (1956), 29-33.

Knoop and Jones 1967 D. Knoop and G.P. Jones, *The medieval Mason*, Manchester 1967.

Knowles 1932 W.H. Knowles, *Trans. Bristol and Gloucester Arch. Soc.*, liv (1932), 167-201.

Knowles 1949 D. Knowles, *The monastic Order in England*, 2nd edn., Cambridge 1949.

Knowles 1951 D. Knowles (Ed.), *Decreta Lanfranci Monachis Cantuariensibus transmissa*, 1951.

Kok 1949 I. Kok, 'De Hollandse Tegel', *Heemschut Series*, lxvii (1949).

Korf 1963 D. Korf, *Dutch Tiles*, London 1963.

Krautheimer 1979 R. Krautheimer, *Early Christian and Byzantine Architecture*, 3rd edn., Harmondsworth 1979.

Kroeber 1952 A.L. Kroeber, 'Stimulus Diffusion', in *The Nature of Culture*, Chicago 1952, 344-57.

Lambarde 1826 W. Lambarde, *A Perambulation of Kent* (1576), London 1826.

Lane 1960 A. Lane, *A Guide to the Collection of Tiles*, London 1960.

Laurent 1922 M. Laurent, 'Guido di Savino and the Earthernware of Antwerp', *Burlington Magazine*, xli (1922), 288-97.

Laver 1909 H. Laver, 'Ancient Type of Huts at Athelney', *Proc. Somerset Arch. Soc*, lv (1909), 175-80.

Lawrence 1960 C.H. Lawrence, *St. Edmund of Abingdon*, Oxford 1960.

Leach 1978 R. Leach, 'An Investigation into the Use of Purbeck Marble in medieval England', Crediton 1978.

Leask 1955-66 H.G. Leask, *Irish Churches and monastic Buildings*, Dundalk 1955-66.

Leech, forthcoming — R. Leech, 'Excavations at Catsgore, Somerset', forthcoming.

Leland 1530 — J. Leland, *Itinerary, c.* 1530.

Leland 1769 — J. Leland, *The Itinerary of John Leland the Antiquary*, vii, part 2, appendix to 3rd edn. published from Stowe's transcript, 1769.

Lerat 1956 — L. Lerat, 'Les Fibules gallo-romaines', *Annales littéraires de l'Université de Besançon*, iii (1956), 1-48.

Lethaby 1906 — W.R. Lethaby, *Westminster Abbey and the King's Craftsmen*, London 1906.

Lethaby 1925 — W.R. Lethaby, *Westminster Abbey re-examined*, London 1925.

Levison 1920 — W. Levison, Introduction to Edition of Constantius of Lyon *Vita Germani*, 1920.

Levison 1941 — W. Levison, 'St. Alban and St. Albans', *Antiquity*, xvi (1941), 337-59.

Lewis 1736 — J. Lewis, *The History and Antiquities of the Isle of Thanet*, London 1736.

Lewis 1939 — A. Lewis, 'Roger Leyburn and the Pacification of England 1265-7', *English Hist. Rev.*, liv (1939), 193-214.

Lewis 1945 — N.B. Lewis, 'The Organisation of indentured Retinues in fourteenth-century England', *Trans. of the Royal Hist. Soc.*, xxvii (1945), 29-39.

Lewis 1971 — L. Lewis, 'Bedale through Georgian Eyes', *Country Life*, cxlix (1971), 464-7; 'Tales of Old Bedale', *ibid.*, 554-8; 'Bedale Hall, Yorkshire', *ibid.*, 592-5.

Lewis 1975 — L. Lewis (Ed.), *Hird's Annals of Bedale*, North Yorks. County Record Office Publications, no. 2, 1975.

Liversidge 1968 — J. Liversidge, *Britain in the Roman Empire*, London 1968.

Lloyd 1883 — H.R. Lloyd, 'Clyffe-at-Hoo Rectory House', *Arch. Cant.*, xv (1883), 255-8.

Luff 1952 — S.C. Luff, 'A Survey of primitive Monasticism in Central Gaul *c.* 350-700', *Downside Review*, lxx (1952), 180-203.

MacFarlane 1945 — K.B. MacFarlane, 'Bastard Feudalism', *Bull. Institute Hist. Res.*, xx (1945), 160-80.

MacFarlane 1973 — K.B. MacFarlane, *The Nobility of later medieval England*, Oxford 1973.

Mackenzie 1933-4 — W.M. Mackenzie, 'Clay Castle Building in Scotland', *PSAS*, lxviii (1933-4), 117-27.

Maillé 1930 — Marquise de Maillé, 'L' Église cistercienne de Preuilly', *Bulletin monumental*, (1930).

Malden 1911 — H.E. Malden (Ed.), *VCH*, Surrey, iii, London 1911.

Mann 1977 — J.C. Mann, 'The Reculver Inscription', in Johnston 1977, 15.

Martin 1904 — J.B. Martin, 'Inscriptions chrétiennes découvertes à Lyon', *Bull. Arch. de Comité*, xli (1904), xli-xliv.

McCourt 1972 — D. McCourt, 'Roof-timbering Techniques in Ulster; a Classification', *Folk Life*, x (1972), 118-30.

Marks 1979 — R. Marks, 'The Glazing of the Collegiate Church of the Holy Trinity, Tattershall (Lincs.)', *Archaeologia*, cvi (1979), 133-56.

Margary 1955 — I. Margary, *Roman Roads in Britain: I South of the Fosse Way-Bristol Channel*, London 1955.

Markham 1912 — C.A. Markham, 'Barnwell Castle, Northamptonshire', *Assoc. Archit. and Archaeol. Soc. Reports and Papers*, xxxi (1911-12), 525-38.

Matthew Paris 1872-3 — Matthew Paris, *Monachi Sancti Albani Chronica majora*, H.R. Luard (Ed.), P.R.O., London 1872-3.

Merion-Jones 1976 — G.I. Merion-Jones, 'Some early and primitive Building Forms in Brittany', *Folk Life*, xiv (1976).

Mesqui 1979 J. Mesqui, *Provins: la Fortification d'une Ville au Moyen Age*, Paris and Geneva 1979.

Mesqui 1980 J. Mesqui, 'Les Portes de Provins et de Château-Thierry et la Défense des Entrées au XIIIᵉ Siècle', Lecture at Château Gaillard 10th conference, September 1980.

Miles and Saunders 1970 T.J. Miles and A.D. Saunders, 'King Charles' Castle, Tresco, Scilly', *Post-Med. Arch.*, iv (1970), 1-31.

Morley 1976 B.M. Morley, 'Hylton Castle', *Arch. Journ.*, cxxxiii (1976), 118-34.

Munier 1963 C. Munier (Ed.), *Concilia Galliae, Corpus Christianorum Series Latina*, cxlviii, Turnhout 1963.

Murray 1935 K.M.E. Murray, *Constitutional History of the Cinque Ports*, Manchester 1935.

Nairn and Pevsner 1965 I. Nairn and N. Pevsner, *The Buildings of England: Sussex*, Harmondsworth 1965.

Nairn, Pevsner and Cherry 1971 I. Nairn, N. Pevsner and B. Cherry, *The Buildings of England: Surrey*, Harmondsworth 1971.

Nash-Williams 1950 V.E. Nash-Williams, *The early Christian Monuments of Wales*, Cardiff 1950.

Neilson 1928 N. Neilson (Ed.), *The Cartulary and Terrier of the Priory of Bilsington, Kent*, London 1928.

Neilson 1932 N. Neilson, 'The Domesday Monachorum', *VCH* Kent, iii, London 1932. 'Introduction to the Kent Domesday,' *VCH* Kent, iii, London 1932.

Nenquin 1953 J. Nenquin, *La Nécropole de Furfooz, Dissertationes Archaeologicae Gandenses*, i, Bruges 1953.

Newman 1969 J. Newman, *The Buildings of England: West Kent and the Weald*, Harmondsworth 1969.

Newman 1976 J. Newman, *The Buildings of England: North-east and East Kent*, Harmondsworth 1976.

Nicaise 1935 H. Nicaise, 'Les Carreaux en Faïence anversoise de l'ancienne Abbaye d'Heckenrode', *Bulletin des Musées d'Art de d'Histoire de Bruxelles*, (1935), 92-105.

Nichols 1826 N.H. Nichols, *Testamenta vetusta*, 1826.

Nichols 1845 J.G. Nichols, *Examples of decorative Tiles, sometimes termed 'Encaustic'*, London 1845.

Norris 1977 M. Norris, *Monumental Brasses: the Memorials*, London 1977.

Norton 1981 E.C. Norton, Review of Eames 1980, *J.B.A.A.*, forthcoming.

Oman 1926 C. Oman, *Castles*, London 1926.

O'Neil 1945 B.H. St. J. O'Neil, 'Criccieth Castle, Caernarvonshire', *Arch. Camb.*, xcviii (1945), 1-51.

Page-Phillips 1972 J. Page-Phillips, *Macklin's monumental Brasses*, 2nd edn. of revised version, London 1972.

Painter 1971 K. Painter, 'Villas and Christianity in Roman Britain', in Sieveking 1976, 156-75.

Painter 1975 K. Painter, 'A fourth Century Christian Treasure found at Water Newton, England, in 1975', *Rivista di Archeologia cristiana*, li (1975), 333-45.

Painter 1977 K. Painter, *The Water Newton early Christian Silver*, London 1977.

Palm 1959 T. Palm, 'Die Holz und Rindenkäfer der süd- und mittelschwedischen Laubbäume', *Opusc. Entom.*, suppl. xvi, 1959.

Pantin 1959 W.A. Pantin, 'Chantry Priests' Houses and other medieval Lodgings', *Med. Arch.*, iii (1959), 216-58.

Parker 1882   J.H. Parker, *Domestic Architecture in England*, 1882.

Parkin 1970   E.W. Parkin, 'Cogan House, St. Peter's, Canterbury', *Arch. Cant.*, lxxxv (1970), 123-38.

Peacock 1977a   D.P.S. Peacock, 'Bricks and Tiles of the Classis Britannica: Petrology and Origin', *Britannia*, viii (1977), 235-48.

Peacock 1977b   E. Peacock, *Rhizophagidae. Handbooks for the Identification of British Insects*, London 1977.

Peelen 1922   I.C.E. Peelen, *Guide*, Delft 1922.

Peers 1978   C. Peers, *Middleham Castle; Guide Pamphlet*, London 1978.

Percival 1976   J. Percival, *The Roman Villa*, London 1976.

Perks 1948   J.C. Perks, 'The architectural History of Chepstow Castle during the Middle Ages', *Trans. Bristol and Gloucester Arch. Soc.*, lxvii (1948), 307-45.

Perks 1954   J.C. Perks, 'The Development of Corfe Castle in the 13th Century', *Proc. Dorset Nat. Hist. and Arch. Soc.*, lxxvi (1954), 62-6.

Petersson 1958   K.G. Petersson, 'Ett Gravfynd från Klinta, Köping sn., Öland', *Tor*, iv (1958), 134-50.

Philp 1957   B.J. Philp, 'Recent Discoveries at Reculver', *Arch. Cant.*, lxxi (1957), 167-84.

Philp 1958   B.J. Philp, 'Discoveries at Reculver 1955-57', *Arch. Cant.*, lxxii (1958), 160-6.

Philp 1959   B.J. Philp, 'Reculver: Excavations on the Roman Fort in 1957', *Arch. Cant.*, lxxiii (1959), 96-115.

Philp 1960   B.J. Philp, 'Excavations at Reculver, 1958', *Arch. Cant.*, lxxiv (1960), 182-6.

Philp 1968   B.J. Philp, 'The Discovery of an elaborate Roman Drying-oven at Reculver', KAR, no. 13 (1968), 12-4.

Philp 1969   B.J. Philp, 'The Reculver Inscription', KAR, no. 17 (1969), 18-20.

Philp 1970a   B.J. Philp, *The Roman Fort at Reculver*, 6th edn., 1970.

Philp 1970b   B.J. Philp, 'Reculver Excavation Group: The Roman Fort – 1969', KAR, no. 20 (1970), 31-2.

Philp 1981   B.J. Philp, *The Excavation of the Roman Forts of the Classis Britannica at Dover, 1970-77*, Dover 1981.

Piggott 1976   S. Piggott, *Ruins in a Landscape*, Edinburgh 1976.

Piggott 1978   S. Piggott, *Antiquity depicted*, London 1978.

Platt 1962   C. Platt, 'Excavations at Dartington Hall, 1962', *Arch. Journ.*, cxix (1962), 208-24.

Platt and Coleman-Smith 1975 C. Platt and R. Coleman-Smith, *Excavations in medieval Southampton*, Leicester 1975.

Pool 1966   B. Pool, *Navy Board Contracts 1660-1832*, London 1966.

Potts 1920   R.U. Potts, 'St. Austin's Abbey, Canterbury', *Arch. Cant.*, xxxiv (1920), 139-47.

Potts 1934   R.U. Potts, 'The Plan of St. Austin's Abbey, Canterbury', *Arch. Cant.*, xlvi (1934), 179-94.

Powicke 1947   M. Powicke, *King Henry III and the Lord Edward*, Oxford 1947.

Powicke 1953   M. Powicke, *The Thirteenth Century 1216-1307*, Oxford 1953.

Pugh and Saunders 1968 R.B. Pugh and A.D. Saunders, *Old Wardour Castle; Official Handbook*, London 1968.

Purslow, n.d.   D.F. Purslow, *The Effect of Specimen Size on the Life of Timber in Contact with the Ground*, Princes Risborough, n.d.

Purslow 1969   D.F. Purslow, *The Natural Durability Classification of Timber*, D.o.E. Forest Products Research Laboratory, Technical Note no. 40, 1969.

Rackham 1909   R.B. Rackham, 'The Nave of Westminster Abbey', *Proc. of the British Academy*, iv (1909).

Rackham 1926   B. Rackham, *Early Netherlands Majolica*, London 1926.

Radford 1957   C.A. Ralegh Radford, *Acton Burnell Castle: Official Guide*, London 1957.

Radford 1961   C.A. Ralegh Radford, 'Acton Burnell Castle', in Jope 1961, 94-103.

Radford 1971   C.A.R. Radford, 'Christian Origins in Britain', *Med. Arch.*, xv (1971), 1-12.

Ramm 1971   H.G. Ramm, 'The Tombs of Archbishops Walter de Grey (1216-55) and Godfrey de Ludham (1258-65) in York Minster and their Contents', *Archaeologia*, ciii (1971), 101-47.

Reed 1872   F.H. Reed, *Illustrations of Tattershall Castle*, London 1872.

Renn 1975   D.F. Renn, 'An Angevin Gatehouse at Skipton (Yorkshire, West Riding)' in De Bouard 1975, 173-82.

Renn 1977   D.F. Renn, 'The Gatehouse', in Barton and Holden 1977, 74-5.

Renn 1981   D.F. Renn, 'Canterbury Castle in the early Middle Ages', in Bennett, Frere and Stow 1981, 70-7.

Rhys 1919   J. Rhys, 'An Inscription at Penmachno', *Arch. Camb.*, (1919), 201-5.

Richmond 1955   I.A. Richmond, *Roman Britain*, Harmondsworth 1955.

Richmond 1961   I.A. Richmond, 'A new Building-inscription from the Saxon-Shore Fort at Reculver, Kent', *Antiq. Journ.*, xli (1961), 224-8.

Richmond 1966   I.A. Richmond, 'Industry in Roman Britain', in Wacher 1966, 76-86.

Ridgway and King 1959   M.H. Ridgway and D.J.C. King, 'Beeston Castle, Cheshire', *J. Chester Arch. Soc.*, xlvi (1959), 1-23.

Rigoir 1968   J. Rigoir, 'Les Sigillées paléochrétiennes grises et oranges', *Gallia*, xxvi (1968), 177-244.

Rigoir and Meffre 1973   J. Rigoir and J.F. Meffre, 'Les Dérivées des Sigillées paléochrétiennes du Groupe atlantique', *Gallia*, xxxi (1973), 207-63.

Rigold 1954   S.E. Rigold, 'Three medieval Portrait Galleries', Lecture to the Society of Antiquaries of London, 11 November, 1954.

Rigold 1962   S. Rigold, 'Notes on Maidstone Buildings', *Arch. Journ.*, cxxvi (1962), 252-4.

Rigold 1964   S.E. Rigold, 'Two Kentish Hospitals re-examined: St. Mary, Ospringe, and SS. Stephen and Thomas, New Romney', *Arch. Cant.*, lxxix (1964), 31-69.

Rigold 1966a   S.E. Rigold, 'Bishop Waltham's Palace', Lecture on site to the Royal Archaeological Institute, 23 July, 1966.

Rigold 1966b   S.E. Rigold, Review of W. Horn and E. Born, *The Barns of the Abbey of Beaulieu*, *Antiq. Journ*, xlvi (1966), 356-7.

Rigold 1967a   S.E. Rigold, 'Early Indents in Laon Cathedral', *Trans. Monumental Brass Soc.*, x (1967), 275-82.

Rigold 1967b   S.E. Rigold, 'Indents of Chalice Brasses in Bruges', *Trans. Monumental Brass Soc.*, x (1967), 283-4.

Rigold 1967c   S.E. Rigold, 'Petrology as an Aid to Classification of Brasses', *Trans. Monumental Brass Soc.*, x (1967), 285-6.

Rigold 1967d   S.E. Rigold, 'Excavations at Dover Castle', *J.B.A.A.*, xxx (1967). 87-121.

Rigold 1969   S.E. Rigold, 'Excavations at Dover Castle, principally in the inner Bailey', *J.B.A.A.*, xxxii (1969), 54-104.

Rigold 1970   S.E. Rigold, 'The Roman Haven of Dover', *Arch. Journ.*, cxxvi (1970), 78-100.

Rijken 1966   I.A.J. Rijken, 'Behoorde Schip van Capelle tot Vloot van Prins Maurits', *De Echo van het Zuiden*, 4 November, 1966, 1.

Roach Smith 1850   C. Roach Smith, *The Antiquities of Richborough, Reculver and Lympne*, London 1850.

Roach Smith 1852	C. Roach Smith, *Report on Excavations made on the Site of the Roman Fort at Lympne, in Kent,* 1852.
Rollason 1979	D.W. Rollason, 'The Date of the Parish Boundary of Minster-in-Thanet, Kent', *Arch. Cant.,* xcv (1979), 7-17.
Ross 1967	A. Ross, *Pagan Celtic Britain,* London 1967.
Rous 1485	J. Rous, 'Life and Acts of Richard Beauchamp, Earl of Warwick', *British Library,* Cotton MS Julius E IV Art. vi. fo. 24 (1485).
Roussell 1974	A. Roussell, *Norse Building Customs in the Scottish Isles,* London 1974.
Routledge 1902	C.F. Routledge, 'Excavations at St. Austin's Abbey, Canterbury', *Arch. Cant.,* xxv (1902), 238-43.
Rymer 1816	T. Rymer, *Foedera,* London 1816.
Sadler 1980	A.G. Sadler, *The Indents of lost monumental Brasses in Cornwall, Devon, Somerset and Wiltshire: Appendix,* Ferring-on-Sea 1980.
Sailhan 1978	P. Sailhan, 'Typologie des Archères et Cannonières', *Bull. Soc. de l'Ouest et des Musées de Poitiers,* xiv (1978), 511-41.
St. John Hope 1895	W.H. St. John Hope, 'The Atchievements of Edward, Prince of Wales', *Vetusta monumenta,* vii (1895).
St. John Hope 1902	W.H. St. John Hope, 'Excavations at St. Austin's Abbey, Canterbury: I, The Chapel of St. Pancras', *Arch. Cant.,* xxv (1902), 222-37.
St. John Hope 1913	W.H. St. John Hope, *Windsor Castle, Country Life,* London 1913.
Salzman 1952	L.F. Salzman, *Building in England down to 1540,* Oxford 1952.
Searle 1902	W.G. Searle (Ed.), *Chronicle of John Stone, Cambridge Antiq. Soc.,* xxxiv (1902).
Séjalon 1892	A.R.P.H. Séjalon (Ed.), *Nomasticon cisterciense,* Solesmes 1892.
Sellye 1939	I.G. Sellye, *Les Bronzes émaillés de la Pannonie romaine, Dissertationes pannonicae,* ser. 2, viii, Budapest 1939.
Sheppard 1889	J. Brigstocke Sheppard (Ed.), *Literae cantuarienses,* Rolls Series 85, 1889.
Sherlock, n.d.	D. Sherlock, 'Medieval Floor Tiles in Suffolk Churches', *Suffolk Churches Historic Trust,* i, n.d.
Sherlock and Woods 1982	D. Sherlock and H. Woods. *Excavations at St. Augustine's Abbey, Canterbury, 1972-78, Med. Arch.,* Monograph series, forthcoming.
Sieveking 1976	G. de G. Sieveking, I.H. Longworth and K.E. Wilson, (Eds.), *Problems in economic and social Archaeology,* London 1976.
Simpson 1940	W.D. Simpson, 'Tonbridge Castle', *J.B.A.A.,* v (1940), 63-72.
Simpson 1946	W.D. Simpson, ' "Bastard Feudalism" and the later Castles', *Antiq. Journ.,* xxvi (1946), 145-71.
Simpson 1960	W.D. Simpson, 'The Building Accounts of Tattershall Castle, 1434-72', *Lincs. Record Soc.,* lv (1960).
Simpson 1976	F.G. Simpson, *Watermills and military Works on Hadrian's Wall,* Kendal 1976.
Smallcombe 1946	W.A. Smallcombe, 'Communal Burial Chamber at Park Place, near Henley-on-Thames', *Berks. Arch. Journ.,* xlix (1946), 42.
Smart 1972	A. Smart, *The Renaissance and Mannerism outside Italy,* 1972.
Smith 1943	R.A.L. Smith, *Canterbury Cathedral Priory,* 1943.
Smith 1975	P. Smith, *Houses of the Welsh Countryside,* R.C.A.H.M. (Wales), London 1975.
Smith 1979	G.H. Smith, 'The Excavation of the Hospital of St. Mary of Ospringe, commonly called "Maison Dieu"', *Arch. Cant.,* xcv (1979), 81-184.
Sotheby 1981	Sotheby, *Catalogue of British Coins,* etc., sold on 18th February, 1981.

Sprott 1719   T. Sprott, *Chronicle c. 1270*, Oxford 1719.

Stafford 1971   F. Stafford, 'Insects of a mediaeval Burial', *Science and Archaeology*, vii (1971), 6-10.

Stanley 1882   A.P. Stanley, *Historical Memorials of Westminster Abbey*, London 1882.

Steen 1958   F.W. Steen, *A short History of Halnaker House*, privately published, 1958.

Stenton 1965   F. Stenton (Ed.), *The Bayeux Tapestry*, London 1965.

Stevens 1952   C.E. Stevens, 'A Lady of Quality from Roman Devonshire', *Trans. Devonshire Assoc.*, lxxxiv (1952), 172-7.

Stevenson 1858   J. Stevenson (Ed.), *Chronicon Monasterii de Abingdon*, Rolls Series, London 1858.

Stone 1955   L. Stone, *Sculpture in Britain. The Middle Ages*, Harmondsworth 1955.

Straton 1909   C.R. Straton (Ed.), *Survey of the Lands of William, first Earl of Pembroke*, Roxburghe Club, London 1909.

Streatfeild 1878   J.F. Streatfeild, *Collection of Prints*, privately published, 1878.

Streeten 1977   A.D.F. Streeten, 'Excavations at Lansdowne Road, Tonbridge, 1972 and 1976', *Arch. Cant.*, xcii (1977), 105-18.

Stukeley 1776   W. Stukeley, *Itinerarium curiosum*, 1776.

Summerson 1955   J. Summerson, *Architecture in Britain 1530 to 1830*, Harmondsworth 1955.

Swanton 1975   M.J. Swanton, 'A fragmentary Life of St. Mildred and other Kentish Saints', *Arch. Cant.*, xci (1975), 15-28.

Symonds 1913   H. Symonds, 'The documentary Evidence for the English royal Coinages of Henry VII and Henry VIII', *Brit. Num. Journ.*, x (1913), 127-71.

Tatton-Brown 1980   T. Tatton-Brown, 'The Use of Quarr Stone in London and in east Kent', *Med. Arch.*, xxiv (1980), 213-5.

Taylor 1944   M.V. Taylor, 'Roman Britain', *JRS*, xxxiv (1944), 85.

Taylor 1961   A.J. Taylor, 'White Castle in the thirteenth Century: a Reconsideration', *Med. Arch.*, v (1961), 169-75.

Taylor 1969   A.J. Taylor (Ed.), *Château Gaillard III*, London and Chichester 1969.

Taylor 1979   A.J. Taylor, *Harlech Castle: Official Guidebook*, London 1979.

Taylor and Taylor 1965   H.M. and J. Taylor, *Anglo-Saxon Architecture*, Cambridge 1965.

Tester 1973   P.J. Tester, 'Excavations at Boxley Abbey', *Arch. Cant.*, lxxxviii (1973), 129-58.

Thomas 1959   C. Thomas, 'Imported Pottery in Dark Age western Britain', *Med. Arch.*, iii (1959), 89-111.

Thomas 1976   C. Thomas, 'Imported late-Roman Mediterranean Pottery in Ireland and western Britain — Chronologies and Implications', *Proc. Royal Irish Academy*, lxxvi (1976), section C 245-55.

Thomas 1979   C. Thomas, 'Saint Patrick and fifth century Britain: an historical Model explored', in Casey 1979, 81-101.

Thomas 1981   C. Thomas, *Christianity in Roman Britain to A.D. 500*, London 1981.

Thompson 1904   E.M. Thompson (Ed.) *The Customary of the Benedictine Monasteries of St. Augustine, Canterbury, and St. Peter, Westminster*, Henry Bradshaw Soc., xxvii (1904).

Thompson 1914   A.H. Thompson (Ed.), *Visitations of religious Houses in the Diocese of Lincoln*, Lincoln Record Soc., vii (1914).

Thompson 1953   F.H. Thompson, 'Excavations at Reculver, Kent, 1951', *Arch. Cant.*, lxvi (1953), 52-9.

Thompson 1957	E.A. Thompson, 'A chronological Note on St. Germanus of Auxerre', *Analecta Bollandiana*, lxxv (1957), 135-8.
Thompson 1960a	M.W. Thompson, 'The Date of 'Fox's Tower' Farnham Castle, Surrey', *Sy. Arch. Coll.*, lvii (1960), 85-92.
Thompson 1960b	M.W. Thompson, 'Recent Excavations in the Keep of Farnham Castle, Surrey', *Med. Arch.*, iv (1960), 81-94.
Thompson 1974a	M.W. Thompson, *Tattershall Castle, Lincolnshire*, (National Trust), London 1974.
Thompson 1974b	M.W. Thompson, 'Bolingbroke Castle', *Arch. Journ.*, cxxxi (1974), 314-7.
Thompson 1976	M.W. Thompson, 'The Construction of the Manor at South Wingfield, Derbyshire', in Sieveking 1976, 417-38.
Thompson 1979	E.A. Thompson, 'Gildas and the History of Britain', *Britannia*, x (1979), 203-26.
Thompson and Greene 1970-2	F.H. Thompson and J.P. Greene, *Norton priory Excavations*, 1970-2.
Thorne 1934	W. Thorne, *Chronicle. 14th Century* (Ed. and trans. A.H. Davies), Oxford 1934.
Tomlin 1976	R.O. Tomlin, '*Notitia dignitatum omnium tam civilium quam militarium*', in Goodburn and Bartholomew 1976, 189-209.
Torr 1933	J.B. Torr, 'The Arms of James II at West Malling', *Arch. Cant.*, xlv (1933), 234-40.
Toulmin-Smith 1906-10	L. Toulmin-Smith (Ed.), *The Itinerary of John Leland*, i-v, London 1906-10.
Tout 1920-33	T.F. Tout, *Chapters in mediaeval administrative History*, Manchester 1920-33.
Toy 1939	S. Toy, *Castles: a short History of Fortification*, London 1939.
Toy 1953	S. Toy, *The Castles of Great Britain*, London 1953.
Toynbee 1964	J.M.C. Toynbee, *Art in Britain under the Romans*, Oxford 1964.
Toynbee 1973	J.M.C. Toynbee, *Animals in Roman Art and Life*, London 1973.
Treharne and Sanders 1973	R.F. Treharne and I.J. Sanders, *Documents of the baronial Movement of Reform and Rebellion 1258-1267*, Oxford 1973.
Turnbull 1979	D. Turnbull, 'Some Problems about the Origin of Criccieth Castle', *Fort*, ix (1979), 52-68.
Turner 1851	T.H. Turner, *Some Account of domestic Architecture in England, from the Conquest to the End of the thirteenth Century*, Oxford 1851.
Turner 1863	E. Turner, 'The Priory of Boxgrove', *Sx. Arch. Coll.*, xv (1863), 83-122.
Turner and Parker 1851	T.H. Turner and J.H. Parker, *Domestic Architecture of the Middle Ages*, i (1851), 154.
Unwin 1918	G. Unwin (Ed.), *Finance and Trade under Edward III*, Manchester 1918.
Urry 1960	W. Urry, 'Two Notes on Guernes de Pont Sainte-Maxence: Vie de Saint Thomas', *Arch. Cant.*, lxvi (1960), 92-7.
Urry 1967	W. Urry, *Canterbury under the Angevin Kings*, London 1967.
Vallance 1925	A. Vallance, 'Harty Church, Sheppey', *Arch. Cant.*, xxxvi (1925), 73-82.
Vallance 1936	A. Vallance, *English Church Screens*, London 1936.
Vis and De Geus 1926	E. Vis and C. De Geus, *Althollandische Fliesen*, Amsterdam 1926.
Wacher 1966	J.S. Wacher (Ed.), *The Civitas Capitals of Roman Britain*, Leicester 1966.
Wadmore 1886	J.F. Wadmore, 'Tonbridge Castle and its Lords', *Arch. Cant.*, xvi (1886), 12-57.
Wallenberg 1934	J.K. Wallenberg, *The Place-names of Kent*, Uppsala 1934.

Wander 1978   S.H. Wander, The Westminster Abbey Sanctuary Pavement', *Traditio*, xxxiv (1978), 137-56.

Ward 1932   G. Ward, 'The List of Saxon Churches in the *Textus Roffensis'*, *Arch. Cant.*, xliv (1932), 39-59.

Ward-Perkins 1937   J.P. Ward-Perkins, 'Late medieval Flemish inlaid Tiles in England', *Antiq. Journ.*, xvii (1937), 442-3.

Ward-Perkins 1940   J.P. Ward-Perkins, *London Museum Medieval Catalogue*, London 1940, 229-53.

Weever 1631   J. Weever, *Ancient Funeral Monuments*, London 1631.

Wegner 1965   M. Wegner, *Schmuckbasen des antiken Rom*, Münster 1965.

West 1981   J.J. West, 'Wattlesborough Tower, Alberbury', *Arch. Journ.* cxxxviii (1981), 33-4.

West and Plouviez 1976   S. West and J. Plouviez, 'The Roman Site at Icklingham (Suffolk)', *East Anglian Archaeology*, iii (1976), 63-125.

Wheeler 1932   R.E.M. Wheeler, *Report on the Excavation of the prehistoric, Roman and post-Roman Site in Lydney Park, Gloucestershire*, Reports of the Research Committee of the Society of Antiquaries of London, ix, Oxford 1932.

Whittingham 1970   S. Whittingham, *A thirteenth-century Portrait Galley at Salisbury Cathedral*, Salisbury 1970.

Whittingham 1975   S. Whittingham, *Medieval Portrait Busts at New College, Oxford*, London and Chichester 1975.

Whitton 1949   C.A. Whitton, 'The Coinages of Henry VIII and Edward VI in Henry's Name', *Brit. Num. Journ.*, xxvi (1949), 56-89, 171-212, 290-332.

Wild 1976   J.P. Wild, 'The Gynaecea', in Goodburn and Bartholomew, 1976, 51-8.

Williams 1872   G. Williams (Ed.), *Official Correspondence of Thomas Beckynton*, Rolls Series 56, London 1872.

Williams 1899   S. Williams, 'An ancient Welsh Farm-House', *Arch. Camb.*, xvi (1899), 320-5.

Willis 1868   R. Willis, 'The architectural History of the Conventual Buildings of the Monastery of Christ Church in Canterbury', *Arch. Cant.*, vii (1868), 1-206.

Willis and Clark 1886   R. Willis and J.W. Clark, *Architectural History of the University of Cambridge*, Cambridge 1886.

Wilson 1965   D.R. Wilson, 'Roman Britain in 1964', *JRS*, lv (1965), 199-220.

Wood 1950   M.E. Wood, 'Thirteenth-century domestic Architecture in England', *Arch. Journ.*, cv (1950), supplement.

Wood 1965   M.E. Wood, *The English medieval House*, London 1965.

Woodruff 1936   C.E. Woodruff, 'The Sacrist's Rolls of Christchurch, Canterbury', *Arch. Cant.*, xlviii (1936), 58.

Woodruff and Danks 1912   C.E. Woodruff and W. Danks, *Memorials of the Cathedral and Priory of Christ in Canterbury*, London 1912.

Wray 1932   F.W. Wray, *The Text of the Kent Domesday*, *VCH* Kent, iii (1932).

Wylie 1914   J.H. Wylie, *The Reign of Henry V*, Cambridge 1914.

Zachrisson 1909   R.E. Zachrisson, *A Contribution to the Study of Anglo-Norman Influence on English Place-names*, Lund 1909.

COLLECTANEA HISTORICA

ESSAYS IN MEMORY OF STUART RIGOLD

PREFACE

'Riggy', as Stuart Rigold was affectionately known to all of us, died suddenly on 5th July, 1980, within a year of his retirement as Principal Inspector of Ancient Monuments and Public Buildings at the Department of the Environment. This commemorative volume is not the place for an appreciation of the man and scholar that Stuart was and, in any case, obituary notices have already appeared elsewhere (e.g. *The Times*, 7th July, 1980; *Arch. Cant.*, xcvi (1981), 429-30.)

Apart from anything else, Stuart's death deprived his friends and colleagues of the opportunity to contribute to the *Festschrift* that he so richly deserved. With this partly in mind, I suggested to the Kent Archaeological Society, on whose Council and Publications Committee Stuart had served for many years, the publication of the present volume of essays dedicated to his memory.

It is no small measure of the esteem in which we all held Stuart that so many essays, reflecting his many scholarly interests, were readily forthcoming within a necessarily short time. I am personally in the debt of all contributors to this volume for their willing co-operation, which rendered my editorial task not only a labour of duty to a friend of many years' standing, but also such a pleasant experience.

Votum solvi libens laetissimus merito.

ALEC DETSICAS

THE PUBLISHED WORKS OF STUART EBORALL RIGOLD

COMPILED BY DAVID SHERLOCK

The three-hundred-odd articles, notes and reviews that Stuart Rigold wrote in only thirty-three years surely make him one of the most prolific writers of his time in his various fields. His output reached a peak in 1969 with two official guidebooks, twenty articles and five reviews on subjects ranging from Shropshire and Lincolnshire to Kent and from Roman hair-styles to medieval cruck-buildings. He was also his own competent draughtsman and illustrator and his reconstruction drawings are worthy of particular mention (see for example nos. 149, 152-3, 250).

I have tried to make this bibliography as complete as possible but there are doubtless other odd notes hidden in more obscure publications. How Stuart would have enjoyed providing these himself! For help with the search I thank particularly Christopher Miscampbell and Robert Thompson.

Analysis
(Many items will be found indexed under more than one category.)

NUMISMATICS: 1, 3, 5, 8, 9, 13, 15, 19-20, 23, 27, 32, 42, 46-7, 59, 63, 76-7, 79-80, 89, 92, 101, 103, 106, 108, 110, 130-1, 144, 146-7, 160, 167-8, 173-4, 185-8, 196, 198, 203-9, 220, 224, 226, 235-6, 241-4, 249, 260-1, 263, 267, 271, 285, 287, 295-6, 300-3; *Reviews of Sylloges*: 38, 90, 127, 129, 143, 161-2, 183, 199, 254, 294; *Sceattas*: 31, 62, 81, 92, 222, 237-40, 258, 274, 284, 304-5, 313-4; *Jettons*: 32, 35, 42, 64, 82-3, 92, 108-10, 148, 188-90, 209-10, 212, 217, 223-6, 244, 259, 262, 275-6, 278, 286-7, 300-2, 306-7, 315, 316.
ROMAN: 27, 61, 92, 106, 113, 145, 155, 170, 235, 291.
MEDIEVAL HISTORY AND ARCHAEOLOGY: 6, 7, 16, 17, 25, 33-7, 40, 43, 48, 51, 53, 58, 61, 83, 91, 99, 107, 111, 125, 128, 130, 134-5, 141, 144, 149, 153, 163, 166, 178-9, 182, 193, 195, 198, 200, 204, 212, 225, 230, 234, 244, 248, 251, 255, 263, 265-7, 270, 276, 296, 308, 310-12, 315; *Brasses*: 65-7, 218; *Seals*: 16, 185, 190, 246-7, 262, 277, 287.
MEDIEVAL ARCHITECTURE: 21, 28-9, 41, 49, 50, 53, 55-6, 68-73, 84-7, 94-7, 100, 115-22, 125, 133, 136, 138-9, 142, 150, 154, 156-9, 164-5, 176-7, 191-2, 194, 201, 215, 227, 229, 245, 249, 252-3, 279-81, 288-91, 298-9, 308; *Guidebooks*: 4, 10-12, 14, 18, 22, 26, 30, 39, 45, 52, 60, 104-5, 145, 184, 221, 257, 273; *Timber-framed buildings*: 24, 44, 54, 74-5, 78, 88, 93, 98, 102, 112, 114, 123-4, 126, 132, 137, 140, 151-3, 172, 175, 180-1, 197, 213, 215, 231, 250, 264, 269, 293; *Bridges*: 169, 179, 201, 211, 214, 228
KENT: 22, 34, 39, 44-5, 50, 53, 55-6, 74-5, 83, 88, 92, 94, 98-9, 102, 111-24, 134-6, 145, 151,

154-5, 165, 170-1, 178-9, 195, 205, 213-5, 229, 234, 270, 274, 276, 283, 303-5, 310-2.
MISCELLANEOUS: 2, 57, 195, 216, 219, 232-3, 256, 268, 272, 282, 298, 309.

1947

1. 'Coins of Malta', *Seaby's Coin and Medal Bulletin*, no. 353, p. 397.
2. 'The Twrch Trwyth', *Seaby's Coin and Medal Bulletin*, no. 353, p. 398.

1948

3. Review: *Hamburger Beiträge zur Numismatik 1947-8, Br. Num. Journ.*, xxv, pt. 3, 347-8.

1949

4. *The Pyx Chamber, Westminster Abbey*, Ministry of Works Official Guide, 4 pp. See also 221.
5. 'The Trail of the Easterlings', *Br. Num. Journ.*, xxvi, pt.1, 31-55.
6. 'Excavations by the Shaftesbury Historical Society, at Castle Hill, Shaftesbury 1947-49', *Proc. Dorset Nat. Hist. & Arch. Soc.*, lxxi, 54-7.

1950

7. 'Pottery from a late medieval Well-filling and other medieval Finds from St. John's College, Oxford, 1947' (with E. M. and H. M. Jope), *Oxoniensia*, xv, 44-62.
8. Review: J.G. Milne, C.H.V. Sutherland and J.D.A. Thompson, *Coin Collecting, Br. Num. Journ.*, xxvi, pt. 2, 222-3.

1951

9. 'A Hoard of English Groats and Flemish double Patards from Norham Castle, Northumberland', *Br. Num. Journ.*, xxvi, pt. 3, 348-50.

1952

10. *The Chapter House, Westminster Abbey* (with J.G. Noppen), Ministry of Works Official Guide, 23 pp. See also 221.
11. *Totnes Castle, Devon*, Ministry of Works Official Guide, 7 pp. See 16, 21.
12. *The Moot Hall, Elstow* (with J. Godber and T.W. Bagshawe), Beds, County Council Official Guide, 5-8.

1953

13. Review: R.P. Mack, *The Coinage of Ancient Britain, Br. Num. Journ.*, xxvii, pt. 2, 222-4.

1954

14. *Titchfield Abbey, Hampshire* (with Rose Graham), Ministry of Works Official Guide, 12 pp.
15. 'An imperial gold Coinage in Southern Gaul in the 6th and 7th centuries?' *Num. Chron.*, 6th ser., xiv, 93-133.
16. 'Totnes Castle: Recent Excavations by the Ancient Monuments Department, Ministry of Works', *Trans. Devon Assoc.*, lxxxvi, 228-56. See 11.

1955

17. 'Shank Castle, Cumberland', *Trans. Cumb. & West. Antiq. & Arch. Soc.*, liv, 144-50.
18. *Nunney Castle, Somerset*, Ministry of Works Official Guidebook, 12 pp.
19. Review: J.D.A. Thompson, *Inventory of British Coin Hoards, A.D. 600-1500, Br. Num. Journ.*, xxviii, pt. 2, 425-6. See also 20.
20. Review: J.D.A. Thompson, *Inventory of British Coin Hoards, A.D. 600-1500, Arch. Journ.*. cxiii, 169-70. See also 19.

1957

21. 'Totnes Castle' *Arch. Journ.*, cxiv, 177-8. See also 11.

1958

22. *Maison Dieu, Ospringe, Kent* (with G.C. Dunning), Ministry of Works Official Guidebook, 23 pp. See also 50, 276.
23. 'Finds of St. Edmund memorial and other Anglo-Saxon Coins from Excavations at Thetford', *Br. Num. Journ.*, xxix, pt. 1, 189-90.

24. 'The timber-framed Buildings of Steventon', *Trans. Newbury & Dist. Field Club*, x, no. 4, 4-13.
25. 'The Stone Head' in P.W. Gathercole, 'Excavations at Oakham Castle, Rutland', *Leics. Arch. & Hist. Soc. Trans.*, xxxiv, 36.

1959

26. *Yarmouth Castle, Isle of Wight*, Ministry of Works Official Guide, 14 pp. See also 257.
27. 'Coins' in Mrs. Murray Threipland and W.J. Davies, 'Excavations at Caerleon', *Arch. Camb.*, cviii, 132-3.
28. 'Pevensey Castle', *Arch. Journ.*, cxvi, 236.
29. 'Martello Tower No. 60, Pevensey Bay', *Arch. Journ.*, cxvi, 236.

1960

30. *North Elmham Saxon Cathedral*, Ministry of Works Official Guide, 12 pp. See also 43, 288.
31. 'The two primary Series of Sceattas', *Br. Num. Journ.*, xxx, pt. 1, 6-53. See also 62.
32. 'Medieval and later Coins and Jettons' in P.A. Rahtz, *Pleshey Castle First Interim Report*, Essex Arch. Soc. Monograph, 24.
33. 'Stone Objects' in P.A. Rahtz, 'King John's Palace, Clipstone', *Trans. Thoroton Soc.*, lxiv, 43.
34. Review: W. Urry, *The Normans in Canterbury*, *Med. Arch.*, iv, 174-5.

1961

35. 'Jettons' and 'Ring' in J.G. Hurst, 'The Kitchen Area of Northolt Manor, Middlesex', *Med. Arch.*, v, 288 and 294.
36. 'The Supposed See of Dunwich', *J.B.A.A.*, xxiv, 55-9. See also 193.
37. Review: J.C. Dickinson, *Monastic Life in Medieval England*, *Arch. Journ.* cxviii, 260-1.
38. Review: Anne S. Robertson, *Sylloge of Coins of the British Isles, 2, Hunterian and Coats Collections, Anglo-Saxon Coins*, *Med. Arch.*, v, 341-2.

1962

39. *Temple Manor, Strood, Rochester, Kent*, Ministry of Public Building and Works Official Guidebook, 16 pp. See also 53.
40. 'Excavation of a moated Site at Pivington', *Arch. Cant.*, lxxvii, 27-47.
41. Review: E.A. Fisher, *The Greater Anglo-Saxon Churches*, *Arch. Journ.* cxix, 364-6.

1963

42. 'Coins and Jettons' in J.G. Hurst, 'Excavations at Barn Road, Norwich, 1954-55', *Norf. Arch.*, xxxiii, 170-1.
43. 'The Anglian Cathedral of North Elmham', *Med. Arch.*, vi-vii, 67-108. See also 30, 48, 288.
44. 'The Distribution of the Wealden House' in E.M. Jope, 'The Regional Cultures of medieval Britain' in I. Ll. Foster (ed.), *Culture and Environment*, Essays in honour of Sir Cyril Fox, 351-4.

1964

45. *Eynsford Castle, Kent*, Ministry of Public Building and Works Official Guidebook, 15 pp. See also 149, 179, 310.
46. 'Coin' in J.G. and D.G. Hurst, 'Excavations at the deserted medieval Village of Hangleton', *Sx. Arch. Coll.*, cii, 139.
47. 'The coin' in Helen O'Neil, 'Excavation of a Celtic Hermitage on St. Helen's, Isles of Scilly, 1956-58', *Arch. Journ.*, cxxi, 66.
48. 'The Anglian Cathedral of North Elmham: Two Corrections', *Med. Arch.*, viii. See 43.
49. 'Ashlar Fragment' in Ernest Greenfield, 'Excavation of a bombed Site in Chapel Street, Exeter', *Trans. Devon. Assoc.*, xcvi, 376.
50. 'Two Kentish Hospitals re-examined: S. Mary, Ospringe and SS. Stephen and Thomas, New Romney', *Arch. Cant.*, lxxix, 31-69. See also 22, 56.
51. Review: F.T. Wainwright, *Archaeology and Place-Names and History*, *Med. Arch.*, viii, 315-6.

1965

52. *Portchester Castle, Hampshire*, Ministry of Public Building and Works Official Guidebook, 24 pp. See also 70.
53. 'Two Camerae of the Military Orders', *Arch. Journ.*, cxxii, 86-132. See also 39.

54. 'Frocester Court Tithe Barn', *Arch. Journ.*, cxxii, 209-11.
55. 'Two Kentish Carmelite Houses — Aylesford and Sandwich', *Arch. Cant.*, lxxx, 1-28.
56. 'Two Kentish Hospitals re-examined: Addenda and Corrigenda', *Arch. Cant.*, lxxx, 29. See also 50.
57. 'Introduction' in Alan Sorrell, *Living History*, 7-10.
58. Review: H. Halbertsma, *Terpen, Tussen Vlie en Ems*, *Med. Arch.*, ix, 227-8.
59. Review: M. Dolley, *Anglo-Saxon Pennies*, *Med. Arch.*, ix, 230-1.

1966

60. *Baconsthorpe Castle, Norfolk*, Ministry of Public Building and Works Official Guidebook, 15 pp. See also 289.
61. 'Recent Investigations into the earliest Defences of Carisbrooke Castle, Isle of Wight', *Château Gaillard* iii, 128-38.
62. 'The two primary Series of sceattas: Addenda and Corrigenda', *Br. Num. Journ.*, xxxv, 1-6. See also 31.
63. 'An Elizabethan Hoard from Thornton Abbey, Lincs.' *Br. Num. Journ.*, xxxv, 200-1.
64. 'Jetton' in C.F. Tebbutt, 'St. Neot's Priory', *Proc. Camb. Ant. Soc.*, lix, 54.
65. 'Petrology as an Aid to Classification of Brasses', *Trans. Mon. Brass Soc.*, x, 285-6.
66. 'Indents of Chalice Brasses in Bruges', *Trans. Mon. Brass Soc.*, x, 283-4.
67. 'Early Indents in Laon Cathedral', *Trans. Mon. Brass Soc.*, x, 275-82.
68. 'Netley Abbey', *Arch. Journ.*, cxxiii, 187-8.
69. 'Warnford Church', *Arch. Journ.*, cxxiii, 189-90.
70. 'Portchester: The inner Bailey and the Priory Church', *Arch. Journ.*, cxxiii, 193-5. See also 52.
71. 'Christchurch Castle', *Arch. Journ.*, cxxiii, 204.
72. 'Bishops Waltham Palace', *Arch. Journ.*, cxxiii, 217.
73. 'King John's House, Romsey', *Arch. Journ.*, cxxiii, 220.
74. 'Some major Kentish Timber Barns', *Arch. Cant.*, lxxxi, 1-30.
75. Review: R.T. Mason, *Framed Buildings of the Weald*, *Arch. Cant.*, lxxxi, 252-4.
76. Review: Hans Hermann Vökkers, *Karolingische Münzfunde der Frühzeit*, *Num. Chron*, 7th ser., vi, 361-2.
77. Review: *Dona Numismatica*, Walter Hävernick Festschrift, *Num. Chron.*, 7th ser., vi, 363-4.
78. Review: Walter Horn and Ernest Boin, *The Barns of the Abbey of Beaulieu and its Granges of Gt. Coxwell and Beaulieu-St. Leonards*, *Antiq. Journ.*, xlvi, 356-7.
79. Review: M. Dolley, *Viking Coins of the Danelaw and of Dublin*, *Med. Arch.*. x, 225-6.

1967

80. 'The Coin' in P.A. Rahtz, 'Whitby 1958, Site two', *Yorks Arch. Journ.*, xlii, 72.
81. 'Silver Sceatta of Eadberht from Caistor', in J.B. Whitwell, 'Archaeological Notes 1966', *Lincs Hist. and Arch.*, ii, 46-7.
82. 'Jetton' in A.J.F. Dulley, 'Excavations at Pevensey, Sussex, 1962-6', *Med. Arch.*, xi, 229.
83. Excavations at Dover Castle 1964-66', *J.B.A.A.*, xxx, 87-121. See also 111.
84. 'Duxford Chapel', *Arch. Journ.*, cxxiv, 229-30.
85. 'Bottisham Church', *Arch. Journ.*, cxxiv, 251.
86. 'Swaffham Prior, Churches of St. Mary and SS. Cyriac and Julitta', *Arch. Journ.*, cxxiv, 252.
87. 'Burwell Church', *Arch. Journ.*, cxxiv, 254-5.
88. 'Fourteenth-century Halls in the East Weald', *Arch. Cant.*, lxxxii, 246-56.
89. Review: D.M. Metcalf, *Coinage in the Balkans, 820-1355*, *Num. Chron.*, 7th ser., vii, 308-9.
90. Review: *Sylloge of Coins of the British Isles, G. Galster, Royal Collection, National Museum, Copenhagen, 4, Ancient-British and Anglo-Saxon Coins before Aethelred II, and 7, Aethelred II, and 6, R.B.K. Stevenson, National Museum of Antiquities, Edinburgh, Anglo-Saxon Coins with Associated Foreign Coins*, *Med. Arch.*, xi, 329-30.
91. Review: A.M. Smith, *The Place-Names of Gloucestershire*, *Med. Arch.*, xi, 331-2.

1968

92. 'The Post-Roman Coins' and 'Richborough Today' in B.W. Cunliffe (ed.), *Richborough*, v. Soc. Ant. Research Report xxiii, 217-23 and 253-5.
93. 'The Cherhill Barn', *Wilts. Arch. & Nat. Hist. Mag.*, lxiii, 58-65.

94. 'The double Minsters of Kent and their analogies', *J.B.A.A.*, xxxi, 27-37.

95. 'Monk Bretton Priory', *Arch. Journ.*, cxxv, 322.

96. 'Bolton Priory', *Arch. Journ.*, cxxv, 331-3.

97. 'Harewood Church', *Arch. Journ.*, cxxv, 341-2.

98. 'Two Types of Court Hall', and (with D.C. Mynard) 'Pottery from Canterbury Guildhall', *Arch. Cant.*, lxxxiii, 1-22.

99. 'Floor Tiles' and 'Medieval pottery' in Brian Philp, *Excavations at Faversham 1965*, Kent Arch. Research Group, 1st Report, 44-50 and 54-6.

100. 'Note on the Plan of the Buildings' in S.E. West, 'Griff Manor House (Sudeley Castle), Warwickshire', *J.B.A.A.*, xxxi, 86-7.

101. Review: Philip Grierson, *Bibliographie numismatique, Ant. Journ.*, xlviii, 341.

102. Review: F.W.B. Charles, *Medieval Cruck-Building and its Derivatives, Med. Arch.*, xii, 229-31. See also 126.

103. Review: P. Berghaus und K. Schneider, *Anglo-friesische Runensolidi im Lichte des Neufundes von Schweindorf, Br. Num. Journ.*, xxxvii, 199-201.

1969

104. *Lilleshall Abbey, Shropshire*, Ministry of Public Building and Works Official Guidebook, 16 pp.

105. *Titchfield Abbey, Hampshire* (with Rose Graham), Ministry of Public Building and Works Official Guidebook, 20 pp.

106. 'The Coiffures of the Empresses', *Cunobelin*, Yearbook of the Br. Assoc. of Numismatic Societies, 17-21.

107. 'Historical and archaeological Background' in R. Seaman, 'A Find of Stephen Coins at Rayleigh Mount', *Br. Num. Journ.*, xxxviii, 187.

108. 'Numismatica' in D.C. Mynard, 'Excavations at Somerby, Lincs, 1957', *Lincs. Hist. and Arch.*, iv, 86.

109. 'Jettons' in K. Jane Evans, 'The Maison Dieu, Arundel', *Sx. Arch. Coll.*, cvii, 74.

110. 'Coins' and 'Jettons' in P.A. Rahtz, *Excavations at King John's Hunting Lodge, Writtle, Essex, 1955-57*, Soc. Med. Arch. Monograph iii, 78-81.

111. 'Excavations at Dover Castle principally in the inner Bailey', (with A.M. Cook and D.C. Mynard), *J.B.A.A.*, xxxii, 54-104. See also 83.

112. 'Great Pattenden, Marden', *Arch. Cant.*, lxxxiv, 31-7.

113. 'The Roman Haven of Dover', *Arch. Journ.*, cxxvi, 78-100.

114. 'Timber-framed Buildings in Kent', *Arch. Journ.* cxxvi, 198-200.

115. 'Patrixbourne Church', *Arch. Journ.*, cxxvi, 214-5.

116. 'Walmer Old Manor House', *Arch. Journ.*, cxxvi, 215-7.

117. 'Maidstone: The archiepiscopal Precinct', *Arch. Journ.*, cxxvi, 252-4.

118. 'Leeds Castle', *Arch. Journ.* cxxvi, 254-5.

119. 'Battel Hall, Leeds', *Arch. Journ.*, cxxvi, 255-6.

120. 'Leeds Church', *Arch. Journ.*, cxxvi, 256.

121. 'Lympne Castle', *Arch. Journ.*, cxxvi, 260-2.

122. 'Chartham Church', *Arch. Journ.*, cxxvi, 265-6.

123. 'Yardhurst, Daniel's Water', *Arch. Journ.*, cxxvi, 267-9.

124. 'The Demesne of Christ Church at Brook', *Arch. Journ.*, cxxvi, 270-2.

125. 'Topography and Documentation' and 'Plan and Structure of the Buildings' in J.B. Whitwell, 'Excavations on the Site of a moated medieval Manor House in the Parish of Saxilby, Lincs', *J.B.A.A.*, 3rd ser., xxxii, 131-5.

126. Review: F.W.B. Charles, *Medieval Cruck-building and its Derivatives, Antiq. Journ.*, xlix, 175. See also 102.

127. Review: J.D.A. Thompson, *Sylloge of Coins of the British Isles, 9, Ashmolean Museum, Anglo-Saxon Pennies, Antiq. Journ.*, xlix, 163-4.

128. Review: R. Allen Brown, *The Normans and the Norman Conquest, Med. Arch.*, xiii, 292-4.

129. Review: M. Dolley and W. Seaby, *Sylloge of Coins of the British Isles, 10, Ulster Museum, Belfast, Anglo-Irish Coins, John-Edward III, Med. Arch.* xiii, 300-1.

130. Review: L.R. Laing, *Coins and Archaeology, Med. Arch.*, xiii, 304-5. See also 144.

1970

131. 'Medieval coins' in P.A. Rahtz, 'Excavations on Glastonbury Tor, Somerset, 1964-6', *Arch. Journ.*, cxxvii, 56.

132. 'The Village Lock-up at Barley' (with J.C. Wilkerson), *Herts. Arch.*, ii, 113-4.

133. 'A Face carved on a Capital in Orford Church', *Proc. Suff. Inst. Arch.*, xxxii, 90-1.

134. 'Six Copper Alloy Objects from St. Augustine's, Canterbury'. *Antiq. Journ.*, l, 345-7.

135. 'Three Anglo-Saxon Disc Brooches' (with Leslie Webster), *Arch. Cant.*, lxxxv, 1-18.

136. 'Two lost Court Lodges — Longfield and Wooton' (with A. Baker), *Arch. Cant.*, lxxxv, 61-70.

137. 'Note on the Structures' in S.E. West, 'Broome, Suffolk. The Excavation of a moated Site, 1967', *J.B.A.A.*, xxxiii, 100-1.

138. 'Cartmel Fell Church', *Arch. Journ.*, cxxvii, 271.

139. 'Astley Hall, Chorley', *Arch. Journ.*, cxxvii, 274-6.

140. 'Rufford Old Hall', *Arch. Journ.*, cxxvii, 276-7.

141. Review: John Harvey (ed.), *William Worcestre Itineraries, Arch. Journ.*, cxxvii, 319-20.

142. Review: Yves Christe, *Les grands Portails romains, Med. Arch.*, xiv, 222-3.

143. Review: *Sylloge of Coins of the British Isles*, 12, D.M. Metcalf, *Ashmolean Museum, English Coins 1066-1279*, 11, C.E. Blunt and M. Dolley with F. Elmore Jones and C.S.S. Lyon, *University College Reading, Anglo-Saxon and Norman Coins with Royal Coin Cabinet, Stockholm, Anglo-Norman Pennies, Med. Arch.*, xiv, 219-20. See also 161.

144. Review: Lloyd R. Laing, *Coins and Archaeology, Br. Num. Journ*, xxxix, 181-2. See also 130.

1971

145. *Reculver*, Department of the Environment Official Guide, 6 pp.

146. 'Review of the Year', 'Record of post-Roman Hoards' and 'A discourse on Method and Terminology', Br. Numismatic Soc. presidential address, *Br. Num. Journ.*, xl, 193-204.

147. 'Coins' in Stephen Moorhouse, 'Excavations at Burton-in-Lonsdale', *Yorks. Arch. Journ.*, xliii, 97-8.

148. 'Jettons' in V. Russell and S. Moorhouse, 'Excavations near the Bishop's Palace at Nettleham, 1959', *Lincs. Hist. & Arch.*, vi, 26-7.

149. 'Eynsford Castle and its Excavation', *Arch. Cant.*, lxxvi, 109-71. See also 45.

150. 'Dated Buildings relevant to vernacular Practice before before 1550' *Vernac. Archit.*, ii, 10-12.

151. 'The Distribution of aisled Timber Barns', *Vernac. Archit*, ii, 20-1.

152. 'The early medieval Timber Hall' in C.F. Tebbutt *et al.*, 'Excavation of a moated site at Ellington, Hunts', *Proc. Camb. Ant. Soc.*, lxiii, 40, 42-6.

153. 'The Pottery' and 'The Timber-framed Buildings' in J.H. Money, 'Medieval Ironworkings in Minepit Wood, Rotherfield, Sussex', *Med. Arch.*, xv, 107-10.

154. 'The Development of St. Peter's and its Relevance to the primary Work' in T.P. Smith, 'The Church of St. Peter, Canterbury', *Arch. Cant.*, lxxxvi, 107-8.

155. 'Dover', letter in *Current Archaeology*, no. 24, p. 28.

156. 'Compton Wynyates', *Arch. Journ.*, cxxviii, 218-20.

157. 'Polesworth Church', *Arch. Journ.*, cxxviii, 245-6.

158. 'Ford's Hospital, Coventry', *Arch. Journ.*, cxxviii, 251-2.

159. 'St. Mary's Hall, Coventry', *Arch. Journ.*, cxxviii, 253-5.

160. Review: R.A.G. Carson (ed.), *Mints, Dies and Currency, Br. Num. Journ.*, xl, 176-8.

161. Review: D.M. Metcalf, *Sylloge of Coins of the British Isles, 12, Ashmolean Museum, English Coins, 1066-1279, Antiq. Journ.*, li, 364. See also 143.

162. Review: *Sylloge of Coins of the British Isles*, 13-15, George Galster, *Royal Collection, National Museum, Copenhagen*; 17, A.J.H. Gunstone, *Ancient British, Anglo-Saxon and Norman Coins in Midland Museums, Med. Arch.*, xv, 187-8. See also 183.

163. Review: A.E. van Giffen, *De Groninger Sint Walberg, Med. Arch.*, xv, 191-2.

164. Review: R.W. Brunskill, *Illustrated Handbook of Vernacular Architecture, Med. Arch.*, xv, 193-4.

165. Review: Ronald Jessup, *South-East England, J.B.A.A.*, xxxiv, 95-6.

166. Review: Anthony Emery, *Dartington Hall, Antiq. Journ.*, li, 365-6.

1972

167. 'Review of the Year' and 'Concepts of Style in Coinage', Br. Numismatic Soc. presidential address, *Br. Num. Journ.*, xli, 208-217.

168. 'Numismatica' in S. Moorhouse, 'Finds from Excavations at the Dominican Friary, Boston', *Lincs. Hist. &*

Arch., vii, 44-5.

169. 'Timber Bridges at English Castles and moated Sites', *Château Gaillard* vi, 183-93.
170. 'Roman Folkestone reconsidered', *Arch. Cant.*, lxxxvii, 31-41.
171. 'Sturry from 500 A.D. to Domesday' in K.H. Mcintosh (ed.), *Sturry, the Changing Scene*, 11-12.
172. Review: Trudy West, *The Timber-framed House in England, J.B.A.A.*, xxxv, 94-5.

1973

173. 'Review of the Year' and 'Coinage and the Myth of the Renaissance' Br. Numismatic Soc. Presidential Address, *Br. Num. Journ.*, xliii, 169-78.
174. 'Numismatica from Site D' in D.S. Neal, 'Excavations at the Palace and Priory, King's Langley', *Herts. Arch.*, iii, 56-8.
175. 'The Timber Churches of Champagne', *J.B.A.A.*, xxxvi, 26-42.
176. 'Tintagel Old Post Office', *Arch. Journ.* cxxx, 247-8.
177. 'Cotehele House', *Arch. Journ.*, cxxx, 256-9.
178. 'The Middle Darent in History', *Cantium*, v, no. 2, 26-28.
179. 'Eynsford Castle: The Moat and Bridge' (with A.J. Fleming), *Arch. Cant.*, lxxxviii, 87-116. See also 45.
180. 'Piccotts End: a probable medieval Guest House and its Wall Paintings' (with E.C. Rouse), *Herts. Arch.*, iii 78-89.
181. 'The Town House, Barley', *Herts. Arch.*, iii, 94-99.
182. Review: M.W. Beresford and H.P.R. Finberg, *English Medieval Boroughs, Med. Arch.*, xvii, 198-9.
183. Review: *Sylloge of Coins of the British Isles*, George Galster, 13-15, *Royal Collection National Museum Copenhagen, Anglo-Saxon Coins, Cnut*; A.J.H. Gunstone, 17 *Ancient British, Anglo-Saxon and Norman Coins in Midlands Museums, Antiq. Journ.* liii, 319-20. See also 162.

1974

184. *Bayham Abbey, Sussex*, Department of the Environment official guidebook, 29 pp.
185. 'Review of the year' and 'Seals and Titles', Br. Numismatic Soc. presidential address, *Br. Num. Journ.*, xliv 97-106.
186. 'Coins found in Anglo-Saxon Burials' in J. Casey and R. Reece (eds.), *Coins and the Archaeologist, BAR* 201-5.
187. 'Medieval Coins' in P. Rahtz and S. Hirst, *Beckery Chapel, Glastonbury, 1967-8, Glastonbury Ant. Soc.*, 65-6.
188. 'Coins and Jettons' in P.J. Drury, 'Chelmsford Dominican Priory, the Excavation of the Reredorter, 1973', *Essex Arch. & Hist.*, vi, 54-5.
189. 'Jettons' in Eleanor Russell *et al.*, 'Excavations on the Site of the deserted medieval Village of Kettleby Thorpe', *Journ. Scunthorpe Mus. Soc.*, iii, no. 2, 40.
190. 'Jettons and a Seal Matrix' in G. Beresford, 'The medieval Manor of Penhallam, Jacobstow, Cornwall', *Med. Arch.*, xviii, 142-3.
191. 'The post-Conquest Churches of Barton-on-Humber', *Arch. Journ.*, cxxxi, 373.
192. 'Thornton Abbey', *Arch. Journ.*, cxxxi, 373-7.
193. 'Further Evidence about the Site of "Dommoc" ', *J.B.A.A.*, xxxviii, 97-102. See also 36.
194. 'Bradwell Priory Chapel' (with P. Woodfield) in D.C. Mynard, 'Excavations at Bradwell Priory, 1968-73', *Milton Keynes Journ. Arch. & Hist.*, iii, 63-5.
195. Review: F. Hull (ed.), *Catalogue of Estate Maps, 1590-1840, in the Kent County Archives Office, Arch. Cant.*, lxxxix, 230-1.
196. Review: C.H.V. Sutherland, *English Coinage, 600-1900, Post-Med. Arch.*, viii, 147-9.
197. Review: C.A. Hewitt, *English Cathedral Carpentry, Arch. Journ.*, cxxxi, 431.
198. Review: Françoise Dumas-Dubourg, *Le Trésor de Fécamp, Num. Chron.*, 7th ser. xiv, 220-1.
199. Review: R.P. Mack, *Sylloge of Coins of the British Isles*, 20, *Ancient British, Anglo-Saxon and Norman Coins in the Mack Collection, Antiq. Journ.*, liv, 330.
200. Review: H.E. Jean Le Patourel, *The Moated Sites of Yorkshire, Med. Arch.*, xviii, 238-40.
201. Reviews: David Martin, *Bodiam Castle Medieval Bridges* and *Hastings Augustinian Priory, Med. Arch.*, xviii, 240-1.
202. Review: A.N. Hume *et al.*, *Five Artifact Studies, Post-med. Arch.*, viii, 152.

1975

203. 'Review of the Year' and 'Coins and Museums', Br. Numismatic Soc. Presidential Address, *Br. Num. Journ.*, xlv, 116-26.

204. 'The Sutton Hoo Coins in the Light of the contemporary Background of Coinage in England' in R.L.S. Bruce-Mitford, *Sutton Hoo* i, 653-677.

205. 'The Gilton (grave 41) Tremissis and the Sarre Coin Necklace' in Richard Avent, *Anglo-Saxon Disc and Composite Brooches, BAR* 11, 69-72.

206. 'The Coins from J.S. Wacher's Excavations' in Colin Platt and Richard Coleman-Smith, *Excavations in medieval Southampton 1953-1969*, ii, 330-1.

207. 'Coins' in Hugh Chapman *et al.*, *Excavations at the Bishops Palace, Lincoln 1968-72, Soc. for Lincs Hist. and Arch.*, 29-30.

208. 'The Coins' (part) in M.J. Hammerson, 'Excavations on the Site of Arundel House in the Strand, W.C.2, in 1972', *Trans. Lond. & Mx. Arch. Soc.*, xxvi, 242.

209. 'Coins' in P.L. Drewett, 'Excavations at Hadleigh Castle', *J.B.A.A.*, xxxviii, 133-5.

210. 'Jetton' in R.A. Hall 'An Excavation at Hunter Street, Buckingham', *Records of Bucks*, xx, pt.1, 120.

211. 'Structural Aspects of medieval Timber Bridges', *Med. Arch.*, xix, 48-91.

212. 'Window Glass' and "Boy-Bishop" Token' in P.L. Drewett and I.W. Stuart, 'Excavations in the Norman Gate Tower, Bury St. Edmunds Abbey', *Proc. Suff. Inst. Arch.*, xxxiii, 251-2.

213. 'The Town Hall' in K.H. McIntosh (ed.), *Fordwich, the Lost Port*, 145-7.

214. 'The Structure of the Bridge' in Lilian Thornhill, 'A double-moated Site at Beckenham', *Arch. Cant.*, xci, 158-60.

215. 'The Fordwich Stone and the Church Porch' in K.H. McIntosh (ed.), *Fordwich, the Lost Port*, 131-2.

216. 'Semantically beastly to the Welsh', letter to the editor, *The Guardian,* 30th September.

217. Review: G. Berry, *Medieval English Jettons, Br. Num. Journ.*, xlv, 97.

218. Review: J.M. Lewis, *Welsh Monumental Brasses, Post-Med. Arch.*, ix, 277.

219. Review: F. Sandgren (ed.), *Otium et Negotium*, Studies in onomatology and library science presented to Olof von Feilitzen, *Antiq. Journ.*, lv, 434.

220. Review: Philip Grierson, *Numismatics, Br. Num. Journ.*, xlv, 97-8.

1976

221. *The Chapter House and Pyx Chamber, Westminster Abbey*, Department of the Environment Official Handbook, 36 pp. See also 4 and 10.

222. 'The Incidence of Imitation among Anglo-Saxon "Sceattas" in the Light of archaeological Excavation', *Proc. Internat. Numismatic Symposium, Warsaw and Budapest*, 185-91.

223. 'The Jettons' in M. Farley, 'Saxon and medieval Walton, Aylesbury', *Records of Bucks*, xx, pt. 2, 290.

224. 'Coins and Jettons' in Peter Drewett, 'Excavations at Bolingbroke Castle, Lincs., 1973', *Post-Med. Arch.*, x, 24-5.

225. 'Jettons and a Bulla' in P.J. Huggins, 'The Excavation of an 11th-century Viking Hall and 14th-century Rooms at Waltham Abbey', *Med. Arch.*, xx, 125-7.

226. 'The Coins and Jettons' in George Lambrick and Humphrey Woods, 'Excavations on the second Site of the Dominican Priory, Oxford', *Oxoniensia*, xli, 220-1.

227. 'The Significance of Building A' in J.H. Parfitt, 'A moated Site at Moat Farm, Leigh, Kent', *Arch. Cant.*, xcii, 177-81.

228. 'Structural Aspects of medieval Timber Bridges: Addenda', *Med. Arch,*. xx, 152-3. See 211.

229. Review: D.I. Hill, *Christ's Glorious Church, The Story of Canterbury Cathedral, Arch. Cant.*, xcii, 258-9.

230. Review: P. Addyman and R. Morris (eds.), *The archaeological Study of Churches, Arch. Cant.*, xcii, 263-4.

231. Review: David Martin and Barbara Mastin, *An architectural History of Robertsbridge* and H.M. and U.E. Lacey, *The Timber-framed Buildings of Steyning, Med. Arch.*, xx, 211.

232. Review: A.N. Hume, *Archaeology and the Colonial Gardener* and *Maryland Historical Magazine* 60, *Post-Med. Arch.*, x, 187-8.

233. Review: John Harvey, *Early Nurserymen, Post-Med. Arch.*, x 189.

234. Review: A.J. Willis, *Church Life in Kent, being Church Court Records of the Canterbury Diocese, Post-Med. Arch.*, x, 192.

235. Review: M.H. Crawford, *Roman Republican Coinage*, *J.B.A.A.*, cxxix, 96-7.

1977

236. 'Small Change in the Light of medieval Site-finds' in N.J. Mayhew (ed.), *Edwardian Monetary Affairs*, *BAR* 36, 59-80.
237. 'The principal Series of English Sceattas', *Br. Num. Journ.*, xlvii, 21-30.
238. 'A Check-list of English Finds of Sceattas' (with D.M. Metcalf), *Br. Num. Journ.*, xlvii, 31-52. See also 258.
239. 'A Group of three Sceattas from Excavations at Mucking, Essex', *Br. Num. Journ.*, xlvii, 127-8.
240. 'A Group of "primary Sceattas" from Mucking, Essex' (with W.T. Jones), *Antiq. Journ.*, lvii, 321-2.
241. 'The Evidence of Site-finds and stray Losses for the Currency of medieval Scotland' in D.M. Metcalf (ed.), *Coinage in Medieval Scotland*, *BAR* 45, 61-4.
242. 'Coins' (with E.J.E. Pirie) in P.V. Addyman and J. Priestly, 'Baile Hill, York, a Report on the Institute's Excavations', *Arch. Journ.*, cxxxiv, 144-5.
243. 'Coins' (with J.P.C. Kent) and 'Jettons' in Helen Clarke and Alan Carter, *Excavations in King's Lynn 1953-70*, Soc. Med. Arch. Monograph vii, 286-7.
244. 'Lead Disc, Coins and Jetton' in K.J. Barton and E.W. Holden, 'Excavations at Bramber Castle, Sussex, 1966-67', *Arch. Journ.*, cxxxiv, 60-1.
245. 'Romanesque Bases in and south-east of the Limestone Belt' in M.R. Apted *et al.* (eds.), *Ancient Monuments and their Interpretation*, Essays presented to A.J. Taylor, 99-137.
246. 'Two common Species of medieval Seal-matrix', *Antiq. Journ.*, lvii, 324-9.
247. 'Seal Matrix' in Guy Beresford, 'Excavation of a moated House at Wintringham in Huntingdonshire', *Arch. Journ.*, cxxxiv, 256.
248. '*Litus Romanum* — the Shore Forts as Mission Stations' in D.E. Johnston (ed.), *The Saxon Shore*, C.B.A. Research Report 18, 70-5.
249. 'Architectural Fragments' and 'Coin Identification' in Frances Williams *et al.*, *Pleshey Castle*, *BAR* 42, 78-80, 197-9.
250. 'Discussion of the medieval Buildings' in Rosamond Hanworth and D.J. Tomalin, *Brooklands, Weybridge*, Surrey Arch. Soc. Research Vol. iv, 55-9.
251. 'A Mould for leaden Ventilators from Neath Abbey, South Wales', *Antiq. Journ.* lvii, 334-6.
252. 'Sculptured Block from sub-vault of Misericorde' in Graham Black, 'The Redevelopment of 20 Dean's Yard, Westminster Abbey, 1975-7', *Trans. Lond. & Mx. Arch. Soc.*, xxviii, 200-2.
253. Review: Royal Commission on Historical Monuments, *English Vernacular Houses*, *Med. Arch.*, xxi, 282-3.
254. Review: D.M. Metcalf, *Sylloge of Coins of the British Isles, 23, Ashmolean Museum, Coins of Henry VII*, *Antiq. Journ.*, lvii, 392.
255. Review: D.M. Wilson (ed.), *The Archaeology of Anglo-Saxon England*, *J.B.A.A.*, cxxx, 162-4.
256. Review: Euan Mackie, *Science and Society in Prehistoric Britain*, *Arch. Cant.*, xciii, 229-30.

1978

257. *Yarmouth Castle, Isle of Wight*, Department of the Environment official handbook, 20 pp. See also 26.
258. 'A Check-list of English Finds of Sceattas: Correction' (with D.M. Metcalf), *Br. Num. Journ.*, xlviii, 107. See 238.
259. 'Coins and Jettons' in A.E.S. Musty, 'Exploratory Excavation within the monastic Precinct, Waltham Abbey, 1972', *Essex Arch. & Hist*, x, 156-7.
260. 'The St. Nicholas or "Boy Bishop" Tokens', *Proc. Suff. Inst. Arch. & Hist.*, xxxiv, pt. 2, 87-101. See also 299.
261. 'Une trouvaille dans un Puits à la Cathédrale d' York', *Bull. de la Soc. Franc. de Numismatique*, xxxiii, 393-6.
262. 'The Jettons' and 'Seal Matrix' in J.H. Williams, 'Excavations at Greyfriars, Northampton, 1972' *Northants. Arch.*, xiii, 131-2, 147-8.
263. 'A medieval Coin Balance from Roche Abbey, Yorkshire', *Antiq. Journ.*, lviii, 371-4.
264. 'Structures within English moated Sites' in F.A. Åberg (ed.), *Medieval moated Sites*, C.B.A. Research Report 17, 29-36.
265. 'A hard-wearing Carpet' in P. Drury (ed.), *Synopsis of Contributions presented to the Cambridge Tile Seminar*, 28-30.
266. 'Bede Game', Letter to the Editor, *The Guardian*, 22nd August. See 36.

267. Review: Peter Clemoes (ed.), *Anglo-Saxon England*, i-vi, *Br. Num. Journ.*, xlviii, 119-20.
268. Review: J.N. Green, *The Loss of the Verenigde Oostindische Compagnie Jacht Vergulde Draeck, Western Australia 1656*, *Post-Med. Arch.*, xii, 137-8.
269. Review: I. Bott *et al.*, *Fachwerkkirchen in Hessen*, *Antiq. Journ.*, lviii, 211-2.
270. Review: K.P. Witney, *The Jutish Forest, a Study of the Weald of Kent from 450-1380 A.D.*, *Antiq. Journ.*, lviii, 196-7.
271. Review: Gert Hatz, *Handel und Verkehr zwischen dem Deutschen Reich und Schweden in der späten Wikingerzeit*, Die deutschen Munzen des 10. und 11 Jahrhunderts in Schweden, *Num. Chron.*, 7th ser., xviii, 205-6.
272. Review: D. MacCulloch (ed.), *The Chorography of Suffolk*, *Post-Med. Arch.*, xii, 147-8.

1979

273. 'Thetford Warren Lodge' in F.J.E. Raby and P.K. Baillie-Reynolds, *Thetford Priory, Norfolk*, Department of the Environment official handbook, 18-19.
274. 'Anglo-Saxon "Sceat"' in A.C. Harrison and D. Williams, 'Excavation at Prior's Gate House, Rochester', *Arch. Cant.*, xcv, 27.
275. 'Coins and Jettons' in D.D. Andrews and G. Milne (eds.), *Domestic Settlement, 1: Areas 10 and 6*, Vol. I of J.G. Hurst (ed.), *Wharram, a Study of Settlement on the Yorkshire Wolds*, Soc. Med. Arch. Monograph VIII, 132.
276. 'Additional Documentation, Coins and Jettons, Dressed Stonework, Painted Wall-plaster, Painted Window Glass, Stone Mortars' in G.H. Smith 'The Excavation of the Hospital of St. Mary of Ospringe, commonly called Maison Dieu', *Arch. Cant.*, xcv, 87-90, 127-9, 107-13, 113-5, 115-7, 153-4. See also 22.
277. 'Seal Matrix from Bedford Castle' in D. Baker *et al.*, 'Excavations in Bedford, 1967-77', *Beds. Arch. Journ.*, xiii, 284-5.
278. 'The Counters and a Token' in J.H. Williams, *St. Peter's Street, Northampton, Excavations, 1973-5*, Northampton Development Corporation Archaeological Monograph II, 246.
279. 'The Distribution of early Romanesque Towers to minor Churches', *Arch. Journ.*, cxxxvi, 109-117.
280. Review: Deryck Seymour, *Torre Abbey*, *Antiq. Journ.*, lix, 166-7.
281. Review: H.M. Taylor, *Anglo-Saxon Architecture*, iii, *J.B.A.A.*, cxxxii, 113-5.
282. Review: J.K. Major, *Animal-powered Engines*, *Med. Arch.*, xxiii, 289.
283. (and L.R.A. Grove) 'The View and State of the Commandery of Swingfield, 1529', in F. Hull (ed.). *A Kentish Miscellany*, 102-27.

1980

284. 'The Sceattas' in P. Wade-Martins, 'Excavations in North Elmham Park 1967-72' *E. Anglian Arch.*, ix, pt. 2, 497-9.
285. 'The Coin' in P. Wade-Martins, 'Fieldwork and Excavation on Village Sites in Launditch Hundred', *E. Anglian Arch.*, x, 127.
286. 'Jettons' in Peter Armstrong, 'Excavations in Scale Lane, Lowgate, 1974', *E. Riding Archaeologist*, vi, 72-3.
287. 'Seal Matrix' and 'Numismatica' in P.M. Christie and J.G. Coad 'Excavations at Denny Abbey', *Arch. Journ.*, cxxxvii, 257-60 and 264-5.
288. 'North Elmham Cathedral', *Arch. Journ.*, cxxxvii, 327-8. See also 43.
289. 'Baconsthorpe Castle', *Arch. Journ.*, cxxxvii, 331-2. See also 60.
290. 'New Buckenham Castle', *Arch. Journ.*, cxxxvii, 353-5.
291. 'Thetford Castle', *Arch. Journ.*, cxxxvii, 355.
292. Review: Joanna Bird *et al.* (eds), *Collectanea Londiniensia, Studies presented to Ralph Merrifield*, *J.B.A.A.*, cxxxiii, 99-101.
293. Review: A.L. Cummings, *The framed Houses of Massachusets Bay, 1635-1725*, *Post-Med. Arch.*, xiv, 222-3.
294. Review: G. Galster *et al.*, *Sylloge of Coins of the British Isles, 22 Royal Danish Collection, Copenhagen, Hiberno-Norse and Anglo-Irish Coins*, *Antiq. Journ.*, lx, 392-3.
295. Review: M. Jones, *The Art of the Medal*, *Antiq. Journ.* lx, 403-4.
296. Review: C.E. Challis, *The Tudor Coinage*, *Antiq. Journ.*, lx, 404-5.

1981

297. Review: M.W. Barley, *European Towns, Med. Arch.*, xxv.
298. Review: Eric Getting-Jones, *The Dymock School of Sculpture, Med. Arch.*, xxv.
299. Review: Jean Bony, *The English Decorated Style: Gothic architecture transformed, 1250-1350, Churchscape*, Annual Review of the Council for the Care of Churches, i, 57-9.

FORTHCOMING

300. 'More St. Nicholas tokens from Bury St. Edmunds and Vicinity', *Proc. Suff. Inst. Arch. & Hist.*, xxxv. See also 260.
301. 'Numismatica' in Charmian Woodfield, 'Finds from the Free Grammar School at the Whitefriars, Coventry, *c.* 1545-1557/8', *Post-Med. Arch.*, xv.
302. 'Coins and Jettons' in G. Coppack, 'The outer Court of Fountains Abbey, Excavation of the Wool House and other Buildings', Soc. Med. Arch. Monograph series.
303. 'Coins and Jettons' in D. Sherlock and H. Woods, 'Excavations at St. Augustine's Abbey', Soc. Med. Arch. Monograph series.
304. 'Sceatta' in F. Jenkins, 'Excavations at St. Pancras'.
305. 'Four Sceattas' in *The Archaeology of Canterbury*, Canterbury Archaeological Trust.
306. 'Jettons' in Martin Biddle, *St. Alban's Abbey Chapter House Excavations*.
307. 'Jettons' in Martin Biddle (ed.), 'The Winchester Mint and other numismatic Studies', *Winchester Studies*, viii.
308. 'The Fittings of medieval Burgess Houses at various social Levels', *Rotterdam Papers*.
309. 'Guy Knocker' in A. Rogerson and C. Dallas, 'Excavations at Thetford 1948-1959 and 1973-77', *E. Anglian Arch.*
310. 'The House of Eynsford in Tenure, Office and private Activity' in A.F. Butcher (ed.), *Medieval Canterbury, Essays in memory of W.G. Urry*. See also 45.
311. 'Medieval Archaeology in Kent' in A.F. Clarke and P.E. Leach (eds.), *Archaeology in Kent to A.D. 1500*, C.B.A. Research Report.
312. 'Some Thoughts on medieval Towns in Kent', *Arch. Cant.*, xcvii.
313. 'Eadberht Sceatta from Caister on Sea', *Br. Num. Journ.*, li.
314. 'The Thrysma' and 'The Sceatta' in Philip Crummy, *Aspects of Anglo-Saxon and Norman Colchester*, C.B.A. Research Report 39, 8 and 20.
315. 'Medieval sculptured Stone and 'Jettons' ' in J.K. Knight, *Excavations at Montgomery Castle*.
316. 'Jettons and Tokens', in G.C. Milne, *'The medieval Waterfront Development at Trigg Lane, London'* in *London and Middx. Arch. Soc.*, Special Paper 5.

LANDSCAPES: SOME ANTIQUARIAN MOODS AND FANCIES

RONALD JESSUP

Many and varied were, and still are, the views held by scholars, topographers and literary speculators interested in various aspects of the story of the past. Well-known megalithic monuments, for instance, have been attributed to such diverse peoples as the Phoenicians, the Danes, Gallo-Romans, King Arthur and the Druids of the Ancient British kingdoms. Later the Etrurians, the folk of the so-called Early Iron Age, and even Freemasons were to be added to the list. It was in the progress of the eighteenth and early nineteenth centuries that thought in literature, art and antiquity began to turn from some of the accepted tenets of a perfectionist classical tradition towards romanticism and an expression of individuality. With early architecture especially, but also with ancient monuments, there was a pronounced movement towards emotion and a romantic ideal. The well-to-do started and soon increased their collections of antiquities, ornamented their estates with sham ruins, grottoes and caverns decorated with shining minerals and fossils, with fake prehistoric monuments, sometimes even with stones derived from genuine prehistoric and classical monuments. Gentlemen who had no true relics of antiquity on their estates often set about to remedy their needs by moving genuine monuments from elsewhere, by building monuments to give work to local unemployed labour as for example Solomon's Temple at Buxton, Derbyshire, the curiosity at Hay, Breconshire, and above all the 'Stonehenge' at Ilton high on the Uredale near Masham, North Yorkshire.

Broad discussions of such matters and long arguments upon the challenges of antiquarian moods and fancies were often welcomed by Stuart Rigold, Frank Higenbottam, City Librarian of Canterbury, an acknowledged cryptic-shorthand expert, and myself, the three of us not unused to ultra-enigma variations, as we sat after lunch by the side of the lake in Bletchley Park and occasionally in the Quiet Room of the Club. Both of my colleagues later joined the Kent Archaeological Society. Down the long years after Bletchley, Stuart and I continued our private debates, often in Mill's Parlour at the Society of Antiquaries, wondering which of these 'historical' structures should be given the benefit of official protection. Fortunate powers of memory and a determination that it was essential to look to learn no doubt helped our discussions.

From Bletchley it was possible for Stuart and I to visit two monuments outstanding in their landscape.

At Fawley Mount, Henley-on-Thames, Oxfordshire, John Freeman, a well-known Fellow of the Society of Antiquaries, in 1731 removed the contents of a cist which a careful excavation in 1932 (Jessup 1977, 94) showed to be the typical compact burial chamber of a Roman barrow.

Outside the cist, a structure of trimmed chalk blocks partly covered with flanged roofing-tiles, and on the original surface level, was a large wide-shouldered and narrow-mouthed Roman jar. Such vessels, no doubt used in the burial ritual, are not uncommonly found outside Roman barrows. What Freeman may have removed from the cist to add to his own famous collection of classical antiquities is not known. What he added was revealed in the 1932 excavation, a sight now remembered by very few of us. There were contemporary household pots, pans and bottles, pieces of leather harness, padlocks, fragments of Tudor and other stained glass, bottles of wine wax-sealed with Freeman's crest and some seventy coins, chiefly sets of Maundy money, in a bottle of 'preservative' liquid. A fine alabaster carving of the Martyrdom of St. Katharine of Alexandria gave an air of refined antiquarianism to the whole thing. The story appeared in a long inscription in Latin, dated 8th December, 1731, finely engraved on a panel of glass which was carefully placed along a wall inside the cist. Freeman said that he had buried these objects so that if by chance at some time curious posterity should examine this old rubbish it might find something to give pleasure and perhaps profit since some arts were dying out. He added a detailed description of Henley and a brief account of England, and on a separate panel an engraved diagram of local topography. The relics now seem to have disappeared, but four magnificent pieces of classical sculpture bought by Freeman in 1717 have been loaned to the Ashmolean Museum by the Divine Mercy College, the present owners of Fawley Court, while three remain at the Court. From its site, conical form and structure there can be no doubt that Fawley Mount is a typical Roman barrow. (Jessup 1958).

A megalith unique in Britain, a curiosity in its present landscape but nevertheless a genuine antiquity, had interested both of us. 'Monte de la Ville', a communal burial-tomb and passage grave, now stands in the grounds of Park Place Estate at Wargrave, Henley-on-Thames, Berkshire. Its history is partly told by an inscription: *Cet ancien Temple des Druides découvert le 12me Août 1785 sur la Montagne de St Hélier dans l'Isle de Jersey: A été présenté par les Habitants à son Excellence le Général Conway, leur Gouverneur*. A further dozen lines describe its supposed history and significance in ancient times. The monument, then a stone circle with five side-chambers four complete and one destroyed, in one of which was a coin of Claudius, was in fact discovered during the construction of a parade-ground for the St. Helier Militia on the site of the present Fort Regent. A model of the monument given by the General to the Society of Antiquaries (*Minute Books*, 31, 470; 32, 81) may still be seen in the Society's Collections. In 1788, he had shipped many of the stones in a London-bound barge to his Thames-side estate at Park Place where the monument was rebuilt though with fewer stones and in smaller dimensions than in its original form. A useful plan with a full description and photographs was published by W.A. Smallcombe, then Curator of Reading Museum (Smallcombe 1946) and though the site on strictly private property is now somewhat overgrown, its main features can still be traced.

Horace Walpole was greatly pleased with the acquisition of his near neighbour and complimented him on '. . . the transport of the Cathedral of your Island to your Domain on our Continent', but his opinion that the monument had been restored to its original form was not shared by some authorities though most admired its magnificent landscape setting. On the other hand in his customary severe language Augustus J.C. Hare, compiler of the 1860 edition of Murray's *Handbook* among his many literary works, complained that it was difficult to say who were the greater vandals, the donors or the receiver, but to-day we can recognise a noteworthy piece of romantic antiquarianism, as worthy a curiosity of antiquity as the French genuine prehistoric megalithic tombs which were moved over long distances to serve as tombs in modern cemeteries.

From the remarkable assemblage of prehistoric megaliths in the neighbouring Channel Island of Guernsey (which had long interested us both) no monuments have been removed abroad, but there are many examples of local displacements and re-use. Several deserve a brief mention. At Câtel the well-known statue-menhir uncovered below the chancel of the church in 1878 was carefully erected in the churchyard, while the notable figure-sculpture, La Grand' mère du Chimquière, which once stood in the churchyard of St. Martin, was deliberately damaged and moved to serve as a churchyard gatepost. Both monuments are of local grey granite. They differ much in style and execution though both could be local and independent representations of the primitive so-called 'Mother Goddess', the Great Earth Mother found in various places and of various dates, a creature thought to exercise a benign influence on crops and animals and the source to whom all men returned for rebirth after death. If the diffusion conception of the 'Mother Goddess' is not acceptable to all modern branches of archaeology — and there were indications as we argued that it is not — it can scarcely be denied that there is a likely connection between Guernsey and Brittany. La Grand'mère could possibly have been resculptured in Roman or medieval times. She still received small gifts of flowers and coins on her hollowed head in recent years, much to the annoyance of a local member of the parish. The Câtel statue-menhir may be from the walling of a long passage-grave; it does not seem to have any Christian sanctity preserved from pagan times, unlike the large stone probably from a prehistoric megalith which now stands at the eastern entrance to St. Saviour's churchyard which has been Christianised, or so we thought, by the incision of two crosses.

It is possible that some of the stone benches at the open-air feudal Fief Courts, La Table des Pions near Pleinmont, of de Gohiers and de Longues at St. Saviour's among them, came from prehistoric megaliths, as did a large stone at Dunnabridge Pound on Dartmoor, once the President's seat of a Stannaries Court as Bryan O'Neil, then Chief Inspector of Ancient Monuments reminded us, and Le Perron du Roi in the wall by Forest church, moved more than once, is traditionally said to be part of a dolmen called Le Trépied des Nouettes. At St. Sampson's Harbour a large vertical menhir became a convenient memorial to the Bailiff and President of the States under whose auspices the construction of the Harbour in 1820 was first begun. But at Vale churchyard the famous Druid's Altar of some nineteenth-century historians is but a curious natural formation of the local granite rock: its suggestive form still often misleads present-day visitors. And in some places, including Le Creux ès Fées at L'Erée, Vardes at L'Ancresse, Paradis, Vale and Le Trépied — as in some western parts of Wales — megalithic tombs have been used in modern times as cattle-shelters and stores, as armed posts during the German occupation of Guernsey, and for other utilitarian purposes. In this famous island megaliths take their place in an outstanding landscape of archaeology, history and natural beauty, with no little curiosity, as we too had discovered jointly and severally down the years.

'Riggy' and I by virtue of our Kentish background had a strong love for all antiquarian matters associated with our native county. As an Inspector of Ancient Monuments from 1948 onwards he took an especial interest in vernacular architecture as I did in Roman barrows. Often in his company my own activities included field-work as Correspondent for Kent to the Archaeological Officer of the Ordnance Survey and to the Chief Inspector of Ancient Monuments. But in addition we were also concerned with more widely-spread antiquarian interests.

Some of these interests, covering many years of friendship, can only be briefly mentioned here, and it is only right to say at once how warmly we welcomed and later discussed outstanding well-known works by Glyn Daniel, Evan Hadingham, Barbara Jones and Stuart Piggott.
(Daniel, G, etc. noted below).

At the same time we could greatly enjoy Bertil Almqvist's joyously funny story of The Stones exploring Britain when Dad, Mum, with their children Chip and Pebbles, a cow and a dog, and assisted by Messrs. Holmes and Watson, helped to set up at Stonehenge the first pub in Britain.

In our own county one of the most interesting antiquarian fancies was the pavilion built about 1775 in his garden at Heppington near Canterbury by the Rev. Bryan Faussett. He was a zealous excavator of Saxon burial mounds in east Kent, owner of a vast and noteworthy collection of antiquities chiefly so obtained and inventor of a metal probe to locate 'latent graves without opening the ground'. His Journal from 1757 to 1773, published in 1856 by Roach Smith, is a classic of its kind. Here — first shown to me in 1927 by Gordon Home on a visit to his wife's early home and rediscovered only in 1950 (Jessup 1953) — was the pavilion much as Faussett left it with miscellaneous antiquities and learned descriptions in Latin (1769-1775) hung round the inside walls. The bowl of an early font from nearby Kingston church had been returned to its home and regenerated. Other decorations included a quern-stone used as a cover for a Roman cremation urn, sculptured corbels from Northbourne in east Kent, a terracotta relief from Roman London, an effigy from the tomb of an ecclesiastic in St. Augustine's Abbey, Canterbury, and a remarkable piece of late Romanesque sculpture found in the precincts of the Cathedral. Faussett thought that this sculpture represented King Canute. It is in fact that of a Biblical prophet carved by an artist of great ability, and it can be matched as Professor George Zarnecki pointed out by another relief in the Cathedral Library. Faussett's sculpture was a piece which had been re-used as building material in the 'Aula Nova' or North Hall, and both pieces, executed about A.D. 1190, may have been part of the decoration of the first Almonry Chapel. Most of the pavilion relics were given to the Royal Museum, Canterbury: in view of its outstanding interest the Canterbury sculpture was loaned by the Royal Museum to the Victoria and Albert Museum.

Here at Heppington we recalled certain other 'antiquarian' additions to the landscape. The Bartlow Hills at Ashdon in Essex, the most impressive group of Roman barrows in Britain, were planted with palisade-enclosed trees on their lofty summits. Nash Court at Boughton-under-Blean in Kent was ornamented with two Roman-like barrows aligned typically on the Roman Watling Street, the material found on their excavation in 1948 (Jessup 1951) being obtained from a lake dug in 1798 to improve the Park landscape. (It is only fair to add that I was responsible for suggesting to the Ordnance Survey that the mounds were Roman barrows). A rather different style of ornament is Lanyon Quoit in Cornwall which was rebuilt in 1824 after its collapse nine years earlier, but on a smaller scale. Traces of a mound we had both seen, and it was said locally that a mysterious man on horseback appeared under the original capstone: to us he never appeared. The mood of antiquarian fancy is scarcely passed, for not many years ago Stuart and I saw the floor of a Roman bath and a path made of Roman tiles in the garden of the late Arthur Mee, author of the well-known 'The King's England' series of county books: the material had been rescued from the site of a Roman villa destroyed in the building of a nearby housing estate at Eynsford. Antiquarian moods and fancies exhibit also mock-megaliths though Professor Glyn Daniel's words 'Megaliths in History' which include in time and association a wide range of such monuments is to be preferred as it can admit megaliths created, often accidentally, by farmers clearing their land of cumbersome stones, and for the sake of completeness stone circles laid out by modern Druids.

As an aside, but with some knowledge of its countryside we also spoke of several examples of megaliths associated with Welsh churches. At Llanfairpwllgwyngll a menhir was found under the pulpit of the parish church, and at Yspytty Cynfyn near Aberystwyth the earthern bank surrounding the circular churchyard incorporates three stones derived perhaps from a prehistoric circle. The survival of an element of pagan sanctity again seems possible.

Historical legend and tradition long acknowledged to have had a significant place in the environment of megaliths has often become attached to structures which may not be what they seem. One or two examples must suffice here.

The Three Shire Stones by the Fosse Way where the boundaries of Somerset, Gloucester and Wiltshire meet, or used to meet, consist of a trilithon of oolite slabs with a capstone covering three small damaged stones each bearing the date 1736 and the initial letter of one county name. Camden noted, but without enthusiasm, that the original stones traditionally marked the site of a battle in which Canute was defeated by Edmund Ironside. Celia Fiennes and many later travellers' journals mentioned them. The present large stones were in fact put up in 1858-59 to protect older boundary or mark-stones: three human skeletons and a coin of James II were found in a hole dug for one of the new stones in this modern imitation of a dolmen (Gunstone 1964).

Legend is also attached to some of the 'megalithic' sarsen stones near the prehistoric crossing of the River Medway at Aylesford in our own county. The Upper White Horse Stone which does resemble the form of a horse has no link with the legendary White Horse of Kent, though it may well be part of a chamber-tomb. Nearby, until its wanton destruction, stood the Lower White Horse Stone or the Kentish Standard Stone as local antiquaries preferred to call it. There is nothing but popular fantasy to connect it with Hengist or Horsa or the raising or hiding of the Saxon standard at the Battle of Aylesford c. 445, but it may well have formed part of a megalithic burial-chamber. Here as elsewhere farmers dragged sarsens to the edges of cultivated fields to prevent damage to plough-shares, as we had often seen. Hence grew the eccentric suggestion started, we thought, by Fergusson's journeys in 1867, of a sacred cross-country avenue linking Kit's Coty with the elaborate Coldrum chamber-tomb at Trottiscliffe, the site of a legendary battle in which a 'Black Prince' died.

A small monument known as Lady Darnley's Kit's Coty House was built in the garden of the family seat, Cobham Hall near Gravesend, within a few miles of the original well-known national monument of antiquity. It was in fact an ideal monument to be imitated as a genteel, historical and ornamental addition to a landed estate, and so Humphrey Repton decided when about 1790 he made improvements to the Hall and its grounds for the third Earl. Her Ladyship's Garden on the north side of the house was given a classical pavilion with an appropriate Latin inscription, a grotto named Merlin's Grotto which was purchased by the fourth Earl in 1820 from Ingress Abbey, Greenhithe, once a grange of the Priory of Dartford, and a five-foot high 'dolmen' of sarsens sited on an eminence which was surrounded by a chain or ring of large sarsens placed upright on their longest sides. Nearby an ice-house built according to estate records in 1792 had an entrance partly framed by sarsens. All these structures overgrown and neglected for many years are now cared for with appreciation by the present owners, Westwood Educational Trust, Cobham Hall School for Girls.

How were the sarsens for this miniature Kit's Coty House obtained? The interesting story, one of local legend and of personalities in the antiquarian world of the nineteenth century and later, is far too long to relate fully here. Such stones are a very common feature in local surface geology; they were used as can still be seen for road-metal, as farm-posts, to mark road banks and in the fabric of local churches. Lady Darnley's stones came chiefly from the nearby hamlet of Battle Street; but the place-name is in fact derived from a personal surname and has no connection with the burial-place of a chieftain who died in a battle of long ago, or with a possible prehistoric megalith — and a site was marked on earlier editions of large-scale Ordnance Survey maps — thought to be traditionally called The Warrior's Grave. Druids and warrior have gone and there is no evidence at all of the existence of a prehistoric megalith.

One large stone placed at the entrance to Sarsen Close, an appropriately-named group of modern houses at Battle Street, is a reminder of an inviting antiquarian fancy, an unproven epilogue, to which several members of the Kent Archaeological Society and Frederick Lukis of Guernsey gave time and attention. The story is well told in a summary by our members, A.F. Allen and the late John H. Evans in *Archaeologia Cantiana*, lxxxi (1966), lvi-lvii.

One other antiquarian fancy, a feature of the landscape of east Sussex, we liked to claim as an historic megalith. Here in Hove Park is a massive piece of conglomerate-sarsen known as the Goldstone. Early nineteenth-century local antiquaries, Douglas and Horsfield among them, saw here a sacred place of the ancient Britons and claimed in this 6-ft. high stone 'one of the largest and most remarkable of the Druidical stones on the South Downs.' Douglas found nothing of interest when in 1812 he excavated round and under the stone. Some twenty-two years later it was removed from its original commanding position in the valley of Goldstone Bottom to which it had given its name at least since 1617 and with 'unfeeling and sacrilege' in Horsfield's words was thrown into a deep pit dug especially to receive it. A later Sussex historian, Mark Anthony Lower, said in 1870 'some archaeologists wish the utilitarian farmer had been buried under it. Without doubt, the Stone had been sacred to the Druids.' It may have been, but by 1902 in certain quarters there were no more doubts. By then it had been carefully raised from its pit, labelled as 'Goldstone, Dolmen or Holy Stone of Druids' and in 1929 it was given a further inscription which recorded the planting of a tree in its now surrounding enclosure to mark the 1000th Meeting of the Ames Lodge of the Ancient Order of Druids and the Centenary Meeting of the Royal Arch Chapter No. 38. The Goldstone and the group of small sarsens about it, all collected from other areas of the South Downs, are now well cared for (Jessup 1975). But where else is there a megalith or a megalithic folly which has given its name to a large municipal area and a well-known football-ground.

But, as 'Riggy' once reminded me, we can always read from *Advancement of Learning* on the opening page of each volume of our *Archaeologia Cantiana*, and so here we can also say with Francis Bacon that Antiquities are history defaced, or some remnants of history which have casually escaped the shipwreck of time, and with Caleb Colton remind ourselves that

> To look back to antiquity is
> one thing; to go back to it
> is another.

TWO ROMAN ZOOMORPHIC BROOCHES
FROM RICHBOROUGH*

S.A. BUTCHER

The two plate brooches illustrated in Fig. 1 belong to a distinctive type which is widely distributed in the Roman Empire. Fig. 1, no. 2, (AM Laboratory no. 7351711; Bushe-Fox 1949, 148, 229, Pl. LIV) has the outline of a horse in spirited movement. The head is shown naturalistically in full relief but the rest of the body is flat and bears the pin and catchplate on its reverse side. The pin is missing but it was originally hinged on a bar held by two lugs behind the rump.

The decoration gives a spotty appearance to the animal: there is a row of four round cells for enamel on the flank and a panel with three shallow rings (not enamelled) down the line of the shoulder, while the neck bears another three rings.

Miss Justine Bayley (AM Laboratory) reports that the enamelled cell nearest the head has traces of turquoise; the second and fourth spots are completely full of (?) green enamel and the third is empty. Analysis of the metal shows it to be a brass with some lead and a little tin. This alloy is typical of first-century brooches (Bayley and Butcher 1981) although the only evidence so far available for the type would allow a second-century date (Böhme 1972, 41); the Richborough brooch was associated with pottery of up to A.D. 200.

There is a number of close parallels for the Richborough horse. One is shown in the British Museum *Guide to the Antiquities of Roman Britain* (2nd edition 1958), 22, no. 42, fig. 11. Its provenance is unknown. Another from Charterhouse-on-Mendip was seen in Bristol Museum (VCH *Somerset*, i, 1906, 338). In this example the enamel spots on the flanks are alternately red and blue, while the quincunx of spots on the rump is red, except for a blue spot in the centre. Elsewhere in the Roman Empire similar brooches have been found: e.g. Besançon (Lerat 1956, 39, Pl. XVIII 300, 301, both from the river Doubs), Mandeure (Lerat 1956, 39, Pl. XVII, 299).

The brooch Fig. 1, no. 1 (AM Lab no. 7351528, Bushe-Fox 1949, 118, 50, Pl. XXIX) shows a lion with the head in relief turned to face outwards while the rest of the body is flat. Again there were spots of enamel on the body; most of them red, though two contained turquoise. One of the eyes contained traces of green glass according to Bushe-Fox (1949, 118) but there is now only a thin black layer, presumably an adhesive (J. Bayley). Miss Bayley's analysis of the alloy shows that it is a leaded gunmetal.

As with the horse-brooch the pin was attached to the back of the plate by two lugs with a bar acting as a hinge. The mane of the lion is shown by raised circles round the face with hatching to indicate fur, the eyes are deeply drilled and there are grooves, crudely cut, giving a fierce expression to the muzzle. This is a larger brooch than the horse (40 mm. long against *c.*

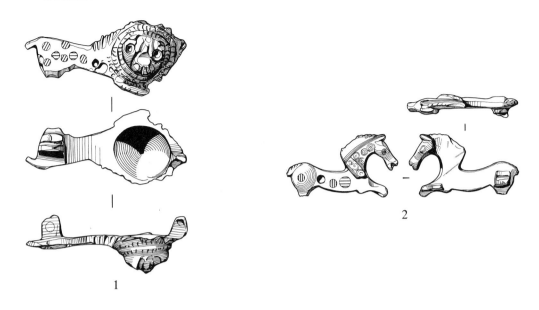

Fig. 1. Zoomorphic brooches from Richborough (½).

30 mm.) and very crudely made. There is a similar brooch from the Saalburg (Böhme 1972, 1059, 40, Taf. 27 where others are quoted from France and from the Tyrol). A shale plaque showing a lion in a similar attitude was found at Jordan Hill in Dorset, where there was a Romano-Celtic temple (BM 1958, fig. 26.8).

Both these brooches belong to a type which is distinguished by a non-naturalistic decoration of enamel in spots on the body and by the representation of the head three-dimensionally whereas the rest of the animal is flat. Other animals represented in this way include leopards: Vindonissa (Ettlinger 1973, 126, Taf. 14, 22), Gyor-Homokgodor (Pannonia) (Sellye 1939, 79, Pl. XIII, 21), two in the Ashmolean Museum from France (nos. 1927, 410 and 411), another from Bessarabia (Ashmolean no. 1927, 413); wild boars: Siscia (Sellye 1939, 79, Pl. XIII, 23), Cirencester (Ashmolean 1927, 415); Bolards (*Gallia*, vi (1949), 323, fig. 43); "Germany" (Ashmolean R. 315); Metz (Museum); a leopard with its prey from Augst (Ettlinger 1973, 126, Taf. 28, 10).

Recently it has become clear that some classes of zoomorphic plate brooches have religious associations: the type showing a horse and rider in very crude outline has been found on a number of temple sites (Butcher 1977, 54; fuller discussion in Leech, forthcoming) while both Anne Ross (1967) and Miranda Green (1976) have discussed this figure type in relation to Celtic mythology.

The general type represented by the two Richborough brooches has not been found in known religious contexts (although the two horses from the River Doubs (Lerat 1956) were probably votive), but it is always possible that brooches from disturbed or uncertain contexts may have been deposited as votives at a minor shrine or with a burial. The animals represented all have strong religious connotations. The horse is well-known as a cult animal amongst the Celts (cf. Ross 1967, Ch. 7) while the lion was adopted from Mediterranean art for its funerary symbolism (Toynbee 1973, Ch. IV) and its appearance on pipe-clay figurines establishes its votive character (e.g. at Kelvedon, *Britannia*, iii (1971), 333). The leopard and prey shown on the Augst brooch is also a funerary image but the series of brooches showing a leopardess in a very distinctive attitude suggests a story or myth to which we do not have the key. The animal is shown reclining, with its head raised and turned sideways: this hardly fits the Dionysiac associations of the leopard where it usually figures as the god's mount or (in pairs) pulling his chariot. Wild boars, shown on the brooches in typically defiant pose, were frequently represented on Celtic cult objects.

It is of course possible that the animals shown on these brooches were used purely decoratively, but it seems significant that those chosen can all have religious associations and that each is shown in a very specific attitude. There are other types of plate brooch with zoomorphic outlines, for instance those which are completely flat and have larger areas of non-naturalistic enamelling on the body; these may be a development of the type discussed here since the enamel fields often include groups of spots. The subjects all have religious associations, and they include some mythical creatures such as sea-monsters and chimaeras.

The use of brooches as votive offerings is illustrated by the collections from such temple sites as Woodeaton (Kirk 1949), Lydney (Wheeler 1932) and Uley (Butcher in Ellison, forthcoming). It has long been thought that votive trinkets were sold (and possibly made) at such sites. But brooches similar to those found in votive groups are also found in secular contexts and since they are so very portable no single brooch can be used to identify the context in which it is found.

It is suggested that brooches such as those discussed here were obtained on visits to holy places and were cherished as souvenirs, good luck charms, or in some cases perhaps as objects of deeper significance. For all these attitudes parallels can be seen in the wearing of Christian symbols as personal ornaments to the present day. The closest analogy may be with the pilgrim badges of the Middle Ages.

The find-spots of similar brooches are too widely and sparsely scattered in Britain and on the Continent to give any indication of their likely place of origin; their appearance at Richborough, one of the main ports of entry to Britain in the first and early second centuries, might suggest a connection with the Rhineland, but possibly no more than that of the trunk route along which travellers from many parts of the Empire passed to reach Britain. Culturally, they fit well into the combination of classical naturalism with Celtic abstract pattern-making (cf. Toynbee 1964, 343-4) so characteristic of the art of the Roman provinces.

ACKNOWLEDGEMENTS

I am grateful to members of the Ancient Monuments Laboratory, and particularly to Miss Justine Bayley and Dr Barry Knight for information on the analysis and conservation of the Richborough brooches, and to Miss Judith Dobie, of the Ancient Monuments Archaeological Illustrators Section, for the drawings.

THE CONSTRUCTION OF THE SAXON SHORE FORT AT RICHBOROUGH*

STEPHEN JOHNSON

Among the many and varied interests of Stuart Rigold was what would nowadays be called the historical geography of the south-eastern coastline, including the successive waves of defences thrown up round its shores as a response to a variety of threats from mainland Europe. When this interest is linked to the analysis of a standing structure, a facet of the work of the Inspectorate of Ancient Monuments at which Stuart excelled, it may provide a fitting tribute to him within this volume.

The sequence of construction and development at the site of Richborough has been defined in broad outline by the major series of excavations undertaken there from 1922 to 1938. Despite the five volumes of publication spanning this campaign, the major feature now visible on the site, the standing wall of the Saxon Shore fort, has not come in for particularly close attention. Yet, the walls of this installation are one of the country's major Roman monuments, and afford a length of about 350 m. of Roman walling, a considerable portion of which stands to a height of 6 m. or so. This brief paper cannot be regarded as a full survey of these defences, but should be seen as brief notes on the structure, which have a bearing upon the construction-method. I do not intend here to rehearse the archaeological arguments for the precise date of construction of the stone fort (Johnson 1970, 240).

At about the middle of the third century, the ditches of the earth fort were capped or completely filled with clay as a necessary preparation for the construction of the stone walls. The area chosen for this stone construction was roughly centred on the earth fort, but it also included areas to the west and south of the earth fort where occupation of late-second and early-third century date was slight, and which was by then so far on the periphery of the town-cum-port of Richborough that burials had begun to take place in it (Bushe-Fox 1932, 25; Cunliffe 1968, 27-8.). When the walls were built, therefore, they made use of an area which was at the same time strategically dominating, which (probably) overlooked a secure harbour, and which caused distress to few, if any, civilians by taking land in residential use. The only known substantial building, which may have been directly affected, was the large courtyard building on Site III (in the north-eastern corner of the excavated site) which the ditches of the earth fort had avoided. Whether this was in fact the only building of second-third century date in the enclosed area will never now be known, but it is a measure of the importance of the newly constructed stone walls that this, a substantial courtyard building, possibly in origin an official establishment, was considered expendable in the cause of the defence of the site.

Details of the construction of the stone fort walls, in particular the foundation trenches, have been given coverage in the Richborough reports normally at the points where sections across the fort butted up to the masonry defences. A foundation trench of varying widths was dug to a depth of 2½ to 3 ft. (0.76 - 0.91 m.), and in this were placed loose packed stones with a capping of chalk. There are slight, though not significant, differences between the recorded sections of the foundations of the north wall (Bushe-Fox 1928, 23 and Bushe-Fox 1932, Pl. XLV) and the west wall (30, 50 and Section 33, Pl. L). Above this stone and chalk packing was a layer of timber strapwork, the holes for which were located in several of the excavated sections. This was packed around with more chalk and loose flints, and above this framing, the wall, 10½ to 11½ ft. wide (3.20 m. - 3.50.), was constructed. The wall was built of typical late-Roman rubble masonry with layered core-work incorporating flints, chalk, brick and other stone (including in one or two places still visible portions of the marble casing of the Monument). It was faced with Kentish ragstone carefully cut into square or rectangular blocks, interspersed with double tile courses. On the exterior face, the walls rise with no offset visible at present, though section 33 in the third report (Bushe-Fox 1932, Pl. L) shows what appears to be a plinth course at ground level. On the interior, there seems almost universally to have been at least one, if not two, offsets at low level.

Excavation has shown that a foundation in many respects similar to that of the fort walls, of flints capped by a layer of chalk, ran north — south above the remains of the early buildings on site III and above the filling of the inner earth fort ditch. This foundation was about 13 ft. (3.96 m.) wide on average, 2 ft. (61 cm.) thick, and had, running down its eastern side, a double row of large stake-holes some 4 ft. deep and spaced some 4 ft. (1.21 m.) apart. This was clearly intended to be the foundation for the eastern wall of the fort, but the excavators surmised that it in fact was never so used. To the strong arguments in support of this view (Cunliffe 1968, 245), notably the digging of pit 26 which was filled in the last quarter of the third century (if not a trifle earlier) and which cut through this foundation, can be added the difference in height of 5-6 ft. between the course of this wall foundation over the tops of the destroyed building on site III and over the fill of the inner fort ditch (Bushe-Fox 1928, Section 12, Pl. XLIV). This rendered the foundation unsuitable for use, and the east wall was in fact built further east, whence it has now toppled. Portions of it lie at the foot of the scarp which forms the site's eastern edge. The presence of the east wall foundation was soon forgotten, its site doubtless filled in with building debris. Pit 26, surely intended as a well for the new walled post, would probably not have been deliberately sunk through the foundation of flints and chalk 2 ft. (0.61 m.) thick.

Substantial portions, however, of the other three sides of the defences survive. They enclose a roughly rectangular area, though on inspection, neither the west wall nor the north wall is truly straight (see below). The external facing of the walls is similar, though not identical, consisting normally of seven courses of limestone rag facing between every double tile-course. The facing of the south wall, apart from the bottom-most courses buried by the accumulation of soil, has been largely removed, leaving large areas of core-work exposed within which the remaining portions of the knapped-off tile-courses are still visible. The position of the put-log holes (for scaffolding) cannot be made out.

The southern part of the west wall is better preserved. Here, although much of the facing at lower levels has been robbed away, substantial portions of the upper registers remain and show a remarkable consistency of building throughout its length of 230 ft. (70 m.). The external facing, interrupted only by the externally projecting rectangular bastion, runs in level stone courses, seven between each row of double tile-courses. At the lower levels, put-log holes,

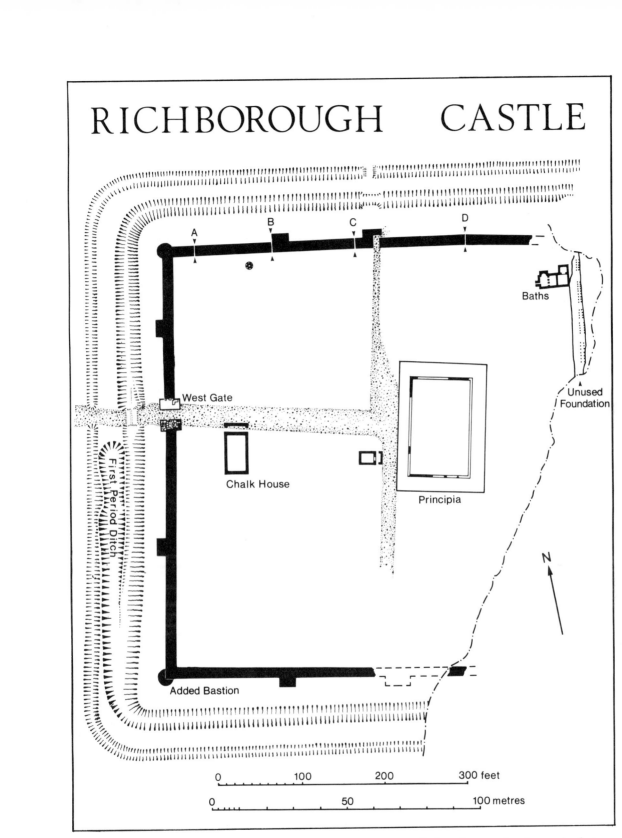

RICHBOROUGH CASTLE

A B C D

Baths

West Gate

Unused Foundation

First Period Ditch

Chalk House

Principia

N

Added Bastion

| 0 | 100 | 200 | 300 feet |

| 0 | 50 | 100 metres |

Fig. 2. Richborough Roman Fort. Plan of the late-Roman walled enclosure, showing main features mentioned in the text. The positions of the main breaks in building sections are shown lettered A, B, C and D in the north wall.

aligned vertically, were placed consistently within the fifth course of masonry above the tile-course (Plate I). Above the double tile-course at or near ground level, the first and second registers (a register = seven rows of facing capped by a double tile-course) of facing are missing. The third and fourth registers exhibit the design described above. Above this the facing and the corework are in much smaller dimensions, so that the complete register is encompassed not within *c.* 1.20 m. (4 ft.) as was the case lower down, but within a height of 0.9 m. (*c.* 3 ft.). At this level, the put-log holes, such as can be seen, appear to lie in the middle course of stone. This arrangement, too, appears to run along the whole length of the wall, since it is discernible wherever the wall reaches the required height. One further feature of note in this portion of the walls is the use of *tegulae* in places for the tile-courses.

The northern part of the west wall and the north-west angle survive only a few courses in height, and further detailed analysis of the facing of the wall is not possible. The north wall itself, however, affords considerable scope for analysis on both interior and exterior faces and is different in detail from the south and west walls. The facing of this wall exhibits work by at least four, and probably five, building gangs, whose styles of masonry construction were very similar in all but the minutest detail. The precise points at which these gangs joined can be pin-pointed by small changes of technique and materials. Working along the north wall from west to east, the first building-break occurs at a point, 25 ft. (7.62 m.) from the north-west corner. This building-break is visible only on the inner face of the wall (the outer face survives only one course high at this point) and is characterised by a number of single tile-courses which do not correspond in level on either side of the point where two gangs' work met.

The next building-break on the north wall lies behind or just west of the rectangular bastion on the wall. In the Richborough reports, a series of sections cut into the layers next to the interior of the fort walls is described. In one of these (Bushe-Fox 1932, 53), an offset plinth, running from the north-west corner along the fort wall, was described as coming to an end some 120 ft. (36.6 m.) from the corner. This lies almost immediately behind the projecting bastion on the exterior face of the wall and is suggestive of a change in building technique. Slightly east of this, as far as can be judged at present, came the building break in the standing wall. This is characterised by a change in facing materials at low level on the interior (flint on one side of the break becomes ragstone on the other, and vice-versa) (Plate II). On the exterior face, at a point some 2.50 m. east of the external tower, there are slight but subtle changes in the wall facing either side of the building-break. To the west, the facing is the grey ragstone with few distinguishing features, except in the lowest register, where flint replaces it. East of the building-break, in the lowest register the ragstone returns, and in the second and fourth registers there is a greater admixture of varied forms and colours of stone in use. Unfortunately, much of the facing in other registers is missing from here eastwards for a few metres. At the actual building-break, there is a vertical crack running down the wall.

Progressing eastwards again, the next building break lies just west of the postern-gate tower. On the internal face, it is marked, among other things, by the beginning of double tile-courses at about 40 cm. from ground level and an abrupt switch from ragstone to flint facing immediately above it. Externally, the building-break shows distinctively only at a low level where the double tile-course above the lowest register of facing changes abruptly in level. The slight variation in stone colours, seen in the section of walling to the west of this building-break, does not continue into the new section, and in addition, the put-log holes are in a different location. West of the break they occur, as on the west wall, in the fifth course in each

PLATE I

Richborough Roman Fort, west wall. The remains of the externally projecting rectangular bastion.

PLATE II

Richborough Roman Fort, north wall interior. Break between two building sections.

register. East of the break, and round the postern turret the put-logs occur in the third register immediately above the tile-course and in the fourth register in the fourth (middle) course. This system is continued along the stretch of north wall east of the postern-tower, with the addition of an extra series of put-log holes in the fifth register. A large nearly square chalk block in the fourth register near the postern entrance may have been a building inscription (Plate III).

The final building-break is by far the most obvious and impressive, for at a point 85 ft. (25.9 m.) from the present end of the north wall the wall makes a slight, but distinct bend in direction. On the interior face at this point a double tile-course at about 50 cm. from ground level suddenly is replaced in ashlars, and there are traces of a vertical crack in the core-work above. On the exterior, a facing style which had become increasingly adventurous in its use of ironstone, chalk and ragstone blocks, producing in parts a mosaic effect (particularly in the fifth the sixth registers) changes in the eastern section to a plain grey style (Plate IV), except in the fourth register, where a series of larger chalk blocks and ironstone interrupts this pattern. In addition, the put-log holes change location again, in the third register they are in the course above the tile-courses, in the fourth, in the second course above the tiles, and in the fifth, in the fourth course of eight rows of small blockwork. This may even mean that there are two separate phases of put-log holes, suggesting two separate building campaigns on this portion of the wall. This blockwork is so uniform and small that, in the sixth register, nine courses of it are required to fill the same height of wall as in the portion of wall built immediately west of the break.

Two types of bastion project externally from the walls: at the north-west and south-west corners are projecting three-quarters round solid bastions: at intervals, roughly half-way between the gates and the angles, are rectangular bastions, sometimes solid at the base, but hollow at a higher level. The two corner bastions are not the same. At the north-western corner, though only a couple of courses remain, the bastion is of one build with the wall and the centre of the radius from which it is drawn lies within the fort wall thickness. At the south-western corner, the bastion is an addition to the wall, though this is not now obvious. Antiquarian engravings suggest that the bastion clasped round the angle of the walls, and the radius of the circle lies at the meeting-point of the exterior face of north and south walls.

None of the five surviving rectangular bastions stands now above above 4 ft. (1.20 m.) high. All of them were clearly hollow, or earth filled, above a solid foundation. The side walls were 90 cm. thick, and were assured of a close bond with the fort walls by the provision of extra, intermediate, tile-courses, visible up to full height of the scar in the masonry which was the point of junction between bastion and wall. At least one intermediate floor, to judge from the remains of holes for substantial timber framing at a height of 4.87 m., was provided within the turrets (see Cunliffe 1968, 31, for a sketch of this in the western bastion on the north wall), but no trace of the method of access to this space has been found. Where sufficient masonry survives in the outer face of the fort wall behind the bastions, there is no visible doorway at this level. The presence of a chamber at a higher level in these bastions is suggested strongly, however, by the remains of a tiled drain outlet at ground level in the northern bastion on the west wall. This must be a chute from a latrine at an upper level. It is clear that these bastions were planned as part of the fort from the first, since the outer fort wall facing behind the bastion-emplacements is less carefully finished than the wall facing always intended to be on view.

The main gate lay on the west wall, and has been fully described in the published reports

PLATE III

PLATE IV

Richborough Roman Fort, north wall exterior, showing the external wall of the postern turret (with the lion's head sculpture) and part of the wall-facing east of it.

Richborough Roman Fort, north wall exterior. The join between building sections showing contrasting styles of masonry and patterning.

(Bushe-Fox 1926, 29-35). It consisted of a pair of opposed rectangular towers flanking an entrance passage some 11 ft. (3.35 m.) wide. The towers projected beyond the wall-line on inner and outer face of the fort wall to provide a pair of guard-towers to which access was gained from the interior part of the entrance passage. It is worth noting the difference in foundation construction between the northern and southern gate towers. The southern one had two bottom courses composed of large re-used stones, consistent over the whole area occupied by the tower. Under the northern one, however, the foundation line of the fort wall was laid out, and the portions of the tower which projected east and west beyond this needed extra stone and flint foundations.

The postern gate on the north wall is concealed in the projecting rectangular bastion at approximately the centre of the fort wall. The entrance passage, not appreciably narrower than the main entrance in the west wall, turns a right-angle as it enters the fort. The postern turret, like the others, has extra tile-courses at its angles, and a beam-hole at high level within the thickness of the fort wall above the gateway arch suggests that the wall-walk behind it was reinforced with timber. On the exterior face of the postern tower, a piece of sculpture, thought to be a lion's head and mane, is visible within the fourth register. This is an unusual position for re-using a piece of sculpture, and it may be that the piece was striking enough to form a figurehead.

The defensive ditches round the walls of the fort were a natural concomitant to the defences. They consist of a pair of ditches separated from the walls by a wide berm, and the inner ditch is in general wider and slightly deeper than the outer. They follow a course roughly parallel to the fort walls, but not uniformly so. Along the southern flank of the west wall, there are in fact three ditches, the middle one actually running the closest parallel to the fort wall, but, according to the excavators, dug in error, backfilled, and replaced by the normal double ditches at a later, but not necessarily significantly later, stage.

Thus far the description of what can be seen on site or gleaned from the published account. The conclusions to be drawn from this mass of information are rather more tentative. With only isolated portions of the fort walls now standing and receptive of study — mainly the southern part of the west and most of the north walls, an assessment of the overall programme of construction at Richborough is difficult to make with any accuracy. Notable, however, are the differences in technique between the south/west and the north walls. The south and west walls (southern part at least) have all the appearance of having been constructed as a unit, in a style of masonry very carefully worked and finished, so that, if different building gangs were employed, this fails to show. A difference was noted, however, in their topmost courses, and this may show that the wall-tops had to be finished off by a different gang in a later stage of the building campaign. Since the bastion at the corner of these walls was added after the walls were put up, it may be suggested that they were constructed first of all the walls now visible. Possibly contemporary with this was the digging of a single ditch on the western side, and the construction of the east wall foundation, not in fact used.

The relationship of the west wall with the east — west road, probably always the main road into the site, has not been clarified. The main west gate accommodates a roadway which is not quite at right angles to the west wall; in fact the road line is followed by the so-called Chalk House on site VII, and is almost at right angles to the abandoned east wall on site III. This would have produced a fort, originally planned as roughly square, but the northern part of the west wall, and possibly the north wall were laid out or marked out and not yet built.

In the second phase of building, the single large ditch on the southern part of the western side was filled in, the gateway was constructed, overlying the laid foundations of the northern part of the west wall, and the northern part of the west wall (on a slightly odd alignment because of the presence of the main gate tower) and the north wall completed. The foundation for the east wall was abandoned, and the east wall eventually sited some distance to the east. At this stage also, the south-west corner bastion may have been added to the circuit, and the double ditches round the whole circuit dug. The difference in construction between the west and the north walls suggests that more urgency was suddenly required over the completion of the fort, since gangs of builders, who were concerned to finish the job rather than to bring it to absolute perfection, were drafted in to complete the task.

The magnitude of the building task at Richborough needs no overestimation, and the historical context for which I have in the past argued on strictly archaeological dating evidence might also hold good for the story reflected by the standing monument. After the barbarian raids of the mid-270s, a start was made throughout mainland Europe in securing key towns, cities and military installations against the repetition of such a threat. One focal point in the defence of Europe was the zone later known as the Saxon Shore, on the south-eastern British coastline, and the Continental coasts opposite. Started in the years after 276-7, the building of Richborough assumed no recognisable urgency until about 285-6, when a new commander was appointed to carry the fight in the Channel to the pirates.

THE LATE ROMAN WATER-MILL AT ICKHAM, KENT, AND THE SAXON SHORE*

C.J. YOUNG

Among Stuart Rigold's many and various interests was the development and subsequent uses of the forts of the Roman Saxon Shore. This paper, which discusses a posible ancillary dépôt for those Saxon Shore forts lying in east Kent, is offered as a tribute to his memory and his particular interest in those forts.

A large area of Roman occupation lies east of Ickham on and near the southern bank of the present course of the Little Stour, 500 m. upstream of its confluence with the Wingham River. It lies midway between the Roman city of Canterbury and the town and military dépôt of Richborough (Fig. 3). In the Roman period its communications would have been good. A minor road crosses the site and would have linked with the road from Canterbury to Richborough (Margary 1955, 31–3). The site would also have had good communications by water to the east, since at this time the Wantsum was an open navigable channel between Thanet and the mainland (Hawkes 1968, 224–30). This would have made it easy to move by boat from the Ickham site to either Richborough or Reculver or, even, further afield to Dover.

The area of settlement was extensive, but large parts of it were destroyed by gravel extraction between 1973 and 1975. During this period the Ashford Archaeological Society carried out a salvage and rescue excavation of many features. For a period of six weeks in 1974 the present writer carried out a full-time excavation of a small part of the site, concerned mainly with the fourth-century water-mill discussed below. Because much of the archaeology could only be salvaged from in front of the draglines much information must have been lost. Nonetheless enough information was recovered to give a clear idea of the use of the area in the Roman period. At that time the course of the Little Stour lay a little to the south of its present line (a post-medieval canalisation) and into it ran a series of ditches. The area was heavily waterlogged and large quantities of timber and leather were preserved in the peaty deposits filling the old river-course and ditches. In between these ditches there had been considerable occupation throughout the Roman period, evidenced by wells, various timber structures and large quantities of artefacts. The most substantial structures were two water-mills on the buried river-course, one of the second century and one of the fourth century. There was also evidence for metal-working in pewter, bronze and, possibly, iron. A full report of the excavation is in preparation and will be published in due course.

*The excavation at Ickham was the result of collaboration between many people. I am particularly grateful to Jim Bradshaw for his unstinting help and advice during and after the excavation, and for placing all his records and finds at my disposal. I am most grateful also to Bob Spain and David Brown for their comments on the water-mill and the metal-work respectively.

About 1100 m. south of the site, on higher ground, surface finds indicate a large Roman masonry building. Field-walking on this site in 1978 discovered five lead seals (Hassall and Tomlin 1979, 350–3), all of the fourth century. Three of these were stamped with the head and titles of the Emperor Julian as Augustus (A.D. 360–363), and one was of the Emperor Constantine II and is dated A.D. 337–340. The last seal, which was square, did not bear an imperial inscription but was stamped as coming from Smyrna. Such seals were most probably used for sealing goods needed for official military or civilian purposes. A concentration of such seals, found as surface finds, must indicate that this building had official connections of some sort in the fourth century.

This paper discusses the possibility that the site at Ickham was an official or military establishment in the fourth century. It is probably reasonable to assume a connection between the excavated area on the banks of the Little Stour and the unexcavated building to the south. The excavated area is clearly industrial and lies on the flood-plain. The undug building had much greater pretentions and its slightly distant siting can be accounted for both by a desire to position it outside the industrial area and to place it above the risk of flooding. The possible official connections of the building have been discussed above.

Within the excavated area there was a high level of activity in the fourth century. Apart from the structures discovered there were very large quantities of artefacts, both metal and ceramic. There were also considerable numbers of fourth-century coins. Much of this activity was industrial.

Apart from the water-mill (see below) there was considerable evidence of pewter manufacture. Large quantities of pewter were found, including bowls and jugs. Some of this material had been cut up for scrap and other objects had been partially melted. There was also working debris from pewter manufacture. Among the large quantities of iron and bronze objects there were some unfinished objects (cf. Appendix 1, no. 13) and a fair amount of bronze scrap.

Because of the nature of the excavation little evidence of metal-working, other than the artefacts, was discovered. The major structural evidence was of the water-mill, which will be discussed fully in the final report by Mr. R.J. Spain. This account is a brief summary only.

Because of the waterlogged nature of the site many of the structural timbers of the mill were wholly or partly preserved. An existing channel of the Stour had been revetted and, in places, floored, with wooden planks fixed to uprights and stretchers to make a race c. 3 m. wide and at least 28 m. long. A similarly constructed head-race, half of the width of the main race, continued the channel upstream.

At two places along the main channel timbers of a larger scantling had been used, presumably to support a heavier superstructure such as the mill-buildings themselves. Adjacent to the upstream one of these was a scouring pit in the river bed and it was in this area that the main concentration of mill-stone fragments was found. Considerable quantities of metal-work and large numbers of coins were found in the channel.

A second channel, 4 m. wide and over 1 m. deep, lay c. 20 m. to the south of the main one. This had probably been dug deliberately and was revetted with hurdles fastened to stakes in the banks. It had contained a sluice-gate or weir and presumably formed a by-pass for the mill-stream. Of the weir there remained the base-sill wedged across the channel, a timber 1.7 m. long and c. 0.25 m. by 0.25 m. in section. A second timber 2.4 m. long and of similar section lay in the channel bed where it had fallen. This was presumably the top beam of the weir. Both timbers were rebated to take either paddles or a gate.

On the land between the two channels, above the waterlogged levels, was a number of post-holes. These presumably held timbers which formed part of the mill-building. There can be litte doubt that these structures are the remains of a water-mill, comprising one channel forming the mill-race, with one or, perhaps, two wheel emplacements, a by-pass stream used to regulate the flow through the mill-race and a mill building on the intervening island.

Few Roman watermills have been found in Britain. Apart from the two at Ickham there was the one at Haltwhistle Burn, dug in 1907 by F. Gerald Simpson (Simpson 1976, 26–43), surrounded by a ditch and rampart, which was presumably built to supply the garrison of that part of Hadrian's Wall. There is the possibility that the channel through the turret on the east side of Chesters Bridge was a mill-leet also (Simpson 1976, 44–9), again constructed to supply the garrison of Hadrian's Wall.

A third possible watermill was discovered at Fullerton, Hampshire, in 1964 (Wilson 1965, 217), on the site of a villa. It lies 15 km. north-west of Winchester and presumably supplied that city. Other evidence for mechanical milling, in the form of items of machinery such as the spindle from Great Chesterford (Liversidge 1968, Fig. 81) or large millstones, comes from

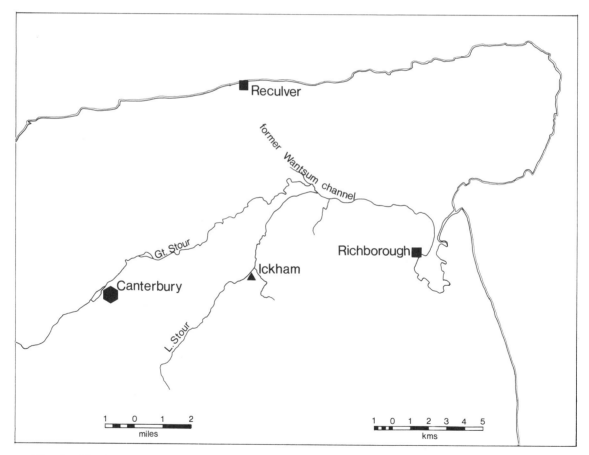

Fig. 3. North-east Kent in the Roman period, showing the Ickham site and major settlements only.

small or large towns. It can therefore be suggested that in Britain, as might be expected, mills were constructed to supply large communities. It is also possible that a fair proportion may have had military connections.

At Ickham in the fourth century there was clearly an extensive industrial area combining metal-working with corn-milling, presumably intended to supply the various needs of a large body of people. The nearest major centres of population were the town of Canterbury and the two Saxon Shore forts of Reculver and Richborough. To the first there was good road communication, to the two forts there were presumably excellent water links. Water-borne transport would have been particularly important for the movement of bulk commodities such as grain or flour.

There are several reasons why it is unlikely that in the fourth century Ickham existed to supply Canterbury. Firstly, given the distance of the former from the latter, it would surely have been possible to locate a mill and industrial area closer to Canterbury. Secondly, it is likely that any mill supplying Canterbury would have been on the Great Stour with the advantage of direct water-links to the town. Thirdly, it seems inherently likely that the varied needs of the inhabitants of Canterbury for different types of metal-work would have been supplied by workshops within the town itself and not by a dépôt some 8 km. distant. Finally, the combination on the one site of corn-milling and various sorts of metal-working suggests central organisation of the needs of a community which seems unlikely in an urban context, even in the late Roman empire.

Such a combination and central organisation are far more appropriate to the supply of official needs of the inhabitants of Canterbury for different types of metal-work would have been identified in Gaul (Percival 1972, 120-132) and sometimes postulated for Britain. This last hypothesis could be built upon the closeness of the industrial area and the presumed prestigious building 1100 m. from it (see p. 33, above), except that, as we have already seen, this building itself had official connections.

An additional argument for an official rôle for the Ickham site is the character of the metal-work and particularly of the copper-alloy objects. In general, the range of material is similar to that found at Richborough. More cogently, there is a number of objects which are normally held to be possibly official in origin. Examples of these are illustrated and described in Appendix 1 (Figs. 4, 5). A preliminary examination of the metal-work by Mr David Brown, on whose notes Appendix 1 is based, has identified one crossbow brooch and fragments of two others, at least ten belt buckles (only seven illustrated), including two of Hawkes and Dunning's Type IA, one of Type II, and one of Type IIIA (Hawkes and Dunning 1961; Hawkes 1974), and other belt fittings including one propeller stiffener and three flat stiffeners, including one (no. 13) which was never completed, and omega-shaped and amphora-shaped strap ends. There are also at least two spur terminals.

The official connections of certain classes of metal object, particularly belt fittings, has long been recognised. During the fourth century the military belt, the *cingulum*, was the badge of military or civilian official authority (Tomlin 1976, 191). Obviously, not all fittings are from such belts and stray finds of fittings from such belts do not necessarily indicate that the find-spot is an official establishment. Of the material from Ickham, the Type IIIA buckle (no. 9) and the three belt-stiffeners (nos. 11-13) are likely to have come from broad military belts (cf. Clark 1979, 265-9, 286-91). The strap ends could have come from either *cingula* or possibly non-official belts, although examples do of course occur on military sites also. Although the other buckles probably come from less explicitly official belts, they too are found in military contexts elsewhere and so are not precluded from official use.

There is thus evidence for several military belts from Ickham; propeller stiffeners are earlier than flat stiffeners and could not have been used on the same belt. The two flat stiffeners are also likely to have come from separate belts since they are so different in style and finish. The fact that one of them appears not to have been completed suggests that such fittings may actually have been made at Ickham.

Crossbow brooches also have some official connection. They are shown in official contexts on sculptures, mosaics and ivories, but this does not mean that all crossbow brooches belonged to officials (Clark 1979, 262-3). On the other hand, the occurrence of parts of three such brooches on a site where undoubted official belt-fittings were also found, strengthens the possibility of the brooches being official also. Similarly spur-terminals (no. 18) can also occur in official or non-official contexts, but could be held, in contexts with official connections, to reinforce those links.

The mixture of activities at Ickham, the site's proximity to a building with official connections, and the pressure of undoubted items of official insignia, combine to suggest that the site was some sort of official works dépôt. The official establishments that Ickham most probably served were the Saxon Shore forts at Richborough and Reculver.

These are the closest concentrations of official manpower to Ickham. There would have been easy communication from the mouth of the Little Stour to either fort along the Wantsum channel. The Ickham site was, indeed, probably the nearest practicable site for a water-mill to provide flour for Richborough and Reculver, since the Little and Great Stours were probably the only rivers in the area at that period capable of powering a mill. Once it had been decided to site a military water-mill at Ickham, it is not surprising that other industrial activities should occur there also. It is even just possible, though not proveable, that water-power may have been used for purposes other than milling corn. It is known, for example, that on the Moselle water-mills were used for sawing stone in the late Roman period (Richmond 1966, 83).

Ickham, therefore, was most probably in the fourth century an official works dépôt for local units of the Saxon Shore, supplying them with flour and metal-work. The presence of the lead seals may suggest also that it was used for storage. It should not be regarded as a full-scale *fabrica*, the imperial arms factories recorded in the *Notitia Dignitatum* (Jones 1964, 834-6). There were few of them and, according to the *Notitia*, none were located in Britain apart from a clothing factory or *gynaeceum* (Wild 1976, 54). They were also far more specialised in their products (Jones 1964, 834) than was the case at Ickham. A much better parallel would be the legionary works compounds at Corbridge. These again fulfilled a number of industrial functions at some little distance from the garrisons that they served (Collingwood Bruce 1978, 95-7).

Any army which is static for any length of time develops numerous ancillary services to fulfil its various needs. Many of these services, for reasons of convenience or necessity, will be sited away from the garrisons they serve. Little is known of the provision of such facilities for the late Roman army in Britain or elsewhere, but it would seem that the Ickham site was part of one such dépôt intended to service part of the defensive system of the Saxon Shore. As such it is yet another pointer towards the complexity of late-Roman military organisation.

APPENDIX 1

Some late-Roman metal-work from Ickham (Figs. 4, 5)

(based on notes by David Brown)

All objects discussed here are copper-alloy. The dimension given for belt-fittings is that indicating the width of the belt.

1. *Crossbow brooch* (55). Solid knobs, cast in one piece, hinged pin, chamfered foot with irregular ring-and-dot. L 77 mm. This corresponds with Keller's types II and IV, dated *c.* 340-380. (Keller 1971, 26-53).

2. *Fixed-plate triangular buckle* (88). D-loop now broken, fastened with three rivets, chamfered edges. L 52+ mm. Mr Brown has drawn attention to this type of buckle when discussing an example from Cirencester. An example from Woodeaton, Oxon., (illustrated alongside, W) shows the complete type. Other examples are known from Shakenoak, Oxon., (Brodribb, Hands, Walker 1971, Fig. 46, 65) and Brackley, Northants. The type is undated but fits into the range of fourth-century metal-work (cf. Bushe-Foxe 1928, Pl. XX, 42).

3. *Oval buckle plate* (400). Roughly oval plate of sheet bronze, now broken away from buckle loop. Three-rivet fastening, in this case reinforced by a fourth. W 30 mm. One of four examples; the type is discussed in the Lankhills report (Clark 1979, 270-2) when a mid-fourth century date (*c.* 340-360) was favoured as the period when the type was most common. However, there are notable exceptions, generally from very narrow belts, of 400 and later.

4. *Rectangular buckle plate* (11). Small rectangular plate, fastened by two rivets. Four ring-and-dots ornament the plate. W 23 mm. This piece could go well with the loop, no. 6. The decoration ties in with that on the omega strap-end, no. 15.

5. *Open-work buckle plate* (1930). Fragment of open-work plate with chamfered and notched edge. W 25+ mm. (originally *c.* 40 mm.). This is a plate for a Hawkes and Dunning Type II buckle. The loop itself may have been a plain oval cast in one, or a moveable loop. A fragment like this from Cirencester is discussed in Hawkes 1974 when the former dating is revised to suggest 'the middle decades of the fourth century'.

6. *Small buckle* (3) without plate. W 30 mm. cf. no. 4.

7. *Buckle* (393). One-piece loop with stylised animal heads; flat on back. W 32 mm.

8. *Buckle* (200). One-piece loop with stylised animal heads; flat on back. W 32 mm. These two are examples of Hawkes and Dunning type IA buckles, for which the present favoured date seems to be the last third of the fourth century (Hawkes 1974, 387).

9. *Buckle* (1076). Zoomorphic heads grip the pin bar. W 39 mm. This is a Hawkes and Dunning type IIIA buckle. Two examples from Lankhills confirm the projected dating of *c.* 370 onwards to *c.* 400 or 410. The buckle in the Dorchester belt is of this type (cf. Bushe-Fox 1949, Pl. XXXII, 67-8).

10. *Propeller-shaped belt-stiffener* (322). Plain, chamfered edges; two rivets. Width (of belt) 33 mm. The occurrence of this type of fitting has been discussed in the Maryport report (Brown 1976). Stiffeners from belts of this width are mid-fourth century, say second or third quarter (cf. Bushe-Fox 1949, Pl. LIII, 209).

11. *Flat belt-stiffener* (483), inlaid with niello; stamped; chamfered edges. L 63 mm. This piece is not matched at present; niello was being used quite a lot in north France and Belgium in the

last quarter of the fourth century. There is an inlaid stiffener from Namur (Böhme 1974, Pls. 129, 13) which will date around *c.* 400. The Ickham piece is probably of the last quarter of the fourth century.

12. *Flat belt-stiffener* (337). A very slender piece, chamfered edge; two rivets; broken across top. L 58+?3 = 61 mm. This piece is a good match for the stiffeners on the Dorchester belt, and on comparable belt sets from Nijmegen, Wijster, Rhenen 824 and 833 (all illustrated in Böhme 1974, Pls. 84, 71, 63, 62). These belt sets all have stiffeners of two sizes, and this piece corresponds with the smaller size. The only difference is that the parallels all have a central rivet-hole which this lacks. If this identification is correct, this piece is going to be late, *c.* 390-410.

13. *Flat belt-stiffener* (1058) with a channelled surface. It is a rough unattractive piece; it has a hole in it. There is a rivet-hole through one end, but the other end has never been drilled. L 94 mm. It is again not exactly paralleled, but identification seems sure; the state of the object seems to suggest that it was never finished. A channelled piece (illustrated by Böhme 1974, Pl. 147), comes from a context of *c.* 390-410, but is *not* a good parallel. The width of the belt is as good an indication of date as anything else. Belts, and stiffeners, of this width are not earlier than the last quarter of the fourth century (see Brown in prep. on a stiffener from Carrawburgh).

14. *Omega-shaped strap-end* (97). Two pieces soldered together at one end, plain save for cut-out pattern around belt rivet. W 30 mm.

15. *Omega-shaped strap-end* (154). Two pieces soldered together at end; three ring-and-dots. W 20 mm. Three other smaller examples were found. At Lankhills two examples were found in graves dated 350-370 and 350-390 (Clarke 1979, Fig. 36, nos. 534, 75, pp. 282-3). This corresponds with Keller's dating of *c.* 340-370 for the type (1971, 64-5).

16. *Amphora-shaped strap-end* (424). Stylish *pelta*-cut-outs. The metal is uneven and split on the back, making it uncertain whether the piece has a back-plate or merely a split butt. W 27 mm. Two examples are recorded at Lankhills in graves dating 350-380 and 370-410 (Clark 1979, Fig. 36, nos. 26, 489, p. 281). This corresponds with Keller's dating of *c.* 350-390 for the type (Keller 1971, 65-6).

A fragment of another was found (cf. Bushe-Fox 1928, Pl. XXI, 47; Bushe-Fox 1932, Pl. X, 19; Bushe-Fox 1949, Pl. XXXVII, 119, for examples from Richborough).

17. *Oval guard* (156) from a knife handle. L 23 mm.

18. *Terminal of a spur* (1044). The rivet in the disc terminal was capped by a sheet of bronze with a notched edge. The fourth-century dating, *c.* 330 onwards, discussed in the Maryport report (Brown 1976) is confirmed by the recent study by V. Giesler (1978).

A second similar piece was found.

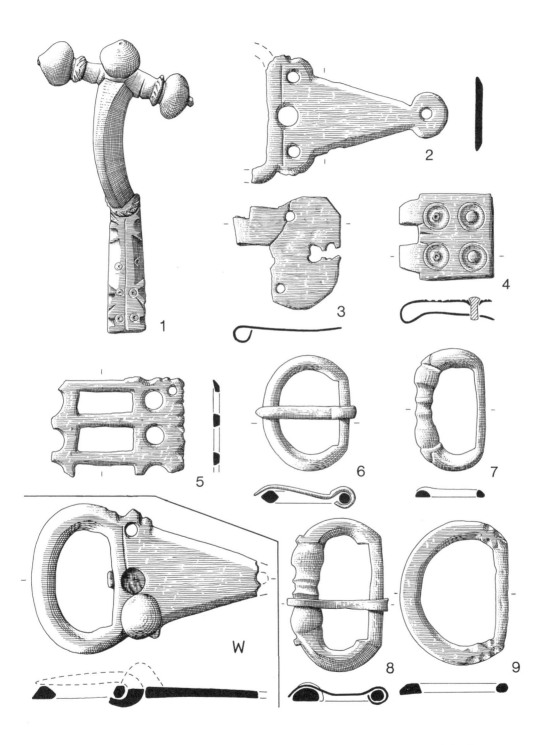

Fig. 4. Late-Roman copper-alloy objects from Ickham, Kent: nos. 1-9 (1:1).

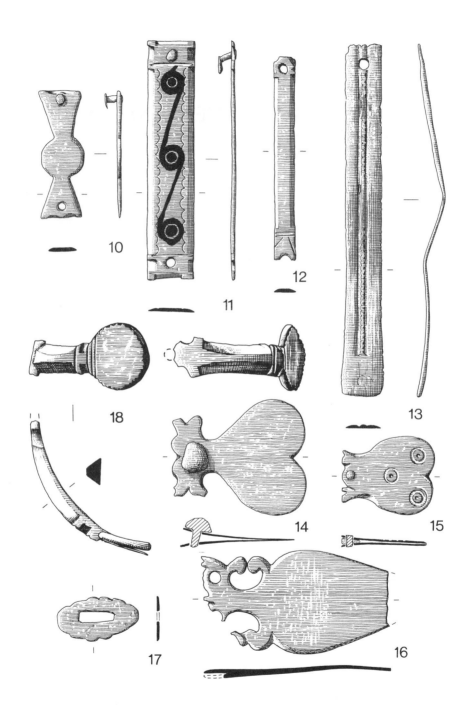

Fig. 5.   Late-Roman copper-alloy objects from Ickham, Kent: nos. 10-18 (1:1).

RICHBOROUGH, RECULVER AND LYMPNE: A RECONSIDERATION OF THREE OF KENT'S LATE-ROMAN SHORE-FORTS

BRIAN PHILP

The sad, untimely death of Stuart Rigold has at least provided this opportunity to review three of the late-Roman coastal forts in Kent. It is, as Stuart would so readily have seen, an apparent sequel to the excellent volume with the same title, written by Charles Roach Smith just 131 years ago (Smith 1850). It is also an opportunity for me to acknowledge the kindly interest and help of Stuart Rigold in the work of the Kent Archaeological Rescue Unit (C.I.B. team) over more than 20 years in Kent archaeology.

RICHBOROUGH

Charles Roach Smith clearly knew the Roman site at Richborough very well. Its high upstanding walls, its close proximity to Sandwich and the attention of many antiquarians, particularly Boys and Rolfe, had made it a well-known site. Leland (Leland *c.* 1530) had described the fortifications, identified the site as *Rutupiae* and noted even then that 'mo antiquities of Romayne mony than yn any place els of England'. Roach Smith published a useful plan of the fort and the north postern gate, several fine elevations, numerous finds including pottery, glass, brooches and he also listed 1279 coins (Smith 1850, 1). He also recorded finds made during the cutting of the railway in 1846 and during the excavation in 1849 of the large amphitheatre, some 400 m. from the south-west corner of the fort.

Even after the intense activity of the first half of the nineteenth century at Richborough, sporadic activity continued. Finally, in 1922, the Society of Antiquaries of London launched a major programme of excavation that was to last for the next 16 years. This great work was carried out under the direction of J.P. Bushe-Fox and at one time involved large numbers of unemployed people, many students and a number of well-known specialists of the day. About two-thirds of the interior of the fort was cleared, the two external ditches were emptied and other areas trial-trenched. Predictably, the evidence of structures, features and finds was prodigious and made Richborough the paramount Roman military site in southern Britain. Bushe-Fox was able to publish, again through the Antiquaries, four complete volumes (Bushe-Fox 1926, 1928, 1932, 1949) on his work and even to consider a fifth and final volume. His untimely death in 1954 prevented its completion, and it was not until 1968 that it was eventually published with some 18 contributors under the editorship of Barry Cunliffe (Cunliffe 1968). Appropriately, that volume also included two short sections by Stuart Rigold on the 'Post Roman Coins' (p. 217) and 'Richborough Today' (p. 253). In volume V, Cunliffe followed Bushe-Fox and opted (p. 245) for the construction of the fort under Carausius (A.D.

286-293). Even then Stuart Rigold had warned (footnote, page 262) that the coins did not preclude a pre-Carausian date and suggested a construction possibly under Probus, a view confirmed in 1970 (Johnson 1970).

Discussion

The excavation of Richborough was undoubtedly a major advance in our knowledge of Roman military activity in south-eastern Britain and it gave an important view of military activity over a span of nearly 400 years. It was, however, unfortunate that for more than three decades the vast scale of the operation dwarfed all other Roman sites in the south-east and thus tended to over-emphasise the importance of Richborough. Since then 17 seasons of work at Reculver (Philp 1970a) and the ten years non-stop campaign at Dover (Philp 1981), both major military sites very much adjacent to Richborough, have demonstrated that there were several major changes of emphasis and have also provided material for Roman military history over a much wider area.

It seems clear from the Bushe-Fox excavations that Richborough marked one of the initial landing places of the Claudian invasion forces in A.D. 43. The pair of long defensive ditches which relate to this phase was traced over some 2131 ft. (650 m.) and yet delimits an area of only 492 ft. (150 m.) in maximum width. It seems highly likely that the defended area would have been very much bigger and perhaps even rectangular in plan. Indeed an enclosure some 10-20 ha. in area seems likely to be nearer the original size and, if this is accepted, then a very considerable degree of erosion must have taken place. If so, this has very considerable implications for the whole site and its possible harbours. The initial camp seems to have been expanded into a permanent base extending even beyond the defensive ditches and to have included a grid of metalled roads and also granaries.

The site appears to have been in constant use throughout the second half of the first century, and it must be that significant natural or artificial harbour facilities existed then, probably to the north-east. During Flavian times a grand marble-cased *quadrifrons* was constructed on a huge concrete foundation, perhaps to commemorate the conquest of Britain. At this time it is probable that Richborough was truly the 'Gateway to Roman Britain'.

If the finds from the site are a true reflection of the overall occupation, then it seems that subsequently there was a marked decline in the degree of settlement. Cunliffe notes (Cunliffe 1968, 243) "a sharp decrease in the amount of pottery and coins found on the site", after the middle of the second century. It seems unlikely that the site was actually abandoned and indeed the large courtyard building at least, perhaps a *mansio*, was constructed and rebuilt several times in the second and third centuries.

What then was the connection of the *Classis Britannica* with Richborough in the first and second centuries? As an important military base during the second half of the first century, it must be that it was serviced by the *Classis Britannica* for most if not all that time. It is quite possible that Richborough was one of the fleet bases on the British side of the Channel but before the time of the large-scale production of fleet tiles with the familiar stamp. This could explain the general sparsity of fleet tiles at the site. If so, then a defensive circuit could have existed here and the possibility that this lay either in the area since eroded or in the large area still unexcavated, must be given serious consideration. Certainly, the large courtyard building could support some such arrangement for it could represent a *mansio* located in the extra-mural settlement of such a naval base. Indeed, very little other meaningful explanation of its function and role has been offered.

Whatever the precise role and disposition of the *Classis Britannica* at Richborough in the late first and early second century, it seems clear that the marked drop in activity at Richborough coincides with the construction of the major fortified base and harbour, with its sea wall and pair of lighthouses, at nearby Dover in the period 130-140 (Philp 1981). Dover took on the role as gateway to Roman Britain; for with its shorter Channel crossing and safe anchorage it attracted much of the trade from Richborough. Any *Classis Britannica* connection with Richborough may have declined suddenly, or even ceased.

Clearly, the impact of the 'New Harbour' of Ptolemy at Dover was inevitably considerable. Certainly, some such change could help explain why only a single *Classis Britannica* stamped tile has been recorded at Richborough and why only comparatively few *Classis Britannica* tiles (Fabric 2) have been found re-used in the walls of the later shore-fort.

What must be equally significant is that when there was a major redeployment of troops in the south-east at the beginning of the third century, because of growing Saxon raids, Richborough seems to have been neglected. The major fleet base at Dover (Period III) was abandoned about 208 and never rebuilt. Instead, a new coastal fort appeared soon after at Reculver, a site visible from Richborough, probably as part of Caracalla's (or his successors') scheme ('Saxon Shore' Phase I) and dating from perhaps 212-225. Possibly the Richborough harbour had partially silted by then, or more likely the military emphasis had moved from the Channel to the East Coast. Whatever the precise reason it seems clear that Richborough was eclipsed for several decades, at least until the triple ditches were cut to enclose the decaying *quadrifrons*, which was then probably serving as a watch-tower, at about the middle of the third century. The large courtyard building, which was respected by this apparent signal-station, seems to have remained in use.

Not long after this and presumably in reaction to a marked increase in Saxon raids, the 'Saxon Shore' system (Phase II) was greatly expanded with the construction of at least six new forts. Richborough then was not neglected and sometime about 275-285 the six-acre fort was constructed, clearly superseding the courtyard building and the triple-ditched enclosure, but still enclosing the great *quadrifrons* and respecting the principal road axis. To judge by the abundant coin evidence the military occupation thereafter appears to have been continuous, though apart from two temples, the large amphitheatre, two internal masonry buildings and a small bath-house, evidence of corresponding structures was seldom recorded during the excavation.

It seems clear that it was at the end of the fourth century and very early in the fifth century that Richborough once again came into its own as a site of outstanding significance. Something like 26,000 coins of this period (out of a total of more than 56,000) have been found on the site, and the contrast with the other 'Saxon Shore' forts and civilian sites is so great that the circumstances at Richborough must have been exceptional. The most acceptable notion (Richmond 1955) is that Richborough had by then resumed its role as the gateway to Britain, or more probably had become the gateway *from* Britain. If so, it is an irony of history that the site witnessed both the conquest invasion and the spasmodic withdrawal of troops that eventually led to the collapse of Roman Britain. Uniquely, therefore, it seems that Richborough represents both the dawn and dusk of Roman Britain.

RECULVER

Whereas Charles Roach Smith wrote up Richborough in considerable detail and with such significance in terms of the shore-fort, he had rather less scope at Reculver (Roach Smith 1850,

175). More than three centuries earlier Leland had visited the site and noted 'ther hath bene much Romain mony fownd abowt Reculver'. More helpfully, the Rev. J. Battely (Battely 1711), who died in 1708, recorded massive foundations of a hypocausted building and deep rectangular 'cisterns', north of the fort, which had been exposed and then destroyed by erosion. Roach Smith quoted Leland, summarised Battely and illustrated coins and small finds. He readily accepted the *Regulbium* of the *Notitia* as Reculver. He also published an estate map of 1685 which shows the complete outline of the Roman fort with the Saxon and medieval church at its centre. It also shows the cliff edge just north of the fort, a single ditch on the east side and a single western entrance. Roach Smith went into some detail on the famous church and finally claimed that it incorporated an original Roman building.

Roach Smith was followed by people who offered comments on the site, but did little original work, though a useful survey was published in the *Victoria County History* (1932). In the 1920s some peculiar diagonal trenching in the interior, carried out by workmen under the orders of Major Gordon Home, located a substantial masonry wall and hinted at the existence of a south gate. The details were never published. In 1951 two trenches were excavated behind the fort wall by F.H. Thompson (Thompson 1953), which showed an internal bank and two internal offsets of the wall and generally confirmed the view that the fort, like all the others of the 'Saxon Shore', had been built at the end of the third century.

It was not until 1952 that a programme of large-scale work began which was to be carried out for most of the next 17 years. This work, under the direction of the present writer, began with six years of rescue-work on the foreshore west of the fort (1952-1957). Here, as winter storms smashed down the low cliffs, a dozen Roman wells, several Roman pits, a cremation-burial and part of the metalled road into the fort, were recorded and soon published (Philp 1957, 1958). Much large-scale excavation inside the fort, both cliff-top rescue and orthodox research, from 1958 to 1969 revealed massive detail (Philp 1959, 1960, 1961, 1968, 1969, 1970b). This work was suddenly interrupted in 1970 when the major rescue-excavation at Dover demanded immediate attention. The whole Reculver team and most of its equipment and resources were moved to Dover for a crisp 8-week programme of work on the west side of the town where the construction of the A20 dual-carriageway was about to destroy large areas of ancient Dover. That crisp programme, extended and still continuing non-stop some 10 years later, has covered some 8 acres of Dover and located and saved the missing 'Saxon Shore' fort and also two totally unpredicted forts of the *Classis Britannica* (Philp 1981). This programme, the most extensive programme of excavation ever carried out in a Kentish town, has resulted in a 'long pause' in the Reculver programme which will certainly be resumed on completion at Dover.

Although several fundamental problems remain to be resolved at Reculver during the resumed programme, much of the basic Roman evidence has emerged (Philp 1970a).

Discussion

It is now clear that the site was first occupied in Roman times at about the middle of the first century A.D. A small earthwork seems to have crowned the low hill upon which the later shore-fort and church now stand. Although only the ditches on two sides of this earthwork have been found, it seems likely that it represents a fortlet of the conquest period. At that time the site lay perhaps a mile from the open sea to its north, yet on the banks of the wide tidal Channel which then separated Thanet from the mainland. After this, the site appears to have remained largely deserted until the early third century when an 8-acre stone fort was built over the centre of the hill. The new fort was roughly square in plan, had rounded corners and almost certainly a substantial gatehouse in the centre of each of its sides. It was protected by double ditches certainly on the east and on most of the south sides. Its walls were built of Kent ragstone, over a flint pebble foundation with an external face of ragstone blocks. The wall was 10 ft. (3 m.) thick at the base and reduced by two internal offsets to about 8 ft. (2.45 m.) It had a wide internal bank, but lacked courses of bonding bricks and external towers. Thus its basic structural characteristics, even before the extensive programme of excavation, were clearly in sharp contrast to most of the other shore-forts and were clearly typologically earlier, though this basic fact was missed by all early writers, including Collingwood. Internally, traces of the *via principalis*, the *via quintana, via decumana* and the *intervallum* road have been found. These frame a massive *principia* and at least five long buildings, probably all barracks. Elsewhere there is a small internal bath-building, ovens, pits and minor features. Both the south and east gates had a single carriageway flanked by a guard-room.

The date of the construction of the fort at Reculver is of special interest. The evidence of coins and pottery found in the rampart-bank near the east wall in 1957 and 1963 strongly suggests a construction date no later than the first quarter of the third century (Philp 1959). The famous Reculver inscription identifies one Rufinus as consular governor at the time of the fort's construction. If this was Aulus Triarius Rufinus (Richmond 1961), then this would have been in 210-216, but epigraphically even a date at the end of the second century is not impossible (Mann 1977).

The wider historical implications must now be considered. Large-scale excavations at Dover in 1970-77 demonstrated that the fleet's *Classis Britannica* base there was abandoned in about 208, as part of the massive support for the Severan campaigns in northern Britain. These campaigns were concluded by about 212, following the death at York of Septimius Severus in 211 and it was left to Caracalla to achieve a lasting peace-treaty. These events in the north were coinciding with increased Saxon raids on the shipping-lanes and the south-east. The Dover squadron never returned to build its Dover base and must have been redeployed elsewhere. It seems certain that the *Classis Britannica* must have been involved, to a greater or lesser extent, in the resulting anti-Saxon measures that clearly contained a major naval element. These measures included the construction of at least three large naval forts (Reculver, Brancaster and Caister-on-Sea), perhaps more (such as Carisbrooke), and it is highly likely that the *Classis Britannica* was attached to all, or some, of these. It must now be accepted, following the discovery of forts built by the *Classis Britannica* at Dover and Boulogne, that the fleet could have built some, or even all, of the early 'Saxon Shore' forts. There is now certain evidence that the fleet assisted in some way with the construction of the Reculver fort. At least 40 tiles of *Classis Britannica* manufacture (Fabric 2) were built into the later church and others were built into the east gate-house. Peacock was prepared to accept (Peacock 1977a) the existence at Reculver of an unknown deposit of local clay, virtually identical to the unique Fairlight Clay of the Hastings Beds, to explain this presence. A much better, simpler and more likely explanation is that these were simply some of the normal Wealden tiles made by the *Classis Britannica* that reached Reculver. Just why Peacock was unable to accept that, though large quantities of the tiles could reach Dover and Boulogne and probably Richborough, they would not have been shipped the extra dozen miles to Reculver. is difficult to understand. At the very least the *Classis Britannica* was supplying some tiles at the time of the fort's construction; equally, they could have been responsible for much or even all of the building work.

It is not yet possible to determine the duration of the Period I occupation at Reculver, be it by the *Classis Britannica* or the *Cohors I Baetasiorum*, or indeed both. Certainly there was some rebuilding later in the third century which may well have coincided with the late third-century expansion of the 'Saxon Shore' fort system (Phase II) of which both Richborough and Lympne clearly formed part. There was also activity in the fourth century, but again to what extent this corresponded with other 'Saxon Shore' fort sites is a question which must await more work for its solution. The coin sequence at Reculver seems to end with coins of Magnentius, although the absence of later issues may be more accidental than meaningful as happened at Portchester (Cunliffe 1975). However, the general absence of large numbers of late fourth-century coins, as found at nearby Richborough, is very noteworthy and there can be little doubt that the roles of the two forts at that time were substantially different. The probability is that Reculver was then almost, if not entirely, abandoned and that it had been superseded by the port and fort at Richborough.

LYMPNE

Whereas, Roach Smith wrote fully on Richborough and rather less on Reculver, he made very special efforts at the little-known site at Lympne. Indeed in 1850 he undertook the only large-scale excavation ever carried out on this site (Smith 1852) to a standard that was ahead of his time. Apart from details by Leland and Stukeley, all that was really known was that the remains of a substantial fort (known as Stutfall Castle) lay near the end of Stone Street, probably equated with the *Portus Lemanis* of the Antonine Itinerary, and was later garrisoned by the *Numerus Turnacensium*.

Roach Smith published a plan of the extant walls; he excavated an internal bath-house, the main east gate, a west postern gate and a massive masonry building at the upper, north end, perhaps the *principia*. The fort appeared to cover more than 10 acres, it had walls 10-12 ft. (3-3.65 m.) thick, semi-circular external bastions and was built of ragstone with occasional courses of brick. His finds included 261 coins, mostly dated between 250 and 350 and also various small-finds. Of special interest were eleven tiles stamped CLBR, or a variation of this, which he readily identified as the mark of the *Classis Britannica*, the Roman fleet in British waters. His most spectacular find, rebuilt into the east gate, was a barnacle-encrusted altar dedicated to Neptune by 'Aufidius Pantera, prefect (of the) Clas. Brit.', a discovery of outstanding importance in coastal studies.

In 1893-94, minor excavations by Victor Horsley (Taylor 1944) located some masonry at the southern limit of the site and this was clearly part of the otherwise 'missing' south wall of the fort. In 1976-78, three short seasons of research excavation were carried out by Barry Cunliffe (Cunliffe 1980). One of the objectives of this work was to locate the implied *Classis Britannica* base, similar to the fort found at Dover in 1970, which Roach Smith may have missed. No trace was found, but more re-used material was discovered. At the same time the east gate was re-examined and an improved plan obtained; two more short lengths of south wall were located and another 9 stamped tiles and 21 coins recovered. Cunliffe then went on to produce a radically different plan of the fort to replace that offered by Roach Smith and this is discussed below. Finally, in 1978-80 the Kent Archaeological Rescue Unit, under the direction of the writer, carried out a series of minor rescue-excavations in the West Hythe area

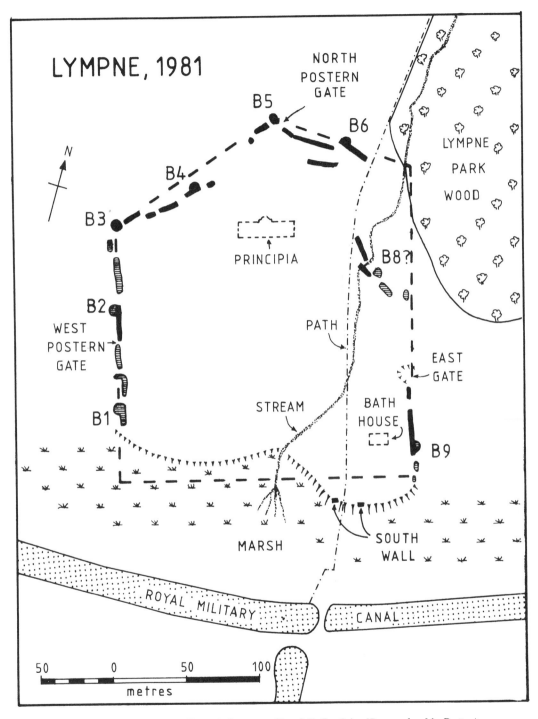

Fig. 6. The Roman Fort at Lympne (Stutfall Castle). *(Drawn by M. Dutto.)*

and located a major storm-beach which contained a large quantity of Roman material, including many tile fragments of *Classis Britannica* type (Fabric 2) and a single worn stamp. Although this work is to continue the evidence does already indicate a strong connection with the fleet.

Discussion

As at Dover, the evidence at Lympne is now sufficient to indicate the presence of major bases of both the *Classis Britannica* and the 'Saxon Shore' system. The evidence for the former now includes at least 25 stamped tiles, re-used building materials, the famous altar and the eroded material in the recently discovered storm-beach. It seems certain from all this that the *Classis Britannica* had a base somewhere nearby and that this, too, took the form of a fort, very much like that at Dover. If so, then it, too, may have served a single squadron of about ten warships and a garrison of 600-700 men. The altar, dedicated about 140, may well have been placed at the edge of an attached military parade-ground, from where it could have been washed into the sea during subsequent early erosion.

It seems clear from the work of both Roach Smith and Cunliffe that such a fortified base does not lie beneath the later 'Saxon Shore' fort, but it must be that its ruins were at no great distance when Stutfall Castle was built, thus paralleling the situation at Dover.

Three options arise from this. These are:
1. That the naval base survives and remains to be found;
2. That only part of the naval base has been removed by erosion;
3. That the base was entirely removed by erosion.

To judge from the Roman material in the storm-beach, the barnacles on the altar and the long history of erosion on this coast the probability is that any such base has already disappeared. However, the continued work by the Unit on its long-term Kent Coastline Survey may yet find further evidence.

There is little doubt about the function of the 'Saxon Shore' fort on the lower slopes of the hill, though its exact internal arrangements are far from clear. Like Reculver and Richborough, it had a small internal bath-house and like Reculver and Brancaster it seems to have had a large *principia*, though probably of rather different form. It clearly had walls on all sides, a large east gate and small posterns on the north and west sides. What clearly needs greater consideration is the basic shape of the fort's plan. Roach Smith produced a largely pentagonal plan, but Cunliffe has recently proposed a neat rectangular arrangement, mainly based on five considerations. These are:

1. The suggestion that three bastions on the north side (nos. 4-6) joined the fort wall at right-angles (Cunliffe 1980, 255);
2. That bastion 3 could 'have been D-shaped in plan if attached at a right-angled corner' (Cunliffe 1980, 254).
3. That the bastions were roughly equally spaced;
4. The presumption that the west wall of the fort had slid at least 60 m. downhill and the east wall at least 55 m. downhill;
5. An attempt to produce a plan similar to those at Richborough and Portchester.

Unfortunately, none of these considerations is anywhere near conclusive and the pentagonal plan suggested by Roach Smith (Smith 1852, 5) still seems to be the best reconstruction based on the available evidence. The five points are now considered in order.

First, if bastions 4 and 6 did meet the walls at right-angles, then they would fit both rectangular and pentagonal plans. The key point is bastion 5 where the evidence is inconclusive (Cunliffe 1980, Fig. 18).

Second, the statement that bastion 3 could have been D-shaped does not help; for on either plan this bastion would mark a realignment of adjacent walls and would thus *not* be D-shaped. What survives looks rather more like a three-quarter attached bastion that could fit either scheme. Certainly the small trench dug here (Cunliffe 1980, Fig. 17), only 9 ft. 7 in. (3 m.) long, 3 ft. 4 in. (1 m.) wide and only 1 ft. 8 in. (50 cm.) deep, was inconclusive for it failed to locate any part of the actual fort wall.

Third, the very roughly equal spacing of some of the bastions could again reflect either plan.

Fourth, whilst it is likely that most of the fort wall may have been moved to some extent, there is no direct evidence that the east walls have moved by such a massive amount. Indeed, where there has been substantial movement, as at the north-east corner where the small stream has broken through, the walls have mostly fallen. How then, if bastion 3 moved 196 ft. 9 in. (60 m.) downhill and bastion 4 downhill by at least 98 ft. 4 in. (30 m.), has about half the intervening length of fort wall (still standing up to 13 ft. (4 m.) high) remained largely upright and even maintained a largely satisfactory line? It looks close to its original position.

Finally, of five other shore-forts built at the end of the third century, three (Dover, Bradwell and Burgh Castle) had plans that were trapezoidal, whereas only two (Richborough and Portchester) had plans that were rectangular. Clearly, the contemporary forts offer a variety of plans, with the main option perhaps just being in favour of a trapezoidal form. Clearly at Lympne, where the steep slope of the hill was a major consideration, a pentagonal plan against the slope is still the most likely possibility (Fig. 6). Only large-scale excavation will finally resolve the matter. So, too, could this resolve the question of the original shore-line. Cunliffe has suggested that it could be 262 ft. 4 in. (80 m.) back beneath the fort far beneath the present site of the east gate. More probably it lies only 16 ft. 4 in. - 32 ft. 9 in. (5-10 m.) from the present site of the slumped south wall of the fort.

The coin list from Lympne seems to suggest an occupation starting no earlier than about 250 and probably nearer 270. It also suggests a general absence of paid troops later than about 350 in sharp contrast to the coin list from Richborough, but perhaps rather like the coin list from Reculver. Clearly, the changing emphasis between these three forts and particularly with that at Dover, is of great significance to our understanding of late-Roman military activity along the Kent coast.

SOME ROMAN ARCHITECTURAL TRADITIONS IN THE EARLY SAXON CHURCHES OF KENT

T.F.C. BLAGG

What is almost certainly the earliest piece of Saxon architectural decoration in England is one which until now has generally been considered to be of Roman date: the column base from the arcade between the nave and the presbytery of St. Pancras' church at Canterbury. The excavator thought that the columns had been taken from 'some Roman building of good period' (St. John Hope 1902, 228), and Taylor and Taylor have commented (1965, 146) that the piece 'had a properly-formed base, indicating that it was a re-used Roman column'. It is indeed competently carved, with two filleted tori separated by a scotia, set above a tall plinth. Most Romano-British column bases do have similar torus mouldings. The general opinion was, therefore, not unreasonable; underlying it, however, was an assumption which might be questioned, that a column base of this type and quality would not have been carved at the time when the church was built.

Now, however, it is possible to compare it with the writer's Corpus of 456 column bases from Roman Britain. The St. Pancras base is exceptional in four respects. It has a step between the lower torus and the plinth, a feature found on no other base in the Corpus. That it had a plinth is relatively unusual; the feature occurs on 31.7 per cent. of all Romano-British column bases, but more particularly, on only 17.7 per cent. of those from such major urban sites as Canterbury. Moreover, the plinth is exceptionally tall, at 190 mm., in relation to the mouldings, which are 126 mm. high. On all double-torus bases from Romano-British civilian sites the mouldings are greater in height than the plinth. Thirdly, the height of the mouldings of the St. Pancras base is equivalent to only 0.26 of the diameter of the shaft, a smaller ratio than on any double-torus base in the province, indeed, between half and quarter the normal proportionate height. Finally, the base has no mouldings above the tori; 89.9 per cent. of bases from civilian sites have a cyma or cavetto moulding; 7.2 per cent. have only a bead or fillet; only 2.9 per cent. have no mouldings at all (Blagg 1980, 34). Had this base been discovered at the site of a Roman auxiliary fort in north Britain, some of these unorthodox features might have occasioned less surprise. In a place which was once a major Roman town, this base is so unusual in its detail that it is highly improbable that it is Roman.

The placing on tall plinths of column bases with low torus mouldings is a feature which does not appear to develop until the fifth and sixth centuries A.D. in the area of the Mediterranean. Early examples include the church of St. Demetrios, Salonica (c. 470; Krautheimer 1979, ills. 81, 82), the basilica of S. Apollinare in Classe at Ravenna (532/6-549; Deichmann 1969, Abb. 53, 54) and the cathedral at Grado (571-9; Krautheimer 1979, ill. 244). These bases do not normally have a cyma or cavetto moulding above the tori, the possession of which is a feature

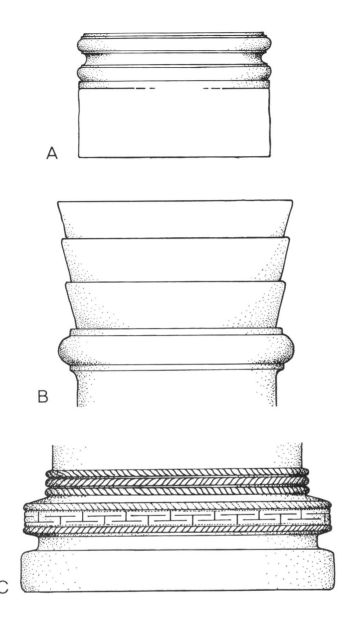

Fig. 7.   Early Saxon Ornament: A. Column Base from St. Pancras' Church. Canterbury;   B. Column Capital
from Reculver Church;   C. Column Base from Reculver.
Scale: A and C, 1:10; B has been sketched to approximately the same scale, based on Roach Smith 1850, 198, with
corrections from the writer's observations.

of western provincial rather than of metropolitan architecture in the early empire. Another such provincial feature is, however, retained by the St. Pancras base: the equal diameters of its torus mouldings; in the Mediterranean area it is normal for the lower torus to be the greater. The column base from St. Pancras' church at Canterbury is, therefore, one carved in the Roman tradition; but a tradition transmitted not from Roman Britain, but through the ecclesiastical architecture of the late Roman and Byzantine Mediterranean.

Any claim that the two columns from the church at Reculver were re-used Roman work has long since been abandoned: as Clapham justly remarked, 'they are almost certainly of the period of the church, as their decoration differs entirely from Romano-British work' (1930, 24). Nor, however, does their decoration closely resemble other Saxon architectural carving. Earlier writers about the church at Reculver have described the ornament of the capitals and bases without attempting to account for it (Taylor and Taylor 1965, 506, and bibliography, 509). It is, however, of particular interest to attempt to find the sources of the ornament, to illuminate the organisation of early Saxon church building, and the origins of the architectural ideas and of the craftsmen concerned.

The capital is relatively plain. It consists of three inclined fasciae above a necking with a projecting astragal, or half-round, moulding. The fasciae convert the square plan of the top of the capital to the circular plan of the column shaft. The base is more elaborately decorated, with a collar of three beads ornamented with cables, a projecting square-cut torus, a scotia, or hollow moulding, and a plinth which is circular in plan. On one base the torus has a compressed key pattern with cable mouldings above and below (Fig. 7). The torus of the other base consists of a triple bead. Roach Smith's illustration of this base (1850, 198) showed all three beads as decorated with a cable, in the same manner as those of the collar, but only on the lowest is one still visible. The columns consist each of eight drums, diminishing in height and increasing in diameter towards the bottom.

The fasciae of the capital have been likened to those of the architrave of the Ionic and Corinthian orders, but this is misleading, for the fasciae of an architrave are inclined downwards and outwards, whereas those of the Reculver capitals are inclined downwards and inwards. It would seem better to regard the latter as a version of the impost block placed above the capital proper, a feature first found in the Mediterranean area in the fifth century, in such churches as S. Giovanni Evangelista (423-34) and S. Apollinare Nuovo (490) at Ravenna (Deichmann 1969, Abb. 26, 184-5) and S. Demetrios, Salonica (470; Krautheimer 1979, ills. 81, 82). Its function was to expand the bearing surface of the capital beneath the springing of the arches which the column supported, and its development coincides with the increasing use of the arcade in place of the horizontal entablature in the nave of basilican churches. During the fifth and sixth centuries the impost block became a decorative element in its own right. The capitals of the presbytery of S. Vitale at Ravenna, luxuriantly decorated though they may be, are formally little more than two superimposed impost blocks above a neck moulding (Deichmann 1976, Abb. 16, 76-80). Among the many variant treatments which proliferated, the original nature of the Corinthian and Composite capitals might become totally lost (cf. Kautzsch 1936, Tafn. 34-43).

The use of ornamental motifs on the mouldings of column bases can certainly be traced back to the early years of the Roman empire; in Italy, such decorated bases were still being carved in the fourth century and later (Wegner 1965, 26 ff., 82 ff., 87). Bases in the Capitoline Museum and in the Palazzo dei Conservatori at Rome (Wegner 1965, Pls. 13c, 29b) provide good examples of the use of the cable motif on the mouldings, notably to form the lower torus. In Britain there are only half a dozen certain or possible examples of decorated bases, all but one from Cirencester; it thus seems most unlikely that the Reculver mason was copying from a locally-found Romano-British survival. The incidence of decorated column bases in other western provinces has not been studied. Admittedly, I have not so far found any very close parallel for the detail of the Reculver bases. Nevertheless, it does seem clear that in general they derive from a familiar, if relatively uncommon, Roman type. The profile of the base, with its collar and square-cut torus, is similar to that of the column bases of S. Apollinare in Classe at Ravenna (532/6 - 549; Deichmann 1969, Abb. 53, 54). This lends support to the inference made in discussing the Reculver capitals, that the form and decoration of the columns derive, though in a manner different from the St. Pancras base, from late Roman and early Byzantine ecclesiastical architecture.

The missionaries who came from Rome to Ethelbert's kingdom in the year 597 brought back the Christian religion and Latin literacy, two of the fundamentals of late-Roman civilisation which Roman Britain had once possessed. The church builders who followed them restored a third essentially Roman tradition which had also been lost after the fourth century: an architecture of mortared brick and stone, of columns and arched openings. Different versions of this tradition are observable, even among the small number of buildings, which survive from the seventh and eighth centuries, both in the varying uses made of tile and stone in their wall construction, and in their architectural embellishment. If this paper has pointed to the Mediterranean area as the ultimate source of the latter, that should not be thought to imply that the influences came directly from that quarter. Churches were being built in Merovingian Francia, and further work may succeed in defining a source closer to the kingdom of Kent for the masons and craftsmen who worked there. That would call for a wider consideration of the planning and constructional detail of the buildings than has been possible in this short offering to the memory of Stuart Rigold. It would have been characteristic of his learning that he might have suggested the answer.

IN TEMPORE IUSTINI CONSULIS:
CONTACTS BETWEEN THE BRITISH AND GAULISH CHURCHES BEFORE AUGUSTINE

JEREMY K. KNIGHT

> There was near by, on the east of the city, a church built in ancient times in honour
> of St. Martin, while the Romans were still in Britain, in which the Queen, who, as
> has been said was a Christian, used to pray. In the church they first began to meet
> . . . until when the King had been converted to the faith, they received greater liberty
> to preach everywhere and to build or restore churches.
> Bede, *Historia Ecclesiastica Gentis Anglorum*, i, 26 (trans. Colgrave and Mynors).

Bede's concern was with the church of the English, as his title states, not with that of the
sub-Roman British, but one would like to know more of the churches which were restored,
even though the impossible claim that a church was dedicated to a fourth-century bishop
within a decade of his death should warn us against putting too much weight on his precise
wording. The cult of Martin of Tours (*obit.* 397) was closely associated with the Merovingian
royal house and the Canterbury dedication no doubt derived from relics brought from Paris by
Bertha and her party shortly before 588 (Chadwick 1959, 181). In his own time, however,
Martin had been a leader of the ascetic evangelical wing of the Gallo-Roman Church and the
possibility of contact between this ascetic movement and the Romano-British Church cannot
be ruled out, particularly since recent archaeological discoveries (e.g. Poundbury: Green 1967-
1975; Water Newton: Painter 1975, 1977; Icklingham: West and Plouviez 1976; also Thomas
1981) have modified our view of this Church as a select congregation of rich villa owners or
high thinking Pelagians.

Ten years ago, discussing the way in which the Romano-British Church seemingly left so
little mark on its successors, Anglo-Saxon or British, Kenneth Painter suggested that 'the
failure (of the villa owners) to produce a missionary such as Martin of Tours resulted in their
losing the leadership of British society when the government of the Empire withdrew its
support. . . the lack of interest by the British aristocracy in proselytising the masses. . . left the
unromanised people. . . open to domination by the invaders. . . it was the failure of the villa
owners to establish Christianity as the basis of the new social order that led to the
disappearance of their own order.' Of the Christians of the post-Roman Celtic-speaking West
he wrote 'their faith seems to have been an entirely new affair, unconnected with the fourth
century Christianity of the upper class. . . whose tenants in town and country were almost all
pagan,' (Painter 1971, 166-8). One might perhaps take this argument a stage further by
recalling the rift in western Christianity at this time between the wealthy landowners and urban
office holders, some of whom adopted Pelagian ideals, and the populist ascetic movement
embracing such men as Martin, Germanus of Auxerre, Victricius of Rouen and Constantine

III, most of whose leaders were army men. It is possible that this embodies a larger social conflict within late-Roman society, but in terms of Church history it is an example of what W.H.C. Frend, writing of the Donatists, described as one of the fundamental divisions of Christian history, between 'the orthodox Catholic church. . . based upon an urban episcopate and ordered hierarchy and. . . the Church of the Holy Spirit, of enthusiasm. . . individualistic and intolerant' (Frend, 1952, 112-13). We may be dealing not with a negligent failure to produce a leader for the new age, but with two different views of the place of the Christian Church in society. To the one, the idea of producing a Martin of Tours in the way which Painter suggests might have seemed absurd, even repugnant. The British dignitaries who confronted Germanus of Auxerre in 429 and the *potentes* or *domini cati rhetorici* ('? well educated and subtle men of authority') — possibly clergy (see Hanson 1968, 109-112) who seemingly despised Patrick as an ill-educated enthusiast may have thought likewise. Martin of Tours once dreamt that the devil came to him disguised as Christ, in the Imperial robe and with the gemmed diadem and gold shoes of an Emperor, demanding to be worshipped. Martin hesitated, then replied 'The Lord did not say that he would come in a purple robe and glittering diadem. I will only believe in a Christ who comes in the clothes and form of his passion, bearing the wounds of Christ' (Sulpicius Severus, *Vita Martini c.* 24). It is an odd story, but one wonders what Martin would have made of the Christ-Emperor of the Hinton St. Mary mosaic.

Martin's name was probably not unknown in Roman Britain during its final years. His friend and colleague Victricius of Rouen was in Britain in 395-6 at the request of his Gallic episcopal colleagues to settle a dispute within the British Church (*De Laude Sanctorum*, i). The statement of Orosius (*Historia Adversus Paganos*, vii, 40) followed by Bede (*Historia Ecclesiastica*, i, 11) that Constans, son of Constantine III was a monk has aroused little comment among historians. It is very doubtful whether there were monks in Britain at this period, for there were few monasteries then even in Gaul — perhaps eight to a dozen (Luff 1952, 182; Grosjean 1957a, 159-61), but whilst ruler of Gaul Constantine obtained the election of Heros *"vir sanctus et beati Martini discipulis'* (Prosper of Aquitaine, *Chronicle*, n. 1247) to the see of Arles and of Lazarus to that of Aix-en-Provence. Lazarus, like John Cassian, was a protégé of that patron of early Gallic monasticism Bishop Proculus of Marseille. Heros and Lazarus had been involved in the bitter disputes at Tours which followed Martin's death, when his aristocratic successor Brice had been deposed and appealed to Rome. At the Council of Turin (398), they had been his leading accusers. When Arles fell to the *magister militum* Constantius in 411, Heros tried to protect the fallen Constantine III by ordaining him as priest. Later, both bishops fled to Palestine, Heros being replaced at Arles by Patroclus, friend and familiar of the *magister militum*, whilst Remigius, who had been deposed from Aix in favour of Lazarus, was re-instated. Complicated quarrels ensued, in the course of which Pope Zosimus, in two letters written to the bishops of Africa in 417 (Jaffé 1885, 329 and 340) attacked Heros and Lazarus as creatures of the fallen tyrant, forced upon an unwilling episcopate and people. These quarrels were, of course, intimately connected with those relating to Pelagius. Zosimus had declared Pelagius innocent of holding dangerous opinions, whilst the two Gallic bishops, in Palestine, pressed formal charges against him. Constans, son of Constantine III, had left the monastic life when his father elevated him to Caesar and in view of the Pelagian proclivities of sections of the British Church, it is of interest to find his father securing the election as bishop of a man who was a disciple of Martin and a fervent opponent of Pelagius himself.

During Constantine's usurpation in Gaul, St. Honoratus founded the monastery of Lerins.

By about 430 it had produced a brilliant generation of men who dominated the sees of southern Gaul and in some cases had specific links with Britain — Hilary of Arles, Lupus of Troyes, who before entering Lerins about 425 had been married to Hilary's sister and who visited Britain in 429; Eucher of Lyon. At Riez (Basses-Alpes) two successive bishops, Maximus (434-460) and the British-born Faustus (468- *c.* 480) were ex-abbots of Lerins. Germanus of Auxerre was not a Lerins graduate, but was closely associated with several of the group and his life, by Constantius of Lyon, is dedicated to Eucher's successor Patiens. It cannot be wholly coincidence that the Latin-inscribed memorial stones of western Britain show by their use of the formula *Hic Iacet* an origin in central or western Gaul in the very period dominated by this influential and close-knit group.

Constantius of Lyon's *Vita Germani* is dedicated to Patiens, Bishop of Lyon 469-475 + (Duchesne 1910, 163) and Censurius, Bishop of Auxerre *c.* 480-510 (Duchesne 1910, 436-445- the chronology of the bishops of Auxerre is confused in this period). It was probably written *c.* 480-490 (Levison 1920). Constantius is at home with Roman official ranks and titles, and where he does not know the correct title he uses a descriptive phrase. Thus he knew that Germanus held the rank of *Dux*, with authority in more than one province, but evidently did not know his official title. It is sometimes objected that this account conflicts with the separation of civil and military office under the late Empire, but Constantius does not say that Germanus held a civil service post before becoming *Dux*, but only that he practised law — a subject which was a staple part of late-Roman education. He may possibly have been *Dux Tractus Armoricani*, whose command extended from the Garonne to the Seine. This might account for his later acting as *patronus* for the citizens of *Lugdunensis Tertia* (i.e. Armorica), much as an ex-legate of *Legio II Augusta* had, much earlier, apparently acted as patron of the *civitas* of the Silures (*RIB* 311). It would also have made him particularly suited for the mission to Britain in 429. for his post would have entailed official contact with his colleagues of the *Litus Saxonicum*. Lupus of Troyes would have acted as his adviser on technical theological matters, for he belonged to the Lerins school of anti-Pelagian doctrine sometimes misleadingly called 'semi-Pelagian'. It was semi-Pelagian only in that it opposed the extreme pre-destinarian views of some of the followers of Augustine. The cast list for the first visit (*Vita Germani*, 12-18) includes the group of Pelagian notables holding official (? urban) office, a man holding *tribuniciae potestatis* — possibly a chief magistrate, if not a rather grand circumlocution for a military tribune, and the British bishops, who are quite distinct from the Pelagians and whose orthodoxy is not called in question. In all, we see, if somewhat vaguely, a normal late-Roman society. The subsequent visit to the shrine of St. Alban has the air of a post-conference excursion and does not imply that the synod was held at Verulamium. London or Canterbury would be the most likely venues.

Germanus's second visit (*Vita Germani*, 25-27) must lie in the period 440-445 and both Grosjean (1957) and Thompson (1957) have argued for 444-5. It dealt with a localised out-break of Pelagianism and, if we are comparing like with like (the geography of both visits is vague), we receive a somewhat different impression of Britain. Germanus is met on arrival by Elafius 'first man of that region' (*regionis illius primus)* and Constantius's usual accuracy with official titles suggests that he is not describing an official Roman office, though he may be using *regionis* with specific connotations, perhaps even, as Frere (1978, 414) implies, for a civitas. Germanus's companion on this occasion was Severus, Bishop of Trier, remembered (*Vita Lupi*, ii; Bede, i, 21) as the evangelist of the peoples of *Germania Prima* and presumably familiar with the problems of a sub-Roman society with barbarian elements. The Pelagians were condemned by the British bishops in formal synod and exiled — presumably by the civil power.

Not all contacts between Britain and Gaul in this period were one way. The literature of the period is full of well-born Christians fleeing from the barbarians to Provence, Africa or the East, and it is no surprise to find Britons among them. Salvian mocked their Gallic counterparts for acting on the text 'when they shall persecute you in one city, flee unto another.' A Dumnonian woman who claimed the title *clarissima femina* was buried at Salona in Dalmatia in 425 at the age of 30 (I.L.C.V., 185; Stevens 1952) and at Arles a fragment of the lid of a re-used sarcophagus has the epitaph of Tolosanus *Britannus Natione* cut over its sculptured dolphins. (Benoît 1954, no. 98, 67-8). This uses a version of the *Hic Iacet* formula and a date of *c.* 420-60 is indicated. Patrick may have been in central-northern Gaul perhaps *c.* 435-50 (Thomas 1979, 88), though this is disputed (Hanson 1968, 128-30). Had he got as far as Lerins, he could have met a fellow countryman in the person of Faustus. Born in Britain *c.* 400-405, he moved to Gaul, seemingly with his family — or at least his mother, and lived in Lyon before entering Lerins *c.* 425-30. In 434, he became Abbot of Lerins and in 460 Bishop of Riez. Preacher, writer and theologian, he was a friend of Avitus of Vienne and Sidonius Apollinaris, both of whom refer to his British origin (Avitus, *Letters*, iv, '*ortu Britannum*'; Sidonius, *Letters*, ix, 9). Sidonius's letter, written *c.* 465, tells how he had managed to intercept and copy a new book by Faustus which Riochatus, a British cleric ('*antistes et monachus*') was carrying back to '*Britannis tuis*'. Riochatus may have been a Breton rather than a Briton, for Sidonius calls him 'twice exile in this world' (? as a monk and as a British emigrant to Armorica), but the episode shows that Faustus remained in touch with his fellow countrymen down to his last years and that the British Church at that date still possessed churchmen who were in touch with one of the leading theologians of southern Gaul and received complimentary copies of his latest book.

The epigraphic evidence for contacts between Britain and Gaul in this period was examined thirty years ago by Nash-Williams (Nash-Williams 1950 = E.C.M.W.). The core of his conclusions concerned the *Hic Iacet* formula which occurs on many of the fifth to seventh century Latin-inscribed memorial stones of western Britain. This originated in Italy in the late third century and spread thence to southern and central Gaul, where it appeared about A.D. 420 and enjoyed a restricted vogue in the period up to about 460. It reached western Britain in the mid-fifth century. A broader survey of the development of a Christian epigraphic tradition in Britain and Gaul may serve to put these conclusions into perspective.

By continental standards, Romano-British tombstones are rare outside legionary fortresses, the northern frontier zone and a few special cases like Bath. Of the fifteen examples from London (*RIB* 9-23), six are of legionaries, two of civil servants and one of a Greek. The same basic pattern recurs through most of the civilian areas of Britain, with the sparse series heavily biased towards the army, foreign immigrants and an early date. Of the distinctive late type using the formulae *Dis Manibus et Memoriae* or *Memoriae* only three occur, two from London and one from Silchester (*RIB* 16, 23, 87). This is in contrast with, for example, *Lugdunensis Prima*, where Audin and Burnand were able to assemble 170 example of the third and fourth century, only 7 (4 per cent) of which showed some possible hint of Christian influence or sympathy (Audin and Burnand 1959, 1959a). This was a very flimsy foundation for any British tradition of Christian epigraphy to build on, and the subsequent insular tradition of Latin-inscribed memorial stones must be a new introduction from outside and not a stem grown from

Romano-British roots.

This is even true to some extent in Gaul, where the fourth-century Christian epitaphs are not derived from the late Gallo-Roman types studied by Audin and Burnand, but from the third-fourth century Christian tradition of Italy and the central Mediterranean. The earliest, a lost stone from Lyon (I.C.G. 62; *CIL* xiii, 2351), bears a consular date of A.D. 334, within the lifetime of Constantine the Great. There are others from Lyon, Vienne and Autun in the Rhône Valley and from western Gaul around Bordeaux, the Pyrenees and the Charente. They are quite distinctive (Fig. 8) and there is nothing like them in Britain before or after 410. The two latest-dated examples are both of A.D. 405 and when the sequence resumes after the barbarian invasions with a stone of A.D. 422 from Lyon, much has changed. The fourth-century series is well represented in Aquitania and were the tombstones of the contemporaries of Ausonius of Bordeaux and Martin of Tours. The new series belongs mostly to Provence, the Rhône Valley and the Narbonne-Toulouse area. They use the initial formulae *Hic Iacet* or *Hic Requiescit*; replacing the older *Depositio* or *Recessit*. They are closely related to the beginnings of the insular series (Fig. 9). The evidence for their date comes almost exclusively from Lyon, where there is a sequence of six dated stones of A.D. 422, 431, 438, 447, 448 and 449 (I.C.G. 35, 44, 53, 68, 532; *CIL* xiii, 2353-7, 11207; Martin 1904). After this is a gap of almost twenty years until a fresh series starts using the longer formula *Hic Requiescit in Pace* or related forms, the earliest of this group being of A.D. 467 (St. Romain d'Albon, Drôme — N.R. 134; *CIL* xii, 1791) and 469 (Grigny near Lyon — I.C.G. 87; *CIL* xiii, 2361). The insular series thus goes back to a Gallic group with a date bracket of A.D. 420-60.

The novelty of the insular Latin-inscribed series has prompted suggestions of Gallic missionaries or of direct influence from Lyon-Vienne, where the bulk of the *Hic Iacet* stones is found, but there are now sufficient *Hic Iacet* stones in areas like Vendée and the Bordelais to form a western French group which could have inspired the insular series. The French stones are, however, mostly rectangular marble or fine stone plaques or slabs set horizontally over the grave, quite unlike the 'standing stone' form of the insular series. Radford (1971, 8) has suggested that Roman milestones may have served as the immediate model for the form of the insular stones and a fifth-century British chieftain, who saw the name and titles of a Roman Emperor displayed thus, might well be tempted to emulate him. This fusion of Gallic import and Romano-British form needs to be seen against the background of the mechanics of cultural borrowing and diffusion (e.g. Kroeber 1952, 344-5).

A comment on continuity is also necessary. Of the three epigraphic phases, phase 1 — the fourth-century pagan series using *Dis Manibus et Memoriae* — is found in both Britain and Gaul. Phase 2 — the fourth-century Christian series using *Depositio* or *Recessit* — is found only in Gaul. Since the Gallic phase 3 stones — the fifth-century Christian series using the formula *Hic Iacet* are themselves an introduction into Gaul from outside and are not directly derived from the phase 2 stones, we cannot safely use the similar discontinuity between our phase 1 and phase 3 British stones as evidence of discontinuity between Romano-British Christianity and its insular successor, since no one doubts the continuity of Christian tradition in Gaul at this period. Similarly, though it is tempting to cite the failure of the British series to use the post 460 *Hic Requiescit in Pace* series as evidence of disruption of contacts with Gaul after 450, it is doubtful whether this conclusion is valid. One of the most striking features of the Early Christian epigraphy of western Europe is its division into self-contained local groups confined to a province, a geographical area, or a single city. Each of these normally takes its

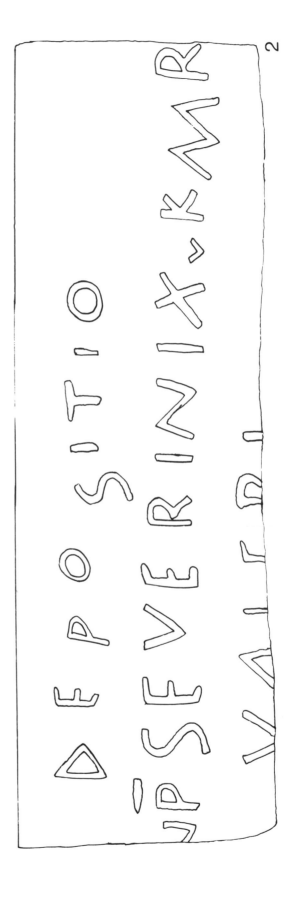

Fig. 8. Fourth-century inscriptions from Gaul. (Not to scale).

1. 'Basilius was buried on Sunday, January the 22, in the year after the sixth consulship of Honorius' (A.D. 405.)

   Square tile found in a grave in the cemetery of the demolished church of St. Ausone, Angoulême (Charente) in 1882, placed vertically behind the skull. Finds made at the same time included late-Roman pottery (? from burials) including one grey-ware pot with the graffito *Lea Vivas*, a second graffito *Aloqia Vivas In Deo* and a sculptured "Aquitanian" sarcophagus. (N.R. 277; *CIL* xiii, 1118).

2. The Presbyter Severinus was buried on the 15th of February. . . Valerius (? erected this memorial).

   Rectangular stone slab, heavily trimmed at edges, found *c.* 1887 built into the fabric of the church of St. Just in the village of Valcabrère on the southern edge of the Roman town of *Lugdunum Convenarum* (St. Bertrand de Comminges, Haute-Garonne). Now built into the internal west wall of the nave. There is another inscription, of A.D. 347, from the same church. (N.R. 296; *CIL* xiii, 300).

starting point from the memorial stones of a neighbouring area — the Gallic borrowing of *Hic Iacet* from Italy is an example — and thereafter usually develops its own tradition with little if any external borrowing. Thus the failure of the insular series to utilise later phases of the Gallic epigraphic tradition does not prove that links with Gaul were cut — indeed ceramic evidence shows that in some respects at least they were not.

Hydatius (*Chronicle* an. 162, p. 27) and Bede (*Historia Ecclesiastica*, i, 21) saw the murders of Aetius and Valentinian III in 454-5 as the watershed marking the end of Roman rule in the west. The mint of Trier continued to strike to the time of Valentinian III and Theodosius II, and gold of Valentinian III is known from such late-Roman military sites in northern Gaul as Furfooz (Belgium) and Famars (Nord) (Nenquin 1953, 20; Bersu and Unverzagt 1961, 187), whilst the military graves of Böhme's phase III (400-450) also relate to this final Imperial occupation (Böhme 1974). There is no good reason to doubt Gildas's claim that as late as 446-454 the British *civitates* could appeal to Aetius for intervention in Britain, even if the wording of the 'appeal' is clearly his own. The death of Valentinian coincides exactly with our last glimpse of the Romano-British church, debating, but seemingly not adopting, the Easter Cycle of Victorius of Aquitaine (Hanson 1968, 67-9).

The problems of the subsequent British emigration to Gaul are too large to be discussed here, but a few relevant details may be picked out. The emigrants were Christians and *Romani* with their own leaders and their own bishop; Mansuetus, who took his seat at the Council of Tours in 461 along with his Gallic colleagues (Munier 1963, 148). They were a significant piece on the Gallic military chessboard and the Praetorian Prefect Arvandus came badly unstuck when he tried to incite the Visigoths to attack them, not realising that they were being wooed as allies by the Emperor Anthemius. Arvandus was condemned for treason in 469 (Sidonius *Letters*, i, 7). Their ambiguous position is similarly shown in another letter of Sidonius to the British leader Riothamus (iii, 9) of 472. Sidonius was Bishop of Clermont in *Aquitania Prima*, the neighbouring province to *Lugdunensis III* where the British were settled and someone's slaves had run away to join them. They might equally have run away to join any similar group, but it is doubtful whether Sidonius would have written to a Gothic or Frankish leader asking him to return runaways. These scraps confirm Gildas's account of how the British organised themselves under their own *tyranni* and so for the moment preserved their way of life, civil, ecclesiastical and military. When this was no longer possible in their own land, they tried to preserve it by organised emigration, much as the Puritans, a thousand years later, transplanted their secular and church government to New England. The villa owners and urban office-holders, as a class, can hardly have survived this period of turmoil. With their economic and political power base destroyed, their influence on the British Church must have ceased. The future, as Painter saw, was with these who regarded themselves as the heirs of Germanus and Martin. Whatever the complexities of the Patrician problem (Hanson 1968; Thomas 1981) or the obscurities of Ninian, our sources (Bieler 1968) show vigorous missionary activity in areas outside the boundaries of *Britannia* and the Latin-inscribed memorial stones of Wales suggest similar but anonymous endeavour within. Bieler's words on Ninian can be applied elsewhere — 'All that we can say is that. . . the sources. . . portray a British Bishop in a Roman border province who preached the Gospel in a territory beyond the Empire'. Such a picture of vigorous missionary activity accords ill with one of a Church which within Britain itself withered on the vine.

From about 475 onwards we are faced with new problems — the narrative of Gildas

Fig. 9. Early fifth-century Christian inscription from Vienne. "Here lies Martinus, who lived 2 years, 2 months and 3 days. In Peace." Marble slab from the cemetery of the demolished church of SS. Gervais and Protasius, Vienne (Isère), destroyed during the construction of a railway in the nineteenth century. Now in the *Musée lapidaire chrétien*, St-André-le-Bas, Vienne, (I.C.G. 422 A; *CIL* xii, 2126).

(Thompson 1979), the import of Mediterranean and French pottery, the impact of the spreading Anglo-Saxons. Fulford (1978, 127-8) would date the Mediterranean fine wares to *c.* 475-550 and suggests a link with Gildas's period of prosperity, but they are now known in quantity on some Spanish and Portuguese sites and the vagaries of their commerce (Hayes 1972, 456-60) may owe more to Theodoric and the disruption of the Mediterranean consequent upon Justinian than to insular affairs. The British finds of the Atlantic sub-type of *sigillée paléochrétienne grise* = Tintagel ware D (Rigoir 1968; Rigoir and Meffre 1973; Thomas 1959, 1976) and of western French coarse wares of Tintagel ware E (Thomas, *loc. cit.*) continue the evidence for Gallic contacts seen in the memorial stones. By the seventh-century with ware E probably still current, the *Vita Columbani* (97) and *Vita Filiberti* (*c.* 40-41) refer to *Brittones nautici, naves Brittanicae* and to ships sailing to Ireland in the waters around the Loire estuary. The former may have been Bretons, but such evidence as we have for the development of monasticism, the transmission of texts and the development of insular script show this to have been a vital formative period. Riochatus has shown us textual transmission in action *c.* 475 and the *Vita Martini* seems to have reached Ireland by 460 (Babut 1913, 267-75) whilst Gildas may have seen the *Passio Albani*, written in the Auxerre region *c.* 515-40 (Levison 1941, 349-50.) Bieler (1949, 272) would see the earliest, majuscule, form of insular script emerging *c.* 550 in the larger British and Irish monastic houses from a continental background whose closest surviving representatives are fifth-century Italian. Insular miniscule followed *c.* 600-650. This agrees well with the first appearance of half-uncial letter forms on the memorial stones.

One further piece of evidence needs consideration, if only to explain the title of this article. The inscription from Penmachno in Gwynedd recording that it was set up *In Tempore Iustini Consulis*, 'In the time of Justinus the consul' (Rhys 1919; E.C.M.W. 104), was probably only the final element of a lengthy inscription on the now lost right-hand face of the stone, but it uses a dating era based on the consulship of the penultimate consul (*cos.* 540), an era used only at Lyon and in *Lugdunensis Prima*. There is evidence that Penmachno was an important early Welsh monastery and this unique post-consular dating suggests a British cleric in Lyon or in a nearby monastery such as Grigny or Ile-Barbe long enough to become familiar with local dating formulae. (There is probably a numeral missing from the end of the inscription). Two generations later we are in the presence of other, greater clerics, exiled for the love of God to those parts of Europe where barbarian settlers had earlier inhibited the foundation of monasteries — Columbanus in those parts of Gaul where the dead were buried with weapons and jewellery; Felix in East Anglia and Fursey at Péronne; Augustine in Kent.

A TWELFTH-CENTURY RE-BUILDING AT ST. AUGUSTINE'S ABBEY, CANTERBURY

CHRISTOPHER MISCAMPBELL

During excavations at the abbey in 1974 and 1975 by the Department of the Environment large quantities of stone were discovered on the south side of the choir of the abbey church from which it was possible to establish a rough building history of the choir. A report was written, and, together with other recent excavation reports, will be published in a forthcoming monograph of *Medieval Archaeology*. This article concentrates on one period of the abbey's history: the fire of 1168 and the subsequent partial re-building of the abbey as evidenced by the mouldings on the worked stone excavated and by documentary sources.

The abbey was burnt in 1168. We do not know the extent of the damage. According to Thorne, "the church was in great part burnt. . . and in this fire many documents perished and moreover the very shrine of St. Augustine and many saints of the place were woefully damaged" (Thorne 1934, 94). The surviving north wall of the nave shows no sign of burning, nor does the section of fallen wall excavated on the south side of the choir in 1974-75. Both these walls are considered to be of pre-fire construction. We know that replacing of stonework took place at St. Augustine's but from the ground plan it does not look as if the church was re-built with a stone vault, so the re-building was probably not as extensive as Thorne implies. (Though the choir aisles and choir apsidal chapels were probably vaulted).

Even so, the post-fire work is interesting because it is so similar to the post-fire work at Canterbury Cathedral. In general, the use of marble for shafts (Bony 1949 and Bony 1965) and Caen stone for facing and worked surfaces and in particular the use of chevron dog-tooth and roll mouldings for window arches and rib-vaults is paralleled by similar work in the cathedral. The earliest examples at the cathedral of chevron dog-tooth and roll-mouldings are from 1176 on the ribs of the choir aisle vaults (Gervase 1930, 17-8) while the window arches of the Trinity Chapel (1182) and the corona seem on inspection to be exactly the same as the *voussoirs* excavated from the abbey. A fragment of classicizing Corinthian capital was also excavated. All these pieces of stone and marble were excavated outside the south apsidal chapel on the south side of the choir of the abbey.

Because St. Augustine's was burnt five years before the cathedral, it cannot, therefore be assumed that the re-building took place before the great internal re-building of the cathedral. The abbey was burnt on 29 August, 1168 (Thorne 1934, 94), a date towards the end of the building season. Assuming that restoration did not begin until the spring of 1169, that still leaves five years before the cathedral fire of 1174. According to Gervase, the cathedral choir was re-built from 1174-1180 a period of six years after the fire there. The Trinity Chapel, a smaller area, but one which needed to be built from the undercroft upwards took from 1179 to

1184, six years also (Gervase 1930, 11-9). From examination of the fallen wall in the choir of the abbey it is evident that the outer walls were basically unharmed by the fire (although pointed windows were inserted into the wall later). The outer walls of the cathedral choir also appear to have been relatively undamaged so the situations are similar in that respect. However, the cathedral no doubt had the money to complete the eastern arm very quickly because of donations pouring in after the murder of Thomas à Becket. The abbey had no such timely martyr to increase its revenues, and may have been much slower in finishing its restoration work. Relations between Clarembald, Abbot of St. Augustine's, and the rest of the monastery may also have delayed the re-building of the choir. Thorne mentions that the monks violently opposed the installation of Clarembald, which was done by Henry II in 1161 and "did (not) suffer him either to enter the chapter house or to celebrate mass or perform other solemn services in the church" (Thorne 1934, 94-5). However, after noting the fire of 1168, Thorne later mentions that the monks let Clarembald run the administrative side of the cathedral because of the uneasy time caused by the quarrel between Becket and Henry II (Thorne 1934, 95). It is possible that one of the reasons was so that a common plan for re-building could be agreed on, and when Thorne later recounts that one of Clarembald's supporters incurred "debts and heavy obligations" with the Common Seal it suggests that he had gone beyond the agreed plan for re-building the church. After the fire at the cathedral there were monks who were content to have it repaired cheaply and quickly and no doubt they existed at St. Augustine's, too. There is some suggestion of money being borrowed for the restoration programme. A letter from the Pope to the King recommending Roger as the new abbot in 1179 says that the King should not allow Roger to be further troubled for debts to the Jews (Thorne 1934, 110). Simon, Abbot of St. Albans from 1167-1183, is known to have incurred debts to the Jews in maintaining his abbey (Boase 1953, 270). Whatever work was done between 1168 and 1173, must have stopped in that year because Abbot Clarembald was removed from office by the Pope after successful petitioning by the monks, and, in revenge for this (so Thorne says), Henry II seized the property and revenues of the abbey which he held until 1176 (Thorne 1934, 110-1; Urry 1960, 94). Adam of Charing and John Fitzvivian paid the abbey revenues into the Royal Treasury after allowing sums for the support of the monks (Urry 1960, 94). The Pipe Rolls record these payments but no mention is made of money set aside for building work on the abbey so it seems that no work was done for three years from 1174 to 1176. (Pipe Rolls, vol. 19, 1173-4, 1; 1174-5, 221; vol. 25, 1175-6, 209). This suggests that the rebuilding of the church after the fire had already taken place or that whatever work was needed was not essential and therefore money was not forthcoming from the royal coffers.

It seems more possible that the second option is nearer to the truth than the first. In 1176 the King restored the revenues of the abbey and in the same year the monks chose a new abbot, Roger, who had been the custodian of Thomas à Becket's tomb at Christchurch (Thorne 1934, 100). He brought some of Becket's relics from the cathedral ('a great part of his blood which he shed, a certain small portion of his head cut away, along with a considerable part of the brain of the said martyr') (Thorne 1934, 100), and no doubt the monks believed they could have a place of pilgrimage to rival Christchurch. In 1179 Roger went to Rome to be blessed by the Pope (Thorne 1934, 107. 1176 according to Sprott; Sprott 1719, 124) and in the same year the abbey became independent of the archbishop's visitations, both of which are signs of the abbey's recovery after its seizure by Henry II. Following from this may come the Papal Bull issued by Alexander III (1159-1184) which confirms the church of Faversham "for the repair of our church which has been burnt" (i.e. St. Augustine's Abbey) (Elmham 1858, 4-29; Thorne 1934, 115). The bull is not dated by year but is between bulls of 1178 and 1179 as dated by the editor of Thomas of Elmham. There are two other papal bulls mentioned by Elmham, this time in his *Chronologia*, the first dated by him to 1172 and confirming the churches of Minster and Faversham, the second dated 1173 and confirming the churches of Faversham and Milton. (Sprott notes all three bulls together; Sprott 1719, 125-6). Even if the first papal bull mentioned above is as early as 1172, it only shows, as do the others, that the abbey monks were still collecting money to re-build their church and they would have been unable to do any re-building until, at the earliest, King Henry II had restored to them their revenues in 1176.

Gervase, while apparently an eye-witness of the fire at the cathedral in 1174 does not mention either the fire or the restoration of the abbey. It is difficult to know what to make of this omission. He may have not wanted to belittle the magnificent rebuilding of the cathedral or it may be that the work at the abbey was not so extensive or innovatory that it merited comment. Since the outside of the abbey appears, from surviving fragments, to have remained intact until the thirteenth century, he may have missed seeing the interior refurbishing of the abbey. That the new work might not have progressed very far is suggested by Roger coming from the cathedral and being determined, as a new abbot, to outdo the cathedral in splendour by re-building the eastern arm in a style fit to receive the relics of St. Thomas à Becket. The lack of large amounts of comparative material at St. Augustine's prevents us from knowing how 'Gothic' the abbey became. The use of late Romanesque detail would not have prevented it from being a Gothic church since Christchurch has details exactly similar to St. Augustine's (the dog-tooth arch). However, the fact that 50 years after the transitional re-modelling, work was again begun, this time on lengthening the windows to increase the light into the choir suggests that the re-modelling had been confined to grafting the new style onto the Romanesque church.

While the above discussion has not proved that the transitional work at St. Augustine's was done before that of Christchurch, it has at least shown that the work could have been earlier or at the very least that the work was contemporary with the rebuilding at the cathedral. As such, it is very advanced for architecture in England.

ACKNOWLEDGEMENT

The writer is grateful to Stuart Rigold for reading through and giving advice on this article.

SOME TOMB RAILINGS IN CANTERBURY CATHEDRAL

JANE GEDDES

In Canterbury Cathedral there are four tombs protected by very similar sets of iron railings. The tombs belong to the Black Prince (*d.* 1376), Archbishop Courtenay (*d.* 1396), Henry IV (*d.* 1413) with his wife Joan of Navarre (*d.* 1436) and Archbishop Chichele (*d.* 1443). The tombs were built over a period of sixty years, so the question is why they should all have similar railings (Plates V-VIII).

The railings all have elaborate corner and intermediate stanchions. These have an enlarged castellated top, and moulded vertical bars are attached to the lower section of the stanchions. Between the stanchions are narrower, plain vertical bars. These are held by a sturdy base plate and, around the top, by a crenellated edging. A characteristic feature of the crenellated bar is the application of repeating moulded motifs, either a fleur de lys, or lion's head, or both (Plate V). This description applies to all the railings, but around the tomb of Archbishop Chichele the crenellated bar is further decorated with a spikey cresting of star flowers and fleur de lys (Plate VI). Furthermore, the decorative details on Chichele's railings are picked out in red and gold paint. The paint has certainly been renewed, but it could easily be a replacement of the original paint as the tomb is highly coloured. Chichele's railings are by far the grandest. His cresting is also found on gates closing the north choir aisle from the transept: these may be reproductions.

Chichele's tomb on the north side of the choir provides the only fixed point in the history of these railings. On February 5, 1426, the chapter at Christ Church appealed to Chichele to remove a prisoner who had sought sanctuary by clinging on '*per clausuram ferream vestri novi monumenti*'. The episode caused '*tam sterpitum terribilem circa chorum*' and obviously upset the monks very much. (Sheppard 1889, iii, 146-7) Chichele's tomb and railings were thus installed by 1425 although he did not gain formal permission from the chapter to erect them until April 1432. (Sheppard 1889, iii, 159) Such a procedure was a mere formality. A similar time-lag occurred with Bishop Beckynton's tomb at Wells: he was congratulated on completing his tomb in 1449 (Beckynton 1872, 264) but the altar in his chantry was not dedicated until 1452 (Register of Beckynton I, 1934, 175).

The Black Prince had hoped to be buried in his chantry in the crypt. He had been granted a papal dispensation to marry his cousin Joan of Kent and founded a chantry in recompense for this, in 1362. (Sheppard 1889, ii, 388, 423; Hussey 1936, 34.) When he died in 1376 it was decided to bury him with maximum honour between the southern piers of the Trinity Chapel where his tomb could be seen by all the visitors to Becket's shrine. St. John Hope reckoned that the railings were 'some thirty years later than the tomb.' (St. John Hope 1895, 1).

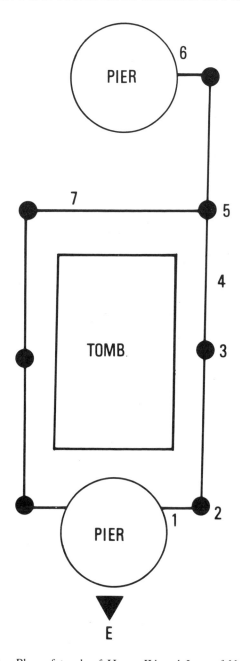

Fig. 10. Plan of tomb of Henry IV and Joan of Navarre.

Bishop Courtenay likewise had no say in the final arrangements for his burial. He had humbly requested to be buried in Maidstone churchyard but, at the King's instigation, was buried just east of the Black Prince, in Canterbury Cathedral. (Duncan 1898, 55; Beazeley 1898, 49-50; Sheppard 1889, iii, 41) So, his tomb railings must also have been made after his death.

In his will, Henry IV requested to be buried in the cathedral 'after the discretion of my cousin the archbishop', Thomas Arundel. (Nichols 1826, 17) In June 1413, his body was brought in solemn procession to the cathedral where it was kept on a hearse, with candles burning night and day, and ninety banners painted with arms around it, all costing £100. (Wylie 1914, 47-8). What exactly happened after that is not clear. It seems that the magnificent alabaster tomb and effigies were not made until his wife Joan of Navarre died in 1436. The expenses of her funeral included a hearse and torches. (Woodruff 1936, 58) It is possible that Henry lay on his hearse all this time because, according to Woodruff and Danks (1912, 191) who do not quote a source, the hearse was not sold off until after Joan's death. Henry IV's chantry on the north side of the Trinity Chapel ambulatory was dedicated to Edward King and Confessor in 1439 by the Bishop of Ross, (Stone 1902, 26) so perhaps the tomb was made at the same time.

Regardless of when the tomb was made, it is clear that Henry IV's railings were not designed for their present position. Those around the other tombs are all a perfect fit. The plan in Fig. 10 shows the anomalies around the royal tomb:

1.   The crenellation next to the pier has been cut off to make the horizontal bar fit;
2.   The crenellated bar on the corner stanchion has a fixing hole pierced through it which is not matched by a corresponding hole in the stanchion;
3.   The middle stanchion has holes for attaching three moulded bars but there are only two bars, on the exterior faces;
4.   There is a jagged join in the crenellated bar, unlike the normal butt joints. It disrupts the spacing of masks and fleur de lys;
5.   There is a break and weld in the crenellated bar at the turning point of the corner stanchion;
6.   Along the top edging bar there are pierced holes for the insertion of vertical bars. The latter could never be fitted because the edging bar passes over the broad base of the pier. This contrasts with the neat fit of the north-east stanchion on the Courtenay railings. Here the standard is in a similar position and its moulded base is specially elevated to fit over the base of the pier;
7.   The crenellation only runs a short way round the west end of the tomb and then stops, leaving the rest of the closure plain.

It is hard to interpret the original disposition of the railings from these observations. They were probably intended to close a free-standing tomb or tombs on four sides, like Archbishop Courtenay's, and were subsequently cut up and extended across the whole bay length. The relative position of the stanchions may have changed during the move: the crenellated bar is bent in a very casual fashion across them, in contrast with the crisp fold on the other tombs (Plates IX-XI). Henry IV's tomb has seven stanchions but a regular tomb like Courtenay's only needs six, hence the possibility of reused railings from two tombs.

If these railings were made before the construction of Henry IV's tomb, then it seems likely that the whole series was commissioned in connection with the construction of Chichele's tomb in 1425. Chichele ordered the smartest for himself and perhaps decided to install the rest after the episode with the felon. Chichele's rails cross the whole bay, protecting both his tomb and the choir; Henry IV's prevent access to Becket's shrine, but Courtenay's and the Black Prince's railings only protect their own tombs.

Henry IV's railings could have come from two possible locations: either they could have surrounded his hearse from c. 1425 until the tomb was built, or they could have come from the

PLATE V

Tomb of the Black Prince, Canterbury Cathedral.

PLATE VI

Tomb of Archbishop Courtenay, Canterbury Cathedral.

PLATE VII

Tomb of Henry IV and Joan of Navarre.

PLATE VIII

Tomb of Archbishop Chichele.

PLATE IX

Detail of tomb of Archbishop Courtenay.

PLATE X

Detail of tomb of Archbishop Chichele.

PLATE XI

Detail of tomb of Henry IV.

first tomb of his son, the Duke of Clarence, who died in 1421. In 1417 Clarence requested in his will to be buried 'at the feet of my father' (Nichols 1826, 194), presumably one bay to the east of Henry IV, where Archbishop Wooton now lies. Then, in 1439, Clarence was dug up and reburied with his wife Margaret Holland, together with her first husband John Beaufort, in the chapel of St. Michael, off the south transept. (Stone 1902, 26; Sheppard 1889, iii, 170) The railings could have been moved from Clarence's and/or Beaufort's tombs in 1439 and installed with difficulty around Henry IV's, ready for the dedication of Henry's chantry chapel in the same year.

ACKNOWLEDGEMENT

This article could not have been written without the generous help of Dr Francis Woodman.

THE BURIAL OF JOHN DYGON, ABBOT OF ST. AUGUSTINE'S*

JAMES COPLAND THORN

In 1971, St. Augustine's College generously presented the archaeological finds and abbey ruins to the nation. The finds as a collection also contained artifacts found buried with abbots. It is those from John Dygon's burial which Stuart Rigold was intending to publish. He only got as far as having the artifacts conserved and a textile report made on the vestments before he died.

What is known of Abbot Dygon begins with a reference to Brother John Dygon in the Treasurer's Accounts for 1468-69 (Cotton 1939, 69). He became abbot in 1496 with the death of Abbot John Dunster (Potts 1920, 147). He was a guest of Archbishop William Warham in 1503. It is probable that both men attended the state funeral of Henry VII on 9th May, 1509. This was held in the Lady Chapel at Westminster Abbey, attended by archbishops, bishops and abbots of the realm (Stanley 1882, 523). A year later on 10th May, 1510, John Dygon died, and his funeral was probably within a week, as a *congé d'élire* was issued to the prior and convent on 18th May (Potts 1920, 147). No tomb for John Dygon is recorded, but he certainly must have had one, which disappeared at the Dissolution (Weever 1631, 259).

In 1901, the ruined Lady Chapel crypt at St. Augustine's Abbey was cleared of debris and his grave was discovered. A published account states that the grave was almost in the middle of the crypt, and 'his head was enclosed in a large leaden painted mitre, and among the contents of the grave were a leaden chalice and paten, two finger rings and a coffin plate' (Routledge 1902, 242). Only a heavily touched-up photograph of the mitre was published (Evans 1904, 8). A complete transcript of the coffin plate (Potts 1920, 146-7) with the position of the grave (Potts 1934, map) was subsequently published.

Although eighty years have now passed since the discovery of Abbot Dygon's grave, most of the artifacts, with the exception of a missing ring, are still extant, including some hitherto unrecorded items. These were a series of vestments in two boxes which belonged to Dygon, and those of Abbot Roger II (1253-1273). The first box (SAM 297, AML 743710) possesses a label from the former College Museum which states that they are 'Pieces of Abbot Dygon's Vestments', but the brocaded braid fragments in this box definitely belonged to Abbot Roger II as these have been published (Potts 1920, 140). In the second box (SAM 296, AML 743711) another label reads 'Fragments of the gold lace edging to the Chasuble in which Abbot Roger was buried.' This obviously refers to the braids in the first box, and what was in the second were only fragments of Roger's chasuble.

At the bottom of the first box was a detritus of mostly decomposed fibres, lime mortar, splinters of iron, fragments of oak (*Quercus* sp.), and beetle remains (cf. Girling, pp. 88-90, below). It was from this detritus that the most tangible evidence of association of vestments

PLATE XII

Dygon's textiles (a) chasuble fragment with site of *R. parallelocollis* beetle (arrowed).
(b) orphrey fragment obverse and reverse with positions of other textile remains (numbered).

was found. Pieces of the chasuble with lining and a piece of silk damask were adhering to the back of the orphrey (Plate XII). Pieces of chasuble containing beetle remains were also adhering to some of the oak fragments.

The burial artifacts in John Dygon's grave are mostly of lead, fashioned into a mitre with infulae, paten and chalice and a coffin plate. It is only the surviving ring which is made of gilded copper. All the objects appear to be funerary material made for burial. Even Dygon's predecessor John Dunster (*d*. 1496) was buried with lead artifacts of a paten and chalice with a small funerary plate (AML 78203069, 72-74). The chalices from both these graves are of interest, as they show the same construction, with John Dunster's differing in design by having a concave-sided hexagonal base. Most of the known abbots' graves found at St. Augustine's Abbey possess only a small number of lead funerary artifacts, but John Dygon is the only one to have them painted and a coffin plate as well. Some of them had been badly distorted, and the infulae deliberately folded in antiquity. These were probably straightened out shortly after their discovery in 1901, causing damage in the form of stretch marks and cracks evident on the mitre and paten, and the infulae have snapped in several places. Unfortunately, one of the large pieces of infula is now lost, but it was apparently undecorated and badly corroded.

A possible indication of how the lead artifacts were lying when found is afforded by the nature of the corrosion products. Generally, deep pitting has occurred on one side at points of contact with a damp surface, possibly from the oak coffin.

On the back of the mitre near the upturned lip is an area of heavy corrosion, whereas the rest of the painted surface is unharmed. This would imply that the mitre was lying horizontally with the apex propped up in some way. The infulae when in their folded state are corroded on the flat surfaces which has not destroyed the painted decoration (Fig. 12 : 3), but on the missing fragment of one infula (Fig. 12 : 4) the decoration most probably had been obliterated. This is feasible as it had been folded inside out. The character of the corrosion on these infulae suggests that they were lying separately at the bottom of the coffin. The mode in which the infulae were attached is uncertain to some extent, as no rivets were used. It would most probably have been a piece of cord which had passed through the holes in each infula to those possibly in the mitre. Unfortunately, the corresponding holes in the mitre were just large gaps, surrounded by deep corrosion.

John Dygon's mitre with infulae is copied from a pretiosa mitre, which is used on important religious occasions. The altar piece painted by Jaime Huguet (1463-1485) of the consecration of St. Augustine depicts some good examples (Smart 1972, Pl. 68). The painting of Archbishop Warham in 1527 by Holbein, now in Lambeth Palace, shows a mitre very similar to Dygon's. A silverpoint drawing by John Rous (*c*. 1485) shows the length of the infulae (Fig. 12 : 2a), and where they were attached (Rous *c*. 1485). Those of Dygon in comparison are very short, being about 20 cm. long with painted representation of embroidery, and the lead cut as a pinked fringe.

The funerary paten is badly distorted and shows corrosion along one side of the flanged edge. In 1927, the IHS monogram could be clearly seen on the front, as P. Merrett's water-colour shows (Fig. 12 : 5a). The chalice (Fig. 12 : 5) is also badly distorted and shows deep corrosion along one side of its height. This suggests that the paten and chalice had fallen from the usual place on the torso sideways coming into contact with the oak coffin. The two Dygon rings are not described in full, as in another account 'a gold one' is mentioned (Potts 1920, 146), which could refer to the surviving oval ring, as this is gilded (Fig. 12 : 6). This ring is

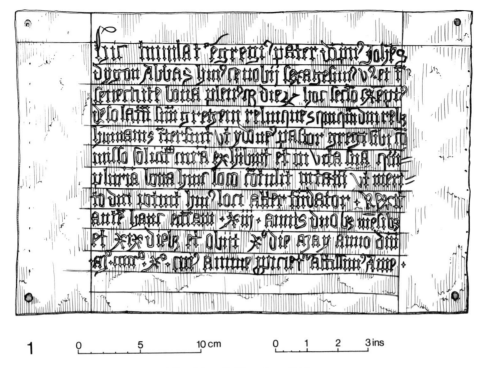

1

Fig. 11. Coffin plate (⅓).

remarkably similar to two other rings which were found on the south side of the abbey (Sherlock and Woods 1982). They differ only in the shape of the stone and its high collet mount in both cases. One is square, the other round, and Dygon's is oval. This may indicate that they are from the same workshop (cf. Bayley, p. 80, below). In each ring the large central stone of rock crystal or colourless glass is made in two parts. This suggests that they may have been soudé stones, i.e. the two layers may have been cemented together by a layer of coloured gelatine to give the impression of a jewel. A comparable gold ring with sapphires, rubies and emeralds was found with Archbishop Walter de Grey (*d.* 1255) in York Minster (Ramm 1971, 126, Pl. LIV).

The lead coffin plate (Fig. 11 : 1) is in a remarkable state of preservation compared with the other funerary artifacts. It is still flexible and uncorroded, which indicates that it was in a different environment. The evidence of this plate-and-oak coffin shows a different method of burial at St. Augustine's, as other abbots are found in stone tombs. None is recorded for Dygon, but it would seem that the burial was protected by some covering above the coffin. Judging from the state of the funerary artifacts, it is assumed to have partly collapsed on to the coffin. A result of this is the shape of the depressed lead mitre (Fig. 12 : 2) which would accommodate no human skull. If this was the case a depression would appear in the crypt floor which, if noticed, would lead to the discovery of the burial.

THE CATALOGUE Part I: Mineral (Figs. 11-12)

1. Funerary Plate (AML 78203075). In perfect condition. Lead sheet 244 mm. high by 373 mm. wide and 3 mm. thick. The upper surface is smooth, whereas the back has a rough granular appearance, and the edges show knife-trimming. In each corner is a small iron nail,

dome-shaped, 6 mm. wide and more than 7 mm. long, one of which is now missing.

On the upper surface are engraved eleven lines of Latin text with abbreviation marks between incised scribe lines. These were set out by two vertical rows of prick marks evenly spaced at either end of the lead sheet. Within these vertical rows were two vertical scribe lines 258 mm. apart, which confined the width of the text. These lines were then cut by thirteen horizontal scribe lines, which were in line with the prick marks. Each line was approximately 17 mm. from the next. The engraved letters show a V-shaped deep cut on the surface with the body of the text being 10 mm. high, but increasing to 15 mm. for ascenders and descenders. A full transcript and translation is published elsewhere (Potts 1920, 146-7) which states that 'John Dygon, the sixty-fifth abbot of this convent' . . . 'ruled this church thirteen years, two months and nineteen days, and died on the tenth day of May in the year of our Lord 1510'.

2.   Pretiosa Mitre (AML 749380). Badly distorted, corroded around the base of the rim especially at the back. The mitre is made of sheet lead 2 mm. thick, cut out, knife trimmed and then folded round into a cylindrical shape with the ends meeting on the sinister side as a soldered butt joint (cf. Bayley, p. 80, below). The sheet was also slightly moulded over the front and back in a convex fashion with an open cleft.

The texture of the lead is smooth over the exterior on which there is painted decoration, whereas the internal surface has a rough granular appearance. Lightly inscribed guidelines exist over the exterior near to the edges, mostly at the back, which were used to outline borders and vertical bands of decoration. Also on the back near the apex is a circle lightly inscribed, 24 mm. in diameter. On the interior the lower portion of the front shows four horizontal scribe lines, the uppermost one being level with the bottom of the cleft. These would have continued on to the back, but are now obliterated by corrosion. Along the cleft borders of the interior is a series of smaller inscribed circles 10-13 mm. in diameter. These were pushed out into spherical hollows by repoussé work. There were eighteen hollows for each border, except on the front of the mitre on the sinister side where there are only sixteen. Over the exterior this repoussé work is separated by a series of 15 mm. long chisel-like cuts. At the apex there are three raised bosses on each side. The whole of the exterior shows a painted representation of a pretiosa mitre, which from the prototype is generally decorated with precious stones and gold. This is shown in great detail on the front of the lead mitre, whereas the back is simplified. The range of colours is small, consisting of black, grey, white and yellow (cf. Knight, p. 81, below). The unpainted areas are a dull purple-red coating which is visible on the borders, bands and large roundels. On the front of the mitre these bands average 30 mm. wide with the vertical band decorated. Three yellow vesica-shaped 'jewels' 31-33 mm. high and 16 mm. wide are symmetrically placed here. The central vesica is surrounded by four white spots. In the horizontal band there are four identical vesica-shaped jewels, badly worn.

The two large roundels differ in diameter, the sinister example being 58 mm. and the dexter 52 mm. Inside is a central lozenge surrounded by four white spots. The areas between the borders and bands are painted with light grey. These zones are approximately 260 mm. high, 130 mm. wide and 40 mm. high at truncation. Over this paint are powdered in each zone about two hundred and fifty spots. These are slightly oval in shape and 6 mm. high in white, and appear to follow the edges of the zones. They also cover the grey interior in a random fashion with an even density and apparently uniform size. These zones of grey with white spots are the only decoration on the back of the mitre.

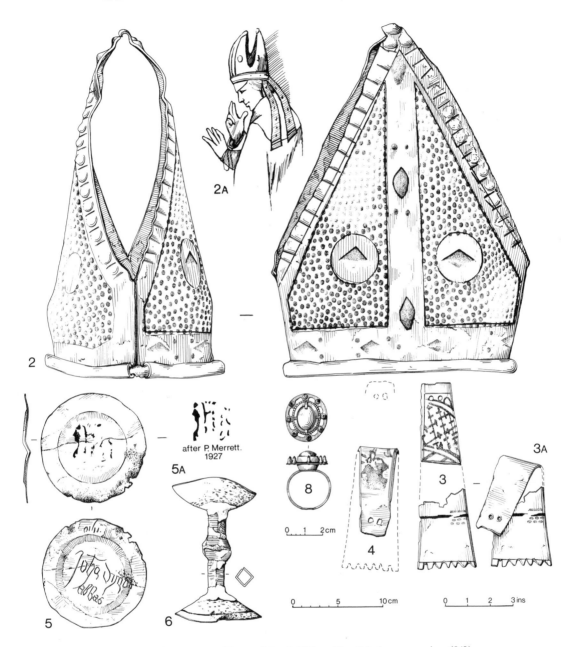

Fig. 12. 2-7 Funerary artifacts of lead (⅓), with gilded copper ring (2/3).

The final colour used was black, which was mainly for outlining the grey zones and some of the vesica shapes. 373 mm. high, 252 mm. wide, 188 mm. deep, 745 mm. approx. for inner circumference.

3. Infula (AML 782310.12) Folded over in antiquity, now broken, the central portion missing. The sheet lead is 2 mm. thick, cut out and knife-trimmed. A smooth upper surface with dull purple-red coating which also covers the chamfered edges. Underneath this coating is

a series of inscribed guidelines, and on the upper piece are two punched holes 4 mm. in diameter, 10 mm. apart. The lower, detached piece has a knife-cut pinked fringe. It would appear that these two pieces are related in shape, trimming and folding. Decoration also occurs on both pieces using the same white paint. A fret decoration is painted with a border of bands and spots, a black band also being used.

4.   Infula (AML 782311) Similar to above, but folded under, lower portion now missing. Badly corroded with amorphous white painted decoration on upper surface.

5.   Funerary Paten (AML 78203076). Badly buckled lead with a diameter of 118 mm. and a thickness of 1 mm. On the obverse the surface shows an inner scribe line of 78 mm. diameter. Matt purple-red over upper surface. Over this are the worn remains of a black painted line over the scribe line and in the centre is a worn IHS monogram. On the reverse of the paten 'JOHN DYGON ABBAS' is incised in the middle and the date '1510' by the flanged rim.

6.   Funerary Chalice (AML 78203078) It is made of 2 mm. thick lead and when complete was 150 mm. high. Much corroded along one side of the bowl and base. The soldered joints have broken away, leaving the stem completely detached. The surfaces of all three components are smooth. The hemispherical bowl is 95 mm. in diameter and shows a compass point in the middle on the inside. The stem is 90 mm. high with a hollow 16 mm. square section. A vertical seam joint occurs down one corner. On this stem is a biconical knop of solid lead which has been soldered on. The base is conical, 93 mm. in diameter at the bottom. The same purple-red colour-coating covers the exterior and a black line is roughly painted on the outside chalice base. The solder lines and joints on the exterior appear grey.

7.   Funerary Ring. Present whereabouts unknown, but lost before 1971.

8.   Funerary Ring (AML 78203077) Gilded copper. The high oval collet contains a centrally mounted jewel. This is a polished dome-shaped rock crystal in two parts, underneath which is a silver gilt foil backing. The jewel was held in place by means of four claws, which were brazed on to the collet; only one now survives. The surrounding mount has a wheel-shaped rim, with intersections on which are eight horns. These are cone-shaped and were riveted to the rim, and topped by green glass cabochons. Only four of these 'stones' now survive complete, with fragments of one other. The hoop is 22 mm. in diameter, and is riveted to the back of the mount. On the opposite side to the mount the hoop is flattened and has a small hole in the middle.

MINERAL ANALYSIS   Justine Bayley

The funerary artifacts (nos. 2-6 and 8) were all analysed by X-ray fluorescence and were shown to be of lead, with tin-lead solder used in the construction of the chalice (no. 6). The solder on the mitre (no. 2) was not examined. The white pigment on the infulae (nos. 3-4) gave stronger signals for calcium than the black pigment, and so may be calcite (calcium carbonate). The Dygon ring (no. 8) was of copper with a small percentage of tin and zinc and rather less lead, which was then mercury gilded. The cabochon green stones on the horns were of glass. The other two rings from St. Augustine's were of similar composition and in these cases it was possible to study the foils used behind the jewel. In the round ring (AML 743661) the foil was of silver containing some copper with a gilded front surface, no mercury detected. The foil in the square ring (AML 765753) was probably the same as it had a gilded front and silver was also detected. Underneath these foils in both collets was a filler of folded-up cloth.

PIGMENT ANALYSIS Dr. Barry Knight

The pigments on the pretiosa mitre were as follows:-

(a) *Black* It was not possible to analyse this colour as a large enough sample did not exist.

(b) *Grey background* Lead carbonate and calcium carbonate, trace of quartz. No other colourant detected. The grey colour probably results from adding carbon black to white paint. The lead carbonate is probably a natural corrosion product, not added in the making of the paint.

(c) *White spots* Calcium carbonate and lead carbonate. The lead carbonate is again probably due to the corrosion of the mitre.

(d) *Yellow jewel (vesica)* Lead carbonate, trace calcium carbonate and quartz. No other colourant detected. The analysis is inconclusive as the pigment might be yellow ochre, which is amorphous and therefore gives no diffraction pattern.

(e) *Purple-red coating* Litharge (PbO) (not red lead). This is a natural corrosion product of lead, not an artificial surface coating. This applies to the purple-red coating noticed on all the funerary artifacts except the coffin plate.

THE TEXTILES Elisabeth Crowfoot

The dark blue worsted twill (no. 9) was a fine quality weave, popular for good class clothing from the fourteenth century onwards, numerous fragments, some finer, but all of similar style, being found in levels of *c.* 1360 and 1499 at Baynard's Castle, London (Crowfoot AML 2126). Some similar twills, red, green and blue, used for fifteenth-sixteenth century vestments in Norway and Sweden, may possibly be imports from England (Geijer 1953/Hoffmann 1964:249, n. 66.) Linen tabby (no. 10), at whatever period, is a universal material for undergarments and linings.

The tablet-weave of the orphrey braid shows an interesting combination of brocading techniques, the silver-gilt borders the earlier method, surface brocading displaying all the metal thread used, the main pattern a wasteful technique found in the thirteenth-fifteenth centuries (V & A Museum), with silver and silk threads changing places on front and back, so that half the metal is unseen. It is a complete piece, woven with four borders. Though small, it could perhaps have been used in the horizontal position below the neck opening of the fifteenth century 'Roman' style chasuble. Such pieces are extremely durable, and were often re-used when the original vestment they decorated wore out.

The tiny silk fragments may also have been re-used. The dye kermes in no. 13 indicates an expensive fabric; the unspun silk of no. 12 suggests a non-European, perhaps Chinese origin. A collection of eighteen small shaped pieces from two silk damasks, which fit together to make a curved border, survive from the tomb of Walter Lyhert, Bishop of Norwich (*d.* 1472). Abbot Dygon's chasuble perhaps had a border, similarly pieced of silk tabby and damask. Its woollen fabric and coarse embroidery, the brass thread a cheap substitute even for silver or silver-gilt, suggest that at this period the abbey was perhaps having to economise on vestments.

THE CATALOGUE Part II: Textiles

Fibre identifications by H.M. Appleyard, F.T.I., and dye identifications by Professor M.C. Whiting, Bristol University.

9. Chasuble? (AML 2793 5) Many small fragments, best *c.* 5.0 by 3.0 cm., most with traces of embroidery. Wool, fibres mostly fine, a few medium, some fragmental medullae, worsted,

dyed dark blue, strong indigotin; threads Z spun both systems, weave regular 2/2 diagonal twill, count *c.* 20/16 threads per cm. Coarse couched embroidery, laid thread with brass metal strip, now green, round a coarse Z. S ply core, degraded vegetable fibre (?flax), couching thread similar to core. The pattern's curved double lines suggest a scroll motif.

10. Chasuble lining? (AML 2793 7) Fragments, largest 5.0 by 5.0 cm., one in folded fragment of No. 9, one adhering to No. 11. Fibre, very badly degraded vegetable, ?flax; spinning Z both systems, weave tabby (plain), count estimated 14/11 per cm.

11. Orphrey (AML 2793 6) (Fig. 12, Plate XII). Brocaded braid with fragments, adhering to the underside, twill and lining (nos. 9, 10) above, silk (no. 12) below; width 4.8, length *c.* 10.5 cm., three probably adjoining fragments, (a) centre 8.4 cm., (b, c) pieces from ends, (c) with cut warps folded underneath. Fibre, braid, silk, no dye detected; warps very slight Z spin, wefts S ply, regular 4-hole tablet weave in chevrons, 19-20 twists and *c.* 22 wefts per cm.; brocading threads, borders silver-gilt strip wound round slightly S-spun silk core, used in pairs, centre pattern silver strip round silk core, pairs, and silk, Z-spun, fours slightly S-plyed. The brocading wefts of the centre pattern go through to the back of the braid when not needed on the surface, the metal and silk threads changing position with one another during the weaving, in successive sheds. The borders, 6.5 mm. wide at the selvedge, and the patterns at either end of the braid, are surface brocaded, the silver-gilt threads turning back on the front after passing round a main-weave weft at the edge of the centre pattern. Design: centre, interlaced diamonds; edges and one end, solid metal surface with single spaced dots from the binding twists, the other end a dotted pattern, diagonals and diamonds.

12. Silk damask (AML 2793 9) Fragment 2.0 by 2.5 cm. adhering to orphrey, and tiny scrap. Silk, reddish-brown, no dye detected; all yarns reeled, double weave, warps one fine, one pairs, wefts one fine, one thick, pattern reversible twill and tabby, count *c.* 16 (8 fine, 8 pairs)/22 (11 thin, 11 thick) per 5 mm.

13. Silk (AML 2793 8) Fragments, best 1.2 by 2.0 cm. Silk, red, dyed kermes (430 ppm); warp very fine, Z-spun, weft reeled, weave tabby, count 40/26-28 per cm. Some scraps deteriorated open weave, but all probably the same fabric.

BEETLE REMAINS Dr. Maureen A. Girling

Beetle remains associated with Abbot Dygon's chasuble (no. 9) have been identified as *Rhizophagus parallelocollis* Gyll., the 'graveyard beetle'. The sub-fossil beetles were noted apparently embedded in brass couched embroidery on the vestment. Channels in the embroidery had the appearance of mould growth along their walls, a factor of probable significance in the beetle life-history. The beetles in the fabric were generally intact but further disarticulated remains, including elytra with an aedeagus and numbers of isolated sternites, proved to be from the same species.

Rhizophagus parallelocollis has occurred in numbers of Pleistocene and archaeological beetle assemblages, often where there is evidence of forest with decaying trees, and in its natural state, the species is probably a predator or a mould feeder in dead, rotten wood. As well as this dead wood habitat, modern collecting records include vegetable refuse, fungi and, significantly, corpses and carrion. There is some dispute among entomologists as to the beetles' food source in these habitats. Blair suggests that the species predates fly maggots feeding on the decaying corpse (Blair 1922, 58, 80-83) whereas Palm favours the corpse itself as the food source (Palm 1959, suppl. 16). Horion believes that the beetle feeds directly on mould but he

b

11a

Fig. 13.   11 Obverse of Orphrey (a) decorated piece with probable adjoining fragment (b) pattern of main area.

quotes other authors who cite the actual decaying coffin wood as providing nourishment for the beetle (Horion 1960). The ecology of *Rhizophagus* has recently been summarised (Peacock 1977b). Whatever the life-cycle of the species, its association with burials, which has earned it the common name 'graveyard' or 'churchyard beetle', provides one illustration of how man's activities have advantaged a particular insect species. In this case the concentration of corpses, mould and mouldy wood and their abundant fly maggot fauna, has provided a widespread expansion of the species' natural dead tree habitat. Until recent historical times, it is probable that graveyards eclipsed the natural habitats for *R. parallelocollis* and although its numbers have now declined with more stringent burial practices, compost provides another man-associated habitat favoured by this species (Johnson 1963, 3-9).

There are two previous records of *R. parallelocollis* from medieval burials, those of Ann Mowbray, *d.* 1482 (Stafford 1971, 6-10), and the fourteenth-century burial of Archbishop Greenfield (Buckland 1979). Both were sealed in lead coffins. Much important data has been provided by the latter example. Investigation of the burial indicated that the manner of interment afforded little chance of insects entering afterwards. Despite this, several hundred specimens of *R. parallelocollis* together with other beetle remains were recorded, which leads to the conclusion that the beetle infestation had arisen from eggs laid while the body was exposed. The absence of a wooden coffin and the lack of adult fly remains have enabled the suggestion to be made that fly maggots provided the beetle food source in the closed system of the coffin.

The examples of *R. parallelocollis* associated with Abbot Dygon may provide some evidence about his funeral. If, as in the case of Archbishop Greenfield, the infestation of the beetle arose from eggs laid directly on the body, this implies a period between death and interment sufficiently long to allow some decay of the body tissues and attack by flies. This might have been provided by a lying-in-state procedure of a few days, depending upon the seasonal temperature. It is almost certain that the medieval churchyard supported large populations of the species which could have entered the adjoining church. Although this conjecture is a likely explanation for the occurrence of the beetles associated with Abbot Dygon, it must be noted that *R. parallelocollis* is also known to enter buried coffins, so this mode of infestation cannot be ruled out.

ACKNOWLEDGMENTS

The author wishes to thank all who helped in the preparation of this report within the Inspectorate of Ancient Monuments, especially David Sherlock and Humphrey Woods, for allowing access to their excavation reports prior to publication; Glyn Coppack and Tony Musty, for identifying and locating the artifacts; John Musty and his staff in the Ancient Monuments Laboratory, who identified and cleaned the artifacts, namely Justine Bayley, Dr. Maureen Girling, Marjorie E. Hutchinson, Eliza Lawler, Gerald Tanner, Dr. Barry Knight and Jacqueline Watson. Thanks are due to Elisabeth Crowfoot, for her work on the textiles and their illustrations, with identifications by H.M. Appleyard, F.T.I., and Professor M.C. Whiting, Bristol University, and to my wife Dorothy for typing the report.

ACTON BURNELL CASTLE, SHROPSHIRE*

JEFFREY WEST

Acton Burnell Castle lies nine miles south-east of Shrewsbury in the landscaped grounds of
Acton Burnell Hall, its low crenellated profile overshadowed by the Wenlock hills. It has been
in the care of the Office of Works and its various successors since 1930, and was one of the
monuments for which Stuart Rigold was responsible as Principal Inspector of Ancient
Monuments for England from 1976 to 1979. It consists of a rectangular building 76 ft. (22.5 m.)
long and 55 ft. (16.5 m.) wide; its three eastern bays are of two storeys, its western bay of
three. There are square angle towers at the corners, and there is a garderobe block attached to
the west. It is shown, already ruined but with its external walls standing to full height, in an
engraving published by S. and N. Buck in 1731. By 1786, it had been partly dismantled to
accommodate and conceal a number of farm buildings (shown in a water colour of that date by
the Rev. E. Williams in Shrewsbury Local History Library); its south wall had been taken
down to a height of 16 ft. (4.8 m.) to form the wall of a barn, the south-west tower and
garderobe block re-roofed and openings wide enough to admit carts made in the north and
south walls. It is a common enough conceit of eighteenth-century landscaping to construct
utilitarian buildings behind a picturesque facade, but less usual to find them hidden inside an
authentic medieval shell. The castle was in this state when it was recorded by Jewitt c. 1840
(Plate XIII). The farm buildings were removed between 1892 (B. 1892, 105) and 1900 (M.P.L.
Watts 31.8) and the north-west tower collapsed during a heavy storm in 1914 (P.R.O. Works/
14/568).

Accounts of the castle have been published by C. H. Hartshorne (Hartshorne 1846),
T. H. Turner (Turner 1851), Dr Margaret Wood (Wood 1950 and 1965) and Dr C. A. Ralegh
Radford (Radford 1957 and 1961). It is generally accepted that it dates from the late
thirteenth century and was the work of Robert Burnell, Edward I's friend and chancellor,
bishop of Bath and Wells and the king's unsuccessful candidate for Canterbury. In this paper I
do not intend to discuss the chancellor's career, nor the architectural detail of the castle which,
with its connections with Burnell's work at Wells and the royal works in Wales, must form part
of a much larger study. What I want to consider is the form of the structure, its use and the
purpose which perhaps lay behind it; this means looking first at three particular points which
concern the roof, the hall and the north-east corner tower. I am grateful to many friends and
colleagues for their help and advice, and in particular to John Blair and Peter Curnow.

The Roof

The upper parts of the south-west tower and the garderobe block were altered when they
were re-roofed in the eighteenth century, but the other corner towers retain their crenellations

PLATE XIII

The interior of Acton Burnell Castle looking north-west *c.* 1840; engraving by O. Jewitt reproduced by Hartshorne (1846, 332) and Turner (1851, between 170 and 171).

and appear to be in their original form. Creasing for a low-pitched roof survives on the eastern face of the north-west tower and the western face of both eastern towers; it does not appear in the rebuilt work of the south-west tower and the garderobe block and is lost where the wall of the castle no longer exists between the eastern towers; see Plates XIII and XVI. Dr Radford noted that it cuts the jambs of the doors leading on to the wall walks, and suggested that it was therefore a later alteration (Radford 1961, 101). The crease is, however, incorporated in the moulded ashlar of the jambs, and its line is reflected in the courses of stonework above it. The apparent discrepancy in height between the roof line and the doors would not in any case present structural difficulties, for the wall walks would have formed leaded gutters below the general level of the roof. The three surviving lengths of crease each amount to less than a quarter of the width of the building, and the evidence is therefore wholly compatible with the existence of two parallel roofs with a central valley and does not necessarily imply a single roof covering the entire width of the building; the existence of a crease on the face of the north-west tower indicates that the roofs ran through from east to west and did not reflect the different internal arrangements in the western bay of the building; corbels projecting from the north wall indicate the position of the principal beams.

The Hall

The windows in the three eastern bays of the north wall clearly lit a room of some importance (Plate XIV), and this has always been interpreted as the hall. Hartshorne's account was written when the southern half of the Castle was obscured by farm buildings, and he suggested, not unreasonably, that the hall was confined to the northern half of the building (Hartshorne 1846, 332). This was repeated by Turner (Turner 1851, 170) and by Dr Wood in her earlier paper (Wood 1950, 63). The internal elevation of the east wall of the castle is shown in Plate XVI; the crude horizontal chase at approximately first-floor level on the southern side of the building should be disregarded; this appears to be secondary and probably relates to the eighteenth-century alterations. The first floor shows (from north to south) a doorway leading from the north-east tower (the rebate shows that the door opened into the castle); the remains of a tall mullioned, transomed and traceried window; a square hatch; a doorway with a monolithic lintel and the scar of an east — west wall above it; another hatch; the remains of another traceried window; and a doorway leading into the south-east tower. From inside the castle, it can be seen that the jambs and lintels of the hatches and the central door are built of finely cut and jointed ashlar, and show no signs of alteration or insertion, although they are partly blocked by facework on the other side of the wall. The reason for this is apparent from the outside (Plate XV), where it is clear that there has been extensive rebuilding: the relieving arches above the hatches are no longer properly centred, the service block which must once have been attached has left no obvious wall-scars, and the canopied feature (perhaps a piscina) that partly blocks the southern hatch shows every sign of being inserted.

The simplest interpretation is that the hatches and door were at some time blocked (perhaps in the fourteenth century, if the piscina is in its original position), and that the outer face of the wall was then rebuilt without reference to their position. When an attempt was made to unblock them (presumably when the farm buildings were removed) they no longer went through the thickness of the wall, and the outer face had to be roughly unpicked — producing the confusing and untidy effect which can be seen today. If the door is an original feature, the scar above it presumably indicates not a dividing wall but a central arcade, with an arch

PLATE XIV

Acton Burnell Castle from the north-east, 1901. M.P.L. Watts 31.11.

(Manchester Public Library).

PLATE XV

(Crown Copyright)

Acton Burnell Castle from the east, before consolidation (*c.* 1930). P.R.O. Works/14/568.

PLATE XVI

(Crown Copyright)

The interior of Acton Burnell Castle before consolidation, looking east (*c.* 1930). P.R.O. Works/14/568.

springing from the monolithic lintel on the door. As Dr Radford has pointed out (Radford 1961, 100), this means that the hall — a remarkable room exactly 48 ft. (14.6 m.) square — occupies the whole of the three eastern bays of the castle.

The north-east Tower

The north-east tower is shown by the Bucks and by Hartshorne as a square crenellated tower similar in appearance to the other three corner towers; a plan published by both Hartshorne (1846, 338) and Turner (1851, Pl. between 170 and 171) shows its first floor lit on two sides by mullioned windows. The north-east angle of the tower fell in 1914, but the western reveal of the northern window survives, and confirms that it was similar to those in the hall; it is therefore unique among the tower windows, all the rest of which have plain chamfered mouldings, just as the room which it lit is unique in the towers by rising to the full height of the hall. The eastern side of the tower was covered by ivy throughout the nineteenth-century (Plate XIV and Turner 1851, 171), which may explain a curiosity in Hartshorne's plan, for it is now clear that the opening in the eastern side of the tower was not a window but a large double-chamfered open arch. Dr Radford suggested that this indicated that the tower originally extended further east, that the arch was probably the chancel arch of the castle chapel and that it had been taken down, perhaps in the late eighteenth or nineteenth century, "to give the ruin a symmetrical appearance" (Radford 1961, 98). This is not supported by the Bucks' engraving, nor by any structural evidence; it would in any case have been more likely at that time for a symmetrical building to be partly dismantled for picturesque effect. A more straightforward explanation of the arch is that the tower formed the principal entrance to the hall, and that it was reached by an external stair. The door from the tower opens into the hall (and is the only surviving one to do so), and it is next to the service hatches, in the position familiar from countless later screens passages. It is not unusual for porches to be given this degree of architectural prominence, and external stairs are common enough, leading to first-floor halls and the principal floors of keeps; there are contemporary parallels at both Wells and Ludlow.

Dating

The date usually given to the castle is *c.* 1284, based partly on stylistic and partly on documentary evidence. Burnell probably began to put together his Shropshire estate before 1263 (Eyton 1858, 127). Edward I was at Acton Burnell from 29 September to 12 November, 1283 (CPR, 72-90, 100-6, 109), during which time the statute of Acton Burnell was passed, so by then the bishop's house was sufficiently complete for him to accommodate the king's household. Edward was briefly at Acton Burnell again in December, and in January 1284 the bishop was given a licence to crenellate "*Mansum suum de Acton Burnel*" (CPR, 110). In July, he was licensed to take timber from the royal forest "for the construction of his manor at Acton Burnell" (*ibid.*, 126), which at least confirms that the licence to crenellate was not retrospective and that Burnell was actually rebuilding or enlarging his house; he was still using timber in February 1286 (CPR, 228). Robert Burnell died in 1292; the death two years later of his heir, his nephew Philip, was followed by a long minority, and it is therefore reasonable to assume that any work begun in 1284 was complete within ten years.

Conclusions

The church, stylistically a few years earlier than the castle, lies immediately to the west of it, and the gable ends of the great aisled barn, very like the one at Bredon, survive 300 ft. (90 m.) to the east. Other buildings must once have existed, probably including a great hall — particularly if the present building was not being built until after the king's visit. Although the castle may have formed no more than the principal lodging, it contained within itself its own hall, chambers and offices, like a keep or later tower such as Warkworth; its very self-sufficiency may have ensured its survival. Like many medieval houses (and not only medieval ones), it can be analysed in terms of a formal progression into increasingly private chambers. The hall is on the first floor, approached up an external stair and through the north-east tower, which served as a suitably impressive porch. In the east wall of the hall were a door and two hatches giving access to the kitchens and other offices — the typical arrangement of an end-passage hall. The room in the south-east tower was presumably a serving room; it has no access except into the hall, and its off-centre windows may indicate the position of cupboards or other internal fittings. The hall itself was an extraordinary anachronism: exactly 48 ft. (14.6 m.) square and divided centrally by an arcade. It was lit on the north by three tall elaborately-moulded windows, by two similar windows on the east and (on the evidence of the Bucks' engraving) three more on the south. All the surviving windows are provided with window seats. There was of course at that date no structural screen (the position of the windows does not permit it), and the arcade precludes a central hearth. There is no evidence for a chimney in any of the surviving walls, but this does not mean that there were none on the south or west sides of the hall; the evidence of a flue rising in the south-west corner of the hall from a fireplace in the undercroft, as well as the consistent use of fireplaces in keeps and tower lodgings, makes this more than likely. A door, one jamb of which survives, led from the northern end of the west wall of the hall into the private chambers. I am reluctant to use the terms "great chamber" and "solar", for it is impossible to say into how many rooms the western bay of the castle was divided, or what their various functions were. Three garderobes were provided to serve the chambers on the first floor, two in the garderobe block and one in the north-west tower. A stair in the south-west tower led up to the inner chambers on the floor above, again served by a garderobe in the north-west tower; most of the structural evidence at this level has unfortunately been lost in the eighteenth-century rebuilding. The western towers, with their garderobes, probably directly overlooked the moat — there is a reference to a *"stagnum"* (P.R.O. C133/63(32)) — since the nearby church presumably lay outside it. Some indication of the functions of the ground-floor rooms is provided by the windows, which are mullioned and traceried on the south and either single or paired lancets on the north; a lower hall seems to have occupied the eastern three bays on the south side, entered and served, like the main hall above, from the east. Beyond, in the western bay, lay a chamber with a fireplace and two mullioned windows; the vaulted room in the south-west tower to which the chamber gives access looks like a strong room and suggests that these may have been the private quarters of the steward.

The castle closely resembles, in general form, a late twelfth-century keep. Its corner towers and exactly square arcaded hall are curiosities, parallels for which are to be found not at Aydon Castle and Little Wenham Hall, which are roughly contemporary, but (as Stuart Rigold pointed out in conversation) in keeps such as Rochester. This is not altogether surprising, given the importance of tradition and association in English medieval architecture. There is a possible local parallel for the persistence (or re-emergence) of the keep form in the late thirteenth century at Wattlesborough (West 1981). For his episcopal palace at Wells, Burnell built a conventional ground-floor hall; in Shropshire, the circumstances were different. He had built up his personal estate from meagre beginnings, not even holding Acton Burnell in chief from the king. In an area dominated socially and politically by the great castles of Shrewsbury, Ludlow, Clun and Caus, he may have seen the possession of a keep (suitably modified for the late thirteenth century) as the most appropriate symbol of authority he hoped his heirs would inherit.

TONBRIDGE AND SOME OTHER GATEHOUSES

DEREK RENN

I first met Stuart Rigold in 1959 when he challenged my over-confident identification of the Canterbury Castle building-stone (see now Renn 1981), so it seemed appropriate to offer his shade a study of another Kent fortification, but one built of very local materials.

On 17 January, 1782, Edward King read a paper to the Society of Antiquaries of London which included an account of Tonbridge castle and more particularly of its great gatehouse (King 1782, 270 ff.). Since his plans and those of subsequent writers (Wadmore 1886, Simpson 1940, Toy 1953) differ in detail, fresh drawings have been made for this study.

Tonbridge Castle consists of a large *motte* with an attached bailey on the north bank of the river Medway. There are foundations of an oval building on the *motte* linked to an ashlar-faced curtain wall (still largely standing) round the bailey. The gatehouse, astride the curtain facing the town, is an astonishing survival, being practically complete and unaltered apart from the loss of its timber floors and roofs. King (1782, 280) dated it to 'the time of King John or at least in the very beginning of the reign of Henry III', Wadmore (1886) to *c.* 1230 and Elliott to perhaps 1220-40, but otherwise opinions have concurred in a date of *c.* 1300, as a copy of such Edwardian gatehouses as those of Harlech and Beaumaris. But the closest similarity of all to Tonbridge is another Clare gatehouse at Caerphilly in Glamorgan, and I believe that both precede the works of Edward I in Wales and Scotland. The evidence for Caerphilly has recently been restated in detail (Johns 1978), and my case for Tonbridge rests not only upon architectural similarity but also upon historical probability and defensive development. Each argument will be enunciated in turn, concluding with some remarks upon the defensive capability of the gatehouse.

DESCRIPTION

The gatehouse (Figs. 15 and 16) is a rectangular four-storey block (including the basement) symmetrically planned with half-round stair-turrets at the angles toward the bailey and with half-round fronts flanking the entrance passage. Apart from the basement it is faced inside and out in Wealden sandstone ashlar said to have come from Quarry Hill only a few miles away, in close-jointed courses about 28 cm. high, with a little brick repair work to the inner faces. Externally, the stone has weathered in places to grey-green, but within the stairs and passages it is still golden brown, variegated with iron stains. Its condition is excellent, apart from a settlement crack in the fore-arch over the entrance. King (1792, 293) says that the ditch in front had been filled in during the previous eight years, and describes the two stone piers of the bridge and the foundation of a large round tower beside the outer end.

The basements (Fig. 15, below) were originally only accessible through openings in the floors

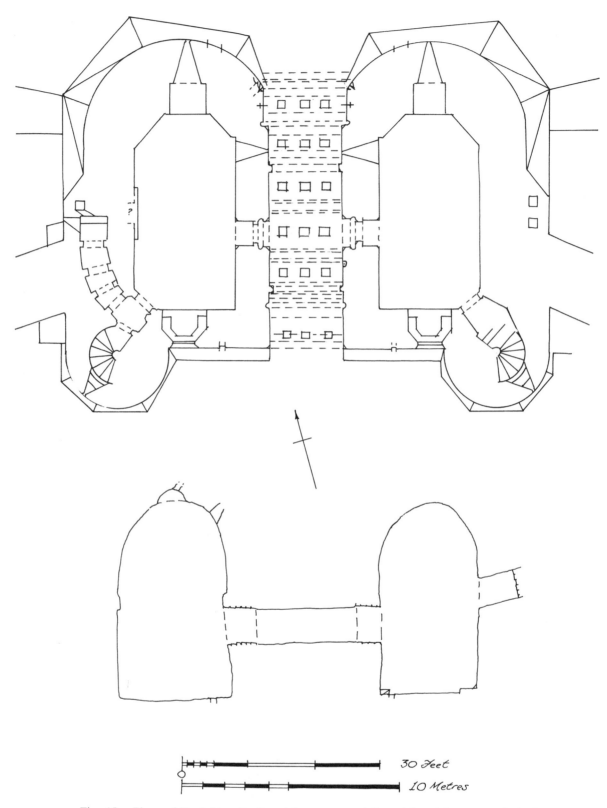

Fig. 15. Plans of Tonbridge Castle gatehouse: ground floor (above) basements (below).

30 Feet

10 Metres

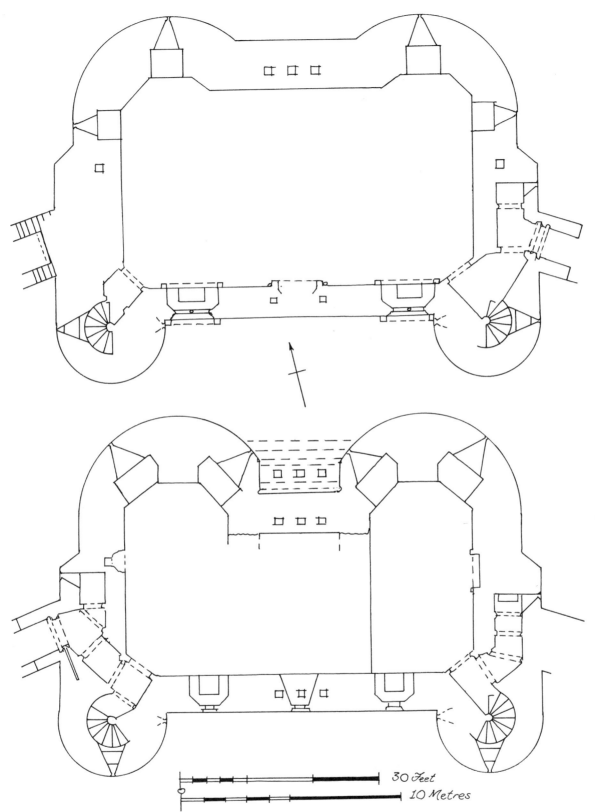

Fig. 16. Plans of Tonbridge Castle gatehouse; second floor (above) first floor (below).

above. The western basement has been re-roofed and the eastern one is reached by an open iron staircase down from the door in the entrance passage. They both have floors of earth or brick and tile; the eastern one has a modern manhole in the centre. Its only original feature is an ashlar-lined shaft about 22 cm. square sloping 3 m. up through the south wall to the top of the batter above ground. A rough plastered recess to the north-west is bricked off at the end — it may have led to the cellars of the house of 1792-93 built across the line of the curtain wall. In the opposite wall a rough tunnel with rubble walls and a segmental brick vault connects with the western basement. This has a similar airshaft (but only 12 cm. square). King (1792, 293) mentions an east — west partition wall, no longer apparent: the northern end has a recess with a drain running out under the foundations, and also a rough shaft about 25 cm. across rising to ground level.

At ground level the gatehouse is surrounded by a sloping plinth, carried round the curved faces in semi-octagonal form to show as cusped spurs (Fig. 15, upper). Outside the curtain wall there are fragments of an added long sloping *talus*. The entrance passage is vaulted with multiple chamfered ribs and defended at each end by a portcullis and doors, with intervening rows of square holes and two arrow-loops facing each other across the passage. In front of the arrow-loops and level with the sill of their embrasures are the pivot-holes for a lifting or turning bridge. The upper parts of the holes are broken away, but they seem to have been 8 cm. in diameter with a shallower outer 'ream' 20 cm. across. At the chamfered angle between the sides of the gate-passage and the curving fronts, at a slightly higher level, wedge-shaped vertical slots have been cut. These, and the damaged stones in a vertical line further round the curving fronts, indicate a timber work here connected with the bridge. Rooms on either side of the passage had a portcullis in front of the door; within, an arrow-loop faced the field and a narrow lancet window the bailey. The latter have side seats and are decorated with a continuous chamfer round jambs and head ending on scroll stops similar to those of the rear-arch of the doorways; another door in the angle gives onto the spiral stair. The stairs spiral in opposite directions, and generally the rooms are mirror images of each other, with two mezzanine arrow-loops. But only the western room has traces (in the east wall) of raking shores for an earlier roof, a cement-covered buttress where old plans show a fireplace, and a passage branching from the stair at its foot terminating in a latring lit by a small obliquely-set lancet. A recess, oval in plan and elevation, alongside the eastern door in the entrance passage looks like a piscina but was probably a lamp-holder.

A modern flat roof with raised lights covers the western room and entrance passage vault, but the stubs of walls indicate that the first floor was originally divided in three; each with a lancet window toward the bailey having one vertical and two or more horizontal iron glazing bars, with trefoiled heads and continuous chamfers within and without the opening. The central window has a vertical shaft through the sill to the entrance passage below, and the flanking windows have side seats. Each rounded front has two arrow-loops set obliquely whose jambs are set obliquely (so causing vaulting problems) in order to strengthen the front, which has casemates for arrow-slits immediately above and below. The west wall has a robbed fireplace, with a square chimney shaft sloping back through the wall; the opposite fireplace has swags of foliage as corbels for the lost hood. Both stairs open onto latrine passages like that already described, but the western one has another doorway (with an external portcullis) leading onto the wall-walk of the curtain rising up the side of the motte. The door has a long bar-hole; most of the other doors in the gatehouse, whatever their size, seem to have been

PLATE XVII

Sculptured head on Tonbridge gatehouse.

(Photo: K.W.E. Gravett)

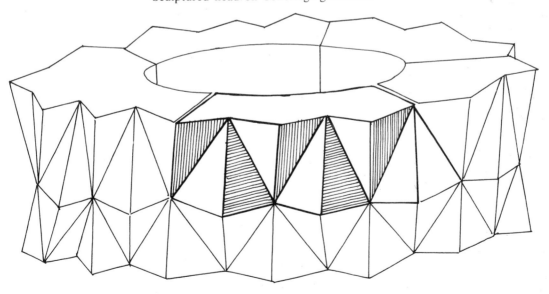

Fig. 17. Fragment of decorated chimney-shaft.

strengthened only by wedging cross-beams into relatively shallow recesses in the side walls. The wall-walk has both parapet and parados carried up against the gatehouse in a series of steep offsets, so as to deflect any enfilading fire from the ditch.

The stairs, with their high (28 cm.) risers, go up past another two mezzanine arrow-loops to the second floor; off the east stair there is a latrine passage and portcullissed doorway, giving onto a steeply-descending stair to the east curtain wall-walk. At this level the arrow-loops face forward and at right angles, with rectangular casemates like the ground floor. The pair of trefoiled windows in the opposite wall is larger and more elaborate than those of the floor below, with an external chamfer and roll-moulding and a rear arch with a filletted roll between cavetto mouldings, plus hood-moulds resting on sculptured heads. These were of remarkable quality, little inferior to those of Westminster or Salisbury (Carpenter 1972; Rigold 1954; Whittingham 1970, 1975) and need a paper to themselves. The interior pairs are male and female (eastern in wimple and hood, western with flowing hair) and the westernmost externally is of a middle-aged man (Plate XVII). Dating must be left to others, but stylistically they are later than the heads of c. 1240 at Brimpsfield (Butler 1959) and Ludlow castles.

The western staircase is continued up in timber to the present wall-head, with an open iron stair turning back into the turret carried higher. The turrets were free-standing, the hollow interior having small slots for a conical roof and a door at a high level giving onto the wall-head towards the field. Between the turrets traces of straight stairs descend toward plain straight-sided embrasures over traces of oillets and large square holes (for hourds?). Elsewhere the wall-head has traces of similar openings (crenels?). There seems little evidence for another storey postulated by Toy (1953, 243) apart from the high spring of the arch from the turrets, the 3 ft. ceiling mentioned by King (1782, 285) and a loose ashlar in the basement with two scroll-stopped chamfers (one hollow-moulded), which do not fit the extant windows.

ARCHITECTURAL PARALLELS

Other loose fragments include sections of weathered sandstone engaged columns carved with a lozenge pattern which might be associated with the Norman capitals found on the motte (Wadmore 1886, 17) and a freestone slab with a smoke-stained concave face opposing a convex one carved in half-pyramids. Five such slabs would fit together to enclose a cylindrical shaft about 20 cm. in diameter, and two such courses would form nail-head decoration (Fig. 17). Almost certainly this was part of a chimney-shaft, fitting typologically between those found at Skenfrith (c. 1225) and Conway (c. 1285) (Wood 1965, 282-4) or Criccieth (O'Neil 1945, 53; Johns 1970, 27) and Conisbrough (Johnson 1980, 88).

Fig. 18 shows the inner east gatehouse at Caerphilly, built 1268-71 (Johns 1971, 1978) and is based on plans made by Sidney Toy before the reconstruction of 1930-33 (see also Oman 1926, 179, and Toy 1939, 188); plans of Tonbridge are superimposed (fine dots). The general similarity is apparent, although Caerphilly's stair-turrets are ¾ rather than ½ round in plan, the flanking projections are not chamfered off and the two-bay chapel at second floor level destroys the symmetry. The Caerphilly gatehouse has a *sloping* shaft from the central window-sill opening as a horizontal slot over the inner end of the entrance passage, also to be seen in the inner north-west tower at Caerphilly and in the gatehouses of Llanstephan (King 1963) and Leybourne, where the idea may have originated (see below).

Cusped spurs to round-fronted towers strengthened their foundation on slopes and beside ditches; most examples occur in south Wales or the Southern March (King and Perks 1956,

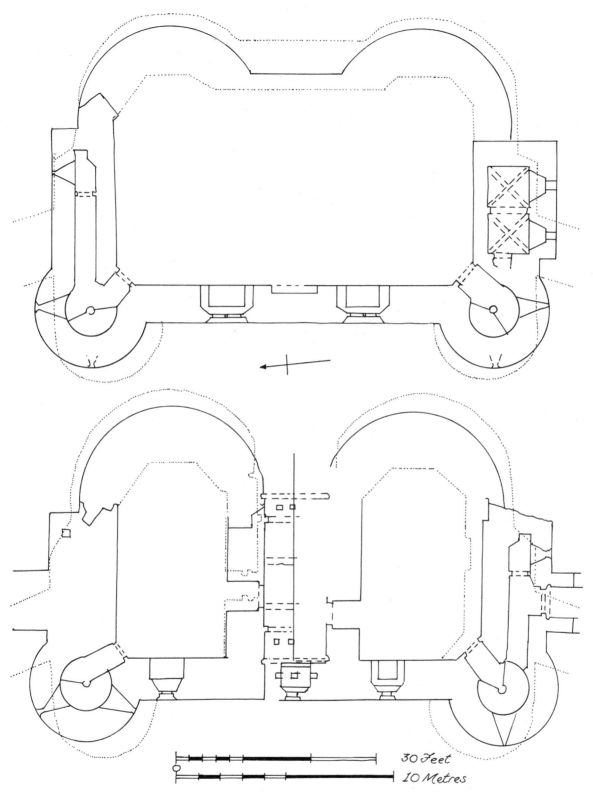

30 Feet

10 Metres

Fig. 18. Plans of inner east gatehouse at Caerphilly castle (after Toy) with Tonbridge super-imposed (fine dots): second floor (above) ground floor (lower left) first floor (lower right). Only half-plans are shown since Caerphilly was entirely symmetrical here.

129) after about 1280, although there are examples in an earlier gate-tower at Caerphilly, and Tonbridge (200 km. from the others) may be equally early in using the idea: the ditch was there before the gatehouse.

THE HISTORICAL SETTING

(See generally Altschul 1965, Lewis 1939, Powicke 1947, 1953 and Treharne and Sanders 1973). Richard fitzGilbert, given the honour of Clare by the Conqueror, also held the manor and castle of Tonbridge and associated manors as a fief of the archbishop of Canterbury. Although his family had acquired the earldom of Gloucester in 1216-17, Richard de Clare III did not take a leading part in national events before the Barons' War, although active in the Degannwy campaign of 1245 and leader of the royal forces in south Wales in 1257. Twenty-five years later, his son Gilbert's failure in the same assignment, and his subsequent rash actions over Morlais castle, left him as little more than life tenant of the Clare estates.

It is the events of the intervening years (1257-82) and particularly the oscillating relationships between the Clares, their powerful neighbour Roger de Leyburn (*fl.* 1251-71) and the Crown which provide substantial reasons for the erection of the Tonbridge gatehouse. In 1257-78 Richard de Clare III had joined the reformers led by Simon de Montfort, although his moderate outlook (and perhaps other influences) led him to change sides at least twice before his death in 1262. In 1259, he obtained licences to enclose the towns of Southwold and Tonbridge with a wall and to crenellate them (CPR 1258-66, 108). Little remains of the town defences at Tonbridge (Streeten 1977), but its licence was the first in Kent (if we except the dubious one for St. Augustine's, Canterbury: Coulson 1979, 83 n. 84) and the only one before 1282 (Allington), although Lagham and Addington just over the Surrey border nearby were licensed in 1262 and 1269 (CPR 1258-66, 199; CPR 1266-72, 395) and Tonbridge town had a second licence in 1318 (CPR 1317-21, 133). Tonbridge castle itself, of course, needed no licence, having been a royal grant of nearly two centuries before, and Richard de Clare III was seeking to strengthen his position in Kent at the time (CPR 1258-66, 99, 493; Dumbreck 1958).

Roger de Leyburn had opposed Richard de Clare III in 1259. Despite his reconciliation with Henry III, Roger was ordered (April 1260) to desist from strengthening his castle at Leybourne or suffer its demolition (CClR 1259-61, 283-4). Leybourne has a gatehouse very similar to that at Barnwell which was said (in 1276) to have been built ten years before (RH II,7). Disgraced for embezzlement, Roger rebelled but was rehabilitated by the end of 1263 as the royal military commander in Kent. Gilbert de Clare made common cause with Roger to re-establish the reform movement, but returned to his allegiance when belatedly given seisin of his estates — and then rejoined the reformers. After the battle of Northampton (1264), he advanced from Tonbridge to capture Rochester — and to lose Tonbridge. He defected to the Crown after Lewes and engineered the escape of Prince Edward. Shortly afterward, Roger Leyburn rescued Henry III at the battle of Evesham, and the *custos* of Westminster Abbey, Robert Beverley, was ordered to give Roger 4000 freestone for building (CClR 1264-8, 190). To secure justice for the Disinherited, Gilbert de Clare captured and fortified London in 1267, and the subsequent peace treaty provided for him to surrender either his eldest daughter or Tonbridge Castle for three years as surety (CPR 1266-72, 144; Rymer 1816, i, 472). The Welsh threat led Gilbert to concentrate on protecting his Glamorgan estates by building Caerphilly Castle from 1262 onward. When Gilbert proposed to accompany Henry III on crusade in 1270, Richard Earl of Cornwall was to hold Tonbridge Castle and Gilbert entertained Edward I there in 1274 on his way to coronation. (See Elliott and Hilton for the later history of the castle.)

In view of the above, it seems very likely that the gatehouse was built by about 1265; Gilbert de Clare was occupied on the defence of Glamorgan from 1268 at the latest, and the break in construction at Caerphilly *c.* 1272-4 (Johns 1978, 31) seems too short an interval to recall the building force and to erect the Tonbridge gatehouse.

TWO CENTURIES OF GATEHOUSE DEVELOPMENT IN ENGLAND

Early Norman gatehouses in England were usually simply walls flanking and arches spanning an entrance passage, but sometimes carried up as a tower (Renn 1977). Rectangular towers flanking an entrance passage defended by doors and a bridge-pit occur in the palace-castles of Henry de Blois: the gatehouse at Bishops Waltham was abandoned by 1182 and perhaps by 1171 (Rigold 1966), and structural analysis at Wolvesey has narrowed its date to 1159 x 71 (Biddle 1969a, fig. opposite 32; Biddle 1969b, fig. 7; Biddle 1972, fig. 9). The King's and Palace Gates at Dover (1168-80: Colvin 1963, ii, 630-33) may have had free-standing predecessors (Rigold 1967, 102).

Round-fronted flanking towers occur in the outer gatehouses at Dover. Stuart Rigold showed me a small excavation in the Norfolk Towers (partly undermined by the 1216-17 siege) which showed the blocked arch of the entrance passage. The Constable's and fitzWilliam Gates (respectively completed and under construction in 1227: Colvin 1963, ii, 636) had a portcullis protecting doors at the inner end of the passage only, as at Skipton (perhaps by 1220: Renn 1975, 78) and Bolingbroke (by 1237: Thompson 1974, 314). Beeston (1220: Ridgway and King 1959, or 1225, Colvin 1963, ii, 559) had no passage length to speak of. Clifford, first recorded in 1233-34 (CPR 1232-47, 25, 41), has an outer gate with portcullis and doors midway along the passage (Iron 1954, 53), similar in position to those at White Castle (1267 x 76: Taylor 1961, 124) and Criccieth (Johns 1970, Turnbull 1979), but Clifford also has an inner gatehouse with a portcullis and doors at the forward end of the passage (R.C.H.M. 1931, 39) a system to be seen at Montgomery (1224-35: Colvin 1963, ii, 740) whilst at the Black Gate of Newcastle-upon-Tyne (1247-50: Colvin 1963, i, 117, fig. 19) the portcullis was one-third of the way along the passage with doors at half-way.

So far we have described passages defended simply by a door or pair of doors fronted by a portcullis. At Chepstow, the outer gate has its door sandwiched between two portcullises and fronted by two rows of openings in the vault; Perks (1948) dates it to 1225 x 70, perhaps by 1245. The asymmetry of the flanking towers can be paralleled in the successive gatehouses at Dyserth (1238-41: Edwards 1912, 275) or the inner gate at Corfe (1247-54: Dufty 1970, 57, from Colvin 1963, ii, 620, or after 1272: Perks 1957, 65). The latter gatehouse is important since it had a portcullis at each end of the entrance passage, with doors behind the forward one and a stair in the rear wall. Mesqui (1980) dated the type to *c.* 1230-40 in France, and Curnow (1979) pointed out that the classic thirteenth-century castle had been achieved by then on both sides of the Channel.

Warkworth has a curious gatehouse, with doors opening forward at both ends of the passage, a portcullis within and arrow-loops in the side walls, all much altered but perhaps originally of the early thirteenth century. Pevensey is unusual in having vaulted ashlar-lined basements to its gatehouse. This was originally free-standing but incorporated in a later curtain by 1274. The confirmation of the commutation of heckage in 1253 (*Curia Regis Roll* 151n.18,

10 Feet
3 Metres

Fig. 19.   Elevations and sections of typical arrow-loops in the Tonbridge Castle gatehouse: on staircase (above) and at first-floor level (below).

CChR 1226-57, 436) may indicate that the gatehouse was built by Gilbert Marshal 1234-40, so linking with Chepstow and Pembroke (see below): there was a comparable plan at Degannwy (1250: Alcock 1967, fig. 2).

The real precursor of Tonbridge (and Caerphilly) gatehouses seems to be that at Pembroke, recently described in detail (King 1978, 88-92, 118). Basically a rectangular block with one round front of uncertain date, it has basements with sloping air-shafts, opposed spiralling stairs in turrets, crooked wall-passages, a latrine block and flights of stairs rising from the wall-head to the turrets. There were design faults compared with Tonbridge: the latrines vented into the courtyard not into the moat, the stairs were unprotected by the passage defences on the court-yard side, which suggests an earlier date: King attributes it to William Marshal (1189-1219), but it could be by one of his sons up to 1245. Mesqui (1980) has designed a code for gatehouse defences, by which we can demonstrate the intermediate position of Tonbridge between Pembroke (1200? 1240?) and Harlech (1284-5: Taylor 1979, 5):

Pembroke   H A.   V A.   H V A,
Tonbridge   A H A.   V A A, A V H A
Harlech   V A H A. A H V A A A A, V H A

(Left to right, outside to inside. A, murder hole (*assommoir*); H, portcullis (*herse*);
V, pair of doors (*vantaux*). Full stop(.) comma(,) indicate an arrow-loop
or door in the side wall protected by the preceding feature)

MILITARY CAPABILITY

The entrance passage demonstrably had a good defence; what of the more offensive aspects of the Tonbridge gatehouse? The arrow-loops have been mentioned in passing, but deserve further description and discussion. They are of Sailhan type IIb/B/2 (Sailhan 1978) (Fig. 19). The outer arris is rounded off and rebated to emphasize the slit (as at Barnwell), and also to confuse the aim of an attacking archer: all the arrow-loops are in shadow at different times of day. The slit has a trefoiled head splayed back part-way through the wall, and a plunging sole terminating in an oillet. The embrasure has a chamfered arch carried on squinches in the case of the stair-loops (Fig. 19, above), but opening into a rib-vaulted casemate in the case of the others. Those facing along the curtain have only a single rib, however. Each loop had a 30° traverse at least and up to 45° plunge so that (even ignoring the unknown potential of the wall-head) there was excellent coverage of the outside of the gatehouse and curtain walls. Towards the bailey there were the turrets and overhanging hourds, and the stair arrow-loops were usable, but the archer would block the stair. The weakest spot was the foot of the curtain, covered by one loop and the latrine windows, which may have been why an extra *talus* was added to the curtain here.

ACKNOWLEDGEMENTS

Many friends of Stuart Rigold have assisted in this study; I must particularly thank Charles Coulson and Cedric Johns, for discussions on the Clares, and the officers of the Tonbridge and Malling District Council, for free access to the gatehouse in the 'close season'.

ASPECTS OF FOURTEENTH-CENTURY
CASTLE DESIGN*

BERIC M. MORLEY

GENERAL CONSIDERATIONS

The castles of the late medieval period have not always received the sympathetic study they deserve. The attitude that they represent only an anticlimax after the great fortresses of the late thirteenth century still permeates much writing. This is unfortunate for it tends to belittle the achievements of their designers and can imply an assumption that the patrons were not clear whether or not they were serious in their intention to have a fortified building. It is better to assume, as a premise, that patron and designer had full choice of the options afforded by experience and opportunity. All the requirements for the defence of a castle against a siege without gunpowder had been developed by the late thirteenth century. Even the arrival of the first generation of siege artillery added little to the arsenal provided by the earlier *petrariae*. Thus innovation in castle design tended to be not in terms of defence but of the castle's rôle as a symbol of the owner's status and power; its ability to impress those both below and above him in social standing. A castle had to be architecturally grand. It had to contain rooms sufficient in size and number to accommodate the elaborate and costly pageantry of the formal life of the well-to-do. If it could outdo its neighbours in originality of design or opulence of architectural detailing, so much the better. The results show a bewildering variety of building in which the relatively simple thread of development from keep to concentric castle is broken, to be replaced by a rich tapestry of styles and ideas.

One way to attempt an understanding of the new situation is to try to abstract the decisions an owner and his designer would have had to have made to produce their particular castle. There need be only four main topics requiring decisions, taken in the following order: planning requirements, defensibility, form, and embellishment. In terms of the tapestry the first two form the weft, the third, the warp, whilst the last is added embroidery. Less figuratively this can be demonstrated in a flow diagram:-

To clarify this I will consider the decisions one by one, defining what is intended as I go.

i. *Planning Requirements*

An owner must ask himself what accommodation he needs in his building; whom he will provide for, and whom he will not; how the rooms will be linked in suites; how they will vary in size, position and elegance to suit their occupants' status. P.A. Faulkner's masterly papers (1958 and 1963) form an essential basis for all work in this field, showing how to spot individual households in a castle and how to divine their relative importance.

There is little point in analysing the way a castle is planned if we do not believe that the planning reflects the social structure of the complete household in residence. But in individual cases the amount of hard historical evidence that exists about the castle's population is often very small indeed. More often than not we are inventing a social structure based on the analysis of the planning: the analysis cannot be seen as corroboration of a structure known from documentary sources. It is very important not to forget this when moving from one building to another: it is too easy to slip into circular argument.

ii. *Defensibility*

The degree of defensibility was a second and independent choice to be made. That it was independent is demonstrated by the fact that schemes of planning identified in a fortified structure can usually be found also in contemporary undefended buildings. Looking back, it is often difficult to decide why a particular level of defence was adopted, from nothing up to a limit imposed, and that not very effectively, by the Royal Licence. But it would be wrong to suppose other than that the decision was carefully thought out, having in mind the local, and in rare instances the national, conditions prevailing. Should a man defend against outlaw gangs or lightly-armed peasant mobs; or against rival lords in that brand of skirmishing that passed for sport among landed ex-soldiers? Should he defend against raiders from across national borders, whether thought of as small gangs or as organized armies? The licences to crenellate give some clue to the answers: otherwise, it is again a question of deduction from the buildings, linked with an assessment of the owner's status and character drawn from the often all-too-scanty historical records.

iii. *The form of a castle*

The late medieval castle could be built in one of many forms. There was no standard and designers dipped into a largely ready-established répertoire. Thus there might be a single dominant element; a keep-like building, or an enlarged gatehouse. The buildings might still wander around an irregular site having a nominal courtyard or bailey: or they might be ranged against a rectangular wall with moat and corner towers. Only the relatively small group of fully-integrated quadrangular castles represents complete innovation.

The two factors already isolated had surprisingly little bearing on the choice of form: the same planning arrangements can often be traced in castles of greatly differing types, as the latter part of this essay should demonstrate. Likewise, the defensive capability chosen seems to bear little relation to the form adopted. In terms of wall thickness, presence of barred doors and portcullises, or the isolation of principal chambers as a stronghold, there are strong and weak examples within each form type. I believe that in this period the patron and designer rarely saw a relation between strength and castle type. Any castle could be provided with the degree of strength required. Size, too, had less bearing on form than might be imagined. There are large and small 'keeps' and gatehouses, whether as a result of the difference in size of the whole establishment, or because, in other cases, a greater or lesser part of the accommodation is provided in this single unit. It may be a whole household or only an enlarged chamber block. The walled quadrangle comes in all sizes, although the fully-integrated type lends itself rather more to the top end of the range.

What then dictated this choice? Was it fashion, or its converse the desire to be different? Was it an individual's assessment of what would impress most? Are there regional preferences?

Can one see individual designers recommending a particular form? At present these questions do not have general answers. In a few individual cases, where the opinion is that the form is continental, rather than insular in origin, one imagines that the owner is trying to impress with something new, copying something seen abroad on campaign. This is probably true, but plenty of other old soldiers built in a thoroughly English manner.

iv. *Embellishment*

This term is intended to cover mainly the detailing of a building. The amount and character of this is clearly a choice available to the builders. But it is to some extent dictated by the material used, usually a local stone, which is not open to choice. Yet, it is the surface work of a castle, the character of its masonry, the design of its windows and mouldings, the extent of its crown-works, rather than its overall form which places it geographically. An example is the 'Durham Palatinate' style of the fourteenth century with its bleak walls, thin, usually diagonal, buttresses, and overhanging crowns (in plan either octagons or diagonally-set rectangles) and with its penchant for displays of armorial shields. It occurs in castles of all form types. However, to see embellishment as merely a reflection of local style is to simplify too much. A man could choose to display his wealth in the quality or quantity of the decorative work on his castle, and he usually did so.

CASE STUDIES

The second part of this essay considers four fourteenth-century buildings, which although different in form and defensibility, seem to share a particular type of planning. That is, they appear not to follow the multiple-household pattern described by Faulkner (1963), nor to exhibit those carefully differentiated architectural details that imply social stratification in so many castles. Although three of them are incomplete, they do each seem to have only a single great hall with a suite of family rooms off. Some other chambers may be separated off for service and servants. Thereafter, they are provided not with further household suites, but with a large number of independently accessible, largely identical, chambers, or occasionally, pairs of chambers. They are not merely simpler than say, Goodrich or Bolton Castles because they are smaller; plenty of smaller castles do display the attributes described by Faulkner. In fact all four buildings (three castles and one undefended house) are large, and belonged to influential families. If the interpretation is correct, they can be seen in terms of planning as occupying one end of a spectrum with Bolton at the other.

i. *Okehampton Castle, Devon*

Okehampton was owned by the Courtenay family; Earls of Devon from 1335. Although their ancestral home, from the fourteenth century they preferred to live at Tiverton Castle acquired in 1293. The castle sits on a steep-sided spur. It was virtually rebuilt in the early fourteenth century (Higham 1977 and forthcoming) with an irregular plan dictated by the site. Its dominant visual element is the new keep on the Norman motte.

Entry to the castle is made through an outer gatehouse at the base of the salient of the spur, along a barbican passage to an inner gatehouse at the crest. The great hall lies through and adjacent to this gatehouse. From its high end a door and stair leads to an upper chamber and to a chamber over the gatehouse. Neither of these retain evidence of garderobes, and it is possible that the northern chamber of the east range was included with these two to form a suite. (See plan, Fig. 20). This last chamber has a vaulted inner room with garderobe and hand

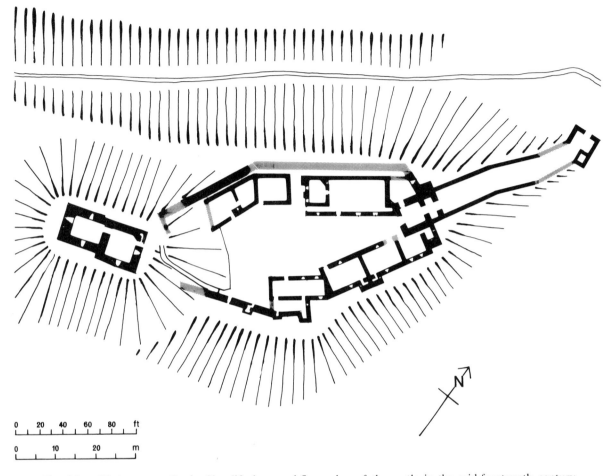

0   20   40   60   80   ft

0   10   20   m

Fig. 20. *Okehampton Castle*. Simplified ground-floor plan of the castle in the mid-fourteenth century.

basin. Together these rooms could provide suitable accommodation for the lord's immediate household. There are common precedents for this position both in respect of being off the high end of the hall and of being part of the gatehouse.

At the low end of the hall is an upstairs chamber with garderobe and fireplace. This could have accommodated a castle official, or would have served, instead or as well, as an office for the lord, enabling him to conduct business elsewhere than in his domestic quarters. If this is correct, it could explain the moulding, the most elaborate to survive in the castle, around the door from the hall to the room below this. Otherwise unremarkable this lower room could be elevated to an antechamber to the lord's office, if an internal stair provided the access between the two.

Away from the hall the castle has a lodging for the chaplain by the chapel, and the possibility of one or two staff chambers above the service rooms alongside the kitchen. There is an upper chamber in the barbican gatehouse. Apart from these the accommodation is in six lodgings, arranged in the south-eastern block and in the keep. Taking the latter first; it is a structure contemporary with the other fourteenth-century work, built over the ruins of a smaller Norman keep. Its upper chambers could serve as two lodgings as each has its own garderobe; access to the inner one was presumably screened off. But they could have been used as a two-room suite. The lower rooms have neither latrines nor fireplaces, and regular use as lodgings seems unlikely.

The range along the south-east side of the ridge forms a typical medieval lodgings block. For parallels, see, for example Pantin 1959, 243-58 and Wood 1965, Ch. 13. The northernmost first-floor room has been mentioned above. That below it was probably used for storage: it has no garderobe, even though provision below that for the chamber above would have been simple. The four other rooms are independent lodgings, all with garderobes. The lower ones are without fireplaces, and for security have only small windows. All the lodgings, including the keep are of similar size and decoration with, for example, only simple pyramid stops to their doors.

Turning to the defensibility of the castle, it is clear that this aspect was by no means neglected. The natural strength of the site, and the ditch south-west of the keep, retained from the Norman period, are enhanced by the long barbican passage from the outer gate, and by the retention of thick curtain walls along the north-west and most of the south-east sides. Where the wall is omitted, above a particularly steep scarp, it is replaced by the formidable outer face of the lodgings block. The keep is interesting for, although in planning terms it has lost the status of principal accommodation usual in Norman keeps, it nevertheless retains its military importance at the higher end of the spur, and it is built with thicker walls than the other lodgings.

ii. *Dartington Hall, Devon*

The evidence suggests that the present buildings were erected by John Holand, Earl of Huntingdon and half-brother to Richard II, when he took possession of the Dartington estate in 1388. He was a younger member of the Holand family, and Dartington would have been his principal residence. Married to the daughter of the Duke of Lancaster, and adviser and chamberlain to the king, his influence grew quickly, and the Holands were soon challenging the Courtenay Earls of Devon as premier family in the county. (Emery 1970, Ch. 3, and Cherry 1979, 90).

It remains a cause of some surprise that the home Huntingdon chose to build at Dartington was an undefended house rather than a castle. There is no obvious reason why this was so. Arriving at the house, the great hall is seen across an entrance court, flanked by rows of lodgings. This much seems to have been Huntindon's work. There is less agreement over the date of an inner court beyond the hall. Only one wall of its far range survives above ground, although part of the plan was determined by excavation in 1962. In his excavation report Platt suggests a date about 1500 (1962, 216-9). However, as part of his wide-ranging study of the house Emery argues for contemporaneity with the rest of the building (1970, 190-202). He rehearses the details with care, but this only serves to highlight the inadequacy of the archaeological evidence and the circumstantial nature of the historical case. In my view we should accept that the date of this court is still unknown. A number of speculations have been hazarded for the use to which the buildings of this court might have been put. A chapel is needed, with accommodation for priests. Otherwise the suggestions involve entertainment or accommodation for members of the Holand family or for privileged guests. Whether the house is considered with or without this range, it remains true that the larger part of the

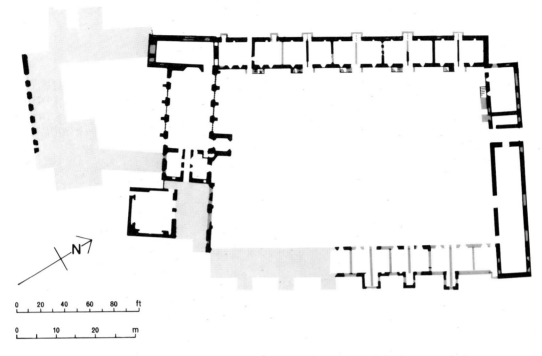

Fig. 21. *Dartington Hall.* Simplified ground-floor plan of the house as built.

accommodation was provided in undifferentiated lodgings.

The great hall had a solar block at its high end with two residential floors above a separately entered basement. At the low end a vice gave access to two small chambers above the porch and to fine chambers on the first and second floors above the buttery and pantry. The four rooms do not interconnect to form permanent suites.

On the east side of the main courtyard there are remains embedded in the existing buildings which, when considered with old drawings, indicate the probable former presence of as many as 28 individual and identical lodgings arranged on two floors along this side. If these were built at the same time as the hall, of only a few years later are the similar lodgings on the west side. These are marginally larger: there are sixteen single-room lodgings and another two available as two-room suites. A further two-room suite existed above the stables as part of the entrance block in the north range. The larger of its rooms could be considered a hall. Thus, it seems likely that there were here between 40 and 50 separate lodgings all but three of them virtually indistinguishable from each other, as can be seen in the Buck's print (Emery 1970, 82-3).

iii. *Middleham Castle, North Yorkshire*

Middleham takes the form of a large Norman keep closely surrounded by a curtain wall. Against three sides of the curtain are two-storey ranges. The exterior of the walls is punctuated by corner towers and by intermediate latrine towers. There is a two-phase gatehouse. The keep is probably of the second quarter of the twelfth century, the curtain of the thirteenth. The buildings against the latter are fourteenth- or early fifteenth-century in date: two main phases seem apparent, though the similarities between them suggest a single intention. That

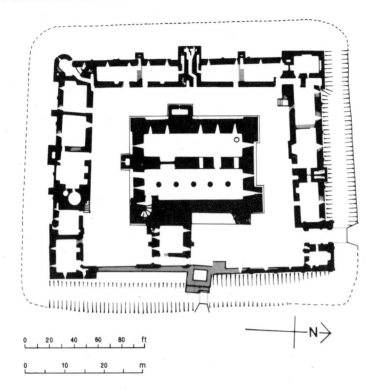

Fig. 22. *Middleham Castle*. Simplified ground-floor plan of the castle *c.* 1400.

must have been to provide adequate lodgings accommodation. At the time the castle belonged to the Nevilles of Raby, with whom it stayed until after the death of Richard Neville, Earl of Warwick in 1471.

The Norman keep had its accommodation on the first floor: a great hall with, beside it, two rooms termed 'privy chamber' and 'chamber of presence' by Peers (1978 edition, 3). A chapel was added to the keep in the thirteenth century, and in the fourteenth the original garderobes on the south and west sides were enlarged and built out as turrets. There is evidence of a second floor contrived in the keep late in its life. Without any doubt, the keep must still have provided the principal accommodation in the fourteenth century.

The new ranges outside offered mainly single lodgings but there was possibly a first-floor hall on the south side. Access to it is unclear, but was apparently up an external flight of stairs through an antechamber to the east. Across the antechamber from the hall was another chamber. This must have been reached up the same stairs, but whether it was entered directly or through the antechamber cannot be seen now. Thus, there is the possibility of a household suite here, albeit with an odd, and avoidable, sequence of rooms. Alternatively, the hall and antechamber stood alone for use by the occupants of the lodgings. These can be considered in two groups; those along the main lengths of the north and west ranges and those elsewhere. The former are fourteen in number, on two floors, more-or-less uniform in size, every one independently accessible and with its own garderobe. All but two of the ground floor rooms have original fireplaces. The second group of lodgings is made up of four chambers in the north-west tower, two or three in the south-west and two in the south-east. There are then two more in the east end of the south range. Of these ten all but three are clearly independent of other chambers; the other three are almost certainly so. All have garderobes. Four no longer have evidence of fireplaces. Finally, there are two floors of accommodation in the gatehouse to be considered apart from the main lodgings and tiny rooms in two of the garderobe towers.

From this it can be seen that although this was not a freshly-built castle, it was modified to have a main suite with possibly a second hall and up to 24 independent single-room lodgings, mostly of a uniform size and with comparable facilities. The modifications did not alter its military effectiveness.

(In this discussion I have ignored the bridges from the keep indicated by Peers. They are probably later, but their presence would not alter the case presented here.)

iv. *Old Wardour Castle, Wiltshire*

Like Dartington, Wardour was built anew in the late fourteenth century. Its licence to crenellate is dated 1393 when the builder, John, fifth Lord Lovel was 48. Little is known of Lovel's family home of Titchmarsh in Northamptonshire. The Wiltshire lands were a new acquisition and gave Lovel a chance to build anew, as his grandson was to do 40-odd years later at Minster Lovell in Oxfordshire. The castle was intended to be fully defensible and takes the form of a tall, compact unit built round a courtyard so small as to be virtually a light-well. Although a little altered in the sixteenth century and slighted after a long Civil War siege, the castle is still an eye-catcher. Its plan is hexagonal, with an enlarged front. The walls were capped with a decorative cornice and corbelled-out hexagonal corner turrets. The quality of the masonry is very fine throughout.

The planning is straightforward in its main arrangement. There is a great hall across the front at first-floor level. From the high end, occupying the north and north-west sides of the hexagon are the family rooms. There is a tall first floor with two rooms, and a lesser floor above, also apparently with two rooms. It seems that the space could have been used as two two-room suites or the inner one on the upper floor could have been taken into the main suite to leave a single second-floor room. Once away from the family rooms the lodgings are gathered onto staircases. At the low end of the hall there is a small chamber and inner chamber on each of two floors above the service rooms. Windows indicate a chamber above the kitchen on the western side of the building. It is unclear how this was reached; probably from the stair in the adjacent south-east angle. From this, access was gained to three floors of identical lodgings in the next, south, side. These are now seen as six independent rooms, but this is probably a sixteenth-century alteration. Originally, they may have been three pairs; chamber and inner chamber. There are then single chambers on the ground floor in the south and north-west sides. Only unheated basements occupy the south-east, north-east and north sides. Returning to the high end of the hall, a small chamber here leads off the private great chamber. But the two above it could have been independently accessible from the northern newel stair.

So much remains, but the last side, the south-west, was removed in the Civil War, taking with it part of each of the adjacent sides. Foundations revealed during conservation work are shown in the official handbook (Pugh and Saunders 1968). They indicate that at least the ground floor was divided into four rooms. A thickening of the wall in the western corner implies a newel stair there. It is impossible to be sure to what it led. The simplest solution is to see the pattern of the ground floor repeated on three upper ones. There would then be six two-roomed suites here with two more on the ground floor. These eight separate lodgings would be increased if some were arranged via mural passages as single rooms, or decreased if

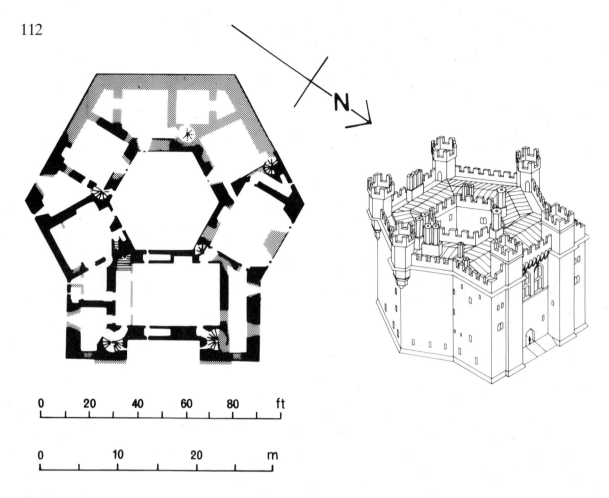

Fig. 23. *Old Wardour Castle*. Simplified first-floor plan of the castle as built. Reconstruction drawing based on the surviving fabric and the *Pembroke Terrier* drawing of 1567 (Straton 1909).

some of the space was taken up with a chapel, otherwise unaccounted for. However, I can offer no proof that this side was not used for one or more major household suites, rather than for independent lodgings. Nevertheless with the pattern set for stacks of undifferentiated lodgings on the other sides, this must be likely here, too. Wardour has to be thought of as a strong candidate for this type of planning.

In all ten lodgings can be identified in the existing structure; five of one room, five of two. The west range could provide up to sixteen more rooms, possibly between eight and sixteen more lodgings.

DISCUSSION

My brief accounts cannot do justice to any uncertainties in the interpretation of individual rooms in the four buildings chosen. In a short essay, based on such damaged structures, this is bound to be so. Yet, there must still be discernible a striking difference between the planning of these very varied buildings and that of such castles as Goodrich, Bolton or Warkworth or even of the much smaller Hylton. (See Faulkner 1963, 221 and 225; Hunter Blair and Honeyman 1954, and Morley 1976, respectively.) The descriptions do, I hope, provide confirmation of the propositions made in the first part of the paper.

By way of conclusion it is necessary to consider why this particular type of planning was chosen. It can be seen immediately that these are not 'castles of livery and maintenance' as defined by Douglas Simpson in 1946. There is, for example, no means in any of them of satisfactorily holding the principal accommodation against the rest; what mathematicians would usefully describe as a necessary, though not sufficient condition for the definition to hold. Of course, the work of a number of historians has shown that we should not expect the lord's companions in a castle to be simply a band of armed retainers. Rather it is the social and functional variety of a lord's familiars that is so striking. Surviving livery rolls include menial servants at one end of the scale and close relatives of barely lower standing than the lord himself at the other. The extent to which the lord could expect attendance by his familiars at all times or sporadically, for a limited duration or for life, in peace or in war, has been much discussed. For these points see, for example, Lewis 1945, Holmes 1957, MacFarlane 1945 and 1973, and Cherry 1979. There is little doubt that the complete household would be a constantly changing mix, even if drawn from the lord's own affinity. Add to this the variety brought with guests and it seems a wonder that a form of planning in which there was any attempt to provide graduated accommodation in set suites could have been contemplated. The problem was probably exacerbated in my four examples. Only one, Dartington, was used as the family's principal residence. In none of the others could one expect even that stable core provided by the lord's private household. When he did use the castle it would have been for two main reasons. First, each castle was the administrative centre for sizeable parts of the owner's estates. Secondly, each one happens to be sited in notably good hunting country: all four had large paled parks. For this second reason it is likely that there were more guests than otherwise at these particular castles, bringing a further influx of retainers and servants, and further extending the social mix. To have had to squeeze such varied groups into the strait-jacket of the closely-ordered suites of a multiple-household castle would have been to risk violating medieval etiquette at every turn. With all the lodgings identical these important distinctions could be made, without prejudice, in other ways, by temporary alterations to the accommodation: that is, by dressing individual chambers with varying qualities of hanging or furnishing, and by the even simpler expedient of putting a greater or lesser number of people in each room. The similarity in planning to that of medieval or modern colleges and hotels is only partly coincidental. They all deal with the problem of housing an ever-changing population.

ACKNOWLEDGEMENTS

I have discussed ideas used in this essay with a number of friends and colleagues; notably of course, Stuart Rigold to whose memory it is affectionately dedicated. Dr Bob Higham has generously shared his own thoughts on Okehampton Castle over the years. But the views expressed in the above pages remain the responsibility of myself alone.

Fig. 21 is based on plans in Emery (1970) by kind permission of the publishers, Oxford University Press.

STEPHEN DE PENCESTRE'S ACCOUNT AS CONSTABLE OF DOVER CASTLE FOR THE YEARS MICHAELMAS 1272 — MICHAELMAS 1274

A.J. TAYLOR

Not the least of Stuart Rigold's services to archaeology in Kent were, on the one hand, his review of the evidence for the position and extent of the harbour of Roman Dover[1] and, on the other, the excavations he carried out within Dover castle itself and shortly afterwards published in two characteristically thorough reports.[2] It may therefore not be inappropriate that one of the contributions to the present volume should be a transcript of the principal surviving record of an earlier royal servant who for more than thirty years at the end of the thirteenth century was responsible, as constable, for the castle's organisation and day-to-day administration, and who also, as warden of the Cinque Ports, watched over the comings and goings of all the great personages and their retinues who crossed the narrow sea during most of the reign of King Edward I.

In a long succession of names that runs from Odo of Bayeux and Hubert de Burgh, through the Lord Edward and King Henry VIII to the Duke of Wellington and Sir Winston Churchill, none has discharged and exercised the double office longer or more directly than Sir Stephen de Pencestre (*d.* 1299). We know with unusual exactitude the time and circumstances of his appointment, a writ dated at Clarendon on 5 December, 1267, telling us that 'he is now about to set forth in all haste to Dover to receive the keeping of the castle by order of the King and Edward his son';[3] and we have a tangible memorial of him in the effigy on his tomb in the church of his native Penshurst.[4] This paper has the strictly limited purpose of printing, with a minimum of annotation, the full Latin text of the earliest enrolled account of his stewardship,[5] so as to make it the more easily available to antiquaries and Kentish scholars in particular, and thereby to serve as a reminder of the variety of the information that is to be derived from such records, especially the writs in favour of Pencestre preserved on the Liberate Rolls as well as his accounts on the Pipe rolls themselves, about cross-Channel traffic in the last quarter of the thirteenth century.

1. Rigold 1970, 78-100.
2. Rigold 1967, 87-121; Rigold 1969, 54-104.
3. *Cal. Liberate Rolls*, vi, 1267-1272, p. 5, no.38.
4. For Dover's place in the Cinque Ports' organisation, see Murray 1935, *passim*, esp. cap. VII; for the name 'Pencestre', Zachrisson 1909, and, less convincingly, Wallenberg 1934, 87, 449.
5. P.R.O, Pipe Roll 2 Edw. I (E 372/118), rot. 36.

Our present account runs from 29 September, 1272, seven weeks before the demise of Henry III, to 29 September, 1274, six weeks after the coronation of Edward I. At the time of his father's death on 16 November, 1272, the Lord Edward was on his way back from crusade, and the news reached him in Palermo. Nearly two years were to pass before he returned, on 2 August, 1274, at the end of an eventful journey through Sicily and Italy, Savoy and France and his own ducal inheritance of Gascony, to the Dover from which he had set sail in August, 1270, and from which he now proceeded to Westminster[6] for his coronation, on Sunday, August 19th, the first such ceremony to take place within his father's newly built abbey church. A particular interest of the account is its many references to Edward's absence oversea 'antequam rex esset rex et postquam fuit rex', to persons travelling through Dover to visit him, and to expenditure arising in connection with his return. Another main interest is concerned with the castle: the great quantities of wine stored and protected against winter cold in the king's cellar, presumably the great vaulted basement beneath the keep; the sale of the pieces of lead left over after the re-roofing of the castle 'houses'; the flour or grain chest bought for the castle windmill, canvas for its sails and ropes for stiffening them; ropes for the bells of St. Mary's Church; a great rope for the wheel of the castle well (how 'great' will be know to those who, seven centuries later, peer down as the custodian's piece of flaming rag circles on its way to unplumbed depths below); bran bought for burnishing the king's arms and armour; firewood for the cellar, to warm it or to store in it.

In the compass of a necessarily short article it is not possible to print a record of this character both in the original Latin and in translation. Scholarship is better served by giving the former, adding notes on items that seem specially to call for comment. Where this course presents difficulties, as for some readers it must, most of them will be resolved with the aid of recourse to R.E. Latham's *Revised Medieval Latin Word-List* (Oxford, 1965).

The account is as follows:

Account of Stephen of Penshurst, constable of Dover castle, of the wards pertaining to the same castle, the issues of the crossing from the king's harbour there, and of divers other his receipts, from Michaelmas at the commencement of the 57th year of King Henry to the feast of St. Edmund the Martyr next following, before the death of the same king, and from the same feast of St. Edmund to Michaelmas in the 2nd year of this present king, being the commencement of his 3rd year, viz. for 2 whole years, i.e. Mich. 1272—Mich.1274, by writ of the king.

Compotus Stephani de Penecestr', constabularii castri Dovor', de wardis spectantibus ad idem castrum, et de exitibus passagii portus regis ibidem, et aliis diversis receptis suis, a festo sancti Michelis incipiente anno lvij° regis Henrici usque ad festum sancti Edmundi martiris proximo sequens, antequam idem rex moreretur, et ab eodem festo sancti Edmundi usque ad festum sancti Michelis anno ij° regis huius incipiente anno tercio, videlicet per duos annos integros, per breve regis.

Idem reddit compotum de £145 11s. 2d. de predictis wardis de anno primo, sicut continetur in rotulo de particulis quem predictus Stephanus liberavit in thesauro. Et de £146 6s. de eisdem de anno secundo, sicut continetur in predicto rotulo de particulis. Et de £99 6s. 8d. de exitibus

---

6. For Edward and Eleanor's journey, by way of Tonbridge and Reigate, and the celebrations at Westminster, see Powicke 1947, 617.

passagii predicti de anno primo, per talliam contra Thomam Salekin[7] tunc collectorem eiusdem passagii. Et de £118 13s. 2d. de eodem passagio de anno secundo per talliam contra eundem Thomam. Et de £4 de firma perquisitorum ville Dovor' de anno primo per manum dicti Thome. Et de £12 3s. de perquisitis eiusdem ville de anno ij° per manum Valentini de Bere tunc ballivum eiusdem ville,[8] de quibus 100s. sunt de catallis Jacobi Judei Dovor' sicut idem Stephanus recognovit. Et de 40s. de fine Reyne Judee ut possit manere in eadem villa per annum. Et de 4s. de cyneribus plumbi remanentis post cooperturam domorum in castro Dovor' venditis. Et de £4 13s. de vendicione cuiusdam shute unius Flandrensis, qui devenit ad manum regis pro forisfacto eiusdem pro falsa moneta. Et de £17 14s. 10d. de denariis provenientibus de placitis et perquisitis diversorum ad januam castri predicti[9] per totum predictum tempus. Et de £75 8d. de denariis provenientibus de perquisitis et placitis et finibus coram eodem constabulario in Itinere suo per partes Quinque Portuum[10] per idem tempus.
Summa £625 12s. 6d.

Et de £50 receptis de thesauro regis per manus Thesauri (sic) et camerariorum anno secundo. Et de £333 6s. 8d. receptis de firma comitatus Kancie et manerii et hundredi de Middelton' anno primo per manus Henrici Malemeins et Willelmi de Hevre tunc vicecomitum eiusdem comitatus sicut recognovit. Et de £133 6s. 8d. de receptis de firma eiusdem comitatus anno secundo per manus eiusdem Willelmi. Et de £50 receptis de firma manerii et hundredi de Middelton' de prima quarta parte huius anni per manus eiusdem Willelmi antequam rex committeret dictum manerium Johanni de Burgo ut dicitur.[11] Et de £20 de exitibus septem hundredorum de Waldis per totum predictum tempus, que hundreda consueverunt aliquando esse in manibus vicecomitis. Et de £40 11s. de xxiiij. doliis vini que fuerunt in celario regis in predicto castro antequam rex esset rex et postquam fuit rex venditis anno primo. Et de £38 13s. de xxxj. doliis de consimilibus doliis venditis anno secundo, de quibus quedam dolia fuerunt debilia et parvi valoris. Et de £4 de fine duorum mercatorum deferencia vina putrida et debilia et omnino inutilia ad prisam regis inde capiend'. Et de £40 receptis de parte vicesime baronum de Sandwico anno primo sicut recognovit. Et de £70 9s. 5½d. de C. quarteriis frumenti et Ciiij[xx] et j. quarterio et vij. bussellis mixtil' de remanent compoti sui redditi coram auditoribus compotorum regis antequam esset rex,[12] sicut idem Stephanus recognovit. Et de £76 18s. de lxx. quarteriis frumenti, cclxxiij. quarteriis ordei, xv quarteriis fabarum et xix. quarteriis avene que fuerunt in granario anno primo et vend' anno secundo, sicut recognovit.

Summa £857 4s. 9½d.
Summa summarum £1482 17s. 3½d.

7.   For Thomas Salekin and his house at Dover, see Kingsford 1909, 130, 191; Murray 1935, 247-8.
8.   Valentine de Bere was appointed bailiff of Dover in April 1274 and died in or before January 1276 (CPR, *1272-1281*, 48 and 128).
9.   For the court of the Castle Gate at Dover, see Murray 1935, 103-4, 111, 119.
10. For the constable's 'Eyres' within the Cinque Ports jurisdiction, see Murray 1935, index, s.n.
11. John de Burgh 'the elder' was granted the constableships of the Tower of London and Colchester for life on 18 December 1273; on the same day he was appointed to the farm of the city of London and the manor and hundred of Middelton, Kent (CPR, *1272-81*, 41); he died in or before February 1275 (CClR, *1272-1279*, 147).
12. 'Auditors of the accounts of the king before he became king': probably, though not certainly, the John of London and Adam of Winchester named later in the present account; cf. n. 28 *infra*.

In thesauro nichil.

Et in quodam cophino empto ad molendinum ad ventum in castro Dovor', canabo ad vela eiusdem molendini, cordis ad eadem vela afforcianda, filo empto ad cordas balistarum, cordis ad campanas ecclesie in eodem castro, quadam magna corda ad rotam putei ibidem, furfure ad arma regis ibidem, busca ad celarium, turis ad vina regis conservanda contra frigus in hyeme, brevibus portandis pro negociis regis in V^{que} Portibus, et aliis minutis et necessariis expensis in eodem castro per predictum tempus, quarum expensarum particule continentur in rotulo quem predictus constabularius liberavit in thesauro, 58s. 6½d. Et in vadiis cuiusdam custodientis quamdam shutam Flandrensem, qui cepit per diem 2d. per Cxxxvj. dies, 22s. 8d. Et in doliis vinorum regis existentibus in celario regis in eodem castro circulandis, barrandis et custodiendis per idem tempus £9 13s. 9d. Summa precedencium misarum £13 14s. 11½d. Et debet £1469 2s 4d. Idem reddit compotum de eodem debito. In thesauro nichil.

Et in passagio Willelmi de Flandr' et familie sue a portu Dovor' usque Whitsand £12 per breve regis. Et Johanni Hardel ad expensas sex equorum regis commorancium in villa Dovor' per ix. dies propter tempestatem et ventum contrarium 15s 6d. per breve regis. Et in passagio Willelmi Bagod versus regem 7s. per idem breve.[13] Et Roberto Mundekin et Salekino Limerik de Sandwico ad reparandam galiam regis et eandem muniendam ad costeram maris custodiendam contra adventum episcopi Cycestr' et Almerici de Monteforti et complicum suorum 26s. 8d. per idem breve. Et xlvj. hominibus navigantibus in eadem galia per mare ad obviandum inimicis regis ad sustentacionem eorundem navigancium £4 per idem breve. Et Ricardo Spaniel servienti castri predicti eunti Parisius ad insidiandum predictis episcopo et Almarico 20s. per idem breve. Et predictis galiotis ad reducendum predictam galiam de Winchelese usque Sandwicum 10s. per idem breve.[14] Et pro quinque ulnis blueti emptis ad

13. One would much like to know the nature of the business on which William Bagod crossed the Channel for consultation with the king, a visit not otherwise known to be recorded. He was one of the six English commissioners appointed by the regents to meet Llywelyn ap Gruffydd or his representatives at the ford of Montgomery on 6 May, 1274, to examine mutual trespasses and kidnappings (nowadays surely a more realistic rendering of *interceptiones* than 'raids') in the march of Wales in breach of the treaty of 1267 (CPR, *1272-81*, 47, 48). Nothing is known of the outcome of the meeting but the indications are that it was negative (Edwards 1940, lii-liii). The fact that no letter touching on it survives in either *Littere Wallie* or *Ancient Correspondence* is consistent with the possibility that the king was given a verbal report, in which case Bagod may have been its bearer and this may be our only indication of it; cf. the verbal account of the disaster at Dryslwyn given to Edward at Bordeaux in 1287, (Edwards 1935, 174).

14. This whole sequence is again of the greatest interest, for no other record of it is believed to have survived. Robert Mundekin and Salekin Limerick of Sandwich are paid 2 marks to repair one of H.M. ships (*galia*=a galley or warship) and provision it to guard the coast against a landing by the bishop of Chichester (Stephen Bersted) and Amaury the youngest son of Simon de Montfort and his accomplices; £4 are paid in wages to the crew of 46 men for patrolling the channel to waylay the (aforesaid) enemies of the king; Richard Spaniel, a sergeant at the castle, receives 20s. for expenses in going to Paris to keep watch on the movements of Amauri and the bishop; and finally the crew are given 10s. for taking the galley back to Sandwich from Winchelsea. Nothing is said of rewards, which must mean (as indeed we know from what happened later) that it all came to nothing. But in December of the following year (1275), not off the coast of Kent but off the coast of Glamorgan, Amaury was captured in the act of attempting to bring his sister Eleanor to Wales to marry Llywelyn, to whom she had been betrothed by her father Earl Simon ten years before (Powicke 1947, 610 n., 647). The juxtaposition of the payments for William Bagod's visit to the king (previous note) and the tracking down of Amauri '*et complicum suorum*' deserves notice, for surely it may be no coincidence

robam Andree de Saukevill existentis in custodia regis apud Dovoriam 9*s.* 5*d.* per idem breve. Et pro caligis et sotularibus emptis ad opus prefati Andree 22*d.* per idem breve. Et pro linea tela ad opus eiusdem Andree 12*d.*[15] Et Johanni de Maidenestan[16] pro Adineto le tailur[17] ad empciones regis per ipsum factas inde acquietandas £13 4*s.* per idem breve. Et pro passagio comitisse Hereford in veniendo ad regem ad partes transmarinas 35*s.* 6*d.*[18] Et in expensis Johannis de Canterworth ducentis unum juvencum cum pullo ad reginam Hispanie ex parte regis 13*s.* 4*d.* per diem breve.[19] Et pro conductione unius navis a Sandwico usque Crotheie (?)[20] cariantis xx. dolia vini ex parte regis ad predictam reginam 20*s.* per idem breve. Et pro togagio et treagio, clavis, maeremio ad gistand', et aliis minutis expensis factis circa dicta dolia 10*s.* 4*d.* per idem breve. Et pro expensis Hugonis de Dovor' et garcionis sui custodiencium predicta vina per ij. septimanas 10*s.* per idem breve. Et pro una carecta conducta ad faciendum quemdam conductum versus Graveshende per Othonem de Gransum et alios fideles regis contra coronacionem suam 11s. per idem breve.[21] Et pro una carecta conducta ad cariandum Ricardum de Uffinton' et Rogerum Dringewater usque Lond' 8*s.* per idem breve.[22] Et Petro de Badelesmere et Simoni le Cunte veniendo ad regem in Vasconia in nuncium £6 per idem breve.[23] Et pro passagio dicti Petri in redeundo de Wasconia 7*s.* 1*d.* per idem breve. Et pro passagio Johannis de Vallibus euntis apud Lugdunum per preceptum regis 8*s* per idem breve.[24] Et pro robis predicti Andree de Saukevill' per annum 26*s.* 8*d.* per idem breve. Et pro tribus ulnis panni ad tabardum eiusdem Andree 5*s.* Et pro calligis, sotularibus, linea tela ad opus eiusdem 6*s.* 8*d.* per idem breve.[25] Et pro una roba ad opus Gerardi de sancto Laurencio perhendinantis in eodem castro 40*s.* per idem breve. Et pro vadiis eiusdem Gerardi commorantis in castro predicto cum ij[bus] garcionibus et iiij[or] equis a die Jovis proxima ante

15. Andrew de Sackville, eldest son and heir of Sir Jordan de Sackville, late of Buckhurst, tenant-in-chief, was a minor in the King's wardship, and was evidently lodged in Dover Castle. By June 1275 he had been married, by the king's precept, to Ermintrude, a damsel of Queen Eleanor the king's consort (CPR, *1272-79*, 192).
16. John de Aula of Maidstone, Clerk of the Marshalsea, an office of the king's household.
17. Adam of Bidik, king's tailor and buyer of the wardrobe; see Tout 1920-33, iv, 369, n. l.
18. Maud de Avenbury, second wife of Humphrey de Bohun, Earl of Hereford and Constable of England, *d.* at Sorges in Gascony 8 October, 1273 (G.E.C., *Complete Peerage*, vi, 462).
19. The king's gift of a bull and bull-calf, no doubt certain to be acceptable to a Spanish recipient, was presumably to Blanche of Navarre who in or about December 1275 married, as her second husband, Edward's brother Edmund of Lancaster (cf. Powicke 1953, 238-41).
20. The reading is uncertain; probably Guéthary, on the coast between Biarritz and St. Jean-de-Luz.
21. The sense is "for the hire of a carriage for Sir Otto de Grandison and other friends of the king to drive to Gravesend", whence they would go on by river and be at Westminster in time for the coronation. Otto (for whose life and career see the article by C.L. Kingsford (1909, 125-95) was the king's closest confidant.
22. Roger Drinkwater and Richard of Uffington have not been identified; possibly subordinates of the preceding carriage party (cf. note 32 *infra*).
23. The nature of the mission (*in nuncium*) on which Peter and Simon travelled to Gascony to the king is unknown. Peter was a knight, possibly related to Sir Guncelin de Badlesmere, Justice of Chester, and certainly employed by Stephen de Pencestre on judicial business within the constable's jurisdiction at Sandwich (*CPR 1272-81*, 69). Simon le Counte is well attested as a mason who worked as assistant to the Gascon Master Bertram (Colvin 1963, i, 368 and n.); note that Simon apparently remained behind in Gascony, whereas Peter evidently came straight back.
24. John de Vallibus was one of four proctors appointed on 27 March, 1274 to represent the king at the Council of Lyons (CPR, *1272-81* 46; Powicke 1947, 713 n.).
25. For Andrew de Sackville, see note 15 *supra*.

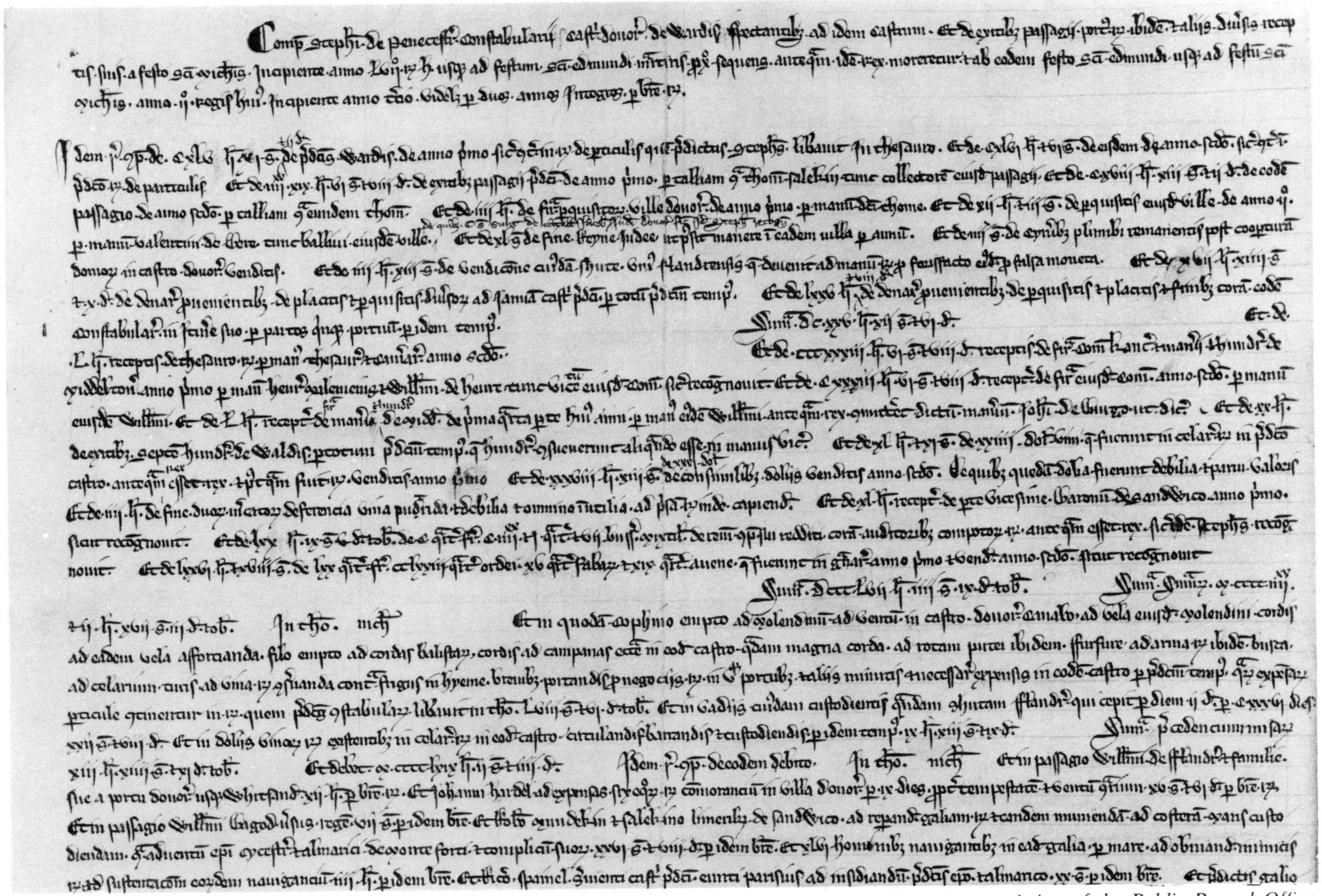

PLATE XVIII

Reproduced by permission of the Public Record Office.

Headings and opening paragraphs of Stephen de Pencestre's account as Constable of Dover Castle for the years 1272–1274 (Pipe Roll, 2 Edward I, E 372/118, rot. 36). (Reduced to 58 per cent).

festum Sancti Barnabe apostoli hoc anno usque diem Sabbati post Gulam Augusti proximo sequentem utraque die computata [7 June— 4 August 1274] 118s. per idem breve.[26] Et pro vadiis Page et Johannis de Barbarie falconariorum regis cum uxore prefati Page, iij^bus garcionibus, tribus equis, a die apostolorum Petri et Pauli anno eodem usque ad predictum diem Sabati [29 June — 4 August 274] 111s. per idem breve. Et pro vadiis predicti de Uffinton' a die Nativitatis Sancti Johannis Baptiste eodem anno usque ad diem Veneris in vigilia exaltacionis Sancte Crucis [24 June — 14 September 1274] 13s. 6d. per idem breve. Et Elie de la Falese et Rogero Dringewater a die Sancti Augustini anno eodem usque diem exaltacionis Sancte Crucis proximo sequentem [28 August — 15 September 1274] 18s. 10d. per idem breve. Et pro expensis prefati Elie a predicta die exaltacionis Sancte Crucis usque festum Sancti Michelis proximo sequens [15-29 September 1274] 2s. 6d. per idem breve. Et pro expensis forincecis circa portum Dovor' £10 per idem breve hoc anno. Et pro expensis predicti Stephani constabularii in eundo apud Mustroil se altero milite pro colloquio inter regem, comitem et comitissam Flandr', morando et redeundo per xix. dies cum passagio suo £10 14s. per idem breve.[27] Et in quodam superplusagio quod idem Stephanus habet in compoto suo reddito et audito coram Johanne de London et Ade de Winton',[28] sicut continetur in quodam rotulo misso ad scaccarium per predictos Johannem et Adam qui est in thesauro et per litteras eorum patentes £121 10s. 5½d. per breve regis. Et pro vadiis unius militis, servientum et vigilum in dicto castro existencium in garnisona anno precedenti £397 7s. 11d. per idem breve. Et pro vadiis eorundem existencium in dicto castro in eadem garnisona hoc anno £331 9s. 2d. per idem breve. Et pro robis eiusdem Stephani, duorum militum et receptoris castri per duos annos, et xiiij servientum equitum, unius atiliatoris balistarum, unius carpentarii, duorum fabrorum anno primo, et decem servientum equitum, predicti atiliatoris, unius carpentarii et unius fabri hoc anno, et xxvij. servientum peditum et xx^ti vigilum per predictos duos annos, et ballivi Dovor' qui fuit proficuator regis hoc anno sals (sic), scilicet pro qualibet roba militis 40s., pro qualibet roba receptoris 20s., pro roba servientis equitis, atiliatoris, carpentarii et fabrorum 13s. 4d., et pro roba servientum peditum 10s., roba vigilis 6s. 8d. et pro roba ballivi Dovor' qui capit robam ut miles 40s., £93 per idem breve. Et pro oblacione et poutura tocius garnisone per iiij dies solempnes in predictis duobus annis de antiqua consuetudine, cum pergameno empto per predictum tempus £4 6s. 5d. per idem breve. Et pro operacionibus castri per predictum tempus £90 9s. 10d. per idem breve. Et pro expensis hospicii eiusdem

---

26. Gerard de St. Laurent was a household knight who accompanied Edward to Palestine, was afterwards with him in Spain (given 20 marks 6 December, 1273, 'ad expensas suas ad nos revertenti ad partes Hispan', C62/49), and whose stay in Dover Castle in June-July 1274 may mean he was assigned special duties in preparation for the king's homecoming. An order (ibid.) to pay him 12 marks arrears of wages 'de tempore quo stetit in servicio nostro in Acon' was made on 8 December, 1273 on the authority of Robert Burnel 'qui a prefato rege mandatum super hoc recepit speciale per litteras ipsius regis patentes'; these letters do not, however, appear to have been enrolled. Later St. Laurent became the first constable of Flint Castle (Colvin 1963, 317, n. 4).

27. For the king's settlement at Montreuil-sur-Mer on 28 July, 1274, of the long-standing commercial and naval quarrel with Flanders, see Powicke 1947, 616 and n. No doubt St. Laurent (preceding note) stood in for Pencestre during his nearly three weeks' absence from Dover, and Pencestre may have accompanied the king on the final triumphal voyage back across the Channel.

28. John of London had been keeper of the wardrobe of Eleanor of Castile (Tout 1920-33, i, 256, n. 2); Adam of Winchester was put in temporary charge of that city as the king's lieutenant during a dispute between the mayor and commonalty (CPR, 1272-81, 60). Cf. n. 12 supra.

constabularii de convencione per idem tempus £293 6s. 8d. per idem breve. Et pro cariagio septuaginta summarum frumenti, xv summarum fabarum, xviij summarum et dimidij avene, CClx et iij summarum ordei de Nunington' et de la Gildeneton' usque ad predictum castrum ad municionem eiusdem 61s. 1d. per idem breve. Et fratribus Domus Dei Dovor' de elemosina regis de exitibus portus Dovor' de ij^bus annis predictis £45 per idem breve. Et pro stipendiis Thome Salekin collectoris passagii Dovor'[29] per idem tempus de convencione 10 marks per idem breve. Et pro passagio fratris Josep de Cauncy thesaurarii regis in veniendo de rege a partibus transmarinis ad partes anglicanas[30] et passagio Roberti Burnel in eundo ad regem et redeundo[31] £9 18s. 4d. per idem breve. Et pro custu Ricardi de Uffinton' et Rogeri Drinkewater et hominum cum armis ipsos conducencium Lond' per preceptum regis 10s.[32] per idem breve. Et pro expensis forincecis dicti constabularii circa custodiam Quinque Portuum anno preterito £10 5s. 4½d. Et pro stipendiis Valentini de Bere ballivi et proficuatoris regis in villa Dovor'[33] £4 per idem breve. Et pro stipendiis captoris prise regis apud Sandwicum per totum predictum tempus £8 per idem breve. Et pro treagio, cartagio et cariagio xxxviij doliorum vini de prisa de Sandwico, de Sandwico usque castrum predictum anno preterito £4 5s. 6d. per idem breve. Et pro treagio, cartagio et cariagio xxxix doliorum vini de eadem prisa a Sandwico usque castrum predictum £4 7s. 9d. per idem breve. Summa misarum per predicta tria brevia £1,511 6s. 1d. Et habet de superplusagio £42 3s. 9d.

Idem Stephanus habet de superplusagio £26 6s. 8d. in rotulo lvj° regis Henrici post residuum Kancie in fine, qui allocantur ei in residuo Kancie in rotulo iij regis Edwardi in compoto suo.[34] Compotus eiusdem Stephani de cameraria Sandwici per idem tempus.

Et pro acquietandis xxviij doliis vini de recta prisa regis apud Sandwicum per totum predictum tempus £28, viz. pro quolibet dolio 20s. de antiqua consuetudine. Et in custu illorum qui traxerunt vina a navi ad terram ibidem et eisdem ponendis in celario regis, et eodem celario conducto, et in oleagio predictorum vinorum, et in doliis predictorum vinorum cuculandis et barrandis per idem tempus 100s.

Summa earundem misarum £33 qui debent allocari ubi voluerit, et aloc' ei in rotulo iij regis in residuo Kancie in fine.

Idem reddit compotum de Ciiij^xx et iij doliis tam de remanencia prise compoti sui redditi coram predictis Johanne et Ade[35] quam de prisa regis ibidem per predictos duos annos sicut continetur in rotulo de particulis quem predictus Stephanus liberavit in thesauro, de quibus in vendicione lv doliorum, et respondit supra de denariis. Et in expensis regis in adventu suo in Angliam xiij dolia per breve regis de predictis brevibus superius allocatis. Et in expensis

29. See n. 7 *supra*.
30. Brother Joseph de Cauncy was Prior of the Order of St. John of Jerusalem in England; the entry may possibly indicate that the king appointed him personally to the treasureship in Gascony at some date before 2 October, 1273, when orders were issued from Westminster for the office to be handed over to him (CClR, *1272-79*, 32).
31. Edward's trusted friend and clerk Robert Burnell, afterwards bishop of Bath and Wells and chancellor of England, was one of those left to guard the realm during Edward's absence oversea (*Powicke 1947*, 583 and n.).
32. Richard of Uffington and Roger Drinkwater remain to be identified, as does the reason for their being sent to London under armed guard or with armed protection (cf. note 22 *supra*).
33. Cf. n. 8; '*profituator regis*', *lit*. 'collector of the king's profits' (see Murray 1935, 5-6).
34. These are references to membranes in the Pipe Rolls of 56 Henry III (1271-2) and 3 Edward I (1274-5).
35. The auditors, John of London and Adam of Winchester.

Beatricis sororis regis in eodem adventu j. dolium.[36] Et in expensis eiusdem constabularii per predictum tempus de convencione x. dolia per ultimum breve superius allocatum. Et Willelmo de Fednes[37] j. dolium per idem breve. Et in expensis Alphulsi filii regis in adventu suo in Angliam j. dolium per idem breve.[38] Et Johanni de Bikenore[39] j. dolium per idem breve. Et in oleagio vinorum existencium in castro Dovor' per totum predictum tempus viij dolia et dimidium.

Summa predictorum doleorum iiij^{xx}x dolia et dimidium. Et remanent in predicto celario castri iiij^{xx}xij dolia et dimidium, de quibus respondit in rotulo sequenti in Kancia (in compoto suo de exitibus Portuum) de xxviij doliis. Et remanent lxiiij dolia et dimidium, de quibus respondit in residuo Kancie in rotulo tercio in fine.

36. There are many references in Pencestre's account to *dolia* or 'tuns' of wine, a 'tun' being the equivalent of 252 old wine-gallons (*Shorter O.E.D.*). Here one may perhaps picture a great reception party in the castle, either in the keep or in 'Arthur's Hall', the excavation of whose remains Stuart Rigold directed in 1967-8 (Rigold 1969, 73-4; Colvin 1963, ii, 636-7), at which 13 tuns were 'expended' on behalf of the king and his household, 1 tun for the household of Edward's sister Beatrice, who may or may not have been accompanied by her husband John of Dreux, Duke of Brittany and Earl of Richmond (G.E.C., *Complete Peerage*, x, 811-14), 1 tun for the household, no doubt already established in embryo, of the infant Alfonso, and 10 tuns for de Pencestre himself.
37. Unfortunately, the single reference to William de Fednes in *CClR 1272-79* does nothing to explain who he was or why he should be favoured with a tun of wine on the present auspicious occasion.
38. Alfonso was only 8 months old, having been born in Gascony on 24 November, 1273; little more than two months later, with the death of his 7-year old brother Henry on 14 October, 1274, he became the king's heir, so remaining until August, 1284, when his own death opened the way for the succession of the then 4-month old Edward of Caernarvon.
39. John de Bickenore and his brother Thomas were two of the king's squires.

BOXLEY ABBEY AND THE *PULPITUM COLLATIONIS*

R. GILYARD-BEER

When one considers the wealth of Cistercian building and documentation that has survived into our own days, it is remarkable that a single abbey of modest size in Kent should provide two pieces of evidence, one structural and the other documentary, for characteristic Cistercian features that are difficult to illustrate elsewhere in so telling a manner. The first of these is the great 'barn' of Boxley Abbey, perhaps the finest surviving specimen in this country of a Cistercian *bâtiment d'exploitation*, as Stuart Rigold recognised (Rigold 1966b, 356-7), combining storage with accommodation for the staff needed for its efficient administration. The second is the subject of this article and is of European import, for Boxley also provides the documentary evidence that establishes beyond reasonable doubt the Cistercian custom of holding the Collation in the cloister alley adjoining the church, and enables its architectural features, rare though they be, to be interpreted on other sites with some confidence.

The ceremony of the Collation goes back to the 42nd chapter of the Rule of St. Benedict. After Vespers the convent was to sit together and listen to a reading before going into the church for Compline, the last Office of the day. The ceremony took its name from the *Collationes* of St. John Cassian, one of the books recommended for the reading. St. Benedict counsels the monks to avoid the historical books of the Bible at this time as being too disturbing for the weaker brethren so soon before bedtime. But apart from its value in settling the minds of the convent before the last Office of the day the Collation served another useful purpose in providing a breathing space during which those monks with special duties, notably the kitchen staff and the guestmaster, could complete their work and rejoin their brethren in time for the full convent to be present at Compline (Delatte 1959, 283-4). From early times it became customary to take a drink during Collation, and Professor Knowles has summarised the development of this into a light meal or 'snack' (Knowles 1949, 457).

The black monks had no fixed place for the Collation. At Abingdon in the thirteenth century (Stevenson 1858, 347) and at Durham in the sixteenth century (Fowler 1903, 86) it was held in the chapter house, and it can be inferred that this was also the case at thirteenth-century Westminster from the fact that, when Collation was finished and the convent had gone to Compline, the church servants were to extinguish the candles in the chapter house (Thompson 1904, 55). In the eleventh-century *Decreta Lanfranci* the ceremony was to begin in the chapter house and continue in the refectory (Knowles 1951, 34-6), whilst fifteenth-century Ramsey held it in the refectory (Thompson 1914, 104).

The white monks did not suffer from this dichotomy, in which the conflicting claims of reading and refreshment were reflected in the use of chapter house and refectory. As might be expected, their *Consuetudines* legislate only for a drink at Collation, for which purpose a monk

PLATE XIX

Cadouin. The abbot's seat in the collation alley.

PLATE XXI

PLATE XX

Melrose. The abbot's seat.

Cleeve. The abbot's seat.

PLATE XXII

Tintern. The abbot's seat.

PLATE XXIII

Tintern. The reader's bay.

PLATE XXIV

Jerpoint. The reader's bay in successive cloisters.

PLATE XXV

Strata Florida. The reader's bay.

PLATE XXVI

Byland. The reader's bay.

PLATE XXVII

Haughmond. The abbot's seat.

was stationed at the refectory door to give any of the brethren admission, an indication itself that the reading was not taking place there (Séjalon 1892, 162). The *Consuetudines* do not say where the reading was to be held, but this was most ingeniously reconstructed by the Marquise de Maillé in 1930 when she pointed out that it can be inferred by collating three passages in the *Consuetudines* (Séjalon 1892, 101-2, 162, 209) which suggest that the Collation was held in the same place as the Maundy and that the Maundy was held in the cloister alley adjoining the church. To this she added evidence from the abbey of Preuilly where, before the rebuilding of the cloister in 1736, Dom Canto recorded that one of the old alleys had been called *de la Collation*, and from the abbey of Noirlac where Abbot Garnier was buried *in parte claustri ecclesiae viciniori dicta collationis* (Maillé 1930, 321-2).

This ingenuity would hardly have been needed had the significance of the Boxley document then been known. The document was published in abstract in 1947 (Atkinson 1947, 157) and in full five years later (Salzman 1952, 448-50), but on both occasions it was treated only on its technical merits as an illustration of medieval building practice and no conclusion about the Collation was drawn from it until 1973 (Tester 1973, 156). It is the well-known contract of 1373 made by the abbot and convent of Boxley with the mason Stephen Lomherst for the rebuilding of their cloister. According to its terms the mason was to build one alley of the cloister each year, the third year being devoted to the alley adjoining the church where he was to build a new processional doorway from cloister to church, insert four new windows in the south aisle no doubt because the more ambitious new alley would mask the old windows, and build a *pulpitum collationis* or lectern for the Collation. Assurance is made doubly sure, so far as the position of the lectern is concerned, by its being referred to in the contract as part of the works on the alley next to the church, and on an endorsement as being in the north alley. The Boxley document therefore replaces hypothesis by certainty.

Turning now to the structural evidence one finds that, just as the most telling documentary evidence comes from England, so the British Isles provide the greatest number of surviving examples of Cistercian cloisters equipped for the Collation. Indeed only two examples can be cited from the Continent, although one of them is the most informative of all. This is at the Cistercian abbey of Cadouin in the Dordogne where the cloister was rebuilt in 1468 under Abbot Pierre de Gaing by the same masons who built the cloister of Cahors Cathedral. The north alley at Cadouin has a stone bench along the church wall and, in the centre of this, an elaborate stone chair bearing the arms of the abbey and of Pierre de Gaing (Plate XIX). Opposite the chair, in a small recess in the alley wall, is a low stone seat. Here, then, is the essential furniture for the Collation: the bench on which the convent sat against the church wall, with the abbot's throne at its centre and the reader's seat facing him across the alley. Only the lectern, the *pulpitum* itself, is missing, perhaps because it was made of wood, and the rarity of these features on other sites is no doubt due to the same reason. For instance it is known that at the great Cistercian abbey of Alcobaça in Portugal the abbot of Piedra on visitation in 1484 ordered that a stone bench with wooden seat and wainscot back should be made in the Collation alley and a chair provided opposite it (Aubert 1943, ii, 23).

The only other Continental example, apart from benches along the church wall which are common to most of the Orders in all countries and not peculiar to the ceremony of the Collation, is at the abbey of Flines-lès-Roches in the Département du Nord, where a half-hexagonal bay projected into the cloister garth from the centre of the Collation alley, to give the reader more light (Dimier 1949, ii, Pl. 114).

Against this the British Isles can provide six examples, of which two are in England, two in Wales, one in Scotland and one in Ireland.

At Cleeve Abbey in Somerset (Plate XX) there is a shallow thirteenth-century ashlar recess with trefoiled head and coved back, set in the centre of the church wall facing into the vanished north alley of the cloister, intended as an architectural frame for the abbot's chair.

At Melrose Abbey in Roxburghshire (Plate XXI) the church wall facing the alley has a stone bench beneath continuous blind arcading. The central arch of this arcade is treated more elaborately than the rest, a decorative emphasis that again marks the abbot's seat.

Tintern Abbey in Monmouthshire provides some evidence not only for the abbot's seat but also for the reader's station. The former (Plate XXII) is in the centre of the church wall facing the cloister, where there are remains of an arched recess now robbed of its dressed stone but representing a stone chair of some elaboration. Opposite it there are slight remains of a rectangular projection into the cloister garth (Plate XXIII) interpreted in the past as the base for a water cistern but on the analogy of Flines and the examples given below more likely to have supported a bay to give the reader more light.

The early cloister associated with the twelfth-century church of Jerpoint Abbey in County Kilkenny (Plate XXIV) has midway in its length the foundations of a rectangular bay projecting into the garth and no doubt intended to house the reader and his lectern, and it is interesting to see that when the south aisle of the nave was pulled down and a new cloister alley was built on its site in the fifteenth century it was provided with an exactly similar bay (Leask 1955-6, ii, 31-2).

Strata Florida Abbey in Cardiganshire (Plate XXV) also has a reader's bay in the same position, this time a shallow half-octagon.

Finally, Byland Abbey in Yorkshire (Plate XXVI) has a rectangular bay in the same place, but here interpretation is less certain because the south wall of the bay is missing and the possibility that it was a porch leading into the garth cannot be ruled out.

The Byland example is a useful reminder that not all bays projecting into the cloister garth were necessarily connected with the Collation. Their position usually enables them to be distinguished from other similar features, for instance from the lavers housed in centrally-planned pavilions intruding on to the garth near the refectory, for which there is evidence at about a dozen sites in Britain, or from the rectangular bay in front of the chapter house entrance at Croxden Abbey which was probably a porch. The thirteenth-century cloister of the Augustinian priory at Norton had a rectangular bay in the middle of each of its four alleys and in a sixteenth-century rebuilding these were kept but were remodelled as half-octagons. They are more likely to have been an architectural embellishment than to have served any practical purpose (Thompson and Greene 1970-2, plans).

In the same way, outside the Cistercian Order seats in the cloister are not necessarily connected with the Collation. Being the usual place for study in several Orders the alley next to the church was often provided with a stone bench, and where a position on this is emphasised, as it is at Lindisfarne Priory by two crude arm-rests, it is likely to mark the prior's place as supervisor of these activities. Accident produced a similar state of affairs at Dryburgh Abbey, where a recess in the north alley seems at first glance a suitable place for a seat but is in fact an early western processional doorway from cloister to church, blocked when the nave was lengthened and a new doorway provided father west.

One exception may be allowed. Evidence from several sources suggests that during the first century of their existence the Augustinian canons of Haughmond Abbey in Shropshire were following customs that were unusually austere but that did not ally them formally to the Arrouaisian or Victorine Congregations of their Order. Near the centre of the church wall facing the cloister at this abbey one jamb remains of a fairly elaborate thirteenth-century chair recess (Plate XXVII). Haughmond may have been holding its Collation in the north alley of the cloister and this, like the white habit its canons continued to wear until 1234, may have been a sign of unusually strong Cistercian influence on its customs.

To return to Boxley, the contract of 1373 leaves no doubt of the intention to rebuild the cloister alley adjoining the church and to equip it for the Collation. It also makes clear that the work was to proceed in sequence round the cloister, the south alley being built in the first year of the contract and the north alley in the third. But the survival of a contract does not prove that the work specified in it was actually carried out. Medieval patrons of building were as liable as modern ones to change their minds and there are signs that this was the case at Boxley. Nor does the mason Stephen Lomherst appear to have been an easy man with whom to transact business, to judge by his later career at Otford (Clarke and Stoyel 1975, 87-8). The document itself shows that the contracting parties were having second thoughts, for it is endorsed with a brief note stating that although it includes the making of a lectern in the north alley this is not to hold good unless it becomes the subject of a new contract. Moreover, recent excavation has revealed that both the width and the footings of the north and west alleys differ from those of the south and east, suggesting that the rebuilding was never completed (Tester 1973, 135).

This evidence suggests that it was the north and west alleys that were rebuilt and that the old south and east alleys were retained, but it is not conclusive and the possibility may still exist that Boxley Abbey, having provided the best documentary evidence amongst the Cistercians for a specially designed Collation alley, may ironically enough never have achieved its ambition.

ACKNOWLEDGEMENTS

I am indebted to the late Mr G.E. Chambers, for his photograph of Cadouin, to Dr. A.J. Taylor, for his photograph of Jerpoint, and to Mr P.J. Tester, for providing details of his excavation and for drawing my attention to Stephen Lomherst's later quarrelsome career.

MEOPHAM: THE PARISH CHURCH OF ST. JOHN THE BAPTIST

H. GORDON SLADE

It is ironical that this paper was the subject of discussion between Stuart Rigold and myself only a few weeks before his death, whilst walking one evening round the Garrison Walls on the Isles of Scilly. I have tried to bear in mind his comments as I remember them and to incorporate his suggestions. It is offered as a tribute to the memory of a generous and profound scholar.

Although described by Hasted as 'a large handsome building', Meopham Church has at first sight little beyond size to recommend it: dark, cold and pauperised, and, until recently, sadly neglected, it is nevertheless one of the largest and most interesting churches in the diocese of Rochester, with a building history of considerable complexity, and examples of window tracery which were a source of great interest to early nineteenth-century antiquaries.

The church, which measures some 140 ft. in length, comprises a large western tower, an aisled and clerestoried nave of five bays, with north and south porches placed centrally, a chancel of three bays and a north chapel. The tower, nave and chancel are buttressed; the roofs of the nave and chancel are high pitched and tiled, those of the aisles low pitched and covered with some patent modern material. The walls are of flint rubble with an admixture of stone, brick and tile, and were formerly rendered. The older dressed work is generally of clunch or Kentish rag, the new is of various stones each one less sympathetic than the last.

The earliest reference to a church at Meopham is contained in the *Domesday Monachorum* (Douglas 1944), and it is possible that there may have been a pre-Conquest church here. The mention in Domesday and in the chrism list in *Textus Roffensis* (Ward 1932) point strongly to a pre-Conquest origin but there is no proof of this. Unfortunately, in the testament of Byrhtric and his wife, Elfswithes, 973-87, which is transcribed by Lambarde from the *Textus*, there is mention that amongst the witnesses at Meopham there was one Wyne the Priest. This is often taken to mean, that he was the parish priest of Meopham, and that therefore Meopham had a parish church. The second assumption relies on the truth of the first for which there is no evidence whatsoever. Equally shaky is the supporting argument that because Meopham belonged to the Archbishop and the Priory of Christ Church there must have been a church because it would have been provided.

The only thing that seems clear is that by the Conquest the religious establishment of Christ Church, Canterbury, held the manor of Meopham. The earliest grant seems to have been made by Eadwulf in 940 which was in fact his own grant of land from King Athelstane. More land came from Queen Eadgitha, the widow of Edward the Elder and a Kentish heiress, *c.* 960 and in 973-87, there was the gift of land by Byhtric. Finally, there were the blanket confirmations of the lands of Christ Church by Ethelred and Edward the Confessor. Some of these charters have been doctored, some are dubious, and some downright forgeries, but no doubt like the 'Donations of Constantine' they served their turn.

What is clear is that until the time of Archbishop Lanfranc the possession of Meopham by Canterbury had meant possession by the Archbishop *and* the monks; but, sometime around 1086, Lanfranc divided the estates of Canterbury between the See and the Priory, and in the course of the division Meopham fell to the latter.

From the architectural evidence it is clear that Meopham was re-built on a large scale during the early thirteenth century. Of this rebuilding there remain the lower stage of the west tower, the south-east and north-east angles of the nave and, possibly although this is not certain, the lower walls of aisles.

The next building phase for which there is documentary evidence comes in the first quarter of the fourteenth century. This is a commission from Archbishop Reynolds to dedicate the Church of Meopham:

> 'Walter, etc, to the venerable brother in the Lord [Peter] by the grace of God Bishop of Corbavia, health and brotherly love in the Lord.
> To dedicate in canonical form the parish church of Mepham in our immediate jurisdiction in the Deanery of Shoreham, newly constructed; and to do all other things known to the pontifical office in this behalf, by the tenor of those present we commit unto you full authority. In witness whereof, etc. Given at Mortelake ii Id Maii, Anno Dni millio ccmd xxvto.
> (Ex Register. Abp. Reynolds, folio 135)

Architecturally this accords conveniently with the nave arcades and clerestory, and supports the tradition that Archbishop Simon of Meopham returned in his greatness to lavish largesse on the home of his youth (except for the fact that he was not Archbishop at the time). This legend derives largely from Lambarde:

> 'It is probable also that the same Bishop [Simon] builte the Church of Mepham, for the use of the poore, which William Courtney (one of his successours) repaired, fower score yeeres after. . .'

Archbishop Simon did not ascend to the Chair of Saint Augustine until 1328. He was archbishop for barely five years, the earlier part being spent in ecclesiastical and political folly, and the last in excommunicate idleness.

Lambarde in turn may have had in mind the foundation of a chantry in the Chapel of St. James le Dene founded by Simon de Meopham — and others — and dedicated in 1327, two years after the dedication '*de novo constructam*'. The legend would appear to have a circumstantial base at least.

What is not at all clear is to what the commission is referring. The words used are '*de novo constructam*' which would seem to be fairly definite and would agree with the building evidence. On the other hand, the commission is to *dedicate*, not to *consecrate*. Canon Wigan, in correspondence, suggests that the words should be taken in a canonical rather than an architectural sense, and argues that re-dedication implies minor works or renewals, whereas had the walls been much affected re-consecration would have been necessary (Gregory IX, Decr. III, tit. xl cap. 6). However, the architectural evidence does argue that the arcades date from the first quarter of the century, and clearly the walls were affected to the point of almost complete renewal. On balance, the building wins by a short head over canon law.

The next documentary date which marches with the building evidence is 1385-86. On 17

November, Archbishop Courtney restored the rectory (that is the office, not the house) to the priory. The rectory had formerly been appropriated to Christ Church, Canterbury, but this had been misappropriated by Archbishop Baldwin (1185-1190). By Courtney's action the monks again became corporately the rector, but the presentation of the vicar rested with the archbishop, and the parish remained in his immediate jurisdiction. Probably to mark this and to put a seal upon the resumption of their rectorial duties the monks beautified the chancel with a new reredos, fragments of which still remain.

Again there is no evidence for archiepiscopal involvement and Philpot's claim in *Vilare Cantianum* that 'Courtney rebuilded the church, which by the onsets of time was shrunk into Delapidation and Rubbis. . .' — which seems to be based on Lambarde — should be discounted.

Further work was undertaken in the mid-fifteenth century when the north and south porches were added, the aisles largely rebuilt and the chancel roof repaired. This seems to have been the last major work carried out before the Reformation.

Because of the disappearance of the first volume of the church wardens' accounts around 1900 our knowledge of the work done before 1789 is based almost entirely on notes made from the missing volume by the Rev. Lewis Woodward Lewis who was vicar from 1875 to 1900.

The great and disastrous restoration of 1858 at the cost of some £1185 left the church much as it is today although work continued for the rest of the nineteenth century and well into the twentieth. Much of this work was unnecessary and nearly all of it injudicious.

c. 1200-1270

The earliest visible parts of the church, which probably date from the first quarter of the thirteenth century are the angles of the nave, the lower part of the tower, particularly the west wall up to the springing of the tower arch, and possibly the lower parts of the aisle walls. The evidence for this is clear. On examination of the tower arch it can be seen that this is of two distinct periods: the main arch with its half-octagonal responds, moulded caps and square-chamfered arch is of the same date as the nave arcades, but it is set into an earlier opening to which it is, apparently, not bonded. This earlier opening is straight-sided with chamfered angles, at the top and bottom of which are steep pyramid stops. The caps are plain blocks with a lower chamfer. Above the caps the wall has been rebuilt, and is only the thickness of the later arch. A similar detail is found in the east respond of the south arcade of the nave. Here again the half-octagonal respond of the later work has been built against, but not bonded to, an earlier straight face, which has the chamfered angle and pyramid stop of the earlier tower arch.

This suggests that the nave arcades of the early church consisted not of arches carried on piers or columns, but rather of solid walls pierced by a series of arched openings. Usually this type of construction is associated with the enlargement of small aisleless buildings by the addition of aisles. Had the nave at Meopham been smaller one would have suggested that it was a thirteenth-century alteration to an eleventh- or twelfth-century church, but the scale of the nave which would have been large for that period in Kent argues against this. An alternative argument can be advanced; the nave, as built in the thirteenth century, was without aisles, and that the opening at the south-east end of the south wall led into a cross aisle.

A church, although on a smaller scale, which exhibits this detail in its tower and chancel (and presumably originally in its now much altered nave) is at Ash, only a few miles away, and similar very simple work can be seen elsewhere in Kent, at Lower Halstow near Sittingbourne, and at Harty on the Isle of Sheppey.

The building of this very large nave before renewing the chancel suggests that it replaced an earlier building of which the chancel was still sufficiently serviceable to wait until the needs of the laity had been satisfied.

Although it is not possible to date precisely the chancel and north-east chapel, the building of which seems on stylistic evidence to cover the years 1240-1265, the sequence of building is in no doubt. First to be built c. 1265 was the chancel. This was of three bays, the bays being marked externally by buttresses, with pairs of angle buttresses at the east end. The western-most buttress on the south side is curiously built against the east wall of the south aisle, but quite independent of it. It is not essential on architectural grounds to have a buttress here as it makes for a clumsy junction between the aisle and chancel. It may indicate an intention, never carried out, to vault the chancel. If this were the intention a buttress would be needed at this point to provide abutment as the chancel wall is not tied into the south-east angle of the nave.

The side windows, of which there are three of this period, two being on the south side, are of the simplest and earliest form of bar tracery and preserve their original form, although considerably and crudely restored. This is of two large uncusped lancets surmounted by quatrefoiled roundel. The form and mouldings are so simple that a date not long after 1240 would be reasonable, especially when the east window of the north chapel is considered, for, though later than the chancel window, it is still early in form.

Within the chancel there is a simple moulded string course running along all three walls. On the south side it acts as a cill to the windows and as a hood mould to the priest's door and the piscina. Before the insertion of the present reredos it rose across the east wall to form the cill for the east window. On the north wall it again forms the cill of the window, dropping to a lower level further west. Unfortunately, the change in level was destroyed when a later door was cut to give access to the north chapel. Where the string has been cut to allow for the introduction of the fourteenth-century reredos this has been most carefully done, the moulding being repaired and returned to the wall.

Although the chancel was designed to be free-standing this has been masked by the building of the north chapel shortly after its completion. This is shown clearly by the relation of the east wall of the chapel to the buttress behind which it joins the chancel; originally, the buttress was free-standing, and on building the chapel it was obviously easier to make the junction between the chapel and chancel against a straight wall than on the sloping offsets of the buttress.

The tracery of the east window of the chapel, which was unblocked and very clumsily repaired in 1874, is now in need of extensive restoration. Nevertheless, it is of the most interesting character and has been cited as an example of early work (Bond 1905, 510; Brandon 1844-47, i, 21, Pl. 21). Its distinctive quality is that the cusping of the tracery springs from the soffit and not from the chamfer plane of the arch, and this is generally regarded as an indication of an early date. Another characteristic of early work is that all the cusps (or more properly foils or lobes) of the trefoils or quatrefoils are parts of equal circles cutting another circle inscribed within them. Both these indicators are to be seen in this window. A further sign of an early date is to be seen in the unequal height and width of the three lancets. This suggests that the designer still saw the window as a triple lancet with superadded tracery.

As originally planned there seems to have been no connection between the chancel and the chapel, both the squint and the doorway being later openings. The arch between the chapel and the north aisle of the nave is a clumsy piece of fifteenth-century work, and whilst it may well replace an earlier opening it could just as easily be a forced opening in a solid wall. This could be corroboration of the theory that the thirteenth-century nave was aisleless. None of the foregoing throws any light, however, on the reason for building a chapel which does not appear originally to have had any means of access to the adjoining church.

An odd feature is the stone drain which carries away the water from the valley between the roof of the chapel and that of the chancel. It is of stone, and built in the thickness of the wall. This was probably because the position of the buttress on the north side of the chancel precluded any other form of outlet that was satisfactory.

Some ten years after the building of the north chapel a new east window was provided for the chancel. What is not clear is whether this was intended from the first but not completed, or whether it replaced an earlier window with tracery in keeping with the side windows of the chancel. Although largely rebuilt in 1874, it seems in its present form to be a careful restoration and follows closely the design shown in Brandon's *Analysis*.

The composition of the east window, which shows a developed form of intersecting arched tracery repays careful study. At its simplest this tracery is nothing but the mullions — a minimum of two being necessary — extended to the head of the window by arcs of the same radius as the head. It was a fashion which never seems to have achieved wide popularity in England, or if it did it was largely and more elaborately replaced by later builders. In Ireland, where it is known as *Switchline* tracery, and in Scotland it remained popular and widespread until the end of the medieval period, one of the largest and latest examples being the east window of the Greyfriars Kirk, Aberdeen, 1518-1532.

The Meopham east window consists of three lights with the mullions extended to the window head in the manner before described. Each of the lancets so formed has a sub-head that in contrast to the acutely pointed main head is based on *equilateral tracery* where the radius of the head is equal to the width of the light. The space between the two heads is filled with a roundel with inverted trefoil cusping, and between the upper heads of the three lancets are quartrefoiled roundels. The head of the window is slightly more acute than an equilateral arch but the difference is so small that it may be a constructional error rather than a designed intention.

As in the tracery of the east window of the chapel the chancel window shows *soffit cusping*. It is to all intents and purposes a decorative addition which could be removed without impairing the structure at all, and the design only a little. Internally, the window is enriched with a moulded rere-arch and label, and with nook-colonettes with foliated capitals.

c. 1325

The next building period would seem to date from the last years of the first quarter of the fourteenth century, and involved a complete reconstruction of the nave and aisles together with new tower and chancel arches.

In the nave the existing heavy piers, or walls, were demolished, leaving only a fragment of the south-east corner visible. In the place of the destroyed work arcades of five bays were erected, the five arches on each side being carried by four octagonal columns and two half-octagonal responds. The columns have simple moulded capitals and bases with standard early fourteenth-century profiles. The arches are not moulded but consist of two orders, each order being square-chamfered. The tower and chancel arches are equally simple, but at the west end

PLATE XXVIII

Meopham Church from the south-east (Petrie Collection 243 KAS)

of the nave it can be seen that the fourteenth-century arch, with its responds, has been set within the early thirteenth-century opening, the sides of which were retained to the level of the springing. Above that level the thirteenth-century work was destroyed and the new arch set back from the earlier wall face.

The nave clerestory consists of four quatrefoiled roundels. This is not a widely used form but did occur in a number of fourteenth-century churches — Cley-next-the-Sea, Waltham Abbey, Great Walsingham being amongst them. The position of the windows above the spandrels of the arcades, and not above the apex of the arches, is awkward visually as it punctuates the wall at the point where weight should appear to be concentrated. Structurally, it prevents the roof being designed with wall posts to the main trusses. Clerestory roundels in a similar position above the spandrels were found at Filby in Norfolk (Brandon 1848). As the cusping and glass of these windows were renewed in 1868 at the cost of £21 19s. 0d. their present form may only be an approximation to their original state.

At the same time the aisles were either re-built or built with large windows, narrower and with lower cills than those existing now, and with steeply sloping roofs. The corbels for carrying the wall plates above the arcades still remain at a lower level than the present aisle roofs. Above the easternmost arch of the south aisle are two corbels at a slightly different level to and more closely spaced than the others. The reason for this is not clear, but a possible explanation is that the south wall of this bay was carried up as a gable, with its ridge at right-angles to the clerestory wall. These two corbels would then have provided the seating for the purlins of the roof so formed.

This massive rebuild fits so well in style with a date 1320-25 that it is difficult to avoid the conclusion that it is the work *de novo constructam* of the 1325 dedication.

c. 1385

If the monks of Christ Church marked their re-appropriation of the rectory and great tithes with some building work this must be looked for in the chancel which was their responsibility. The structure of the chancel clearly antedates the year of resumption — 1385 — but there was an addition to it which would fit with such a theory.

This was the provision of a new reredos, and the apparent re-ordering of the chancel on sub-collegiate lines. In the chancel as originally built the altar had stood against the east wall. The original piscina — which is designed so that the thirteenth-century string course acts as its hood mould — and aumbry show this clearly. In the alteration of *c.* 1385 the altar was moved westward and set in front of a stone reredos. Only the two side jambs of this remain, but they show that it consisted of a central section with two flanking doors. As far as can be seen from the remaining jambs the design of the screen was based on two tiers of cusped panels surmounted by crocketted canopies. The workmanship is of a thoroughly competent standard, and suggests that the screen was ordered from one of the London workshops. In order to accommodate the screen, the thirteenth-century string course had to be cut. This was done with great care, the moulding being returned to the wall on both sides of the screen. At the same time a new piscina was formed below the east jamb of the south-east window to serve the new altar. The space between the screen and the east wall presumably served as a sacristy. A somewhat more elaborate arrangement of a screen forward of the east wall seems to have existed at the neighbouring church at Cobham.

c. 1450

The next major alterations at Meopham took place in the fifteenth century; in the archives of Christ Church there is a record of work carried out to the chancel roof in 1451-52, and as the style of the alterations fits well with this date, it is perhaps safe to assume that the mid-century saw the church being given a fairly thorough overhaul.

The account for the repairs to the chancel was transcribed by R.C. Hussey in 1875:

> 'paid to John Benet for 4000 plain tiles bought of him for the covering of the chancel of the church there, with the carriage at 4*s*. 4*d*. a thousand; 17*s*. 4*d*.: and paid for two quarters 4 bushels of quick lime, bought of the same John for the work of the afore-said chancel, 2*s*. And paid for 3 cartloads of sand bought of John Joskyn at 5*d*. a cartload (curteria); 15*d*. And paid to Richard Elrede, tiles, for tiling the said chancel according to agreement made with him for the job (*ad tascam*) 12*s*. And paid for mending the glass of a chancel window, 20*d*.
> Sum 34*s*. 3*d*.

A comparison with present day prices is interesting: this work would now cost in the region of £4,000.

Apart from the work on the chancel roof, alterations were made to the north chapel, north and south porches were added, the nave aisles were re-fenestrated and given raised wall heads with parapets.

The most curious alterations are those affecting the north chapel. As has been noticed

Meopham Church: East window (Brandon).

PLATE XXX

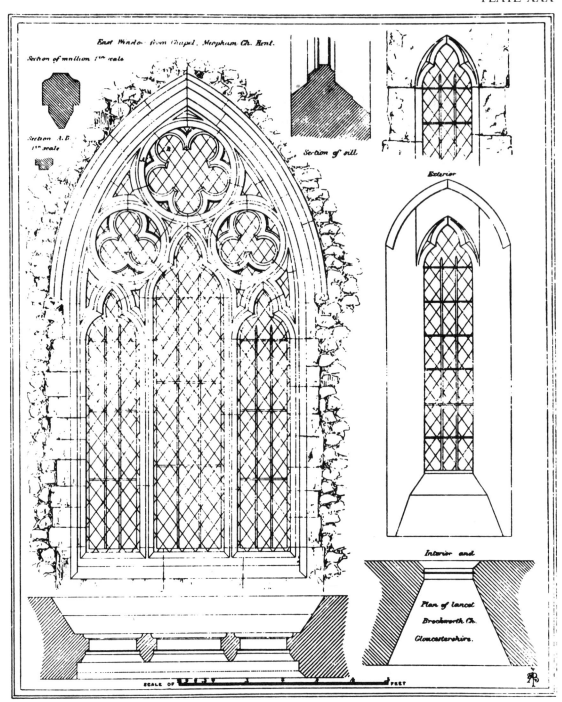

Meopham Church: East window of north chapel (Brandon).

before where the string course in the chancel has been cut to allow for the fourteenth-century reredos the moulding has been returned to the wall, but where it has been cut to allow for the door between the chapel and the chancel there has been no attempt to do this. The position of the doorway at the change in level of the string, the fact that the string does not act as a hood mould or label to the doorway, together with the clumsiness of the break suggest not only that the door is late, but also that until the mid-fifteenth century there was no opening or access between the chancel and the chapel. The arch between the chapel and the north aisle is equally clumsy, and appears to have been broken through an earlier solid wall. This suggests that before *c.* 1452 the chapel was intended for private use, and entered only through the doorway in the north wall. A private chapel in this position is not unusual — and later many became manorial pews — but usually there would have been some opening into the chancel.

Whatever its use, however, before 1452 the reason for linking the chapel with the chancel appears to be connected with the provision of the rood loft. Stairs were cut to give access to the loft in the north-west angle of the east wall of the nave. The fact that the chancel was not on the central axis of the nave, but offset to the south made it possible to do this without disturbing the north respond of the chancel arch, and a straight flight was formed in the thickness of the wall between the chapel and the loft.

At the same time as the stairs were formed, a squint was cut in the chancel wall immediately to the east of the stair foot. The purpose of this squint is puzzling; it gives a view from the foot of the stairs to the high altar in its position in front of the fourteenth-century reredos. Even if it were true that squints were necessary to allow for the elevation of host to be synchronised between the various altars this particular squint would not serve that purpose; and in any case the belief in the synchronization of elevations is something of a mare's nest. A more likely explanation is that at some point in the service it was necessary for the action at the high altar to be visible from the foot of the stairs to the rood loft. There is no sign of an external sacring bell on the east gable of the nave which might have been rung from this position, so possibly it was a means of relaying the action of the priest at the altar to the singers in the loft: this of course pre-supposes a solid tympanum in the archway above the loft and without squints.

The loft of the screen, which has been destroyed, would have been at the level of the springing of the chancel arch. This level is low in relation to the height of the arch, and would have allowed ample space for the rood beam carrying the great rood. A fragment of a carved beam of late-medieval design, and said to be part of the rood beam was still lying in the church in 1936, but it has since disappeared.

At the same time as the screen and loft were erected it is likely that provision would have been made for choir stalls. No traces of these remain, but during the incumbency of Mr Hooper, 1854-75, the chancel was repaired, and in the course of the work a wall was found within the chancel running parallel to the south wall for some 16 ft. and set a few feet in from it. Although this could have been the remains of an earlier chancel, it is more likely to have been the stone sub-structure of the fifteenth-century choir stalls.

The single light trefoiled ogee-headed window in the south-east corner of the chancel must also date from this period. The purpose of these 'High and Low Side Windows' has been the subject of a good deal of esoteric discussion. They were for lepers; they were for anchorites; they were for travellers or the excommunicated to see and hear Mass without entering the church; they were for hearing confessions; they were for ringing the sacring bell; they were to provide light for the priest. Some of these may be valid reasons in some places, but none is a suitable explanation for such a window at Meopham.

In the first place, it is not a true 'High and Low Side Window', it is of the same height and at the same level as the main lights in the earlier window. In the second place, the windows in the chancel at Meopham are large and the light is generous. However, there is another likely explanation. It is possible that the screen (or inner screen) was set well into the chancel beyond the arch, and hard against the jamb of the first thirteenth-century side window. The space, thus created, would be sufficiently deep to contain two altars, flanking the entrance to the chancel without intruding into the nave. This space if ceiled over would have been extremely dark, and even if not ceiled additional light would have been welcome. The aumbry in the cill of this window would therefore relate to the altar on the south side. If there were a double screen at Meopham, projecting into the chancel, ceiled by a deep loft, and providing space for two altars it would become to all intents and purposes a *pulpitum*. Such an arrangement together with the free-standing reredos would have given Meopham a quasi-collegiate plan.

Somewhat similar arrangements exist, or existed at Chislehurst and East Malling in Kent, and Shelsey Walsh in Worcestershire, where there are chantries surviving to the west of the screen. A more developed example at Guilden Morden, Cambridgeshire, shows what was virtually a double screen, which may have been ceiled completely by the loft; and at Compton Basset, Wiltshire, there is an elaborate double stone screen with a deep loft.

The rebuilding of the aisles is clearly seen externally. The original steeply pitched roofs were removed and the wall heads raised. These were finished with flint parapets above a stone string course; this arrangement is best seen on the west walls of the aisles. At the same time buttresses were added; the evidence for there having been none before is that it is only in their upper courses that the buttresses are built in with the aisle walls — that is into the fifteenth-century heightening. The lower parts are built against the earlier walls. The aisle windows were also replaced; the new ones being wider, and with higher cills than the originals, the cills of which can still be seen in the walls below. The tracery of the aisle windows is of standard mid-fifteenth-century design, consisting of three principal cinquefoilded lights with the mullions rising to the upper arched head. The space above the main lights is subdivided into small trefoiled lights — a system now known as *Supermullioned Tracery with Split Y*. All the stonework of the windows is much restored.

The porches are basically mid-fifteenth-century, with small single light side windows, and the mains of moulded timber roofs. They have been much decayed and repaired, and the squared flints on the south porch are probably an eighteenth-century restoration.

Little remains of the pre-Reformation fittings of the church, and that little is generally fragmentary. The most complete survival is the font, octagonal with a simply mouded base, and traceried panels in low relief on the slightly concave sides of the bowl.

Some fragments of medieval glass survive re-set in a window in the south aisle. These are of a somewhat kaleidescopic nature and include two figures: one a palpable St. Catherine, the other an archbishop, said on the slenderest evidence to be St. Thomas à Becket. Apparently much more survived until its destruction in the course of restoration during the last century.

Apart from the piscina and aumbries in the chancel there is nothing to mark the positions of any other altars in the church. However, others are known to have existed — at least by implication as there are references to two chapels.

The earliest reference is found in a licence granted on 25 March, 1327, to Edward and Simon de Mepeham, and John de la Dene, for the alienation of:

'a messuage, two mills, 25 acres of land, 4 acres of meadow, 2 acres of wood, and a rent of 35s., in East Malling, Birling, Northfleet, Meopham and Hoo, to Chaplain to celebrate divine service daily in the Chapel of St James la Dene in the parish church of Meopham; for the souls of Joan de la Dene, Edmund de Mepham, Simon de Mepham and John de la Dene, their parents, relations and benefactors.
(CPR Edward III, 1327-30, p. 30)

Three months later Archbishop Reynolds issued a commission to his suffragan, the Bishop of Corbavia to dedicate the Chapel of la Dene, and its altar (Reg. Reynolds f. 154).

A Lady Chapel is recorded in 1542 when Richard Ardene asked in his will that *'My body be buryed in the chapell of Our Ladye wtin the pyshe churche of Seynt John Baptist in Meopham.'*

The existence of statues in the church did not necessarily mean that there would be an associated altar but the small figure of St. Catherine in glass, and the bequest in 1525 of William Sprever of Dartford that there should be given *'Also to the lighting of St Katheryn in the same church XII pence'* suggests that there may have been an altar dedicated to St. Catherine.

It was probably the same William Sprever who had given an obit rent that a yearly obit should be kept in the church for ever — *'The same rente is by the yere vjs viij d. werof to the pore there is ij s vj d and so remaineth clere iiij s ij p'.* With the suppression of chantries and obits from 1547 the messuage which provided the rent for this was sold.

There was also still surviving in 1809, according to the *Gentleman's Magazine* of June of that year, the remains of the rood screen and a statue of St. Peter.

A feature which has not been touched on so far, and which is difficult to explain is the triangular headed opening in the wall above the chancel arch. It is not accessible for close inspection but appears to be rebated for either a door or a shutter. It may have had some connection with the rood, but a more likely use was to have provided a means of access into the roof space above the chancel. If this is a correct interpretation it may be a further indication that the chancel was vaulted.

The only surviving medieval monument remaining is in the sanctuary — a small brass plate, 3in. high by 15 in. long on which is a Latin inscription, the translation of which reads,

'Here lies Master John Folsham, formerly Vicar of Meopham, who died on the 13th day of June in the year 1455, on whose soul God have mercy. Amen'.

It was moved to the chancel from the floor of the tower in 1905 but its original position is not known. There is also the stone indent of a brass, which was set in the floor in front of the altar in 1859. The brass had disappeared but it, too, had a Latin inscription which was recorded in 1769, and, translated, read:

'I believe that in the last day I shall rise again from the earth and in my flesh shall I see God my Saviour. This faith is buried in my bosom'

From the sentiments expressed this would seem to be post-medieval.

At Harty Church in Sheppey there was a table which incorporated various pieces of fifteenth-century tracery and carving. These came traditionally from Meopham and may have formed part of the screen wainscot. Mr Lewis who became vicar of Meopham in 1875 had previously been incumbent of Harty; possibly he gave these pieces (or the table itself) to his old parish.

Post-medieval

Two pictures survive of Meopham church as it was at the end of the eighteenth and beginning of the nineteenth centuries. One of 1807, from the south-east, in the Petrie collection (243) and the other from the north-east, in a collection of views (*Topographica Cantiana*, v, K.A.S. Library). Apart from the heightening of the tower in 1837 there has been little apparent change externally. Before the raising, the tower was covered by a high and steeply-pitched double-hip cap or helm: in the 1807 picture there appear to be louvred panels in the sides of the lower hips. These together with the size of the cap indicate that it contained the bell chamber.

In all the windows the tracery is much as it is today — in fact considerable trouble has been taken in both drawings to render the tracery as accurately as possible. The aisles had already lost their parapets. It is clear that subsequent restorers have striven to preserve the form of the old building even if its spirit was lost. The only external feature which has disappeared is a small two-light window which had been introduced into the south clerestory between the first and second roundels.

Of the post-medieval work at Meopham that done between 1560 and 1810 was mostly of a straightforward nature concerned largely with maintenance, and very little of it survives to-day. Perhaps the most interesting item is the work carried out on the bells between 1648 and 1655 — a period when this sort of expenditure and effort might not have been expected. The Churchwardens' Accounts for this period have been lost but fortunately Mr Lewis Lewis, a former vicar of Meopham, had copied the entries relating to the bells. From his notes it is not clear whether the bells were completely new, or a re-casting of the medieval bells. There had been earlier bells, as in his will of 1517 Thomas Taylor of Ridley, who was buried at Meopham, left '*To the reparation of the church of Mepham XXd. To the reparacion of the Steple and belles there XXd.*'

An old story recorded in Hasted (iii, 365) suggests that the medieval bells were re-cast:

> 'Within the memory of several antient people of this parish some of the bells of this church being to be new cast, and these being wanting a sufficient quantity of metal to do it, some persons tore off the brass inscriptions from the stones in the church, except that of Folham above mentioned, and threw them into the heating metal to add to its quantity'.

This would agree with the work done in 1651-52 when it seems that the casting was done at Meopham. Then there were no payments for carriage, but there were for coals for drying the moulds, and wood to melt the *Tenner*.

In 1662, shortly after the Restoration the sum of £2 15*s*. 0*d*. was expended on painting the Royal Arms of Charles II. They are painted on boards and surrounded by a deal frame which cost a further guinea. Originally, they hung in front of the vanished musicians' gallery beneath the west tower, but now they are relegated to collect dust in the vestry. Their importance lies not in any intrinsic beauty — the executant was probably an inn-sign painter by trade with only a working knowledge of heraldry — but in the comparative rarity of painted armorials of this period.

A little later in date is the pulpit made for St. Margaret's, Westminster, in 1682 and brought to Meopham at the instance of the vicar, Edward Smedley, who was also a master at Westminster School. He arranged that this pulpit should be set up in Meopham, whence it was taken in 1801, for an entry in the church accounts records 'For part of the pulpit above sub-

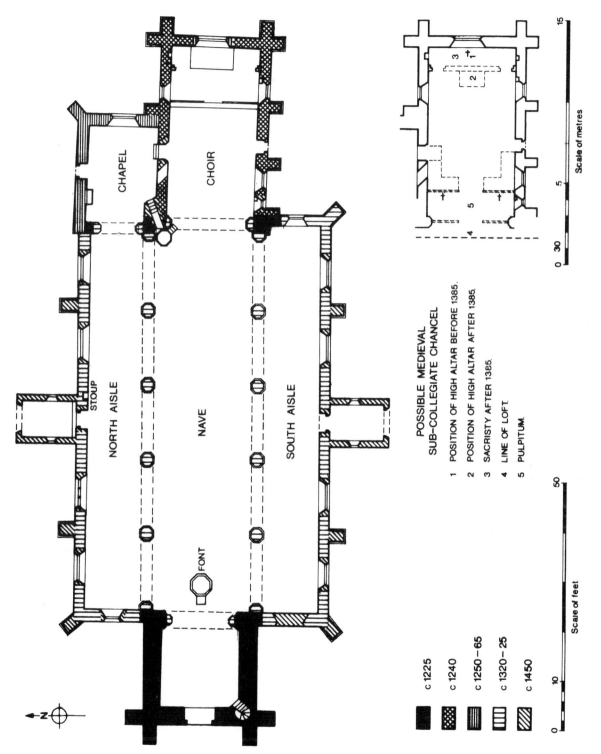

Fig. 24. Meopham Church: Plan.

scription £7 15*s*. 2½*d*..' When it was installed, being a three-decker, it was a high structure, and the preacher reached the top by way of the rood loft stairs from the north chapel. Below was the parson's desk, and under that was the clerk's desk. Unfortunately, in 1859, the pulpit was reduced in height, some of the woodwork being used to make a cupboard, which is now in the vestry.

Hexagonal in plan, the pulpit is carved with winged cherub-heads, — some more finished than others — swags of fruit and flowers, and inlaid panels. One of these is dated 1682, and has the monogram IHS. Who the maker or carver of this distinguished work was, is not known, but the quality of the design is high, and as Sir Christopher Wren was advising on the galleries and fittings at St. Margaret's at the time of its erection, it is likely to have been made by one of the leading London workshops. The carving on the pulpit is very similar to that on the border of the arms of James II in West Malling Church, which must date between 1685 and 1688.

Also surviving are two tables, one of the seventeenth century and one very fine and richly carved early eighteenth-century example. Both may once have served as the Lord's Table — now they support the detritus of modern parochial life.

The installation of the pulpit marked the end of caring for the church; the age of restoration and improvement began, and the tally of damage and destruction has been unceasing ever since. In 1819, the accounts record '*Eighty feet of old oak rail cutaway*': in all probability this was the destruction of the rood screen which still survived in 1804, and some parclose screens. The ceiling of the aisles in 1830 hid what medieval detail may have survived in the roofs. At the cost of £315 the tower was raised 20 ft. to provide a new bell chamber. This was a piece of work of such striking mediocrity that subsequent restorations have failed to improve it in any way. In 1847, the whitewash and any traces of earlier painting were removed from the nave, to be followed four years later by the scraping of the chancel.

1858 saw the church — nave and chancel — re-roofed, re-plastered, re-paved, re-seated and the pulpit butchered at a cost of £1185. This repulsive work is fully recorded in the Building News of September 1858.

The cusping and old glass of the nave clerestory were destroyed in 1868 and in 1874 the east windows of the north chapel and chancel were tampered with, and a new reredos of no merit whatsoever was introduced. The culminating horror was the lining of the lower chancel walls with an encaustic tile frieze in which can be recognised symptoms of most of the fashionable tastes then prevailing. It manages to destroy completely the balance of the mouldings in the chancel and should be greatly admired just now.

There are three mural monuments in the church which merit some attention. One, *c.* 1750 to the memory of various members of the Masters family, by Thomas Beard, is in the north aisle. It is a conventional design of a marble tablet between two Corinthian columns which support a broken curved pediment and an urn. In the chancel are two memorials to members of the Bayley family, one of 1806, by Richard James Wyatt, and the other of 1849, with a bust of Sir John Bayley by Edward Stephens. Both are too chastely austere to compete with the surrounding tilework.

ACKNOWLEDGEMENTS

Apart from the suggestions made by Stuart Rigold, I am deeply indebted to Canon Bernard Wigan for guiding me through the shoals and quicksands of medieval church history in Kent. John Physic provided me with invaluable information on the post-medieval work at Meopham; I am sorry I am unable to share much of his enthusiasm for it.

THE CHURCH OF ALL SAINTS, SHUART IN THE ISLE OF THANET

FRANK JENKINS

INTRODUCTION

The site of the church of All Saints, Shuart, was first revealed on an air photograph taken by Professor St. Joseph of the University of Cambridge (Ordnance Survey 1-inch Map, Sheet 173, N.G.R. 273679). It lies at the south end of a large arable field adjoining the north side of the old trackway going eastwards from Shuart Farm to Hale Farm. Modern methods of agriculture have destroyed the old field boundaries, but this part was a rectangular strip aligned east — west, known in 1630 as All Hallows Close, and renamed Chapel Close on the 1839 tithe map.

During 1978-79, full-time excavations were carried out under the aegis of the Thanet Archaeological Unit, with labour provided by the Manpower Services Commission, directed by the author, assisted by Mr D. Perkins. We are indebted to the owners of the land, the Bursar and Fellows of St. John's College, Cambridge, and their agents Messrs. George Webb and Co., for permission to excavate. Special thanks also to Mr Martin Tapp, the farmer, for making the site available, and for many kindnesses we received as the work progressed. We are grateful to Miss Deborah Kahn, for her report on the stonework, to Mr Peter Gibson of the York Glaziers Trust, for his report on the window glass, and to Mr Mark Horton, for his report on the floor tiles. Thanks are also due to Messrs T. Tatton-Brown and Paul Bennett, who with the excavations team of the Canterbury Archaeological Trust, spent one weekend preparing the whole site for photographing.

THE STRUCTURAL DEVELOPMENT OF THE CHURCH (Figs. 25 and 26)

As only the foundations of rammed chalk remained, the interpretation of the structural development of the church which follows, rests almost entirely upon the evidence provided at the places where certain foundations either abutted or overlapped others.

Phase I

The proto-church was of tripartite form, comprising a nave, a chancel and a sanctuary which was probably square ended. The foundations *c.* 1 m. wide enclosed an area measuring *c.* 16 m. E-W by *c.* 4.8 m. N-S. The tight butted vertical joints between the foundations of the chancel and the sanctuary showed that they had been laid as separate operations, either at the time when the church was first built, or when the sanctuary was rebuilt at a later date. The extant foundations of the sanctuary did not overlie, incorporate or enclose any earlier foundations to prove that they were added at a later date. Hence also taking into account that the original entrance to the sanctuary existed as a gap in the foundations of the east wall of the chancel, it

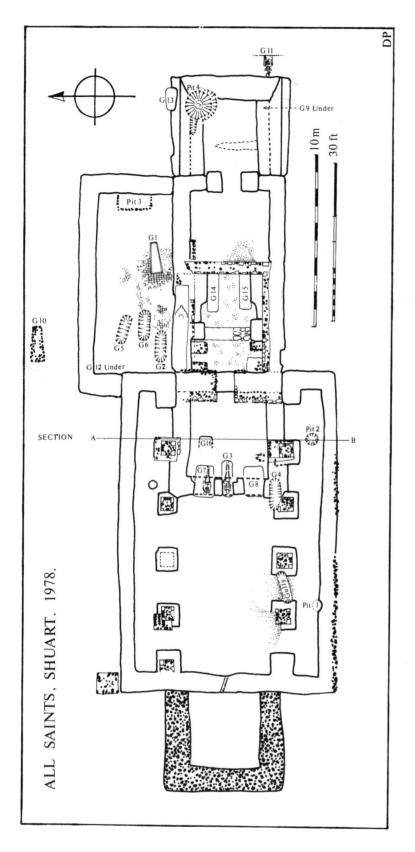

ALL SAINTS, SHUART. 1978.

Fig. 25.   The Church of All Saints: Composite plan.

is assumed that the sanctuary foundations were laid separately when the church was first built.

The chancel, *c.* 5 m. long was divided off from the nave by a pair of L-shaped foundations, one of which projected inwards from the foundations of the north wall, and the other from those of the south wall. The absence of jointing showed that these had been laid as integral parts of the main foundations. They were substantial enough to support a heavy superstructure, possibly vaulting spanning a passage *c.* 3 m. long. The eastern and western halves of this passage were *c.* 2.7 and 3.3 m. wide, respectively, suggesting that the super-structure had been recessed at the west end. The nave was rather small being only 2.8 m. long by 4.8 m. wide.

Phase II

Eventually, the church was altered to provide a nave and a chancel of approximately the same length. This was achieved by pulling down the west wall to extend the nave 5 m. westwards; demolishing the vaulted structure, and replacing it with a less massively built chancel arch, supported on new chalk foundations inserted immediately west of the earlier structure.

Phase III

The Phase II extension at the west end of the nave was pulled down to make way for an aisled nave of five bays. The very few patches of surviving floor material consisted of smooth surface mortar, which had overlapped the chalk foundatins of the Caen-stone faced plinth which had supported the arcading. The earlier chancel arch was demolished to provide a longer chancel, and the foundations for a screen and rood loft were inserted just east of the new chancel arch.

As the order in which the west tower was built is unknown and the arguments for and against a date contemporary with this phase or later appear to be of equal validity, it is pro-visionally assigned to this phase. Only its foundation trenches filled with loose building débris remained, but their plan strongly suggests that the tower had no buttresses or a stair turret. It is noteworthy that the sides and the bottoms of these trenches still retained a smooth hard surfacing of mortar, which was virtually undamaged. This suggests that the foundations had consisted of stone blocks which had been carefully extracted after the tower had been pulled down, and they were neither of flints and mortar, nor rammed chalk.

The material in these trenches consisted mainly of much crumbled green sandstone containing occasional lumps of mortar. Some of the latter bore the casts of barnacles showing that the stones to which they had been attached had been lying in sea-water before being brought to the site as building material.

Phase IV

The north chapel was built on part of the graveyard because near the north-west angle the foundations of its north wall cut through an earlier grave. Instead of tightly butted joints where its foundations met those of the chancel and the nave, there were irregularly shaped fissures filled with soil. The position of the west jamb of the entrance from the south, was marked by the imprint of its moulded base in a patch of mortar resting on top of the foundations of the earlier chancel north wall, which must have been breached when the entrance was installed. The few patches of the floor that had escaped destruction by the plough, bore the imprints of paving tiles *c*. 10 cm. square.

One grave within the chapel had been inserted from floor level. It was covered by a plain, uninscribed stone, but had been robbed of its contents, and back-filled with building débris containing pieces of human bone from at least five skeletons. The other graves could not be related to the floor level for here the plough had been most destructive. All had been opened and filled with rubble containing pieces of human bone at all levels.

The altar had gone, but it seems that it stood in a central position against the east wall, where, much later, a large pit was dug and back-filled with building débris. The filling consisted mainly of much crumbled green sandstone with some pieces of mortar bearing the casts of barnacles, as found in the robber trenches of the west tower.

The presence of many pieces of window glass and pieces of stone mullions in the demolition deposits suggests that new windows were installed at this time. It is also possible that the north-west angle of the nave was buttressed to strengthen the west gable which had developed a structural weakness.

Phase V

Eventually, the church was demolished, and then enough time elapsed for two graves to be dug into the foundations of the east wall of the sanctuary. Then later a smaller church was built over the eastern half of the earlier building. The restoration of its plan is conjectural, because much of its stonework had been removed, leaving only the irregularly dug robber trenches back-filled with débris, and subsequent ploughing had wrought great damage on what had survived those activities. It was built of re-used stone and probably comprised a square-ended sanctuary, a chancel, an aisleless nave, and a west porch.

During this work the earlier damaged foundations of the east wall of the sanctuary were removed and replaced by wider foundations of chalk. New sections were also laid in trenches dug along the inner faces of the foundations of the earlier north and south walls. Others were inserted on each side of the earlier entrance to provide one of decreased width. The area formerly occupied by the chancel was dug out to lay a mortar floor at a depth of *c*. 30 cm. below the level of the tops of the earlier foundations. The walls were then built partly on top of the latter and partly along their inner faces. The west door was the same width as that of the sanctuary. The walls flanking it survived as single courses of chamfered stones at ground level which lined the inside of the entrance.

A porch of the same width as the rest of the building was attached to the west end. All that survived of this were the robber trenches filled with loose débris, but the north-west and south-east angles survived, and incorporated the two easternmost plinths of the free standing columns which had supported the arcading of the demolished nave.

THE STRATIFIED DEPOSITS AND STRUCTURAL FEATURES (Fig. 27)

The only excavated section to reveal a satisfactory sequence of the stratified deposits and structural features, was obtained on a straight line from north to south across the church, *c*. 3 m. west of the east end of the Phase III nave. Because of this the Phase I and IV structures are obviously not included. The numbering of the deposits and structures in the following summary is that shown on the drawn section (Fig. 27).

The Pre-church Deposits

1   The surface of the natural chalk lay at an average depth of *c.* 3 m. below the modern ground level.

2   Above the chalk was a build-up of dark brown loamy soil about 0.7 m. thick and devoid of any archaeological material. Further to the east of this section, it was seen that the rammed chalk foundations of the Phase I church had been laid in a trench dug from the surface of this deposit into the natural chalk.

Phase II

3-4   The rammed chalk foundations of the north and south walls of the Phase II extension at the west end of the Phase I church, were also laid in trenches dug from the surface of that deposit into the natural chalk.

Phase II Demolition

5-6   After the demolition of the Phase II walls thin bands of dark brown loam sealed their foundations.

Phase III

7-8   The rammed chalk foundations of the north and south walls of the Phase III aisled nave were laid in trenches dug from a surface originally a few cm. above that of the ground level contemporary with the Phase II building, but in this section later levelling had evidently destroyed it.

9   While the nave was in use Grave 16 was dug from the floor level.

Phase III Demolition

10-11   After the aisled nave had been demolished a pit (no. 2 on Fig. 25) was dug in the south aisle.

12   This pit was sealed by a thick deposit of soil containing masses of building débris which had been dumped on the remains of the nave floor.

Phase V

13   A robber trench was dug along the line of the north wall of the nave from the surface of the Phase III demolition deposit.

14-15   The north-west and south-west angles of the west porch. Each of these were formed by encasing a plinth of the demolished Phase III arcading with re-used stone.

16-17   All that survived of the west wall of the porch between the two angles was a broken stump projecting a few cm. from the south-west angle into an irregularly cut robber trench filled with loose rubble. Because of the irregularity of the sides of this trench it did not extend entirely into the section, hence it appears to be interrupted by the demolition deposit of the Phase III nave into which it had been dug.

18   The plough soil throughout the site of the church contained scattered building débris.

DISCUSSION

The date when the proto-church was founded must remain an open question.

As a preliminary step in this inquiry, it seems best to state what is known of the history of the western part of Thanet in which it was situated. In 679, the monastery of Reculver was granted land in Thanet called *Uestanae*, meaning the western part of the island. (*Cartularium saxonicum*, 45). This may be the one sulung and one pasture on the shore of Thanet held by Reculver in 949, when the monastery and its estates were granted to Christ Church. (*ibid.*, 880-881), which in 961 acquired the manor of Monkton (*ibid.*, 1065). This infers that Thanet had been divided at an earlier date between the eastern manor of Minster, and the western manor of Monkton, hence the appearance of that division in 1086 in Domesday Book. If then the land owned by Christ Church in the tenth century was actually that marked *Libertas* on the earliest map of Thanet by Elmham drawn in 1410-11, it must have contained the site of All Saints, Shuart (Swanton 1975, Pl. I).

It has been suggested that as the churches of All Saints and St. Nicholas-at-Wade were dependent chapels of Reculver, the ecclesiastical rights of the mother-church may well have originated at an early date, when the monastery actually held the western part of Thanet. (Rollason 1979, 15). If that is true, then the proto-church may have been built between 679 and 949. But it is equally possible that it was founded by the monks of Christ Church in the tenth century, at an early stage in the development of their newly acquired estates in Thanet. As neither of these possible dates can be proved correct, it complicates the problem of assigning a date for Phase II, because we are left with three dates to choose from. Before 961, or soon after 961, or if the proto-church was built after 961, then the Phase II work may have been carried out in the first half of the eleventh century. Before accepting pre-Conquest dates for Phases I and II, it is necessary to proceed one stage further and discuss the probable date of Phase III.

The date of Phase III, which saw the rebuilding of the church on a larger scale with an aisled nave, may be indicated by the presence of one piece of Quarr stone, and many pieces of Caen stone, in the much later demolition deposits. Quarr stone came from the quarries in the Isle of Wight, and seem to have supplied east Kent with building stone only between 1070 and 1120 (Tatton Brown 1980). A few pieces of Caen stone are sculptured and include the following items. A small *voussoir*-shaped fragment with chip carved motives in early twelfth-century style (Fig. 28, 1); two pieces with Kentish Anglo-Norman fret decoration which made its debut at Canterbury in the work of Abbot Wibert (1153-67), and continued to be used until *c.* 1175 (Fig. 28, 2-3); and two small delicately carved pieces of foliage which are certainly twelfth-century work (Fig. 28, 4-5). It seems reasonable to think that the Caen-stone faced plinths for the columns which supported the nave arcading are similarly dated. Finally, there is one plain piece of the same type of stone which has a compass incised mason's mark (Fig. 28, 6). Admittedly, all the dated pieces came from the much later demolition deposits, but strongly suggest that major building work was carried out in the twelfth century, and represent Phase III in the structural development of the church.

The order in which the west tower was built must remain an open question. It is possible that it was built at the same time as the aisled nave in the twelfth century, although its foundation material was entirely different from that of the foundations of the nave, and had been laid separately. It is equally possible that the tower was built at a later date, which would then have involved the demolition of much, if not all, of the west wall of the nave, to incorporate the bonding. As both arguments appear to be equally valid, the west tower is assumed to be part of the Phase III work, but it may belong to Phase IV next to be discussed.

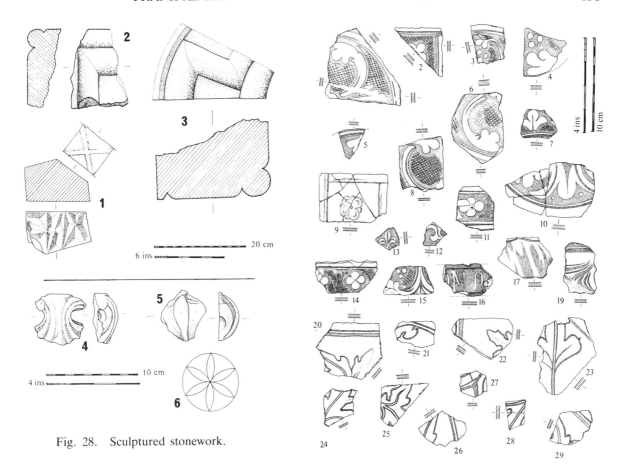

Fig. 28.　Sculptured stonework.

Fig. 29.　Decorated window glass (¼).

Evidence of further major building in the thirteenth century, assigned here to Phase IV, was provided by many pieces of Kentish ragstone recovered from the later demolition deposits. These included a few mouldings, and many pieces bearing tool marks characteristic of that period. There were also many pieces of painted window glass concentrated particularly at the east end of the nave (Fig. 29). A number of these in style and technique closely correspond with a panel of simple *grissaille* glass ornamented with "stiff foliage", dated *c.* 1240, now in the south transept of York Minster. The presence of this glass suggests, therefore, that the Phase IV work included the installation of new windows. Finally, as the north chapel is demonstrably the latest structure to be added to the church, it also belongs to this phase. Hence, it is possible that like the church at St. Nicholas-at-Wade, the church was fully grown by the end of the thirteenth century (Newman 1976, 433).

No evidence was found to show what time elapsed before the Phase IV church was demolished, but a few pieces of information from other sources may be relevant. In 1310, Archbishop Winchelsey endowed three perpetual vicarages for the service of Reculver and its dependent chapels, one being for the chapel of St. Nicholas-at-Wade *with* All Saints thus making it clear that he had united the two parishes (Graham 1952, 1127-31). To what extent the Black Death depopulated the parish in 1348-49 is not known, but the decline of All Saints may date from that time. In any case, the upkeep of two large churches in a rather remote rural parish must have been too much of a financial burden, and in consequence All Saints was neglected in favour of St. Nicholas-at-Wade. The map of Thanet by Elmham suggests that it was still standing at the beginning of the fifteenth century, for it is named, and is shown in its correct position (Swanton 1975), Pl. I). The drawings of the churches are admittedly stylized, but the fact that the towers display individual structural features is interesting. The general impression is that the towers at least are shown as they appeared, and that it is the Phase IV church which is shown. Hence it could be the one referred to in the will of John London proved in 1434 (Lewis 1736, 56). This seems to be corroborated by the many fragments of plain glazed floor tiles of Flemish manufacture, which have been dated possibly late-fourteenth, but certainly fifteenth-century. It is tempting to think, therefore, that as the nave clerestory was added to the church of St. Nicholas in the fifteenth century, All Saints was the source of building materials for that major project (Newman 1976, 433).

According to Leland, who visited Thanet between 1534 and 1543, three of the original eleven parish churches had decayed, but he does not name them (Leland 1769, 137). Lewis, writing in 1734, assumed that one was All Saints, and that Leland meant that its remains were no longer visible (Lewis 1736, 56). This, however, is rather odd because a church was evidently still standing at the end of the sixteenth century, when Philip Symondson undertook the survey for his map of Kent published in 1596. He, unlike other map-makers of his time, shows the churches as they actually appeared. Hence, it is significant that whereas Elmham shows the church with a tower, Symondson does not. In view of the latter's attention to detail, and because he does not show any ruined churches, it seems virtually certain that he depicts the church as it appeared just prior to 1596. It follows, therefore, that the Phase IV church had been demolished at an earlier date, perhaps in the latter half of the fifteenth century, and the one both Leland and Symondson saw was its successor built perhaps twenty years or more later, and assigned here to Phase V.

A return made in 1630, strongly suggests that by that time that church had fallen into ruin, or had been demolished. This states that the glebe belonging to the parish, included a close, called All Hallows Close, on part of which had anciently stood the chapel of All Saints (Hasted 1800, 247. In a letter written between 1695 and 1716, the vicar of Reculver mentions that the chapel was "now dilapidated" (Duncombe 1784, 125). Although this could mean that the ruins were still visible, it is certain that by 1736 nothing remained of either the church or the fences around it (Lewis 1736, 56).

SUMMARY OF PROPOSED DATES

Phase I   Saxon, either before 949, or in latter half of the tenth century.

Phase II   Saxon, either in the latter half of the tenth century, or in the first half of the eleventh century.

Phase III   Norman, in first half of the twelfth century.

Phase IV   In first half of the thirteenth century, completed *c.* 1250. Probably in ruins *c.* 1450 and eventually demolished.

Phase V   In latter half of the fifteenth century. Either in ruins or gone by 1630, but said to be dilapidated *c.* 1695-1716. Nothing visible above ground *c.* 1734.

THE ARCHITECTURAL SIGNIFICANCE OF THE BUILDING WORKS OF RALPH, LORD CROMWELL (1394-1456).

M.W. THOMPSON

The influence of Lord Cromwell's buildings upon his contemporaries was indelibly impressed upon the mind of this writer in a dramatic way. Climbing up Castle Street in Farnham, Surrey, each day in 1958 to carry out work on the castle keep for the then Ministry of Works (Thompson 1960), I had ample opportunity to admire the great brick entry tower to the hall which so dominates the town. Much altered in appearance by the insertion of sash windows, it was then called Fox's Tower, being attributed to the early Tudor Bishop of Winchester by recent antiquaries on no very good grounds except probability. Working through the Winchester Pipe Rolls, or books as they were by that date, I came across a record of erection of a large brick tower at the castle in 1470-75 by Bishop William Wayneflete (Thompson 1960). There can be no reasonable doubt but that this is the tower we see today, which must therefore have been started fourteen years after the death of Cromwell by his executor who was at the same time completing the church and college that he had founded at Tattershall (Marks 1979). Imitation of the Tattershall tower has often been claimed for other fifteenth-century towers or even Tudor gatehouses, but at Farnham the historical sources bring us as close to using the word 'proof' as they are ever likely to permit.

During the next ten or fifteen years I had the good fortune to be closely associated with the surviving remains of Cromwell's major building operations, both ruinous, at South Wingfield Manor, Derbyshire, and at Tattershall Castle, Lincolnshire. He undertook major work at Colleyweston Manor (now entirely demolished) in Northamptonshire, and he was also responsible for the erection of the church at Lambley, Nottinghamshire, although the latter cannot be classified as a major work. It is therefore the first two structures at Wingfield and Tattershall which hold a significant place in late-medieval architecture in England that are the subject of this paper.

A Midlander by origin — Cromwell is a village in Nottinghamshire — the main seat by this time (Cromwell was the fourth baron) was at Tattershall in east Lincolnshire. Three aspects of his life, as outlined in the *Dictionary of National Biography*, deserve emphasis. His existence is first recorded at the Battle of Agincourt (1415) and, as he was still in France as late as 1420, this long period in France during his impressionable youth is likely to have influenced his taste permanently. Secondly, his subsequent political career reached its climax in 1433-43 when he was Lord Treasurer; there is a link between his political office on the one hand and the motivation for, and financing of, the building operations on the other. Thirdly, although married he had no children; the absence of a direct heir meant that there could be ample provision for the posthumous erection of the church and college at Tattershall.

Suprisingly, there is a direct connection between Cromwell and Kent, since a substantial body of his papers passed to the Sidney family and so to Penshurst Place, where they were duly catalogued by the Royal Commission on Historical Manuscripts (Kingsford 1925). Among these papers there is a single building account for Wingfield Manor and five for Tattershall Castle. It cannot be too strongly emphasised that the account for Wingfield is a record of particulars of expenditure describing in detail work carried out, while the accounts for Tattershall are summary records of expenditure which it is difficult to relate to specific construction. The latter have been published by the late Dr Douglas Simpson (Simpson 1960). I have suggested that, if the 'parlour' can be identified with the ground-floor room of the tower (Thompson 1979, 15), then this gives some kind of time-table for its lower and upper parts. I have published the Wingfield account (Thompson 1976) showing that the manor was sufficiently advanced by this date (Christmas 1443) for Cromwell to come into residence. Work evidently started in 1439-40, and may have continued up to 1450. It is clear that the Manor at Wingfield was started later, perhaps ten years later, than the beginning of the work at Tattershall Castle.

Both ruins caught the attention of Victorian architects and we are fortunate that detailed architectural drawings were published in the last century for Tattershall (Reed 1872) and Wingfield (Ferrey 1869). Although these cannot be reproduced here such drawings make the study of the remains much easier.

The restoration works carried out by Lord Curzon at Tattershall Castle (Curzon and Tipping 1929) revealed the existence of an earlier stone castle on the site, indicating that Cromwell had transformed an existing structure and not built on a virgin site. The remains of the brick buildings are pretty scrappy to-day except, of course, the tower, and it is evident that this was the case also in the eighteenth century when the brothers Buck drew their view. The crucial information supplied by that print, however, is that another building, dwarfed by the tower, stood immediately in front of it in the courtyard. Although ruinous the building represented is evidently a hall, its oriel window on the right and its lower end facing the door to the stair turret of the tower.

Our understanding of the tower itself is increased beyond measure by this knowledge. The three ground-floor doors of the tower (Plate XXXI) are one of the most puzzling features; the right-hand one leads into a spacious ground-floor room, the middle one into a vaulted cellar and the left-hand one to the three great upper rooms of the tower. The upper rooms in the tower would serve a similar function to the great chamber at the lower end of the hall at Wingfield, a private suite on a grand scale for the lord. The tower at Farnham, at the lower end of the hall, besides being an entry, no doubt had the same purpose, and so is related to Tattershall not merely by appearance but also by function. The ground-floor room at Tattershall was presumably the parlour, which adjoins the upper end of the hall at Wingfield. This was a sort of common room ('parlour' or 'senior common room' at Cambridge). The vaulted undercroft entered by the middle door no doubt remedied a deficiency in the older hall (the undercroft separating a servants' hall we suggested at Wingfield).

What we appear to have then are the normal ancillaries of a hall built on a grand scale and arranged vertically in an imposing tower which overshadowed the adjacent hall from which it functionally derived. One of the puzzling features of the accounts as Dr Simpson notes

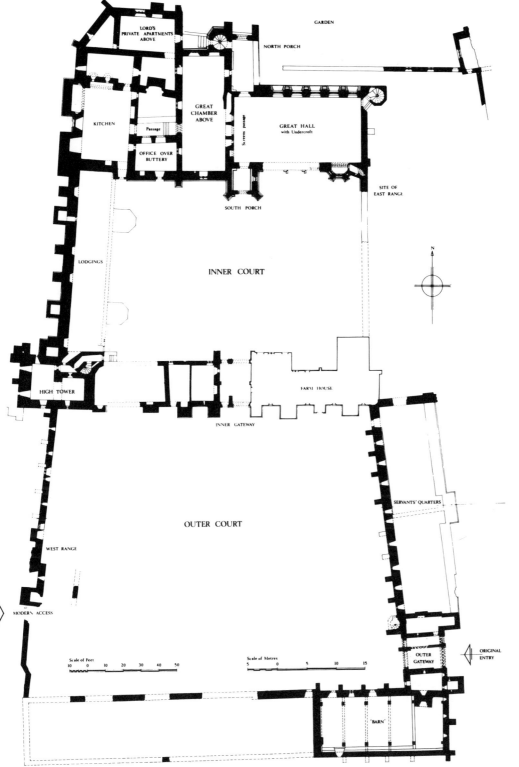

GARDEN

LORD'S PRIVATE APARTMENTS ABOVE

NORTH PORCH

GREAT CHAMBER ABOVE

KITCHEN

Passage

Screens passage

GREAT HALL with Undercroft

OFFICE OVER BUTTERY

SOUTH PORCH

SITE OF EAST RANGE

LODGINGS

INNER COURT

N

HIGH TOWER

FARM HOUSE

INNER GATEWAY

WEST RANGE

OUTER COURT

SERVANTS' QUARTERS

MODERN ACCESS

Scale of Feet
10 0 10 20 30 40 50

Scale of Metres
5 0 5 10 15

OUTER GATEWAY

ORIGINAL ENTRY

'BARN'

(Crown copyright, Reproduced with the permission of the Controller of Her Majesty's Stationery Office.)

Fig. 30. Plan of the Manor of South Wingfield, Derbyshire, as it exists today.

(Simpson 1960, 36) was that the word 'donjon' to describe the tower does not appear until 1445 when the tower must have been complete. If, however, the builders thought of it primarily as an adjunct to the hall, it may well be that they were using the word 'parlour' for the ground-floor room when the tower had only reached that height (Thompson 1979, 15).

The late Professor Hamilton-Thompson had been closely associated with Lord Curzon's restoration work at Tattershall and so was very familiar with the tower. In his classic work on the development of military architecture in medieval England (Hamilton-Thompson 1912, 356-7) the author cited Tattershall as a prime example of the revival of keeps in the later Middle Ages. For a later student of the castle, Dr Simpson, the tower epitomised the 'bastard feudalism' of the later Middle Ages, where the lord required a refuge defensible against his own retainers. The subject has given rise to lively controversy.

A Norman keep had a primary function whereas the Tattershall tower had in essence a secondary function, to serve the adjoining hall. A twelfth-century keep had its door on the first floor; at Tattershall there are three ground-floor doors which made it very vulnerable to attack. We could add to these differences, but none of them alter the fact that the building has been made to look like a keep and was indeed called a 'donjon' by its builders (in its final stages at all events!).

The traveller in Scotland or Ireland cannot fail to be struck by the late medieval towers that abound in those countries. A recently-made distribution map (Smith 1975, 338) showing counts of these tower-houses by counties in Great Britain and Ireland illustrates their very uneven spread over the area: in Ireland, Scotland and the Borders they abound but in most of England and Wales they are rare. The Scottish ones are squatter than the Irish, but both were vaulted at one level and were residential and defensive. The compiler of the map not unreasonably attributed their prevalence in certain areas to the weakness of central government there and the consequent necessity for each owner to fend for himself. Dr Simpson's theories had perhaps more basis in his native Scotland than in eastern England.

One might say that the idea of a tower is always immanent in a castle since it serves both for defence and as a display of the authority of its owner. No doubt in the twelfth century the former consideration was paramount although the latter was important, but in the fourteenth and fifteenth centuries the balance tipped the other way, especially in France and Burgundy. We may recall the residence of the Chevalier Cromwell, as he was called, in France from 1415-20, the construction of Tattershall starting about ten years later when resources permitted. Something of the attitude towards castles in France at this time is vividly demonstrated for us in *Les très riches Heures du Duc de Berry* where the Duke's castles are displayed by the Limbourg brothers as a background to several months in the calendar, or more gratuitously in the mocking of Job and the temptation of Christ. In the latter case, the castle significantly represented the worldly temptation by the devil. In the self-dramatisation so characteristic of the later Middle Ages castles evidently played a very important part.

There is something of the same feeling about the tower at Tattershall with its elaborate machicolations, conical caps (now-vanished) on the corner turrets and the red brick of which it was constructed. Brick was of course a deliberate choice; the church of the college is built entirely of stone. Brick was no doubt cheaper but red was a much more emotive colour. At Farnham ochre was bought to rouge the tower to emphasize the diaper work (Thompson 1960, 88). The same may well have been the case at Tattershall which in its pristine state must have looked like a tower in a manuscript illumination. It is no wonder that people wanted to imitate it!

PLATE XXXI

(Photo: B.T. Batsford Ltd.)

The west face of the great tower at Tattershall Castle, Lincolnshire.

PLATE XXXII

The window of the great chamber and porch to the great hall at South Wingfield Manor, Derbyshire.

South Wingfield lies some 60 miles west of Tattershall, near Alfreton in Derbyshire. Not only is the landscape entirely different, the southern edge of the Pennines as against the Lincolnshire Fenland, but the buildings are in such contrast that were it not for the written evidence we might doubt whether the two structures had been erected by the same person. On the one hand, we have an exotic brick tower where the inference of foreign influence is confirmed by the name of the man in charge, Baldwin, and in the other we have traditional stone used in traditional buildings. The surviving account leaves no doubt that the work-force was entirely English while the level of wages, the ox-drawn wagons and so on suggest a somewhat rustic constructional operation. The writer well recalls a visit to the site with Stuart Rigold, to whose memory this volume is dedicated, ostensibly to inspect the woodwork of the 'barn', when he expressed some disdain for the coarseness of the stonework compared to the finer work of southern and eastern England to which he was accustomed!

Why then should the buildings at Wingfield detain us at all? They form to-day one of the most spectacular ruins in the country, the silhouette of the tall chimneys and jagged remains of the tower being an unforgettable sight; did the living buildings equally impress contemporaries? Quotations from three famous topographers may help us.

William of Worcester, a generation later wrote of '. . *manerium pulcherrimum de Wynfeld prope Derby de lapidibus et cemento. . .*' (Harvey 1969, 72). The manor was not only very pretty but also entirely of stone, not partly timber-framed. For John Leland it was 'but a maner place but yt far passith Sheffield Castle' (Toulmin Smith 1910, iv, 14). What impressed him was that a mere manor-house should be on so monumental a scale that it should overshadow a neighbouring castle. The idea of the large country-house was still an unfamiliar one for Leland. Finally 50 years later, when large Tudor houses were a familiar sight in the countryside Camden spoke of 'where Ralph Lord Cromwell, in the reign of Henry the sixth, built a very stately house considering the age' (Gibson 1695, 493). This indeed puts the matter very neatly: a house planned and designed on this scale and executed in one continuous building operation was very rare in the mid-fifteenth century but commonplace a hundred years later.

There is, of course, no question of courtyard houses being unknown at this period. Haddon Hall in the same county is a good example of a house that grew to its present shape over two or three centuries; it was not conceived in its later form by its original builder in contrast to Wingfield. In some respects the house-plan of the period lagged behind that of the institution: by this date a college had to be designed as a whole, but a house was still seen as detached elements. What is clear at Wingfield is that the designer saw the whole plan from the beginning which he intended to be carried out in uniform stone throughout (not timber for the less important service buildings).

The manor to some extent took the shape of the northward-pointing spur on which it was erected so that it tapered northwards (Fig. 30). The approach was up a valley on the east side leading to the outer gate at the south-east corner. Here a right turn had to be made in the large outer court to pass through a central gateway in the cross-range dividing this from the smaller inner court. Opposite the gate was the porch of the hall which occupied the eastern half of the north range, the western half being filled by the great chamber at right angles to the hall with the kitchen in the corner. The cross-range terminated at its west end in a tower overlooking both courts, not as resplendent as the Tattershall tower (and partly destroyed by slighting after the Civil War siege), but more significantly not here an adjunct of the hall. The west range of the inner court held sets of lodgings with external staircases serving each pair, while the vanished east range probably contained the parlour on the first floor adjoining the hall (Thompson 1976, 426) with what may have been the chapel projecting eastwards from the middle of the range to judge by the conformation of the ground. The hall had a vaulted undercroft, the ground level on the south side corresponding with the floor level of the hall and on the north side with the floor level of the undercroft. There was a porch with a fan vault on the south side and a three-storeyed porch projecting into what was evidently a garden at the tip of the spur.

Looking at this plan (Fig. 30), its essentially traditional origin is clear, the buildings (except the tower) being ultimately an excrescence of the hall, the progenitor of all so to speak. Yet the skill with which they are dispersed is remarkable. The visitor passed through various gradations of increasing privacy until he faced the ultimate chamber and hall. The tower was skilfully placed to command the whole lay-out but only accessible from the inner court. At Tattershall the disposition of the buildings appears to be haphazard, the long ranges squeezed in between the existing moats, but at Wingfield, although recent excavations show there had been earlier structures on the site which were apparently demolished, the unity of the plan is the most striking feature.

The most interesting point about the surviving account which covers the period November 1442 to Christmas 1443 (Thompson 1976) is that it enables us to re-create the sequence in which the manor was erected. It quotes the original contract apparently entered into three years before, i.e. 1439, and by the date of this account the hall, chamber, kitchens and west range of lodgings had been built. This was the minimum required for occupation and, to judge by the cleaning that took place before the arrival of Lord Cromwell, he actually came into residence at the end of the accounting period. There are references to 'outer' and 'inner' courts which clearly had been laid out by this date, but the erection of the other ranges of the inner court and all the ranges of the outer court apparently took place in the following years. Work may well have gone on until 1450 or so if the whole design was complete, and we have no reason to doubt that this was so.

There is nothing surprising about this sequence which is indeed a logical one, although it is interesting to have its written confirmation. However regular the plan, the sequence of construction reflects as it were the development of the house in the Middle Ages. No doubt this would have been the sequence of building in a twelfth-century castle, even if the different buildings were scattered round the bailey and not articulated into one coherent design as they were at Wingfield.

About the architectural significance of the two major works of Lord Cromwell there can be no reasonable doubt. In the case of Tattershall, it was not the function of the tower as an adjunct to the hall that caused most emulation (although this was evidently the case at Farnham) but the display of grandeur that led to so much imitation in towers and gatehouses, particularly in the areas where brick was freely used. A good illustration of the point is the transformation that took place in college gateways in the second half of the fifteenth century at Cambridge but not at Oxford. Although Cromwell put his major labours into the castle that was his main seat, it was courtyard houses of the Wingfield type which by early in the next century were to represent the new style of major country seats. It represented a decisive step towards the Tudor courtyard house in the family tree of which it holds an honoured place.

THE COURT LODGE, HORTON KIRBY

P.J. TESTER

The village of Horton Kirby lies in the valley of the River Darent — an area well known to Stuart Rigold who was familiar with many of its ancient buildings. His investigations at Eynsford Castle and his detailed publication of the evidence in Archaeologia Cantiana *were among the most important contributions he made to the archaeological record of our county. The following notes on the remains of another defended site, just over a mile to the north, are offered as a token of respect to the memory of a fellow medievalist whose friendship I enjoyed for many years and whose profound scholarship was a constant source of inspiration and guidance.*

In September 1977 this house was visited by a group of K.A.S. members during a field excursion, and on that occasion certain features were noted which appeared to call for further investigation. They suggested that despite the drastic alterations in the last century it might still be possible to produce a reconstruction of the medieval arrangement. The place has had an unfortunate architectural history and its study has been neglected by antiquaries. What notice it has received in literature has been mainly derived from a mid-nineteenth-century description by Edward Cresy whose notebook also contains a small freehand sketch-plan (Plate XXXIVA). He wrote as follows:

> The Castle, now called the Court Lodge, stands a short distance from the west end of the Church: in my recollection, and when I made the view in 1811, was entirely encompassed by a Moat, connected with the River Darent, which passed along the western side.
>
> The building originally had some resemblance to the castles of the same period: a structure formed the Gateway, which conducted into a Courtyard surrounded with buildings: the outer walls of which were of rubble stone work, four feet in thickness: the east and south sides of this Court formed the house occupied by the tenant of the Manor. A large Kitchen with a fire place at the west end, at the side of which were windows looking onto the farm yard, beyond which was the Church. Butteries and Pantries were made on one side, and the large oak table occupied one entire side. The Ceiling low, and the joists much discoloured.
>
> The fire place was large, with seats on each side.
>
> Beyond the Kitchen and looking towards the River was a gloomy parlour — the windows at a height from the floor.
>
> The Gates of the entrance after crossing the brick bridge remained, and the key of the Lock is now hanging up beside me. It seems ancient and I dare say was so.
>
> What remained of the original interior, was most rudely handled by Mr. George Smith the Surveyor, who, when he frightfully disfigured the Church and removed its wooden Spire, metamorphosed the old Castle into an indifferent farm house as we now find it.

The Old Castle or Court Lodge seems to have been of a square form, each side about 80 feet, and may have had the character of Hever Castle: the principal rooms towards the River had been long destroyed. The Courtyard of the Interior perhaps of the same size as that mentioned and the fronts of the apartments towards the Court were probably constructed of Timber. The Moat around the exterior was supplied by the river Darenth, which flowed entirely around it, and in the place of the brick bridge of one arch, there was attached to the Gate house a portcullis and drawbridge.

Fig. 31 herewith is redrawn from Cresy's notebook in order to clarify details not readily apparent in the photographic reproduction Plate XXXIVA.

In 1980 I was able by the courtesy of the present occupier, Mr. R.W. Rogers, to make a further inspection and take measurements in order to produce the sketch-plan shown here as Fig. 32. At once it became apparent that the thick rubble wall forming the east side of the medieval rectangular enclosure remains, and its westward returns also survive for part of their length. On the west, towards the river, nothing is visible above ground of the other wall, but I have been shown a position on the grass tennis court where in dry weather it is said to be possible to observe its course. Thus, one is able to establish the lengths of the outer walls and these are found to be greatly in excess of the 80 ft. given by Cresy. Other medieval remains are few, but significant when considered in relation to the circumstantial evidence. No original openings remain on the east side apart from obvious indications of the passage through the range formerly giving access to the courtyard although all evidence of the projecting gatehouse shown in old views (Fig. 33) has long since disappeared. On the south wall, recent removal of the external rendering has brought to light three medieval openings: one is a pointed-arched doorway at first-floor level, rebated for a door opening outwards and hinged on the west side. A short distance to the west are two narrow rectangular windows or loops, one above the other, and the evidence of these three features puts the medieval age of the wall beyond doubt (Plate XXXIIIB). Towards the north end of the east side there is visible, in the angle formed between two modern brick walls, the weathered ashlar of a quoin marking the north-east angle of the medieval enclosure, and from its position it is apparent that part of the east wall north of the gatehouse stood slightly forward of the main line of the range.

Evidently, the west side of the range south of the gateway was of timber, as Cresy suggested. Parts of the framing are still visible at points in the modernised partition standing on this line. The roof has been renewed apart from two steeply cambered tie-beams across the area of the hall, now only visible through a trapdoor in one of the bedroom ceilings.

Attached to the west side of the hall there remains a room with a fine timber panelled ceiling, indisputably the most interesting part of the house and deserving detailed description. Its north wall is timber-framed in two 8-ft. bays, the wall-posts being visible from the modern corridor to the north. An arched opening existed on this side, the shoulder of its arch being cut into the east side of the central post. At the west end, the original wall is missing while the south wall has been partly reconstructed. But the striking feature is the late-medieval ceiling divided by a central cross-beam and narrow moulded ribs into twelve rectangular panels against a background of wide boards laid across the area. At the intersection of the ribs are foliated bosses two of which are surmounted by demi-figures — in one case an angel wearing a dalmatic and holding a shield, and the other a lady wearing a fifteenth-century horned head-dress. There is also a carved head at the junction of the transverse beam with the central post on the north side; it is of a man wearing a *chaperon bourlet* type of headgear also popular in the fifteenth century. There is no certainty that these figures are in their original positions and

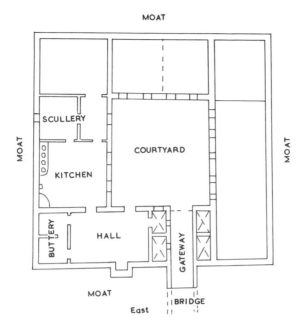

Fig. 31.   Edward Cresy's plan of the Court Lodge. Redrawn from the freehand sketch in his notebook and reproduced here to the same size as the original which is not to scale.

they cannot be taken as firm evidence for dating their architectural setting.

Surface indications of the moat once surrounding the house can be observed and together with the evidence provided by old views show that there was a berm between the water and the walls in contrast to the arrangement seen at Ightham Mote, Bodiam Castle and many other defended sites.

DISCUSSION

On the basis of the recent survey it is possible to assess Cresy's notes and plan in an attempt to reconstruct the original character of the building. Clearly this was a semi-fortified manor house of a type usual in the later Middle Ages, although it is significant that the Patent Rolls for the period 1257 to 1480 reveal no record of a licence to crenellate, a fact throwing doubt on the justification for describing it as a castle. The hall, as Cresy identified it, was in an unusual position for a courtyard house — in the gatehouse range instead of opposite the main entrance or in one of the side ranges. Cresy, therefore, had reason for supposing that the 'principal' rooms might have been on the west side towards the river. A doorway from the courtyard into the remaining hall must have been located in its west wall towards the north end and one would expect the domestic offices to have been near this entrance in accordance with the almost invariable medieval arrangement. But Cresy shows the buttery at the opposite or 'high' end with the kitchen adjoining. There are two possible explanations: either there was a deliberate departure from normal practice from the beginning, or, more likely, the arrangements were altered at a later period to bring the service rooms and kitchen to a more convenient situation in relation to the high table. Most probably Cresy's 'buttery' was

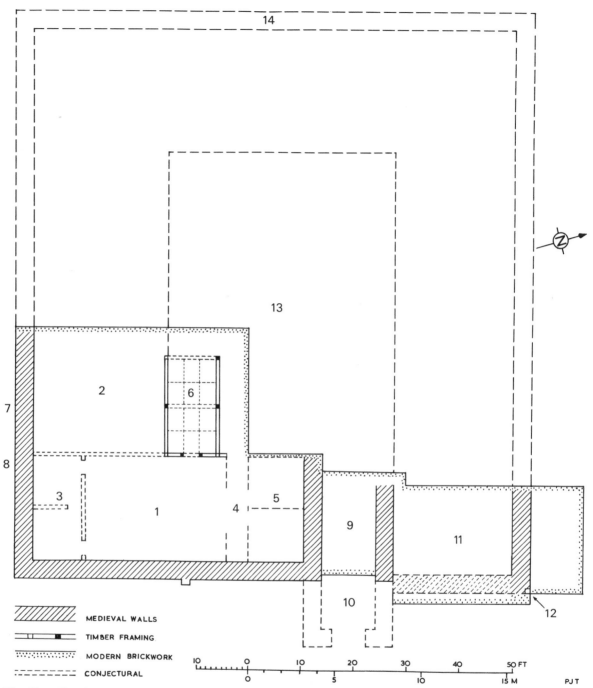

Fig. 32. Sketch-plan of the Court Lodge based on a survey made in 1980, showing the extent of surviving medieval features in relation to the present farmhouse.

1. Site of hall, now subdivided. 2. Area of kitchen, as shown by Cresy. 3. Probable site of original parlour with solar above, shown as buttery on Cresy's plan and reconstructed here on his evidence. 4. Possible site of screens passage. 5. Conjectural reconstruction of medieval domestic offices. 6. Room with panelled ceiling (Plates XXXIVB and XXXV). 7. Medieval windows above and below (Plate XXXIIIB). 8. Medieval doorway at first-floor level. 9. Passage through range, now blocked. 10. Site of destroyed gatehouse shown in eighteenth- and nineteenth-century sketches (Fig. 33). 11. Room rebuilt except for north and south walls. 12. Quoin. 13. Site of courtyard. 14. Approximate line of west wall.

Fig. 33. *(Above)* View of the east side of the Court Lodge, copied from a pencil sketch dated 1786. *(Below)* The same as above, from a water-colour sketch dated 1820. *(Both redrawn for publication by F.D. Hughes).*

Fig. 34.   East side of the Court Lodge at the present time. *(Drawn by F.D. Hughes)*.

originally the parlour with the solar above, the pantry and buttery being at the opposite end of the hall in the normal manner. In the archbishop's palace at Mayfield, Sussex, such a change seems to have taken place. A plan in Margaret Wood's *The English Medieval House* (1965), 52, shows doorways in the low end which *The Buildings of England* identifies as entrances to the service rooms. This is in the fourteenth-century work but at the high end a later buttery is shown behind the dais with the kitchen adjoining, these changes having been made in the fifteenth or sixteenth century. In Cresy's plan the pair of small rooms he marks as the buttery look very much like the pantry and buttery commonly found adjoining in medieval houses. Usually, their doorways were placed close together at the centre, but at Court Lodge they were at the end of the partition to avoid the dais and high table.

The room with the panelled ceiling was obviously a private apartment and may have been added in compensation for the displacement of the parlour from its normal situation behind the dais.

Another uncertainty is whether the hall was ever open to the roof, with a central hearth. I could not ascertain whether there are traces of smoke-blackening on the tie-beams, and it is not impossible that the wall fireplace noted by Cresy was an early feature. Presumably, the existing upper floor in the area of the hall is an insertion, although this cannot be firmly established.

The presence of a doorway at first-floor level in the outer wall near the south-east angle of the hall proves the existence of an upper floor in part of this area, and it is suggested that the opening gave access to a garderobe or latrine — probably of timber and jettied out from the wall to drain into the moat.

On either side of the gateway-passage Cresy shows what seem to be narrow vaulted rooms, each of two bays. No trace of these survives, and it is uncertain what he intended to represent. Possibly, he may have been influenced by recollections of the gatehouse at Hever Castle which has chambers on each side — one narrower than the other as he has drawn. Details of his plan at this point are difficult to interpret, as an experimental reconstruction of what he depicts within the constraints of a correctly dimensioned survey reduces the width of the north range

The Court Lodge, viewed from the north-east.

South side, showing medieval openings. The lower of the two loops is partly concealed by the greenhouse.

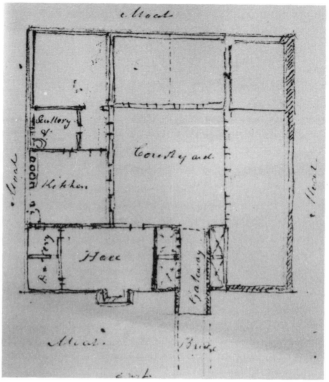

Cresy's sketch-plan, photographed from a page in his notebook.
Approximately actual size.

Demi-figure of an angel holding a shield, from a ceiling boss in the room marked 6 on the plan, Fig. 33.

PLATE XXXV

Carvings of figures with fifteenth-century head-dresses, from the ceiling of Room 6.

to unacceptably narrow proportions. He confidently shows the ranges on the south, west and north sides of the courtyard, although in his notes he describes them as having been long destroyed and conjectures as to their having been partly of timber. This implies that he has reconstructed them schematically and, together with his omission of the room with the panelled ceiling and serious miscalculation as to the size of the 'castle', casts doubt on the strict accuracy of some of the details he describes. His conviction that the house resembled Hever Castle may have been partly responsible: for example, his estimate of 80 ft. square for the outer dimensions is over 18 ft. short of the actual length of the east side of the Court Lodge, although it agrees closely with Hever Castle which is approximately 85 ft. square. Likewise his remarks concerning the former existence of a portcullis and drawbridge may have been based on reasonable supposition rather than remaining objective evidence or reliable record.

In Fig. 32 the original arrangement at the low end of the hall is restored conjecturally except that the south side of the screens passage as shown coincides with an existing transverse beam at ground-storey ceiling-level and there is a significant line of empty mortices under it. Using this as a guide, the proportions of the adjoining features as reconstructed seem convincing, and it may be noted that there is still an opening at the west end of the conjectural screens passage leading into the modern east — west corridor. This could well mark the site of the doorway into the hall even though at present it displays no ancient features. The substantial character of the morticed beam suggests that it played a part in supporting an upper chamber over the service rooms and screens passage, and the entry was therefore of the 'undershot' type often found in medieval houses.

There are no clues as to the primary use of the single-storey apartment north of the gateway passage. Its roof, east and west walls and general internal treatment are all modern. If it ever served as the kitchen, the inconvenience of its siting in relation to the hall could have provided a motive for its relocation in the position shown by Cresy.

ACKNOWLEDGEMENTS

I am grateful to Mr. R.W. Rogers, for permission to examine the interior of his home and for drawing attention to certain details I might otherwise have overlooked. The Kent County Library has kindly permitted publication of part of the Cresy manuscript now retained in Dartford Central Library. Extracts from this have previously been published in the *Transactions of the Dartford & District Antiquarian Society*, no. 11, December 1932. For help in identifying the costume shown on the carved ceiling bosses I am indebted to the Department of Textiles and Dress of the Victoria and Albert Museum. Mr. F.D. Hughes has kindly permitted reproduction of his sketches shown here as Figs. 33 and 34. It was due to his prompting that my attention was drawn to the possibility of investigation at Court Lodge.

THE HOSPITAL OF ST. MARY OF THE POOR PRIESTS, CANTERBURY*

TIM TATTON-BROWN, PAUL BENNETT AND MARGARET SPARKS

INTRODUCTION

For the last decade or so, the surviving buildings of the Poor Priests' Hospital in Canterbury (a Grade I listed building and scheduled Ancient Monument) have been undergoing restoration by Canterbury City Council with substantial grants from the Department of the Environment. During much of this time Stuart Rigold was involved in, and advised on, these restorations, and it seems fitting that an interim report on the building (restoration work has not yet been completed) should be one of the contributions to his memorial volume. Since 1975 the Canterbury Archaeological Trust has been directly involved in the work, carrying out recording work on the fabric and below ground excavation work whenever it has been needed. As a result of this much more has been discovered of the archaeology of the building (which in part probably goes back to the twelfth century), and a detailed report will be published in due course.

East Kent is particularly rich in the surviving remains of its medieval hospitals (Godfrey 1929, 99-110), and Stuart Rigold has long been concerned with the protection, restoration and excavation of many of them. He has been involved particularly with the hospitals in New Romney and Canterbury (Rigold 1964), and most recently with the large scale excavations at the hospital in Ospringe known as the "Maison Dieu" (Smith 1979, 87-91, 107-117). The medieval hospitals of Canterbury are still a particularly fine group, and two of them (St. Nicholas, Harbledown, and St. John's Northgate) which were founded by Archbishop Lanfranc in c. 1085 and are still occupied as almshouses are probably the oldest in the country. As well as this there is the extremely well preserved hospital of St. Thomas-upon-the-Eastbridge, which was founded in c. 1180 and is also still occupied as an almshouse. The Poor Priests' Hospital (founded in c. 1220) is by comparison relatively recent. However, the surviving buildings of the hospital are a remarkably complete group of largely fourteenth-century buildings which have long deserved a more complete study.

In the centre is the stone-built Great Hall with its screens passage and main doors at the south end. Above the hall is a very fine smoke-blackened (from the open hearth) crown-post roof which is very large and, exceptionally, has double rows of collars. South of the hall is an adjoining, but structurally separate, service wing which is entirely timber-framed, and survives remarkably well despite relatively recent refacing in brick on the outside. Rooms in the service wing were entered by three doors in the screens passage and the south-west bay of this wing (facing the river) still has a medieval jetty. At the north end of the hall two doors at either end lead into the undercroft of the solar, which has a recently discovered medieval fireplace in its north wall. The solar above (probably the Master's chamber) is on massive chestnut beams and has a very fine late fourteenth-century transomed window in its east wall. The solar is covered by another splendid crown-post roof at the east end of which was later inserted a bell-cote and clock. North-east again is the chapel which also has a surviving fourteenth-century crown-post roof. This roof is perhaps slightly earlier than the other roofs, as it has much longer and slimmer crown-posts. The hall and chapel and the upper part of the solar had extra floors (and dormer windows in the roof, fire-places and chimneys) inserted in them after 1575, and many of these features have now been removed again in the recent restorations. During these restorations detailed drawings of the building, and various excavations (see below), have been undertaken by the Canterbury Archaeological Trust, and it has been shown that parts of the earlier (late twelfth and thirteenth century) stone buildings still survive within and below the fourteenth century work. A very fine thirteenth-century open hearth was found within the hall (at the opposite end from the fourteenth-century hearth), and an interim report on these discoveries is below.

It is hoped that shortly the newly restored buildings will be opened to the public again as a new archaeological and historical museum for the City, thus enabling the building to be seen again in its original glory.

DOCUMENTARY HISTORY

In about 1175, Lambin Frese, one of Canterbury's moneyers, exchanged his workshop near Christ Church Gate for two adjacent buildings "towards Hottemelne, near the ford". These dwellings, which had previously been leased by Christ Church Priory to Godwin Grom and Gerold the Tanner, were thrown together and a new stone house was built there. Lambin then paid 5s. per annum to the monks for the site which had a street frontage length of 130 ft. and went back 86 ft. to the river at the north end and 80 ft. at the south end. This was confirmed by a Royal Charter in about 1177. The monks of Christ Church gave Lambin Frese 10 marks as an extra inducement to move because it is quite likely that it was a fire in Lambin's workshop which started the great fire in the Cathedral choir in September 1174. (Urry 1967, 199). In about 1180, a great scandal involving many of the moneyers came out (the details are unknown), and most of them had to pay very large sums of money to the king (in one case 1,000 marks). Lambin Frese, however, fled the country and his stone house was taken over by the king and sometime later leased to Adam of Charing, who died c. 1205-7. On his death Roger the Clerk, Lambin's son, managed to re-acquire the site and he in turn sold it to Alexander of Gloucester for 105 marks, who founded the Hospital for Poor Priests in it in about 1220 (Urry 1967).

The archdeacon of Canterbury, Simon Langton, in 1243 persuaded St. Augustine's Abbey to grant to the hospital the church at Stodmarsh and 4 acres of land as he was concerned to increase the hospital's income. This gift was followed by that of the church of St. Margaret in 1271, also from St. Augustine's, who continued an interest in the affairs of the hospital. (St. Margaret's was the parish in Canterbury in which the hospital stood). In 1315, the hospital failed to render an account and the archbishop appointed a commission to look into its affairs. Grants were made to the hospital in 1317, 1327 and 1330, and Edward III on several occasions excused them payment of tax because they were so poor. There was another enquiry in 1343 when there were three priests and a Syndic (or Master) and the buildings of the hospital were said to be ruinous. From the 1370s onwards rebuilding work clearly took place on quite a large scale and Hasted (1800, 187-190) records that in 1373 Thomas Wyke, the Syndic (Master) rebuilt the hospital in stone.

In 1393, Pope Boniface IX granted indulgence to penitents visiting and giving alms to the hospital.

The hospital escaped dissolution with the monasteries but had been the subject of an enquiry in 1534 in the *Valor Ecclesiasticus* when its gross income was said to be £28 16*s*. 1*d*.In 1548, at the enquiry into the hospitals and chantries the income was £32 3*s*. 11*d*. It had no inhabitant but the rector of St. Margaret's Church, and "never no poor priest nor other poor folk [were] harboured or succoured". 200 years earlier in 1343, the income was £36 8*s*. 7*d*., there was a master and three priests, and £5 was spent on hospitality "for which the house was founded". But the house was poor and the buildings always in need of repair.

Archbishop Parker in 1562 found only a Master, a lay man who did not live at the hospital house, then "marvellously in ruin and decay". The burmote of the City of Canterbury, however, conceived a use for the building, and at least from 1572 they rented it. In May 1575, it was ceded to the Crown, and in July that year granted to the Mayor and Commonalty of the city for the use of the poor. The result was immediate repairs to the buildings. Timber, tiles and bricks were bought, and the work continued in 1576. Another campaign, in which windows, stairs and a kitchen are mentioned, was begun in 1587.

The hospital estates engaged the interest of the burmote. There were inspections, perambulations, takings of distress, and recourse to law to reclaim pieces of land. All the land was detailed in 1343, in 1548 and in later city surveys, the last being in 1772 when copies of all previous maps were made.

The hospital buildings were used for three purposes — as a bridewell or house of correction for offenders, as a lodgings for paupers, and as a school for 16 Bluecoat boys, orphans of tradesmen and others in the city, who were to be educated and apprenticed. Items about all these uses occur in the burmote books and chamberlain's accounts of the city. In 1727, an Act of Parliament set up the Poor Priests' Hospital as the Canterbury Workhouse, which it became in July 1728. The Workhouse Guardians still had to "provide for cloath and maintain 16 poor boys and furnish them with all manner of necessaries, and find them good or sufficient diet, lodging and an apartment by themselves, separate from the other poor in the said Hospital". The hospital lands were to provide for the Bluecoat Boys. In 1842, the income was £728, at last a sizeable increase on the medieval £35. £400 was spent on the boys, and the rest used for the paupers in the workhouse.

In 1849, a new workhouse was completed at Nunnery Fields. Part of the Poor Priests' Hospital was in use as the Canterbury Police Station, and part still used by the Bluecoat Boys. When the new middle schools were opened in 1881 the Bluecoat foundation was merged with them, and gave them their name, Simon Langton Schools, from the archdeacon who provided some of the land for the hospital in 1243. Since the late nineteenth century the Poor Priests' buildings have been used as a furniture store, an organ builders' works, the Buffs' Regimental Museum and the City Health Centre.

THE EXCAVATIONS

The following is an interim report of our work; a more detailed final report will be undertaken when reconstruction work is finished, later in 1981.

The four main excavated areas, part of the service wing to the south of the hall (November

1979), the Hall (January 1980), the solar undercroft (February 1981) and the Chapel (1977), indicate at least three major construction phases. These may relate to the stone house of Lambin Frese, the moneyer, constructed *c.* 1175, the conversion of this to a hospital for poor priests by *c.* 1220 and major reconstructions of the building in the late fourteenth century. The complex series of conversions of the building after *c.* 1575 cannot be considered in this interim report.

Area I: The Service Wing.

Small-scale excavations in the south-west part of this area were undertaken by Mr. and Mrs. Stones early in the 1970s. Unfortunately, these have not been published and the notes on them are not with the Canterbury Archaeological Trust.

An area in the north-west corner of the service wing, undertaken to lower the floor for a new stairwell, was excavated to an average depth of 0.50 m. below the level of the undisturbed surface. The earliest levels consisted of at least four small rooms partitioned by small mortared chalk and flint dwarf walls and floored with clay and mortar. (Fig. 35). Room 1, the best-preserved of the four, was cut away by later walls to the west but measured 3 m. north — south and 2.15 m. east — west. The floor of poured white mortar bedded on clay was preserved, and sealed by a thin lens of occupation detritus which yielded a gold quarter noble of Edward III, *c.* 1363-69. The dwarf walls, on average 0.22 m. wide, bore the scar of the original sleeper-beam, which indicated a timber at least 0.13 m. wide. The bed for the sleeper-beam was levelled with a mixture of fragmented tiles and a few oyster-shells. Small lips of plaster rendering projected above the bed of the dwarf wall, suggesting that the wall was faced with plaster after the beam had been laid.

Room 2 had a floor of compact grey-brown clay; very little of this room was within the excavated area. Rooms 3 and 4 were divided by a partially demolished mortared chalk wall, 0.20 m. wide. The floors of both rooms, laid at approximately the same level as Rooms 1 and 2, were of beaten clay. An iron sickle was found lying on the surface of Room 3. No obvious signs of doors joining the rooms were found. The floor of Room 3 was removed and the underlying levels excavated for a further 0.20 m. The clay floor of Room 3 was laid over a thick deposit of clay containing fragmented plaster. This deposit, possibly residue from a de-molished wall, sealed a further sequence of clay floors, indicating earlier rooms underlying those already discussed. The occupation deposits overlying the floors contained a number of small animal and particularly fish bones together with a few oyster and mussell shells. No pottery was recovered. The coin found in Room 1 would suggest that the small complex of rooms was in use immediately prior to the late fourteenth-century reconstruction of this part of the hospital. It is not inconceivable that they were first constructed in the early thirteenth century, but the presence of a further sequence of floors under Room 3 would suggest that they represented the latest arrangement of rooms prior to the late fourteenth-century recon-struction, and that earlier service rooms underlie them.

The north end of Rooms 1 and 4 was effectively the south end of the hall. Here a substantial dwarf wall, 0.30 m. wide and plaster faced, stood proud of the clay floor by 0.30 m. The floor levels of the service rooms were, on average, 0.25 m. below that of the floors in the hall.

Sealing the service rooms were thick deposits of clay mixed with plaster. These deposits were 0.65 m. thick against the hall-service partition wall, tapering to a mere 0.12 m. at the south edge of Rooms 2 and 3. The dumped deposits, probably the residue from demolished clay infilled walls, seem to have been ramped against the partition wall. Divisions in the thickness of the deposit indicate a gradual accumulation, with each horizontal division being a trodden surface. These divisions were probably created as the internal walls were dismantled prior to the reconstruction processes of the late fourteenth-century. Sealing the clay deposits was a thick levelling dump of brown loam containing much domestic refuse. The nature of this deposit would suggest that this was garden soil, brought in from nearby to level the interior prior to the laying of the late fourteenth-century floors. In some areas patches of mortar and chalk rubble separated the two deposits. Construction trenches for the dwarf walls of the late fourteenth-century building also cut the clay horizon, and were backfilled with brown loam. It would, therefore, seem likely that the frame of the new building was probably constructed from the level of the clay deposit, and the garden soil imported once the construction of the dwarf walls, or even the timber-framing, was completed. The dumped loam deposits not only contained midden but also large quantities of thirteenth- and fourteenth-century pottery. Nothing from this post-dates the late fourteenth century.

Sealing the loam deposit were banded layers of trodden clay. These layers, in places extremely disturbed, may be (at least in part) the final levelling of the dumped deposits and in part the surviving truncated remains of a late fourteenth-century floor.

The late fourteenth-century reconstruction consisted of a new partition wall dividing the hall from the service wing, and the division of the area into one room and a passage, leading from a new screens passage to the south end of the building. A second room existed to the east of the passage, with access via a third doorway at the east end of the screens. These rooms on either side of the passage were presumably the buttery and pantry.

The new partition wall dividing hall and service wing was built directly on top of its predecessor. The wall, 0.30 m. wide, was plaster-faced on both sides and still bore the remains of a plate scar which indicated a sleeper beam of at least 0.20 m. width. The lower part of the wall, laid in a construction trench backfilled with loam, was built entirely of roughly-hewn chalk blocks, and butted against the east and west stone walls of the hall.

The west wall of the new room within the excavated area was not so well constructed, though undoubtedly of the same constructional phase. This wall, built mainly of mortared roughly-hewn chalk blocks and the occasional flint, was not of uniform thickness throughout its length. Half-way along the excavated length the wall changed in width from 0.37 m. to 0.43 m. To the west of the wall deposits of mixed clay, loam and occupation detritus indicated that this wall was an external wall separating the internal floors and open ground. The relationship between this wall and the wall dividing the hall and the service wing was not observed as a more recent brick wall obscured the details. The wall was, however, bonded into a second dwarf wall, the south wall of the room. This dwarf wall, still carrying some of the original posts for the present timber frame, was also of chalk-block build and rendered with plaster. The eastern end of the same dwarf wall was located during the cutting of a service trench (Fig. 35). Here the dwarf wall butted against the eastern wall of the room on the east side of the passage. This north — south wall, also of chalk-block build and badly damaged during the cutting of the trench, butted against the small stone quoins of the stone wall at the south end of the hall. Despite the bonding of the walls at the western intersection and the butt joint at the eastern end, these walls are all undoubtedly contemporary; the differing joints probably only relate to different phases of construction. The east and west walls indicate that the whole of the service wing was probably jettied on both sides — the original framing of both jetties having been removed and replaced by brick walls. Mortice holes in the main posts also indicate the presence of the jetties.

Part of another well-preserved dwarf wall was uncovered during the excavation. This wall, the east wall of the passage and still supporting posts for the existing frame, was only partially within the excavated area; it was also trench-built, the construction trench having been filled with brown loam. The west wall of the passage was less substantially built as it did not constitute a load-bearing part of the main frame, but probably supported a simple screen. The wall, 0.25 m. wide and built of rough chalk blocks, was largely removed when the passage was dismantled and the level of the floor reduced in more recent times.

Access to the passage and the rooms on either side of it was by three doors from the screens passage. The main beam over these doors survived above the modern brick wall and mortice holes (as well as stopped chamfers) indicate exactly where these doors stood, and indicate openings 0.65 m. wide on average.

The overall impression gained from the structural evidence below ground and that still surviving in the present frame is that this was the service (and kitchen) area of the building complex. The partially blackened original roof timbers would suggest this to be the case. If this is a correct assumption, then it would present something of an unusual picture, since early kitchens are usually detached from the main building as a fire précaution. A timber kitchen attached to a stone building also seems somewhat unusual since it seems to compound the fire risk. A forthcoming excavation in the large room to the south of the excavated area should help to clarify this point. One final observation should be made: a small section of flint wall survives in the main west wall of the service range. This fragment of wall, earlier than the surviving frame, may indicate the presence of an earlier detached stone kitchen, perhaps associated with the small service rooms demolished prior to the late fourteenth-century reconstruction. An examination of this wall to determine its relationship to the building phases discussed would certainly further our understanding of how this part of the building was used.

Area II: The Hall

The entire area of the hall was excavated to an average depth of 0.75 m. below the level of the modern concrete floor, in advance of the lowering of the floor for the new museum and the cutting of a number of service ducts. In only one small area were the underlying levels investigated. Here, a 1 m.-wide cutting, 1.50 m. north of the late fourteenth-century screens passage, was cut to a depth of 1.30 m. below the concrete floor. A compact clay floor was found that pre-dated the construction of the flint east wall of the hall, which may in origin be part of the late twelfth-century stone house, and which was sealed by a thick deposit of charcoal with large lumps of charred timber and wattles. Though no dating evidence was recovered, the clay floor sealed by possible demolition deposits may relate to the clearance of buildings owned by Godwin Grom and Gerold the Tanner prior to the construction of Lambin Frese's stone house. Further deposits of clay, 0.30 m. thick, banded with lenses of mortar and containing quantities of broken peg-tiles and slate sealed the deposit of charcoal. These deposits were in turn sealed by a layer of mortar and rubble, possibly a construction horizon, which overlay a slight offset, 0.10 m. wide, in the east wall, indicating the separation of the foundation and the wall itself. Above the level of the offset the wall was rendered in plaster. Sealing the mortar and rubble horizon was a thick clay floor which in turn was capped by occupation detritus. The occupation deposit yielded a fairly worn silver penny of Edward I of 1279. The constructional evidence together with the coin would suggest that this floor and the occupation deposit were associated with the earlier (pre-late fourteenth-century) phase of the hospital. These deposits were sealed by a 0.15 m. layer of clay containing plaster, possibly a demolition deposit accumulated during the destruction of internal clay-infilled walls. This was capped by a further sequence of clay floors associated with a later refurbishment of the building.

The sequence of clay floors excavated throughout the area of the hall was associated with a number of constructional features. An early passage existed at the north end of the hall (i.e. at the opposite end to the later screens passage), perhaps separating the hall from the service area. The passage was 1.40 m. wide and flanked on the north side by a mortared flint dwarf wall bearing the scar of a timber plate 0.20 m. wide. On the south side of the passage the screen was flanked by a rotted ground plate 0.12 m. wide; the plate (surviving as a void) was set into the ground at approximately the level of the hall floor. A complex sequence of worn clay and mortar floors was excavated within the passage. Scars in the east and west stone walls indicate a later blocking of the main doors at either end of the passage which gave access to the original hall in the fourteenth century. The width and ragged nature of the infill indicate that these doors may have had stone quoins. Two more doors at either end of the passage on the south side lead into the hall; these were 1 m. wide and had posts flanking narrow mortared tile and flint thresholds, which bore the scars of timber treads. A third door pierced the dwarf wall in the north-east corner of the passage. Though badly disturbed the offset foundation for the late (fourteenth-century) wall of the hall, this door (which was also flanked by posts), may have had at least one step leading down. This step, retained by wide tiles set in clay, indicated that the earlier service area was at a lower level than the hall. This indeed was found to be the case when the undercroft of the solar was excavated in 1981, the floor being considerably lower than that of the hall. No other north-facing door in the passage was located.

The hall measured 8.70 m. north-south by 7.65 m. east — west and had two low stone walls (possible "benches") built up against the main east and west walls. The western 'bench' was well-preserved and stood well proud of the floor. Though disturbed and robbed at the north and south ends, this 'bench' originally flanked almost the entire length of the hall from the line of the screens passage to the line of a small chalk-block wall, at right angles to the bench and some 0.55 m. north of the south wall of the hall. Built into the bench were four square 0.10 m. posts, spaced on average 2 m. apart.

The eastern 'bench' had been entirely robbed and the trench backfilled with clay containing plaster, tile, flint and mortar debris. Three square 0.10 m. posts, undoubtedly associated with a similar 'bench', were found; these were spaced at intervals of 2.52 m. This 'bench', smaller than its counterpart, was located 0.83 m. south of the screens passage and 2.20 m. north of the south wall of the hall. It is possible that the benches were used as beds for the poor priests living in the hospital. Timber stains, perhaps associated with a retaining device for a raised clay platform, were found at the south end of the hall. Though badly disturbed by a modern sewer, scars of timbers were seen, on average 0.12 m. wide and surrounding an area of soft yellow clay heaped against and butting the south wall of the hall. The west end of this feature butted against a low rubble wall at right angles to the west 'bench' and the east end was set 1.25 m. west of the main east wall of the hall. The arrangement indicated a raised platform of clay, perhaps clad with timber, measuring 5.40 m. by 2.50 m.

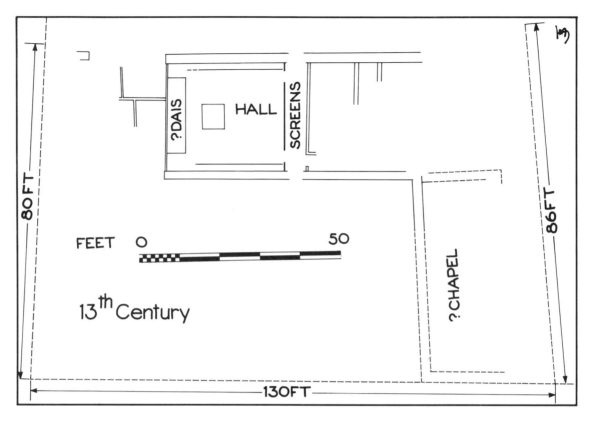

?DAIS   HALL

SCREENS

?CHAPEL

FEET O   50

13th Century

80 FT

86 FT

130 FT

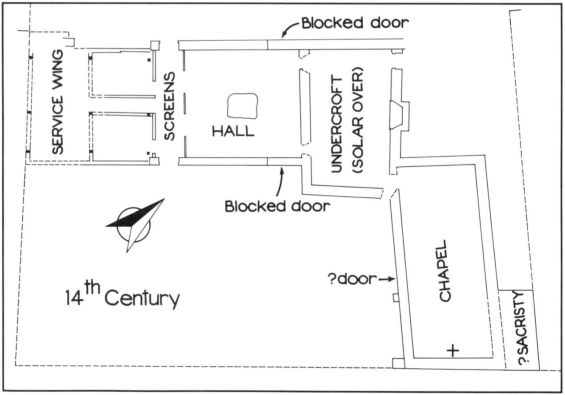

SERVICE WING

SCREENS

HALL

Blocked door

UNDERCROFT (SOLAR OVER)

Blocked door

CHAPEL

?door

?SACRISTY

14th Century

Fig. 36. Plan.

A fine sequence of three central hearths was uncovered to the south of the centre of the hall. The primary hearth, 1.85 m. north — south by 2.05 m. east — west, was constructed entirely of peg-tiles set (end-on) in a bed of clay. This hearth was associated with the first of the clay floors and is perhaps thirteenth-century in date. A thin occupation deposit sealed the floor; this deposit thickened in the area surrounding the hearth and eventually sealed all but the centre of the hearth itself, which was extensively pitted and worn. The occupation detritus surrounding the hearth was sealed by rammed deposits of mortar and chalk, which constituted a bedding for a second clay floor.

A second hearth, 1.63 m. east — west by at least 1 m. north — south, was constructed over the first. This hearth was laid on a mortar bed and had a timber surround. Though badly disturbed, scars for the original timbers, 0.17 m. wide, were discerned in the mortar. Traces of the original pitched tile platform bedded in mortar also survived. This hearth was badly worn and patched and was probably used for a considerable period. The foundations of a third hearth cut the remains of the second. The third hearth measured 1.70 m. by 0.29 m. and was raised well above the level of the contemporary floor, it was probably added to the second phase hearth rather than superseding it. Though partially destroyed, the hearth survived to a maximum height of 6 tile courses, which were set in clay and originally rendered with plaster. This possible 'split-level' hearth arrangement bears a marked similarity to a late thirteenth-century hearth found on 3 Beer Cart Lane in 1979. A considerable depth of occupation debris accumulated over the floor during the period these hearths were in use. Though very few datable finds were recovered from this deposit, it did yield large quantities of small animal and particularly fish bone. Though a few indentations and stake-holes were found (possibly indications of internal furniture), the overall impression is one of a completely open area, with a screens passage to the north, a raised platform or dais to the south, "benches" or storage fixtures to the east and west and a slightly off-centre hearth. The floor was kept relatively clean and was re-surfaced only once during its long life.

These levels were sealed by thick demolition deposits dating to the extensive rebuilding of the hospital during the fourteenth century. The final phase of hearth was demolished and the residue spread over a considerable area. At the same time, the east 'bench' was completely removed, and the resultant hollow filled with clay, plaster and rubble. Also, the timber-framed north and south walls of the hall were dismantled, and the doorposts and frame of the screens passage were removed. A deposit of mortar and rubble, 0.30 m. thick at the base of the east and west walls, and 0.10 m. thick in the centre of the hall, sealed the early levels. This deposit, residue from the partial demolition of the east and west walls, contained very few finds. Two 'piles' of flints were discerned in the matrix of the deposit, close to the east wall. This perhaps suggests that much of the demolished wall material was kept for re-use in the reconstructed building. Much of the original east and west walls was demolished almost to ground level (on average 0.45 m. above the level of the final clay floor). These walls were then rebuilt, using many new roughly-hewn chalk blocks, with three large new windows inserted, probably in both walls. The jambs of the windows in the east wall still survive in part, though all the outside work has gone and been replaced by two tiers of sash windows. The southern ends of both walls were probably left almost intact since small stone quoins, typical of the thirteenth century but not of the later fourteenth century, still survive at their terminal ends on the inside and outside, showing that there was only a timber end-wall.

At the same time, the east and west doors of the original screens passage were probably robbed of their stone quoins and the openings blocked. The excavations in the solar undercroft indicated that the continuation of the east stone wall into the solar was demolished more extensively there than in the hall, since the solar wing was later extended further to the east. At the south end of the hall a new timber frame was erected, separating the hall from the service wing; this was set on a new dwarf wall which was laid directly over its predecessor. A new screens passage was established at the south end of the hall, and a new, more substantial, chalk block wall divided the hall and the solar. The demolition deposits were sealed by extensive deposits of brown loam, containing domestic rubbish with large quantities of thirteenth-century and earlier fourteenth-century pottery. These deposits, similar to those excavated in the service wing to the south of the hall, were capped by a thin deposit of trodden clay, residue from the original bedding for a floor. The floor itself had been reduced by at least 0.10 m. in more recent times, and little survived to suggest internal arrangements within the later hall. However, the foundations of a large central hearth did survive. This foundation, set to the north of centre, indicated a hearth approximately 2.30 m. north — south by 2 m. east — west. The foundation, comprising a bed of large flints set in clay, was constructed after the brown loam had been laid to level the interior of the hall. Though no traces of the bottom of the screens passage were found, the top of the original screens, (a moulded beam), does survive *in situ*. Three doors to the south of this passage gave access to a buttery, pantry and central passage.

The wall dividing the hall and the solar was built of roughly-hewn chalk blocks. This wall, sturdily built to support the solar floor, was laid on an arched pier foundation 1.15 m. thick; it was probably constructed within the shell of the earlier building before the hall walls had been demolished, since the demolition deposits accumulated during the dismantling of the hall walls overlay the foundations. Access to the solar undercroft was by way of one, or possibly two, doors set at either end of the wall. Part of the west door still survives, built of small decorated Caen blocks. The moulding perhaps suggests an early fourteenth-century date. The door flange and an emplacement for a door catch still survive on the east side. This doorway, *c*. 0.70 m. wide on the hall side, may have splayed back to 1.45 m. on the solar side, though it had been partially destroyed when a nineteenth-century fireplace and chimney were erected in the south-west corner of the undercroft. The east doorway is now a large post-medieval affair with brick jambs. It is likely, however, that an earlier medieval door stood here, though no trace of it now survives.

A large number of later post-holes cut all the deposits in the hall. The posts were presumably for internal partitions when the hospital became a workhouse and a school after 1575.

Area III: The Solar Undercroft

This excavation was undertaken in February and March of 1981 to lower the floor, prior to the cutting of service trenches for the new museum. The earliest levels, investigated only in a small cutting in the south-west corner of the undercroft, consisted of a hard mortar floor sealed by a thick deposit of flood silt. This cutting, the deepest of all the trenches cut in the Poor Priests' Hospital so far, indicated the presence of an early half-cellar in this part of the building. The mortar floor overlay the offset foundation of the main west wall, indicating that the half-cellar may have been part of Lambin Frese's stone house. No finds were recovered from the occupation deposits capping the floor and an insufficient area was investigated to determine whether this was actually the moneyer's workshop.

The floor was sealed by thin layers of flood silt mixed with mortar. This deposit was sealed by a 0.22 m. thick dumped layer of grey clay and chalk, indicating an attempt to counteract a rising water-table. Sealing the dumped deposit was a 0.06 m. capping of hard clay, the surface of which was sealed by a compact layer of pebbles. A sequence of at least four clay floors, separated by lenses of flood silt sealed this clay and pebble capping. These floors again indicate that the rising water table continued to be a problem. Sealing the floors was a further dump of grey sandy silt, 0.40 m. thick, indicating perhaps an abandonment of the cellar. This deposit was capped in turn by a further sequence of clay floors associated with at least two parallel east-west dwarf walls (Fig. 36). These walls were probably constructed when a new floor was laid after the cellar had been filled (perhaps in the early thirteenth century). The walls, set only 1.25 m. apart, may have divided the room into two areas, perhaps 3.50 m. wide, separated by a passage defined by the two dwarf walls. As the north end of the early building has not yet been established, this conjectural plan cannot be proved. Both dwarf walls were associated with the main west wall as mortar scars linking the two were observed. The southern dwarf wall, constructed of large flints set in a bed of clay, had two large sandstone blocks set in the fabric of the wall. These large blocks may have supported vertical posts holding the upper floor. An insufficient area of the south dwarf wall was uncovered to determine similar constructional details.

These levels were sealed by dumped destruction deposits, dating to the extensive late fourteenth-century reconstruction of this part of the hospital. Prior to the dumping of these deposits, the east wall of the undercroft was demolished to its foundations. The west wall may also have been extensively demolished, but major rebuilding of this wall in the nineteenth century made this impossible to determine. Nevertheless, a sufficient height of the original plaster-faced lower part of the wall survives to suggest that it was only partly demolished in the fourteenth century. At the same time, new walls were built separating the hall and new solar wing to extend the building to the east. A new north wall, containing a fire-place, was also added. The wall dividing the hall and the solar wing butted against the earlier stone west wall. This wall was trench-built on arched pier foundations from the level of the earlier floor. The foundation was carried up for a further 0.50 m., built free-standing with a 0.10 m. offset, where the wall width narrowed from 1.10 m. to 0.80 m. Similar offsets, stopping at roughly the same level, are seen on the other walls. The new north wall of the solar wing also butted against the earlier west wall. The north-east corner of the hall seems to have been completely reconstructed, the earlier east wall having been demolished to its sub-foundation, and the solar/hall dividing wall carried across for a further 2.20 m. The internal offset for this reconstructed south-east corner of the new solar wing varied in width from 0.42 m. to 0.57 m. This thickened wall foundation was probably due to its proximity to the earlier wall foundation. Elsewhere, the internal offsets were on average 0.25 m. wide; though where the new north wall of the solar wing was carried over the previously demolished east stone wall, the offset tapered from 0.35 m. to 0.10 m. The narrowing of these offsets occured directly over the west edge of this east wall, indicating perhaps that a greater part of the original foundation was re-used in the north wall, and possibly carried through to be incorporated into the south-west corner of the chapel (Fig. 37). The dumped deposits sealing the earlier sequence of floors comprised banded and compacted layers of crushed chalk, mortar and clay. The deposits, on average 0.80 m. thick, contained quite a large quantity of late thirteenth- to early fourteenth-century glazed floor tiles of a Tyler Hill type. These deposits were capped by a compact clay floor.

A single arched door pierced the new north wall. This door, edged with ragstone blocks and decorated with simple chamfer, may have given access to an open yard to the north of the solar undercroft. A threshold of two worn ragstone blocks, one of them fractured, was slightly raised above the level of the floor. Also set in the centre of the new north wall was a hitherto unknown medieval fire-place. The fire-place, 2 m. wide and set back 0.85 m., was largely destroyed by later building alterations and a later drain. However, it still retained one course of moulded ragstone jambs at the bottom on either side. The hearth was fronted by three ragstone blocks with a half-round moulding. The badly disturbed floor of the hearth was of pitched tiles set in a mortar bed. The back walls of the fireplace were of coursed roofing-tiles. A number of bricks were later set into the bed of the hearth to repair areas of wear. A wall supporting the chimney stack, 0.64 m. wide, projected beyond the north wall, and was bonded into it.

In the north-east corner of the solar undercroft was a previously unknown door. The door was set at the point of intersection between the north and east walls of the solar and the south-west corner of the chapel, and gave access both to the exterior and the chapel itself. The thresholds of both doors were of large ragstone blocks. A single Caen-stone quoin block survived on the west side. The doorway leading outside was blocked with a mixture of large ragstone and Caen blocks on the inside face of the solar, and with roughly knapped flints on the exterior. The intervening cavity was filled with unmortared rubble. Some of the original door quoins still survive *in situ*.

A number of windows originally lighted the undercroft — two windows in the east wall (which still survive), and a third (now blocked) in the south-east corner of the undercroft. Other windows may have existed in the now rebuilt west wall.

The floor of the solar undercroft was sealed by a thin deposit of occupation detritus which contained a Genoese *minuto* of Prospero Adorro of 1461. This was in turn sealed by deposits of sand and mortar consistent with bedding for a more durable floor of stone or tile. These deposits were sealed by dumps of mortar, garden soil and clay, containing sixteenth- and seventeenth-century material. These deposits were then sealed by a sequence of sprung floors and a number of brick-built features and post-holes associated with the later life of the building.

Area IV: The Chapel

In 1976, a fragment of a thirteenth-century Purbeck marble engaged column base was discovered in a small trench near the south-west corner. A further small trench cut in the south-west corner of the chapel was excavated in 1977. This small excavation, conducted prior to the laying of a new sprung floor, was cut to a maximum depth of 1.40 m. below the level of the present sprung floor. Two phases for the south wall of the chapel were discovered. The earliest levels excavated consisted of a layer of compact cobbles overlain by crushed chalk and mortar bedding for, perhaps, a tile or stone floor. This possible bedding was associated with a large chalk and flint wall, aligned east — west and roughly at right angles to the east wall of the first stone building. The wall, standing to a height of 0.70 m., may be the south wall of an early chapel — possibly dating to the early thirteenth century — underlying the fourteenth-century wall. The Purbeck marble fragment may also have come from this earlier chapel. The earliest levels were sealed by a 0.50 m. 'dump' deposit of brown loam and chalk; this was then sealed by a compact 0.30 m. deposit of mortar and crushed chalk. The early wall was demolished to the surface of this layer. The top of this layer was heavily compacted and may have been a 'working floor' during the construction of the present south wall of the chapel in the late fourteenth century. This wall re-uses the early wall for part of its foundation and was built of roughly-hewn chalk blocks 0.75 m. thick. The possible working floor was sealed by a further 0.25 m. of compact chalk and mortar debris. This may have been a levelling deposit prior to the laying of the late fourteenth-century floor. However, no traces of such a floor were found in the excavation; these were probably removed in more recent times when the interior of the chapel was lowered. A halfpenny of Edward III of 1344-51 was also found in the trench.

Finally, a number of observations were made when a service trench was cut in 1981, to the south of, and outside the chapel, and the ground level reduced by 0.15 m. prior to the laying of a new flagstone pavement. The service trench (for a new gas supply to the building), uncovered a 0.60 m. wide external offset for the late fourteenth-century south wall of the chapel. The offset was of mortared chalk blocks and was located 0.72 m. below the level of the old pavement. Surmounting this foundation were three courses of ashlared Kentish ragstone blocks. This ashlar work was capped by another course of ragstone blocks with a simple chamfer, which was recessed 0.10 m. from the face of the lower ashlar. The wall face was then carried on up in roughly knapped coursed flints with large ragstone quoins tying the corners. The well-dressed and tightly-fitting ashlar work used in the lower part of the chapel wall (and the east side of the solar wing) bears a marked similarity to the blockwork used in the construction of the plinth of the medieval city wall, in particular, a stretch called "The Long Wall" in the documents, running from the west to the North Gate of Canterbury, which was under construction from 1380 onwards.

A hitherto unknown chapel buttress was discovered when the new pavement was laid. This buttress was bonded into the south wall of the chapel and positioned some 4.1 m. west of the existing south-east corner buttress of the chapel. Only the truncated top was uncovered; this was made of slightly battered ashlared work. This buttress would have come between the two chapel windows, parts of which still survive buried in the fabric of the wall. A previously unknown medieval inscription was discovered over the south door of the chapel, and though badly weathered, a number of letters (including the name RICARDO) can be clearly seen. Further work on this inscription, which needs conserving, would certainly be worthwhile.

A doorway was found at the point of intersection between the chapel south wall and the solar wing east wall. This door, 0.65 m. wide, had a ragstone block threshold, and gave access not only to the solar undercroft but also to the chapel. Two phases of blocking were discerned. A small mortared chalk wall rendered with plaster, and recessed 0.20 m. into the wall, indicated a possible late-medieval blocking. This was sealed by the complete infilling of the doorway in knapped flint on the exterior and rough re-used ashlar blocks and brickwork on the interior of the solar. This was presumably done in the sixteenth century.

Two major areas are still due for excavation: the chapel and the south end of the service wing. These potentially important sites may be examined late in 1981 or early in 1982.

ACKNOWLEDGEMENTS

We are particularly grateful to Canterbury City Council, and in particular Messrs. G.

Couchman and C. Bowley (of the City Architect's Department) and Mr. K. Reedie (City Museums Curator), for access to the building at all times, and for constant help and advice with our recording work. The drawings are the work of Mr. J. Bowen.

THE RECTORY HOUSE AT CLIFFE-AT-HOO

KENNETH GRAVETT

In 1870, the Rev. H.R. Lloyd commenced work on the Rectory House at Cliffe-at-Hoo. He left an account of what he did in *Arch. Cant.* (Lloyd 1883, 255) and illustrated it with an elevation and a plate of fragments of moulded stonework, but unfortunately gave no plan. The Rectory House was sold in April 1972 and, anticipating this and at the suggestion of Mr. R.H. Hiscock, the author visited the house in October 1970, to prepare a plan. He wishes to thank the Rev. J.J. Smith for his kindness in allowing this and also Mr. Hiscock for his assistance with the measurements and the arrangements.

The Rectory House is an isolated building, standing a little over a mile to the south of the church (N.G.R. TQ 733749) and oriented approximately east — west. The church and parish are both large: the living was a rich one and a peculiar of the Archbishop of Canterbury. The Rectory House was of a size commensurate with its importance, having a hall of internal length 37 ft. 9 in. and internal width 24 ft. 9 in. The Rev. Henry Robert Lloyd was sixty when he was instituted in 1869 and was the first resident rector for many years. He also commenced a campaign of restoration at the church (Gray 1978), much at his own expense. At the Rectory House, he recognised the significance of the building and explained how he had discovered and opened up the service doorways. The building to the west of these was entirely his work, the site having been part of the stable yard in 1869, although he found earlier foundations and followed their line. In 1970 the doors were again blocked as the new section was separately occupied. In the plan (Fig. 38) no attempt has been made to plot other than the outline of those parts known to be Mr. Lloyd's work. Stone walls remain of the hall to a height of some 9 ft., and in the rooms to the east, originally of two storeys, to 15 ft. All of the existing roofs are Victorian. The internal walls are plastered throughout and no ancient window-tracery remains. Mr. Lloyd found a fragment of a shouldered ('Caernarvon') arched window and he used this design for all of his new windows, many of them larger than the originals. To match these he chose as design for his new fireplaces a plate of one at Charney, Berkshire, from Turner and Parker (Turner and Parker 1851, 154).

The hall has three doorways in its west wall, a pair 3 ft. 6 in. wide, not quite centrally placed, and another 2 ft. 4 in. wide by the south wall. This led to a stone staircase to the upstairs room, broken treads being found close by in 1870. All the doors are severely plain, with two-centred arches and broach stops at their bases, the two service doors having hollow gated. Here, a 1 m.-wide cutting, 1.50 m. north of the late fourteenth-century screens passage, but the other remains in use. The north wall has a section of flint-and-stone banding outside, as in Cliffe Church, and also has a 3-in. plinth throughout its length and returning along the east wall (exaggerated to show on the plan). The south-western window retains its window

THE RECTORY HOUSE, CLIFFE-AT-HOO — GROUND FLOOR PLAN

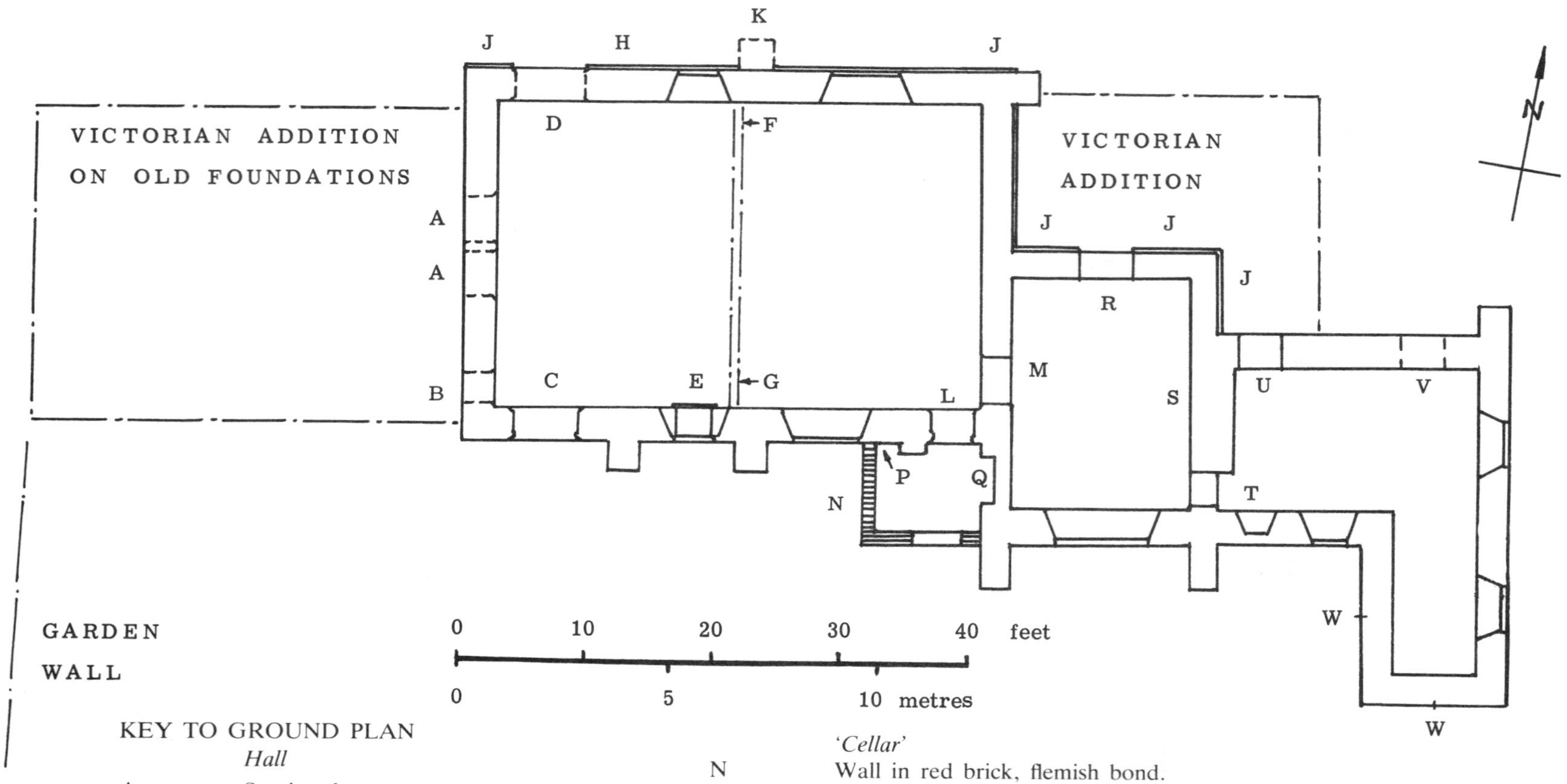

J
H
K
J
D
F
C
E
G
L
A
A
B
VICTORIAN ADDITION
ON OLD FOUNDATIONS
VICTORIAN
ADDITION
J
J
J
R
M
S
U
V
T
P
Q
N
W
W
N
GARDEN
WALL
0 10 20 30 40 feet
0 5 10 metres

KEY TO GROUND PLAN

	Hall
A	Service doorways.
B	Smaller doorway, probably to stairs.
C	Entrance doorway.
D	Blocked entrance doorway.
E	Window with original seats.
F,G	Jacobean timber partition.
H	Area of flint and stone banding.
J	Plinth.
K	Site of buttress.
L	Doorway with moulded label.
M	Parlour door
	'Cellar'
N	Wall in red brick, flemish bond.
P	Window in narrow brick. Mr. Lloyd found window tracery here.
Q	Recess.
	Parlour
R	Pre-1870 front door, cut in medieval wall.
S	Wall thickened for fireplace.
	Room beyond Parlour
T	Niche.
U	Modern door.
V	Blocked door.
W	Position of small, blocked square-headed windows on first floor.

Fig. 37.

PLATE XXXVI

The three doorways at the west end of the hall.

PLATE XXXVII

The south-west window of the hall, showing the seats.

PLATE XXXVIII

The two doors at the south-east corner of the hall.

PLATE XXXIX

Exterior from south-west (from left to right) hall, 'cellar', parlour and room beyond parlour.

seats. That on the north west matches it in size, but the other two have been widened. Mr. Lloyd found broken tracery (of 'decorated' form, with a rebate for a shutter) in the infilling of the south-east window. Both of the doors in the south-east corner of the hall are medieval. One leads to the parlour, the other to a brick porch in Flemish bond, known to Mr. Lloyd as the cellar. This door which has a mutilated label moulding, a flattened roll with a wide frontal fillet, could have lead to stairs, as at Penshurst, or to a passage as at Meister Omers, Canterbury. A floor has been inserted in the hall which is divided by a timber partition and both are of Jacobean date. Two windows upstairs are of brick, probably contemporary with the 'cellar', which dates from c. 1680 and blocks the remains of a window of thin brick.

To the east of the hall are two rooms, both of two storeys, a parlour and an L-shaped room to the east. It is unlikely that these are contemporary, since the plinth on the north wall of the hall is continued around the parlour only. The east parlour wall has been thickened for a chimney and Mr. Lloyd found a Tudor fireplace upstairs here. The chimneys are all Victorian and an extension was made in front of the pre-1870 front door, which had been inserted in the north parlour wall. This extension contains the present hall and stairs. In 1870, the L-shaped room was open to the roof. Mr. Lloyd converted it into a study, with a bedroom above and put fireplaces in the end of the south wing. In 1970, this was the kitchen, the Victorian fireplace being blocked by a solid-fuel cooker, and very few old features were visible. There are two small, square-headed, blocked windows upstairs in the south and west walls. Although the room faces east, there is no sign of the piscina needed for a chapel. Hussey (1911, 228) refers to a chapel in the house in 1338, but it is likely that it was elsewhere. Possibly the rector of Cliffe added a further private room beyond his solar, as at Croydon Palace, and the narrow extension to the south could represent a garderobe, similar in size to that at Old Soar. The plan may be much more complicated, awaiting excavation for its elucidation. The two large buttresses on the south parlour wall may show where an extension has existed, while Mr. Lloyd found many fragments of stone work in the area to the north and believed a chapel to have been on this side. The present block could well have been a central range between two courtyards, as at Croydon. The fragments of stone were collected and built into a garden wall, which ran south from the west end of the new west block and which had largely collapsed by 1970.

Difficult as it is to understand the plan, the dating is even more of an enigma. The plain-ness of the doors and complete absence of roof do not help. The one remaining moulding could date from the second half of the thirteenth century. The horizontal banding of flint and ragstone is found in many churches of north-east Kent, including the early fourteenth-century parts of Cliffe and Higham, and the west tower at Herne of c. 1310. In the absence of better criteria, an early fourteenth-century date can be offered for the hall and parlour, with the L-shaped room a later addition. It is in matters of dating that the author misses the skill and encyclopaedic knowledge of the late Stuart Rigold.

SOME REFLECTIONS ON THE DEVELOPMENT OF THE CENTRALLY-PLANNED HOUSE

P. SMITH

Note

This article is written not only as a tribute to Stuart Rigold whose wide ranging and enquiring mind covered many aspects of vernacular architecture but also in memory of a dear friend of twenty-five years standing, Mr. C.E.V. Owen, of Llanidloes, who helped me to survey the two houses principally illustrated, Plasnewydd (Llanwnnog), and Tŷ-faenor (Abbey Cwm-hir). More than a quarter of a century ago Cecil Owen showed me some half-timbered houses in the Llanidloes area. All but one were built to the local sub-medieval, lobby-entry, central-chimney, pattern. The exception was Plasnewydd. We pondered about the house many times and some years later we discovered a house of a similar plan and age, Tŷ-faenor not far away in neighbouring Radnorshire. Two years ago we decided we should make a complete survey of these two remarkable buildings, and these surveys are published here. Cecil Owen died suddenly at the age of 79 within a fortnight of our last expedition together.

Some months ago I toured some villages in Alsace, a rewarding, indeed an unforgettable experience, not only because it would be difficult to parallel these concentrated village layouts anywhere in the British Isles, not even in those areas where the village is the norm of rural settlement, but also because it would be hard to parallel the conservatism of their construction and to some extent the conservatism of their design. Houses with half-timbered, black-and-white walls abounded, many dated by inscriptions, some as late as the second half of the nineteenth century (Plate XLII). These attractive and archaic buildings were clearly part of a continuing tradition and not a piece of 'vernacular revival'. The houses were all set gable end to the street each with a small courtyard alongside around which stood the farm buildings. The house could only be entered from the yard which itself was entered by a gateway from the street. Each, I was told, was a small farmhouse, whose fields lay outside the village. Indeed this must have been the case, for as one travelled from village to village six or seven miles apart not a solitary building was to be seen in the intervening hedgeless fields.

Occasionally, about once in each village, there would be a house quite different from the rest (Plate XL). It appeared to be of mass-wall construction, though it was impossible to say what material lay under the smooth plaster rendering. Unlike the farmhouses the house stood in its own grounds without associated farm buildings the main front facing the street, and this elevation was formally symmetrical in its design, the front door in the centre, and the windows evenly spaced on each side. 'What houses are these?' I asked my guide, Madame Scheurer, a conservateur from the *Inventaire régional* based on Strasbourg. 'They are priests' houses. We can always recognize a clergyman's house. They are quite different from those of the peasants'.

As I travelled home through Hessen I saw many houses and many villages which appeared to resemble those of Alsace, half-timbered dwellings on two main floors, platform-framed (*zweistöckig*) rather than balloon-framed (*zweigeschossig*), the houses set fairly close together with their yards alongside. Further north in lower Saxony and the Netherlands such houses gave way to the extraordinary aisled long-houses of northern Germany where the peasant lives at one end of an enormous barn which houses all his stock and stores. Nowhere did I see farmhouses which corresponded closely to those which can reasonably be claimed as the commonest British farmhouse type, the stone or brick box, its symmetrical main elevation (facing the main approach) consisting of a central doorway flanked by evenly spaced windows and gable chimneys, a house in its basic conception not altogether unlike the priests' houses I had seen in Alsace but seemingly very unlike the farmhouses.

What are the salient features of the most characteristic British farmhouse type, a house which had its origins in the middle of the seventeenth century, and which by the middle of the eighteenth century was beginning to displace traditional patterns of building in a big way? The first characteristic is a symmetrical main elevation, the second is a siting designed to impress, the main front facing the approach. The third is an inclination to site the house away from the village in its own fields, or at least on the outskirts rather than the centre of the village. The fourth is a tendency to site the house away from its buildings, though this would depend on the social standing of the farmer and the locality; the higher the standing and the more 'lowland' the locality, the more marked would be the tendency to separation. The final development is the evolution of a centralised system of circulation, the house built astride a central passage at one end of which is the front door, and at the other a framed dogleg stair. The fireplaces are nearly always on the gable walls. The passage, stair, and fireplaces are repeated on each floor. The larger houses are built 'double pile' that is with a range of rooms front and back, the central stair passage bisecting both. The smaller houses may have a rear range, but contained in a lean-to under a catslide roof rather than under a second full roof divided from the first by a valley. Alternatively, the house may be planned in the shape of a T, the rear stem containing a kitchen projecting at right-angles to the main block.

All these developments resulted in the British farmhouse looking more and more like the manor-house of a small squire, the suburban villa of a member of the bourgeoisie, or the vicarage of the village parson, and less and less like a farmhouse as such. On architectural grounds it would often be very difficult to distinguish our late eighteenth- and nineteenth-century farmers' houses from those of quite different social groups in a way that it would not be at all difficult in Alsace.[1]

The first centrally planned villa-type houses can be seen either as the culmination of a gradual evolution from the sub-medieval house over half a century, or as the result of a sudden flash of inspiration, as it were, a sudden surge of creative imagination applied to the dwelling problem. By whichever road they arrived it seems reasonable to date the first complete examples to about the middle of the seventeenth century. These first central stair-passage houses are best exemplified not so much in the houses of the great landowners as in those of the middling squires. It is arguable that other major architectural changes are to be associated more with this middle class than with the top *strata* of society. Court and aristocracy seem to have retained the open hall and intercommunicating suites of rooms for reasons of prestige and as a setting for great gatherings long after the middling squires had come to appreciate the comforts and convenience of the completely compartmentalized house.

To understand the changes which the new plan represented it is necessary to go back briefly to its precursor, the sub-medieval house, the house that developed out of the medieval hall-house, but which now incorporated an enclosed fireplace and an overall upper floor. Such houses had become common form in most of Britain south of the Pennines, east of Pumlumon and east of Dartmoor by the beginning of the seventeenth century. Within this area there were significant variations in structure and in plan which there is no space to discuss in detail here. Suffice it to say that such houses, built in a single range, were completely asymmetrical on their main elevation and they lacked any central system of circulation. The middle rooms of the house, whether the hall on the ground floor or the chamber above, were passage rooms and the stairs, usually in the form of winding stairs by the fireplace, opened directly out of the hall and communicated directly with the chamber above. Thus most rooms on the ground floor and all rooms on the first floor are entered through the hall. The entry whether by the earlier cross-passage or the later lobby-entry had no direct link with the stair. One large ground-floor room, the hall, continued to dominate the house. Such house-types had been known in Wales since the mid-sixteenth century. By the early seventeenth century certain changes began to make their appearance.

The first major development was a great improvement in the design of the stair. A framed stair either in the form of a dogleg but more often a well began to supersede the old winding stair set in a recess by the fireplace. The new stairs were often housed in turrets projecting off the rear wall of the hall or occasionally as part of the front porch.

A second change involved the transfer of the service-rooms or kitchen to the rear so that instead of being housed in a continuation of the main range they were placed in an outshut or wing projecting from the rear. The main range thus tended to be reduced from three principal units to two, and the plan became more compact and less strung out.

A third development was the search for formal symmetry in the main elevation. The main door was placed as near the centre of the elevation as practicable, and was often emphasised by a porch, often storeyed.

Such developments paved the way for the centrally planned house but they did not immediately achieve it. By the middle of the seventeenth century a small landowner's house might have the stair and service-rooms in a rear projection and the entry enclosed in a storeyed porch. It might even have an enclosed passage linking the front door with the rear wing. Pool Hall (Crucadarn, Brecs.) had all three yet the stair rises out of the hall (used here in the old sense of living-room and not in the later sense of entrance lobby), through which the first floor was reached (Fig. 38a). Piodau-fawr (Llandybie, Carms.) has a basically very similar plan, hall and parlour on each side of a central passage, leading to a rear wing, this time incorporating a full kitchen rather than a service-room (Fig. 38b). The stair, a very fine well stair, however, opens not off the living room but off the passage, and there is a central stair lobby in the rear wing from which the entry and all other rooms in the house can be independently reached. In this house a system of circulation giving complete privacy had been achieved. Pool Farm is dated by inscription to 1670. Piodau-fawr is undated, but the details particularly of the stair, the classical pedimented internal doorways and the bold plasterwork on the coffered ceiling to the parlour indicate a similar date.

Piodau-fawr suggests the achievement of a centralised circulation as the end product of a series of progressive improvements which can be traced back to the beginning of the seventeenth century. We now turn to two houses probably of much the same date, which imply no such gradual development but a comprehensive ingeniously thought out design which solves the whole circulation problem at a stroke. It presupposes a single master designer — might one say an architect? Both houses are set in the depths of the mid-Wales countryside. Both were clearly the houses of men of rank, but neither are particularly large.

There is not much doubt who built Tŷ-faenor (Abbey Cwm-hir, Rads.). It is almost certainly Richard Fowler who was High Sheriff of Radnorshire in 1656. A rhyme bewailing the relative poverty of Radnorshire runs:

'Radnorsheer, poor Radnorsheer
Never a park and never a deer
Never a squire of five hundred a year
But Richard Fowler of Abbey Cwmhir'.

In the eighteenth century the Fowlers achieved the rank of baronet, by which time they had moved from Tŷ-faenor to a much larger house close to Abbey Cwm-hir, the Cistercian monastery that the family had acquired after the Reformation. Tŷ-faenor (Figs. 39-40) would not strike a visitor from the south of England as the house of a major landed family, but one has to keep the problem of the geography of wealth in mind. The resources which would support only a small estate in Kent would constitute considerable wealth in Radnorshire. Although Tŷ-faenor is by no means a large house, and although it has to-day a very rural appearance, there can be no doubt that it was designed for a man who moved in fashionable circles, not only locally but nationally.

About Plasnewydd (Llanwnnog, Mont.), although a larger house, we know very little. The mansion is not mentioned in the Note of 1630 concerning the Tithes of Carno, although there are repeated references to Lewis Evans of Plasauduon nearby, so one can only conclude it was built some time after 1630. The historian of the parish, Mrs. Andrew Davies, wrote 'nowhere have I been able to trace any history of Gilfach, Plasnewydd, Ty-Mawr or Castell farm', and we have not been able to do any better. Its builder is unknown.

As will become evident Tŷ-faenor and Plasnewydd share a basic idea, the idea of a centralised circulation by means of a stair passage, and as far as we know they are the earliest houses in Wales to have this feature. Both are sited on sloping ground, and their plans relate to the slope in a similar way. Their similarities are much more striking than the differences in construction (stone walls at Tŷ-faenor, timber-framed walls at Plasnewydd) or in design (the rooms one room deep at Tŷ-faenor, and two room deep at Plasnewydd).

Neither house is closely dated. Tŷ-faenor, to judge from its massively detailed stair could be as early as c. 1650. Might we conjecture that it was built in 1656 to celebrate Richard Fowler's appointment as sheriff?

The house is sited on steeply-sloping ground and has four floors including basement and loft. There are two entries, one to the ground floor on the uphill side, and one to the basement on the downhill side. The plan consists of a central passage on each floor at the rear end of which is a dogleg stair. On each side of the passage is a single large room. Assuming the loft was once used as living space (the rebuilding of the roof makes it difficult to be certain on this point) there were four rooms on each side of a central stairway, giving eight rooms in all, each of which could be reached independently of the others from both entrances.

Besides this there was horizontal segregation. Presumably the gentry entered at the first floor, and could live completely segregated (if they so wished) from the kitchens in the basement. The windows on the north (uphill side) are now blocked, and it is difficult to be certain of their original size. The house is now lighted by wide windows on the south (downhill) side only, and these give commanding views over the bosky Radnorshire countryside. Unfortunately, the windows themselves are replacements placed in the original openings and part of the south wall has been rebuilt, clearly on the lines of the original. However, the massively framed front doorway with its richly carved ornate head and the triple diagonal shafts rising from the projecting gable chimneys have all the hall-marks of a mid seventeenth-century building, an interpretation confirmed inside by the richly carved stairway with its remarkably elaborate newels and pierced balustrade.

Plasnewydd would appear on stylistic grounds to be somewhat later than Tŷ-faenor (Figs. 41-42). The stair is less massively detailed and the front door has a plain square head without the enrichment of Tŷ-faenor. Plasnewydd is the larger house, built two rooms deep instead of one (in a sense double-pile although under a single roof). It is of close-studded, half-timbered construction apart from the stone-walled basement set into the hillside, and the fireplaces and chimneys which are partly stone and partly brick. The latter have been largely rebuilt. In our drawing their likely original appearance is restored. The house is again on four floors (including basement and loft). The main entry is again to the ground floor on the uphill side, while there is a secondary entry to the basement downhill. The house again consists of a central passage terminating in a dogleg stair, and on each side of the stair passage is arranged a room, front and back. Thus each room enjoys independent access from the central stair hall; a perfect system of circulation has been achieved. The larger and more important rooms are placed on the rear, downhill side of the house and they command fine views over the countryside. This shows clear thinking, as so many later houses of centralised plan tend to place the more important rooms on the entrance front irrespective of aspect or outlook. The very large mullioned and transomed windows survive more or less intact. Each is ovolo moulded as is the front doorway. It would be useful to have the latest probable date for a mullioned ovolo-moulded window. They are generally employed in the much less skilfully designed Castle House, Monmouth, built for the Earl of Worcester (later Duke of Beaufort) in 1673. The ceilings at Plasnewydd are plastered, but with main beams exposed, each with the characteristic seventeenth-century broad chamfer and ogee stop. The stair, which is again the show-piece of the house has square newels with finials and pendants, moulded balusters, square in section, all consistent with a late seventeenth-century date. On its downhill front the house is completely symmetrical. On its main entrance front is a curious irregularity. On the ground floor, left of the main door are two small windows instead of one large one; an inexplicable variation which mars the otherwise symmetrical design. The main entrance front is now flanked by two rows of farm buildings which add to the formality of the approach. It is difficult to be sure whether they are part of the original design, but they certainly add to its formal impressiveness.

By the end of the seventeenth century the central stair-passage was beginning to gain general acceptance among the squires, whether in a single pile or the more common double pile form. An instance of the former may be cited in Gelli (Trefilan, Cards.) which still retains a set of mullion and high transom windows, and which has the stairs in a rear projecting turret in the old style. A rear range of lean-to-service-rooms was added early on (Fig. 43). At Edwinsford (Llansawel, Carms.) is a good example of a single pile central stair (as at Tŷ-faenor) is contained within the central bay of the house and does not require a projection to contain it (Fig. 44b). At Faenor (Llawhaden, Pembs.) is a similar plan (Fig. 44a).

Fortunately the house is dated 1707 by an inscription, and as at Edwinsford two large rooms stand on each side of the central stairway. Among the double pile houses one might mention Fforest (Brechfa, Carms.) Dated 1724 (Plate XLIV). These houses illustrate a trend which was rapidly spreading among the landowners all over the British Isles, and by the end of the century among their more substantial tenants.

To-day the central stair passage has long been a background to our lives, that we take it very much for granted. As a design for living its advantages seem so obvious and self-evident that we easily forget that it has not been in existence very long, and that it is the result of a conscious act of invention. When the first houses of this type were erected in the depths of the Welsh countryside they must have appeared quite revolutionary. It is hardly conceivable that they were invented locally, yet the basic similarity of their design suggests that the idea was circulating among a few squires at the time. Its precise origin I have not been able to discover. The standard works on the history of architecture have very little to say on its emergence.[2] And yet the appearance of this plan is the most important contribution the seventeenth century had to make to the development of architecture.

It appears that the central stair-passage house would have been normal amongst the landowners by the middle of the eighteenth century, and was by then spreading to the yeomen even in areas so remote as the Eden Valley according to Dr. Brunskill. But I do not think it had become general in this latter class until the Victorian Age. Then innumerable numbers of tenanted farms were erected to this plan (Plate XLV). There can be no county in the country where they are not numerous and in the western coastlands of the British Isles they must be the commonest house type there is, even if we include the single-storeyed cottage in the count of the alternatives.

What is the significance of a type of house that had thus been spreading for two-and-three-quarter centuries? It may be argued that it arose out of the same social changes that had previously produced the sub-medieval, central-chimney, lobby-entry house with a direct entry to the parlour from the front door, changes which are alleged to have arisen from the decline in the status of the farm and household servants as a result of which the landowning or tenant family sought a high degree of privacy for themselves. Certainly the social status of the servants in great houses seems to have been declining since the sixteenth century when it was still the fashion for a nobleman to employ men of rank as servants in his household. Whether a parallel development took place lower down the social scale would be more difficult to determine. Another factor may involve an increasing differentiation among the peasantry, the emergence of some as successful tenant-farmers, and the relegation of others to the status of day-labourers. Again this would tend to the development of a house which conferred privacy and which implied strong social differentiation.

But it seems likely the plan could have developed without such factors. After all the tendency is for all machinery to be improved. One does not have to identify a social change to explain why a motor-car of 1980 is basically a more efficient means of transportation than a motor-car of 1930. Slow improvements of the 'machine à habiter' are probable in the nature of things, and unquestionably the central stair-passage house was a more convenient 'machine à habiter', than the sub-medieval storeyed house, just as the sub-medieval storeyed house was an unquestionable improvement on the earlier hall-house.

If we are to take the central stair-passage house as an indication of technical advance, then perhaps its diffusion can be taken as an indication of progress in a general sense, and this brings us back to our starting point. If this plan became diffused much earlier and more widely in rural Britain than on the Continent, can this be interpreted as one of the *indicia* of the age of British supremacy, the age which really began in the seventeenth century with the establishment of parliamentary government and the beginnings of a great empire? The eighteenth century accession of the Hanoverians consolidated parliamentary government while the great naval victories placed the empire beyond the reach of continental rivals. Under the Victorians the empire reached its apogee now reinforced by British industrial supremacy. For three centuries things had gone very well for Britain which now lives in a state of permanent mystification why things have not continued to prosper. Unfortunately, success is not a law of nature for any nation. Perhaps we can link the dominance of this house type with an age of remarkable success; its beginnings about the time of the Commonwealth, its general acceptance by the landowning classes by the middle of the eighteenth century and its apogee in the nineteenth century when industry and empire raised Britain to a peak of power and influence which are unlikely to be experienced ever again.

1. I must write with caution over contrasts between Great Britain and Alsace in the development of the centralised plan itself, however confident I feel over the other differences. The Alsatian farmhouse often has a type of centralised plan although little attempt is made to express this in a formal elevation. Many are illustrated in the *Inventaire topographique* for Saverne. They have a small entrance hall containing a steep stairway. Behind the hall is a working kitchen, to one side a parlour with a bed alcove to the rear, and on the other side a small parlour with a chamber behind opening off the kitchen.

    The planning of the central area is complicated by the need to fit in an internal stove fired from the kitchen, but projecting into and heating the parlour. A central fire heating the whole house is clearly characteristic of central Europe. It contrasts with the later British fashion of placing the fireplaces on the end walls in order to simplify circulation and the placing of the stairs. This end chimney layout leads more easily to a formally symmetrical elevation.

    The *Inventaire topographique* says nothing about how the Alsation plan evolved or the form of possible predecessors. In the museum at Kommern, however, is re-erected a large number of farmhouses from the middle Rhine region many structurally very similar to those of Alsace, but nearly all having a form of sub-medieval plan, the rooms arranged in sequence, the entry directly into the main room (*herdraum*) and the stair rising out of it. In these houses (mainly late seventeenth - eighteenth century) there is no indication of the development of a centralised plan.

    I have discussed the continental development of the centralised plan with Dr. Karl Baumgarten, the well-known German authority on vernacular architecture, sending him copies of my drawings of Tŷ-faenor and Plasnewydd. He has told me that he would regard such houses as completely uncharacteristic of German rural building.

2. Although the plan is the most important contribution the seventeenth century had to make to the development of domestic architecture the standard works on architectural history have little to say on its emergence and some ignore it altogether, concentrating on the development of essentially decorative ideas based on the grammar of classical architecture. Clearly the symmetrical front and the central stair plan are related but quite distinct ideas. Some of the masterpieces of sixteenth- and early seventeenth-century classical architecture have no contribution whatsoever to make to the improvement of circulation within the house. The earliest plans involving greatly improved circulation appear to be associated (in Great Britain at least) with Sir Roger Pratt, and his designs for Coleshill in 1650. But Coleshill's centralised plan involves a stair hall and not a stair passage and in any case stylistic dating would not place Tŷ-faenor any later than Coleshill! I am not suggesting, however, that the central stair passage house was invented in Radnorshire. I am simply seeking an opinion, on where and by whom? A possible origin of the central stair access is in collegiate architecture, the stair rather than corridor access found in the Oxford and Cambridge colleges where individual suites of rooms are reached from landings. These provide privacy for the occupants in much the same way as does the central stair passage at Tŷ-faenor, but of course these stairs are not linked with the public rooms of the colleges save through the courtyards and the open air!

PLATE XL

Courtesy: Inventaire général

The Presbytery at Geispolsheim (near Strasbourg, Alsace), built in 1759, stands in its own grounds, and has a symmetrical elevation facing the road. It is immediately recognizable as the house of the parish priest, easily distinguishable from the peasant farmhouses which form the rest of the village (see Plates XLI and XLII, *overleaf*).

PLATE XLI

Courtesy: Inventaire général

Geispolsheim, *above*, farmhouses along Rue du Maréchal Leclerc dated 1809, 1783, 1844; *below*, farmhouse dated 1785, Petite Rue du Château. Note the extraordinary concentration of houses each with its yard and buildings. Note the gallery, a common feature in Alsace but whose purpose seems to be forgotten.

PLATE XLII

(Courtesy: Inventaire général)

Geispolsheim, *above* farmhouses along Rue Fer à Cheval, dated 1860 and 1863, *below* farmhouse 10 Rue du Château dated 1845. The archway leading to the yard at the rear is dated 1871.

PLATE XLIII

Early centrally-planned houses, *above* Tŷ-faenor (Abbey Cwm-hir, Rads.), view from downhill showing basement entry. The mezzanine windows light the stair; *below* Plasnewydd (Llanwnnog, Mont.) view from uphill showing the ground floor entry. Note the extraordinary large windows which have been since partly blocked.

PLATE XLIV

(Courtesy: R.C.A.M. Wales)

The Old Rectory (Llanbedr, Denbs.) *above* probably dating from *c.* 1700 may be compared with the Presbytery at Giespolsheim (Plate XL). Both show the clergy in the vanguard of fashion. Fforest (Brechfa, Carms.) *below* is another upper-class house built two-rooms deep with central stairway and gable chimneys. It has a date-inscription 1724 over the door.

PLATE XLV

Typical eighteenth-nineteenth century British farmhouses showing standardisation on the Rennaissance-inspired, symmetrically fronted, central stair-passage design, each house in its own grounds and each apart from its buildings and away from the village centre: *top left*, King's Farm, 1738 (Over Wallop, Hants.); *top right*, Broughall Farm (Whitechurch, Salop); *middle left*, Brick House Farm (Sandbach Cheshire); *middle right*, Pentre-coch Farm (Llanfair D.C., Denbs.); *bottom left*, Wern Philip (Upper Vaynor, Cards.); *bottom right*, Dunstaffnage Mains Farm (Dunstaffnage, Argyll). Note the mass-wall construction (brick or stone) and the sliding windows except at Brick House Farm.

PLATE XLVI

Aldbourne, Wilts., the village green and church. Unlike the Alsatian village Geispolsheim, the centre of which is entirely made up of farmhouses, the centre of Aldbourne is made up of artisans' houses, the farmhouses being either on the outskirts or in the distant fields. Even the artisans' houses clearly follow the conventions of symmetrical design.

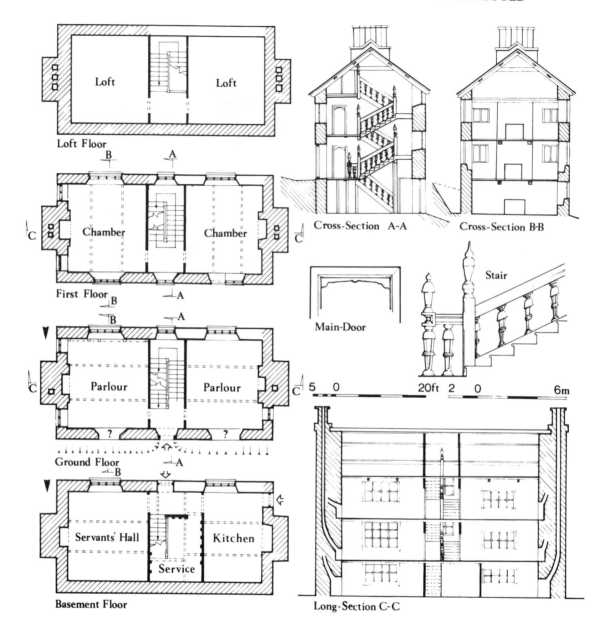

Fig. 39. Tŷ-faenor (Abbey Cwm-hir, Rads.) is the earliest known Welsh example of the central stair-passage plan. Here the stair is not placed in a rear projection (see Pool Hall and Piodau-fawr on p. 212) as was common in the early seventeenth century, but in the body of the house, as became the standard later practice.

Note: for Fig. 38 see p. 212.

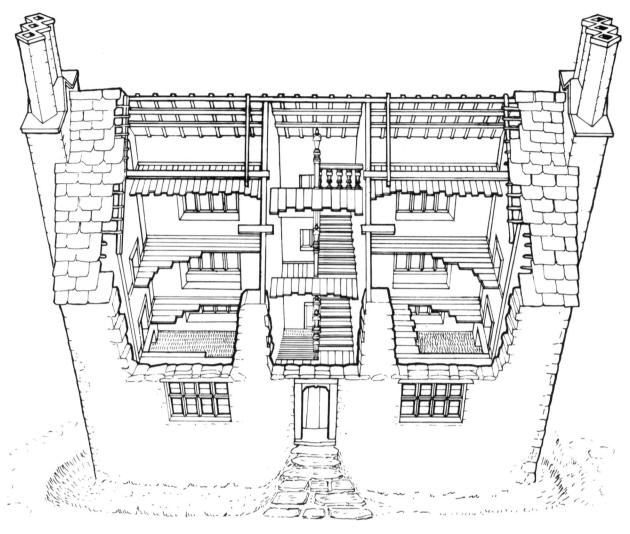

Fig. 40.   A perspective cut-away drawing of Tŷ-faenor. Although the design is advanced (see Fig. 39, *opposite*) the details of the chimney, doorway and stair suggest a mid-seventeenth century date, consistent with the house having been built to mark the nomination of Richard Fowler as High Sheriff of Radnorshire in 1656. In spite of the conservatism of the detail, the plan is as advanced as any that were then being built in England, and must have appeared revolutionary in the depths of the Welsh countryside. Not only could each room be reached independently of the others from the central stair, but there was also horizontal segregation of gentry and servants, the former entering at the front on ground-floor level and the latter entering at the rear at basement level. As at Piodau-fawr there is a full kitchen not merely a service-room. The kitchen is in the basement.

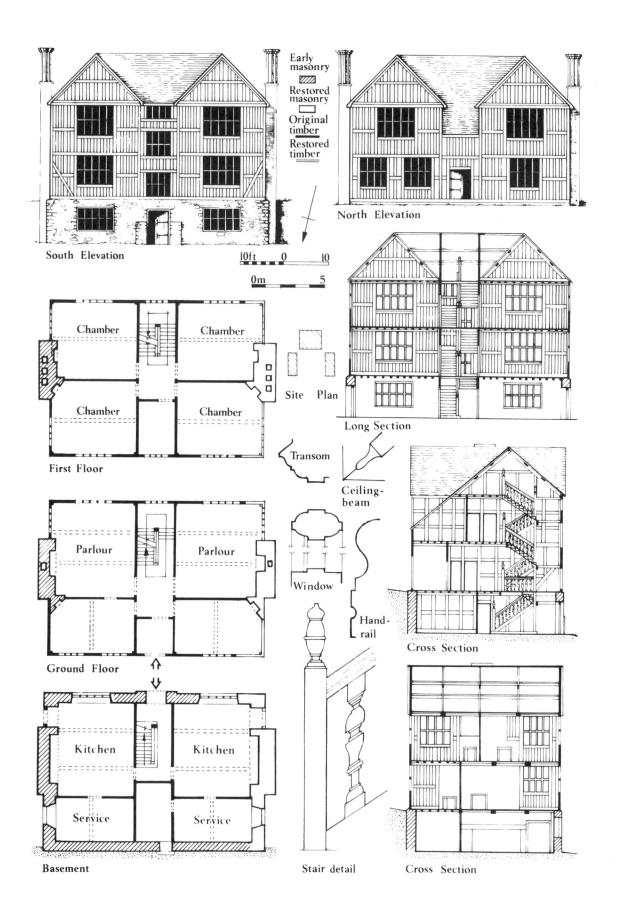

South Elevation

North Elevation

Early masonry

Restored masonry

Original timber

Restored timber

10ft 0 10

0m 5

Chamber Chamber

Chamber Chamber

First Floor

Site Plan

Long Section

Transom

Ceiling-beam

Parlour Parlour

Ground Floor

Window

Hand-rail

Cross Section

Kitchen Kitchen

Service Service

Basement

Stair detail

Cross Section

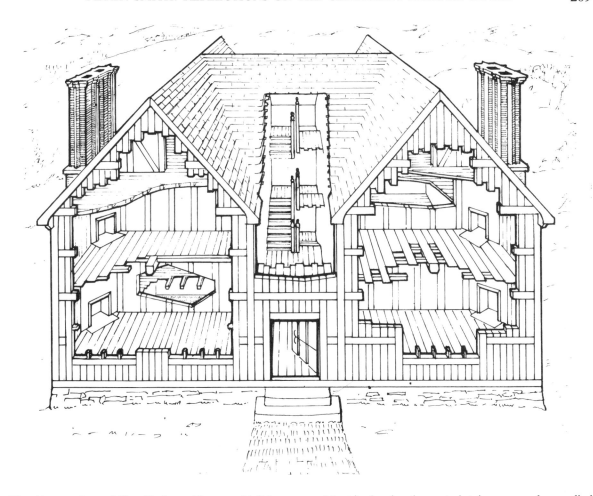

Fig. 41 *opposite* and Fig. 42 *above*, Plasnewydd (Llanwnnog, Mont.), showing the central stair passage plan applied to a house two rooms deep. The use made of falling ground to accommodate basement kitchens and service-rooms clearly recalls the small Tŷ-faenor (Figs. 39-40). A plan showing such mastery of the problems of circulation was rare before the eighteenth century, and when Plasnewydd was first built deep in the Montgomeryshire countryside it must have been a source of wonder to the local country folk till then familiar only with the local sub-medieval, central chimney, lobby-entry plan.

Although the plan is symmetrical the front elevation oddly is not. Why two small windows were provided to the room on the left where one would have sufficed is not clear. Nevertheless, it suggests that the centralised plan and the formally symmetrical elevation are distinct, if related, developments.

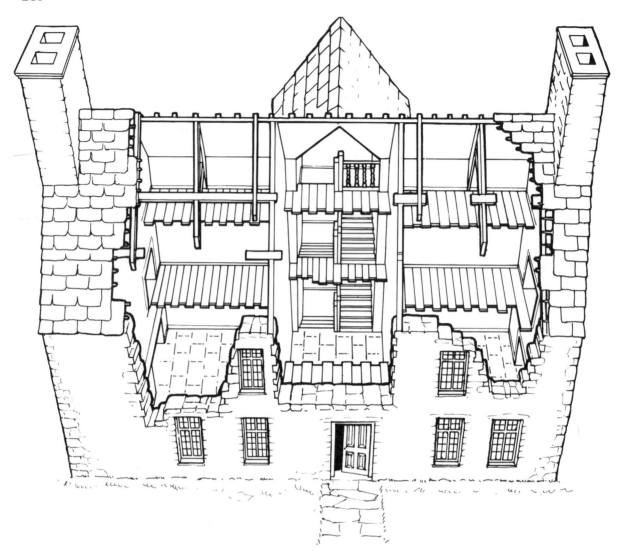

Fig. 43.   Gelli (Trefilan, Cards.) has hall and parlour built about a central entrance passage. The details suggest a date about 1700. The wooden mullion-and-high-transom windows are placed symmetrically about the front door, but all are to one side to accommodate the deep hall fireplace, a departure from absolute symmetry which was common in Wales until *c.* 1850 when the shrinkage of the fireplace with the introduction of coal made it unnecessary. The stair in a projecting turret represents a reversion to the earlier pattern. At an early date service-rooms under a lean-to roof were added at the rear on each side of the stair turret and reached from it.

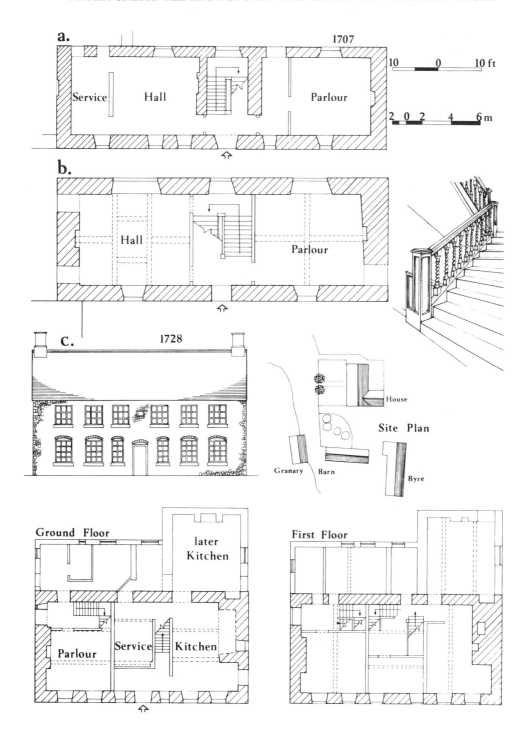

Fig. 44. Early eighteenth-century examples of stairs centrally placed in the body of the house at *(a)* Faenor (Llanwhaden, Pembs.) *(b)* Edwinsford (Llansawel, Carms.) and *(c)* Blaen-y-cwm (Llanuwchllyn, Mer.). Note the typical layout at *c*, the house standing well away from the farm buildings.

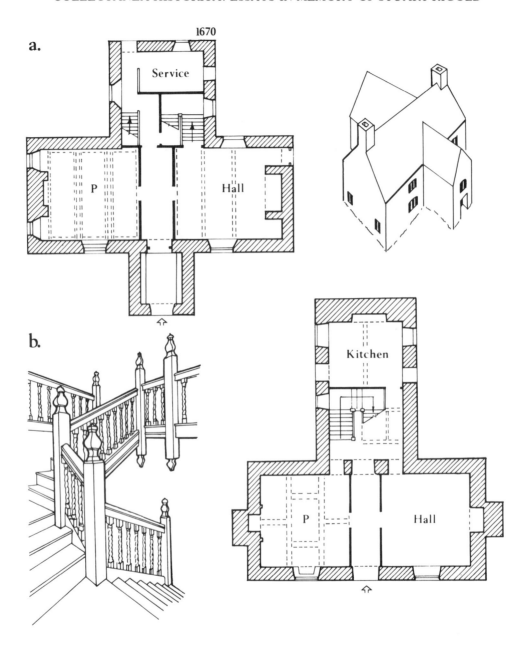

Fig. 38. *a* Pool Hall (Crucardarn, Brecs.) and *b* Piodau-fawr (Llandybie, Carms.), seventeenth-century cruciform or T-plan houses having the service-room or kitchen placed at the rear rather than at one end of the main block as in a sub-medieval house, and the stair in the rear projection. In terms of layout Piodau-fawr represents a marked advance on Pool Hall as at Piodau-fawr the access to the stair is from the passage, not from the hall, thus giving the house a completely self-contained system of circulation. Piodau-fawr is also the more advanced of the two in having a full kitchen rather than a service-room.

THE TIMBER-LACED WALL IN ENGLAND

GUY BERESFORD

Recent excavations of some medieval settlements on the clay-lands in England have revealed a type of timber building of light construction the remains of which may be readily distinguished by the irregular size and poor alignment of the closely set footings of the wall lacing timbers. Buildings of this type had a long tradition throughout the Middle Ages, examples being generally found in the houses of the peasantry, the lesser gentry and in the minor domestic offices of the aristocracy, but the recent excavation of the small late eleventh-century motte and bailey castle at Goltho, Lincolnshire, revealed evidence of timber-lacing in the motte revetment as well as in the walls of the steward's house, suggesting a wider use of this construction. No standing medieval structure of this type has survived into the present century, but houses of similar construction are still being built in parts of tribal Africa today (Andersen 1977, 199–204). The buildings varied in size according to the function for which they were built, but they seldom exceeded 18–20 ft. in width. The research after the excavation of the manorial enclosure at Goltho, Lincolnshire, indicates that their construction was probably the work of the 'village handyman' rather than that of a craftsman skilled in the construction of halls (Beresford, forthcoming).

The size of the post-holes in such buildings indicates that the walls were built of untrimmed timbers usually some 4–9 in. in diameter. In some, like the steward's house in the twelfth-century manorial enclosure at Caldecote, Hertfordshire (Beresford 1977a, 1A, 179–80), the diameter of the posts differed along the lengths of the individual wall (Fig. 45). Although there was this difference in their size, the walls were not divided into bays with principal posts and studs. There was also no apparent link with the posts on one side of the building with those on the other. The posts were usually spaced randomly at intervals between 18 in. and 3 ft. apart and were set up to 12 in. into the ground. An individual feature of these buildings was that the close-set post-holes zigzag their way along the line of the walls by sometimes as much as a thickness of a post.

It was not until the excavation of the well-preserved remains of the early fourteenth-century bower at the sub-manor site at Wintringham, Huntingdonshire, that the significance of this type of building was fully realised (Beresford 1977, B, 224, 229–30; see also Beresford 1975, 37–40). They were then classified as primitive timber buildings. However, since this term is somewhat lacking in description it would seem more appropriate to classify them as having timber-laced walls. The Wintringham bower was 36 ft. long and probably about 18 ft. wide (Fig. 46). The walls were between 18 and 20 in. thick and stood at the time of excavation up to 9 in. in height. The walls were of clay tempered with chopped straw and had been laced with vertical posts set between 3 ft. and 5 ft. apart. The post positions were clearly marked by fine

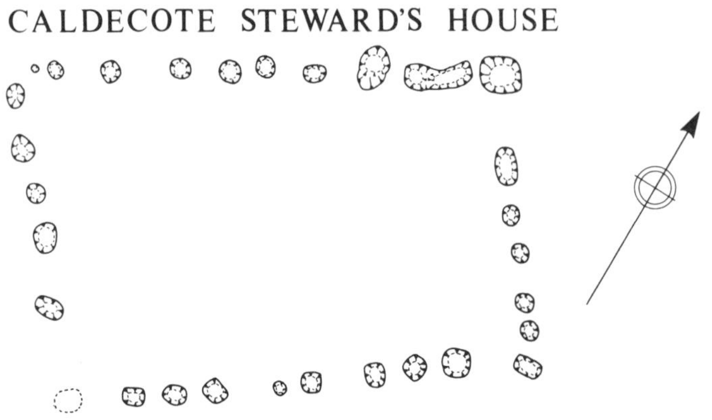

CALDECOTE STEWARD'S HOUSE

Fig. 45.   An example of the remains of a timber-laced wall.

WINTRINGHAM BOWER

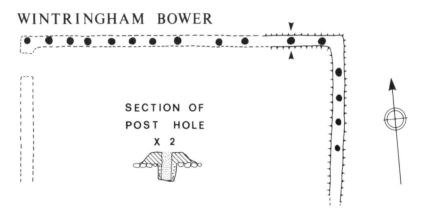

SECTION OF
POST HOLE
X 2

Fig. 46.   Footings of a timber-laced wall.

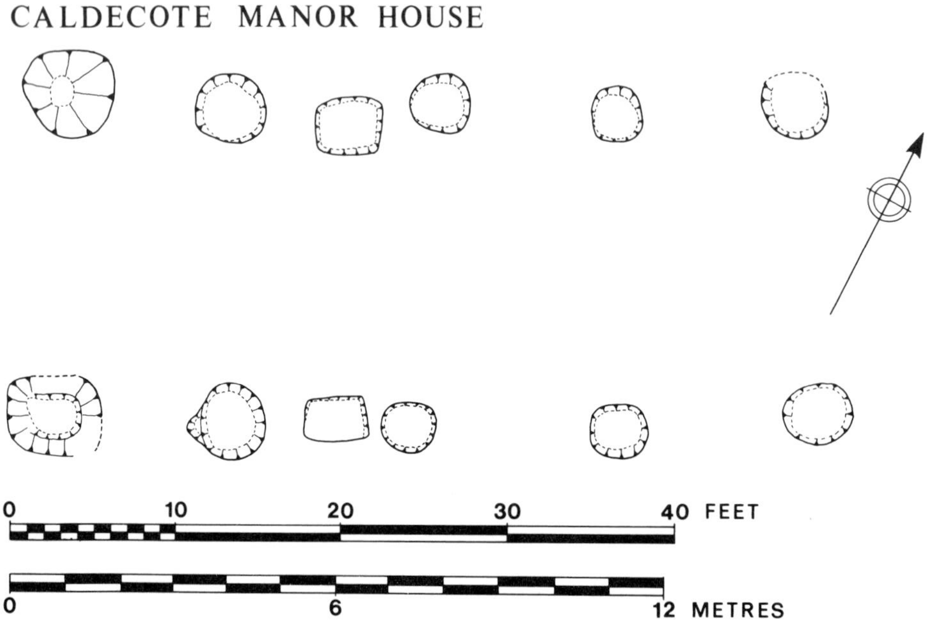

CALDECOTE MANOR HOUSE

0   10   20   30   40 FEET

0   6   12 METRES

Fig. 47.   Examples of a hall built with posts set at bay intervals — a comparison.

soil passing through the remains of the wall down into the post-holes which had been cut through the earlier cobbling into the underlying soil. The post-holes were up to 18 in. deep. The section cut through the remains of the wall clearly shows that the posts were of unsawn timber about 9 in. in diameter and that they were completely surrounded by clay (Fig. 46) inset). The width of these walls explains the poor alignment of the post-holes found in this type of building: either the posts were deliberately placed out of line to strengthen the wall or that their random alignment was immaterial. The construction of the walls resembles that of some African tribal houses today in that both have been constructed with earth-fast posts which have been completely surrounded by clay (Fig. 48) (Anderson 1977, 109-204).

Buildings of this type have an advantage in that timber of inferior quality could readily be used; it was, therefore, an ideal type of building in areas where timber was scarce or in circumstances where the purchase of quality materials was beyond the resources of the builder. Timber, as ash or as hard timbers containing a high proportion of sap-wood, normally classified as perishable or, at best, non-durable when set in earth-fast foundations and exposed to the weather, could readily be used, since they would have been encased in clay and protected from damp, insects and wood-rotting fungi (Purslow n.d.). Further, the thick clay walls would permit the use of posts which were either crooked or uneven in length or thickness. The availability of the necessary materials on the clay-lands and the lack of structural complexity in the design of the buildings were an attraction to the small builder throughout the Middle Ages in these areas. When such buildings were constructed to be used as domestic offices by the side of structurally complex craftsmen-built halls like those of the late-Saxon aristocratic site at Goltho, Lincolnshire (Beresford 1976, 55–56) or at the sub-manor site at Wintringham, Huntingdonshire, in the early fourteenth century (Beresford 1977b, 224–5, 229–30), their construction could not be attributed to the shortage of timber, but to the probability that the builder only employed skilled craftsmen for the construction of his major buildings and relied upon the estate labour, skilled only in the use of timber and clay, to build the domestic offices.

The difficulty in obtaining crushed stone, chalk, slate or other suitable aggregate for the tempering of cobwalls in the 'no stone areas' of the clay-lands probably led to the development of this type of building. Although they had all the appearance of cob construction and probably some of the advantages, too, they must have been easier to erect and could be completed with less skilled labour. The walls only some 18–21 in. thick would have required less material than those of a traditional cob-walled structure and the narrow timber-laced walls would have facilitated the hardening of the clay permitting early occupation of the building – it is said that it took two years to build a cob-walled house of two stories (Clifton-Taylor 1972, 289). Although these buildings could have been constructed with poor quality timbers in some instances, they should not be regarded as poor, mean dwellings. The thick clay walls would have taken up any misalignment of the posts. Indeed, in many manor sites the walls were possibly plastered to resemble stone. Recent research in Brittany, where the tradition of light building construction has persisted until recent years, has demonstrated that such buildings are reasonably durable. There the buildings were of much lighter construction than those which are the subject of this essay and were all about thirty years old when recorded. They were then expected to last, if properly maintained, for another decade or more (Meirion-Jones 1976, fig. 2).

Walls constructed with timber-lacing must not be confused with the type of building like the early thirteenth-century manor-house excavated at Caldecote, Hertfordshire, (Fig. 47) where the posts were also poorly aligned (Beresford 1978, 179–80). In this building the posts were set at bay intervals some 10 ft. apart along each side. The post-holes were sufficiently large to take posts of up to 2 ft. 6 in. in diameter or if dressed some 18–21 in. in section. It could be reasonably postulated that the building had been constructed with interrupted sill-beams, plates and tie-beams. The posts, plates and ties could have been joined by either normal or reversed assembly (Hewett 1962–3, 260–2; see also Beresford 1977a, 234). The large posts would not have been surrounded by clay; the panels formed between the posts, sills and plates would have been, in this period, filled with wattle and daub.

The small diameter of some of the posts together with their close-set irregular alignment would have precluded the possibility of a top plate from being morticed to the posts. There was no evidence to suggest that one had been fixed to selected members. Nevertheless, a plate could have been placed on the top of the wall as in a building of stone, cob or clay-lump. Although the recording of certain vernacular buildings in Ireland (McCourt 1972, 118–30) and

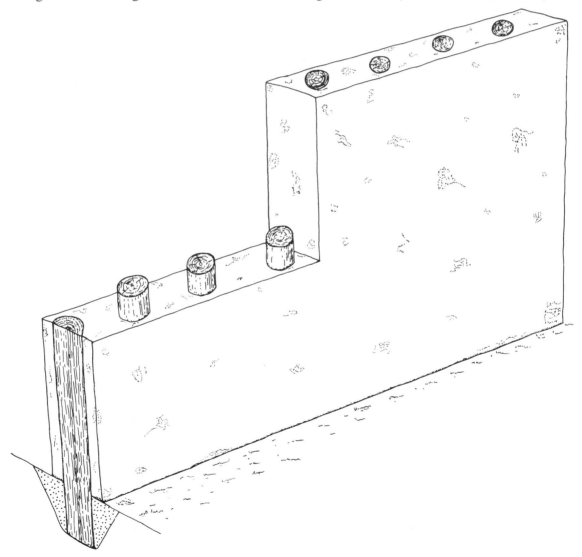

Fig. 48. Reconstruction of a timber-laced wall.

in Devon (Alcock 1966) shows that plates were not always necessary, it seems likely that they would have been adopted in these buildings in order to distribute the weight of the roof evenly along the top of the lightly constructed wall.

Although the slightly rounded ends of some buildings constructed with timber-laced walls suggest that they probably had hipped roofs, the layout in many buildings in this category did not indicate whether the roofs were gabled or hipped. When these buildings were first identified in the early 1970s, it was argued that in those at Barton Blount, Goltho and Wintringham (Beresford 1975, 19–40 and Beresford 1977a, fig. 8), because some amongst their number had no earth-fast foundations beneath the end walls, the complete weight of the roof must have been carried on the side walls and therefore the roofs must have been gable ended. However, such a hypothesis could not really be substantiated since it could also be argued that there could be a need for better end-footings if the building were gable-ended to provide extra strength to permit the infill of the gable itself. Contemporary illustrations are Viking and Norman houses in the British Isles and on the Continent (Petersson 1958, 134–50; Henry 1967, Colour Plate B, and Stenton 1965), but the choice, in some circumstances, must depend upon the availability of suitable building materials and structural technology – especially in timber buildings – to infill a gable of a wide building. Although there are some houses of cob in Devon and of clay-lump in Norfolk which have gable-ended roofs (Clifton-Taylor 1972, 283–4), it is unlikely that they were frequently adopted in buildings constructed with timber-laced walls since many of the slight posts in the end walls could not have reached up to the top of the gable in a high building.

The roof is the most uncertain element in the reconstruction of these houses; there was nothing to indicate the use of a ridge piece supported by either the posts standing on the ground surface or set in earth-fast footings and there was no evidence to suggest the use of outside buttresses to contain the outward thrust of the roof – the tradition of outside buttress, of course, did not persist in England after the middle of the eleventh century. The ridge-piece has had a long tradition dating back to prehistoric times, the function of which is merely that of convenience in the fixing and fastening of the tops of the rafters and not to carry the weight of the roof as many still suppose (Innocent 1971, Impression, 11).

Many reconstructions of medieval houses base the assembly of the roof upon a ridge-piece housed in the fork formed by the crossing of principal rafters at the ends of the building. Although this type of ridge has a long tradition on the Continent, there is no evidence to suggest that it was ever adopted in Britain except in cruck construction (Alcock 1973, fig. 6). Perhaps it is because none have survived. However, a ridge could have been carried in two other ways in such a building: firstly, it could have been supported on king-posts placed on tie-beams and, secondly, it could have been lashed to paired rafters above the point at which they cross close to the apex of the roof. The former, incorporating the use of tie-beams, king-posts and presumably some form of king-post brace, seems too structurally complex to have been built upon walls of light construction. A ridge supported by paired rafters could also have been adopted, but this construction would also require tie-beams to contain the outward thrust of the roof.

However, the collared-rafter roof has, also, a very long tradition and would probably have been the choice of the builders in the Middle Ages for this type of building. The construction had the advantage in that it could have been readily adapted for either a hipped or a gable-ended roof; the collars would have contained the outward thrust of the roof, obviating the necessity of tie-beams and, further, the weight of the roof would have been evenly distributed along the line of the wall through the feet of the rafters onto the plate. The members could have comprised untrimmed timber, as ash, for the roofs of the houses of the peasantry or from prepared timbers for the more important manorial domestic offices.

The longitudinal stability of the roof and the support for the thatch was probably provided by wattles woven between the rafters, a construction favoured in many parts of the British Isles with recorded examples occurring in medieval and later buildings like Higher Tor, in the parish of Widecombe, Devon,[1] Athelney, Somerset (Laver 1909, 175–80) or the Farm House near Strata Florida, Wales (Williams 1899, 320–5). A layer of turf was possibly placed between the wattles and the thatch as in Scotland (Roussell 1974), Ireland (Buchanan 1957, 123–42) and on the Continent (Innocent 1971, Reprint, 214–5), places where the tradition has persisted until the present time. The turves were usually cleaned of surplus earth so that the matted roots could be placed through the wattles or thatching laths. In some counties of Ireland (Buchanan 1957, 123–42), the turves were about 2 ft. wide and up to 20 ft. or more in length running up from the wall plate to the ridge which they overlapped by about 1 ft. The houses may have been thatched with straw, sedge *(carex)*, rush *(juncus)* or furze *(ulex)*.

Documentary evidence and contemporary literary sources dating from the early thirteenth century clearly demonstrate the use of timber and clay in the construction of castles in Scotland (Mackenzie 1933–4, 117–27). In the old French romance *Fergus*, the poet tells how the father of the hero lived in a castle in Scotland overlooking the Irish Sea. The residence was built upon a great rock surrounded by posts interwoven with brushwood and on the summit of the rock there was a tower, not built of stone and lime says the author, but of clay, the high walls of which had crenellated battlements. In England, excavations at Wallingford Castle, Berkshire, have revealed substantial remains of late twelfth- or early thirteenth-century cob-walled buildings within the inner ward (Carr 1973, 159–61) and at Goltho, Lincolnshire, the excavation of a small late eleventh-century motte-and-bailey castle revealed remains of a house constructed with timber-laced walls and evidence of timber-lacing in the revetment of the motte (Beresford, forthcoming). At this clay-land settlement quarried stone was not to be obtained within a nine-mile radius of the site. Since clay walls are resistant to fire and are difficult to demolish without much labour their adoption in the construction of the defences of earthwork castles and their associated buildings was probably more widespread than at present realised. Clay can disintegrate leaving no visible trace on the ground even on sites of buildings where the walls were of cob and up to 3 ft. in thickness like the house excavated at Tresmorn, Cornwall (Beresford 1971, 58–62). Its breakdown in many instances may account for the apparent dearth of structural remains encountered in the excavation of some earth-work castles.

1.   I am most grateful to Dr N.W. Alcock, for drawing my attention to this house.

NEWARK, MAIDSTONE

L.R.A. GROVE

The histories of the two Newarks on the west bank of the River Medway — one at Strood, the other at Maidstone — are sad ones. The hospital at Strood remained only as a site in Newark Yard until at the suggestion of Stuart Rigold the Lower Medway Archaeological Research Group began an excavation there in 1966 the results of which together with a plan were published (Harrison 1969). Maidstone's Newark is perhaps more fortunate in retaining its chapel but the prospects for excavation are poor as the buildings, which possibly remained on the west and north sides, have been demolished and others erected over the foundations. As little has been written critically concerning this Maidstone hospital an opportunity is here taken to bring forward some of the relevant facts. It is curious that Stuart Rigold omitted it in his report on the town's ecclesiastical buildings (Rigold 1962).

The Hospital of Newark or New Work (*novi operis*) in West Borough, Maidstone, was probably built about the year 1261. Its position to the north-west of the west end of Maidstone Bridge has significance especially as it is exactly paralleled by the location of the Strood Newark in relation to Rochester Bridge. There is, however, no evidence for Cave-Browne's statement that Archbishop Boniface who built the hospital was also responsible for the bridge 'connecting, as it would, his hospital with the town and the market' (Cave-Browne). The market was also founded by Boniface in 1261 by a grant of land at 'Petrisfield' which seems likely to have been near 'Petryshull' where the hospital was built (Beale Poste 1847).

Although the archbishops of Canterbury had held the Manor of Maidstone since late Anglo-Saxon times, as shown in *Textus Roffensis*, the *Domesday Monachorum* clearly reveals that a necessary distinction was made between the lands of the primate and those of his monks and this dichotomy was observed by Lanfranc and his successors when it suited them (Smith 1943 and Du Boulay 1966). The monks were very touchy on the subject especially when it concerned religious foundations in Maidstone. In 1196, according to Gervase's *Chronicle*, Archbishop Hubert Walter proposed to found a church of secular priests in Maidstone (Gervase, 536) in order to provide for the many secular clerks employed in diocesan administration. He was bitterly resisted. 'The setting up of a great collegiate church in the diocese, endowed out of the possessions of the archbishopric and peopled by the learned clerks who served the archbishop, might be the first step in transferring the chapter's electoral rights, and even the see itself' (Lawrence 1960). Archbishop Edmund Rich revived the project. The chapter appealed to the Pope and this move resulted in instructions being given to Cardinal Ottoto hold an enquiry and to inspect the site of the proposed foundation (*Calendar Papal Letters*, i, 173). Maidstone was chosen and plans were drawn up by Elyas of Dereham for conventual buildings and a great church for fifty prebends (Gervase, ii, 174). Archbishop Edmund was informed that the appeal had failed (May 1239) and building began. The monks then went to the king and in November of the same year the sheriff of Kent ended operations (*Close Rolls*, 1237-42, 234).

This quarrelling did some good for the details of the 1261 foundation of Maidstone's Newark are only to be found in a confirmation by Prior Roger of St. Alphege and the chapter of Christ Church, Canterbury, on the Sunday before the Feast of the Blessed Virgin 1261 (Cave-Browne, for Latin text). Freely translated into English it runs as follows:

> To all the Faithful in Christ to whom the present writing may come. . . Roger the Prior and the Chapter give greeting, etc. Since our venerable Father Boniface, by the Grace of God Archbishop of Canterbury, would build a certain Hospital at Maydenstane and would give and concede to the same Hospital and the Master and Brethren serving God there and to their successors and would confirm by his charter (as we have clearly seen to be more fully contained in the same) certain lands, possessions and returns, we have given our assent and support under our Chapter seal, as was fitting and reasonable, to these same, namely, all lands, possessions and returns with their appurtenances which the aforesaid Lord of Canterbury bought with his own money in the fields of Peter's Hill [Petryshull] and in other places outside our territory or feof and also a certain meadow which is near the same Hospital and which is called 'Broks', with its appurtenances which the same Lord had in the domain of his Manor of Maydenstane, together with the presentations of the churches of Farnlege [Farleigh] and Sutton with appurtenances which the aforesaid Lord of Canterbury made over to the Master and Brethren. Again giving our consent we have confirmed these and all others which he has obtained justly and peacably. But, however, no prejudice may be produced against us or our successors with those things which pertain to our manor of Farleigh with its appurtenances and which from ancient usage and confirmation we have been accustomed to receive in our same Manor. In testimony of which we have set our seal, etc. Given in our Chapter on the Sunday next before the Feastday of the Birth of the Blessed Virgin Mary in the year of the Lord 1261.

The hospital had a master *(magister)* or warden and a few corrodiars or prebendaries drawn usually from the ranks of the archbishop's pensioner servants (VCH Kent). It consisted of a chapel and buildings part of which survived until recent times in Newark House on the north side of the chapel. This latter was demolished in the 1920s by the local Gas Company.

The cause of the building of this hospital by one who owed his archbishopric mainly to being uncle of Eleanor of Provence, Henry III's Queen, has been ascribed by Matthew Paris (1872-3, 5) to expiation of a local wrong which almost had tragic consequences for Maidstone. The archbishop in the early years of his primacy quarrelled with the Bishop elect of Winchester over an election to the mastership of a hospital in Southwark. He ordered the new master to be clapped in his manorial prison at Maidstone. The bishop-elect sent a body of armed dependants to rescue the master, if necessary by assault, but when they arrived in Maidstone they found that the master had been transferred to Lambeth. So Maidstone was spared trouble and bloodshed and the archbishop apparently had a bad conscience over the whole affair.

The position of the hospital near the west end of Maidstone bridge, in view of the archbishop's palace and on the north side of the medieval London road issuing from Maidstone (until 1781 — now Buckland Road), must have been carefully chosen. Dr. Wilfrid Hooper (Hooper 1936) followed Frank Elliston-Erwood in discounting any connection with pilgrimage ('another mare's nest — the so-called Pilgrims' Chapel') and he pointed out that Newton in his *History of Maidstone* (1741) spoke of it as 'The Hospital for Pilgrims or Travellers dedicated to St. Peter and St. Paul and Thomas Becket'. One suspects that the addition of St. Thomas to the dedication must be traced back to Lambarde and to that master of misinformation, Kilburne, who also regales us with the falsity (Kilburne 1659) that Archbishop Courtenay pulled down the hospital. 'With this respectable backing the story gained a firm foothold, and on the rise of the pilgrimist theory the pilgrims and poor travellers passed by easy transition into Canterbury pilgrims, the hospital became one of their most important hostelries, despite the fact that to reach it and return to the (Pilgrims') Way involved a detour of about six miles while the Chapel was dubbed the Pilgrim Chapel. The story. . . shows how a specious legend can spring up and flourish unchallenged when no one will trouble to scrutinize its credentials' (Hooper 1936).

Time has obliterated the site and only the chapel remains. When the attention of the Reverend Frederick Fitzherbert Haslewood (1803-76) was drawn to this building in 1836 it was in a poor state. An early nineteenth-century drawing in Maidstone Museum shows the east windows emptied of glass and acting as a trellis for climbing plants. In the same collection another drawing, dated 31 December, 1835, is valuable in that it reveals a wall running westwards from the chapel's south wall. It contained a doorway with pointed head and ran for some way. It had a roof for the artist has drawn in the ghost of a gable over the three windows in the west wall of the chapel.

Haslewood has earned our thanks in writing an article about the state of the Chapel for *The Gentleman's Magazine* in 1842. He told of the excavation of ground at the west end of the building in order to erect the elder Whichcord's nave and transepts where 'large quantities of bones were found, including several perfect skulls, the mouths well supplied with teeth, but there were no remains of coffins or of any other substances. The form of the graves was in many instances as easily traced as if they had been dug yesterday, the soil being a stiff clay. I was on the spot daily, and was assured by the workmen that the skulls were found almost invariably with the faces downward, which is remarkable, if their account is to be depended on. That an ancient cemetery surrounded the chapel appears as well from ocular demonstration as from the circumstances that in some old deeds, still in existence, some lands are described as bounded by the cemetery wall. And during the time I occupied Newark House, in carrying a drain across the lawn human bones were discovered; and also on digging holes for clothes'-posts, at a distance of 100 yards from the east of the chapel, and having the house between the holes and the chapel. The house, built at different times, contains nothing of the least interest.'

Some comment over eighty years later from T.H. Oyler, F.S.A., author of *Churches of the Diocese of Canterbury*, is a corrective to Haslewood's statements although Oyler generously stated (in *St. Peter's Church, Maidstone*, 1924) that 'it was fortunate for St. Peter's that such a man was at the helm, or irreparable damage might have been done' before the re-opening of the chapel on the 16th July, 1837. But Oyler emphasized that Newark House contained work of different periods from the thirteenth to the seventeenth century. 'The walls are of good old brick, and there are oak floors, doors, rafters and massive moulded beams. On the West side is what was probably a priest's closet about seven feet long by four feet wide. The banisters of the winding staircase are good, with massive and well-moulded posts, having large cylindrical heads'.

Besides bones the churchyard has produced little. Beale Poste has noted and illustrated a small bronze male statuette of Roman date dug up in the garden 'about twenty-five years since' (Beale Poste 1847). With it were found a Roman lamp and a boar's tusk. A medieval bronze key, now in Maidstone Museum (accession no. 179), was discovered beneath the greensward in front of Newark House under a skeleton buried about 15 in. from the surface. The original entry in the museum register says this was with many others 'one lying on the other, the rest in rows, same depth'. The key was of Ward Perkins' type 1B and may be dated about the middle of the thirteenth century (Grove 1953).

In an account of Maidstone in the early 1830s (S.C.L. 1834) there is the first mention of 'a curious arched way underground. . . now built up'. Haslewood mentioned that the passage 'some years back' had been opened at about 50 ft. from Newark House and the same distance from the River Medway. Its course was traced to the house, 'the cellar of which it may have transversed'. Oyler enlarged on this statement. He placed beneath the house the 'well-built arched passage or tunnel leading downwards towards the Medway' and supposed that on the west side it evidently ran beneath the road and 'was probably connected with some of the Hospital buildings on the North side of the Chapel'. It was strongly built, about 5 ft. in height and 4 ft. wide. Oyler considered that it might be of the same date as the ancient work of St. Peter's. In 1909 excavations on the Newark site at the Gas Works opened the tunnel again when it was observed that it was constructed of Kentish Rag and was about 4 ft. 6 in. in height. Local romantic tradition claimed that it performed the difficult feat of going under the River Medway to the Corpus Christi Fraternity Hall.

From all this written material it would appear that the Newarks of Maidstone and Strood differed considerably in plan. At Maidstone Newark an ancient road ran close to the Chapel on the south side and its graveyard bordered it on the west and north. According to Burgiss Brown's large scale map of Maidstone dated 1884 (1 inch = 5 chains) Newark House was a north — south rectangular building some 50 ft. north of the chapel. If the line of the west side were projected to the south, it would hit the north-west corner of the chapel. Under the house the presence of the cloaca or conduit to the River Medway emphasises the significance of the lay-out which need have been of no great size in order to accommodate ten corrodiars.

I do not intend to deal at length with the architesture of the chapel which in recent years has been described succinctly and adequately by John Newman in Pevsner's *West Kent*. The 1836-37 west end addition by Whichcord Senior (Grove 1962) has been harshly criticised. Newman complained that 'the classic C13 proportions of the building are compromised by Whichcord's mean roof'. In 1847 Beale Poste regretted that 'to enlarge its dimensions such alterations were necessitated as have completely subverted its original proportions'. One suspects that Whichcord's curious barn-like nave with its north and south transepts was really designed to accommodate the west wall of the thirteenth-century chapel which wall he transferred to the west side of the new structure. It may be a fitting place here to mention that the late V.J. Torr (H.R. Pratt Boorman and V.J. Torr, *Kent Churches*, 1954) dated the 'good work in the beautiful Early English chapel' to *c.* 1255, only ten years after Boniface became archbishop. Torr was, I believe, the first to point out the remarkable resemblance of the piscina and three sedilia to those in the Church of St. Mary at Eastling. In 1905 considerable additions — ambulatory, choir vestry and organ chamber — were built on the north side of the chapel which had become a parish church in 1840. I have omitted these from my plan which is adapted from one made by the late L. Mason Apps, A.R.I.B.A., in 1949. Both he and the late Professor A.B. Knapp-Fisher, F.R.I.B.A., F.S.A., worked on the fabric at that period. T.H. Oyler was most

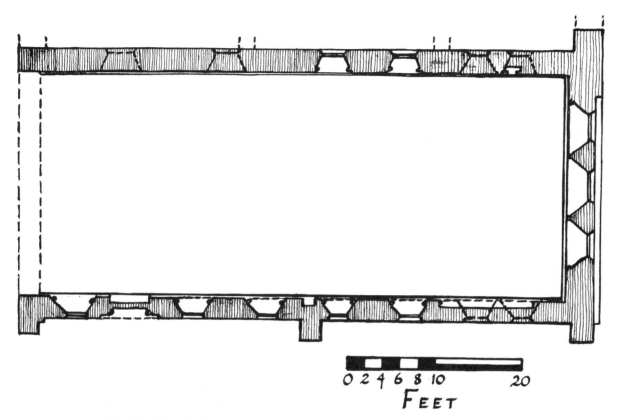

Fig. 49. Newark Chapel, Maidstone — after a plan by L. Mason Apps. 1949.

fond of the trefoil-headed niche over the south doorway. In 1926 he gave a figure of St. Peter to fill it.

Haslewood is our only authority to discuss the chapel's original roof. He saw its timbers and explained that from some remains they appeared to be lined with wood 'probably in former days richly painted'. He had the old decayed roof, 'no doubt. . .the original roof', removed 'because it was constructed with tie beams, which sadly spoilt the appearance of the end windows, which rose at least 10 feet above the tie beams. What remains of it forms part of the present floor joists'.

There was a little damage done to the chapel during the last war. Restoration work began in 1951 under the direction of Knapp-Fisher and Mason Apps. The east wall's restoration in 1959 was supervised by A. Warland, A.R.I.B.A.

The early history of the hospital with its master, chaplain and ten poor residents has been briefly recited by R.C. Fowler (VCH Kent). His list of masters supplements the lists given by Beale Poste and Oyler. Beale Poste also has a list of the corrodiars which he has embellished with notes. In Sudbury's *Register* a corrody for life was granted to John Cozens, servant of the archbishop. Chichele's *Register (The Register of Henry Chichele*, edited by E.F. Jacob) included a corrody given at Saltwood in 1416 to Henry Hampton, his personal valet, after good and laudable service. Hampton was to have sufficient lodging until the end of his life, John

Whyteclyve, vicar of Mayfield and prebendary of Chichester, was a great benefactor of the hospital. In his latter days he was granted a pension out of its revenue. He died whilst visiting Maidstone in 1383 and by his desire was buried in the chapel of the hospital.

Without exception writers have inferred that the hospital quietly disappeared after the foundation of Maidstone College of Priests by Archbishop Courtenay in 1395. A charter of Richard II, witnessed at Leeds Castle on the 2nd August, 1395-6 (*Patent Roll* 19, Richard II, part 1, membrane 2, quoted by Cave-Browne), translated into English reads as follows:

> . . . and we have given licence, on our own behalf and that of our successors, to the same Archbishop that he may have the Hospital of the Apostles Peter and Paul — the New Work of Maydenstone — and all lands, tenements, returns, services and possessions of the same Hospital together with the appurtenances and the advowsons and patronages of the Churches of Suttone, Lillintone (Linton) and Farlegh, appropriated to the said Hospital and existing by our patronage; and he (the Archbishop) may hold the Hospital, the advowsons and patronages from us likewise 'in capite' (as it is said) and he can give and assign them to the aforesaid Master or Warden and his companions, the Chaplains of the said College. . . and similarly the same Archbishop can unite, incorporate and join, for better financial working, the said Hospital and all its lands, tenements, returns, services and possessions with the said College. . .

However, the hospital seems after this transaction to have retained some of its original character, witness the continuance of corrody granting and the fact that in a Maidstone College steward's account of 1424-25 belonging to Maidstone Museum separate accounts appear for the farming of Newark's property.

At the Dissolution Newark was worth £159 7*s*. 10*d*., the College of Priests £211 4*s*. 1¼*d*. In the *Valor* of 1535 the gross value of the College was £212 5*s*. 3¾*d*. yearly and deductions included £2 to each of five poor persons, 'a survival of the old foundation' (VCH Kent). It was suppressed in the first year of Edward VI and then came into the hands of George Brooke, Lord Cobham. Apparently, he soon sold the property. In 1570, William Green of Maidstone devised it by will to his son Gabriel. In George III's reign it belonged to the Reverend Edward Mullins (Newton, *op. cit.*, 31). The Addison family then came into possession. In 1848, the Maidstone Gas Company, in order to provide further space for its growing works, purchased Newark for £2383 from William Addison and Charles Greenstreet Addison. Newark House was used for some time as the manager's office but during the present century was demolished.

The Church of St. Peter has recently become redundant.

A UNIQUE AISLED COTTAGE AT PETHAM

E.W. PARKIN

Petham is an attractive village lying in a hollow of the Downs, 6 km. (4 miles) south of Canterbury, and on the west side of the Roman Stone Street which for over 3 km. (2 miles) forms the eastern boundary of the parish.

It was on June 10th, 1978, that members of the Kent Archaeological Society visited Waltham and Petham, and were shown over Dane Chantry, a handsome brick-and-timber house dated 1628, but with early fourteenth-century internal framing and roof, and a chapel of 1360 at the south end. Among members present were Stuart Rigold and his wife.

Petham, which has several notable medieval houses, held more than a passing interest for Stuart, for it was here, between the two wars that he received his first education at a preparatory school, now no more, before going on to Sutton Valence and Oxford.

DORMER COTTAGE

Dormer Cottage is a detached, but unobtrusive little dwelling, lying beside the main street, close to the centre of the village. It has a thatched roof, hipped at both ends; the thatch coming down to nearly 2 m. (6 ft.) from the ground all round (Plate XLVII), with some external timber framing showing, and with one dormer window protruding from the thatch on the street side.

Inside, one soon realises that the cottage is a very early, and remarkably complete aisled dwelling, even having a timber-and-plaster chimney still in use, one of only three known still to survive in Kent. (The other two are at Marley Farm, Smarden, and at a house called Tilden, near Headcorn.) The house was built originally with three rooms only, a hall with a central hearth, open to the roof, and with a room under each hipped end. Sometime later, the hearth was moved to the north end of the hall, where the framework of the plaster chimney was built over it, leaving the fire visible from both the hall and the north room. Then, in the second half of the seventeenth century, judging by the brickwork, the hearth was converted into two back-to-back fireplaces with a bread oven on the south side, which still exists (Plate XLVIII). At the same time presumably, a floor was inserted to give one extra upstairs bedroom squeezed in under the thatch. In order to give light to this room, the thatch was cut away and a dormer window put in, but cutting through the front arcade plate which formed part of the main framework of the house. To compensate for this, a long blacksmith-made iron was fitted over and around the window opening, and fixed to both cut ends of the plate.

Each of these arcade plates was made from two long oak pieces, joined near the centre by what is known as a scarf joint. The joint in the centre of the street side was lost by the insertion of the dormer, but the one on the east side remains, and is an important

KEY TO DRAWINGS
A   Aisles
AP   Aisle Posts
Ac Pl   Arcade Plate
D1   Original Doorway
GW   Flint Ground Wall
H   Original Position of Hearth
P Ch   Plaster Chimney
S   Shutter (conjectured)
SJ   Scarf Joint
T   Tie Beam
W   Site of original hall window

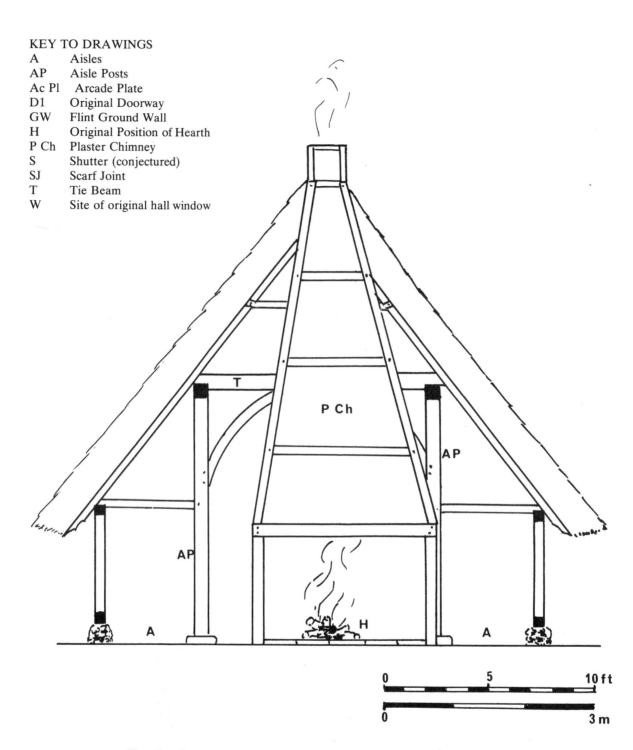

Fig. 50.   Cross-section of cottage, before seventeenth-century alterations.

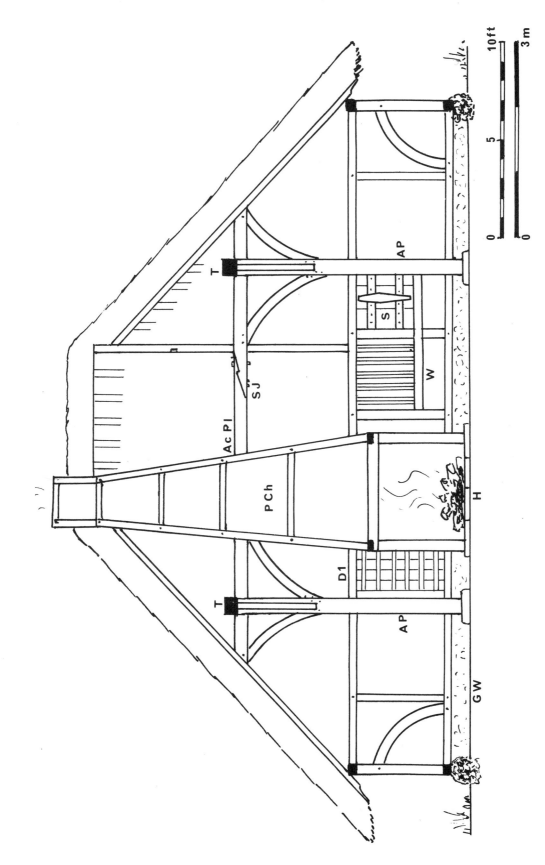

Fig. 51. Equivalent longitudinal section.

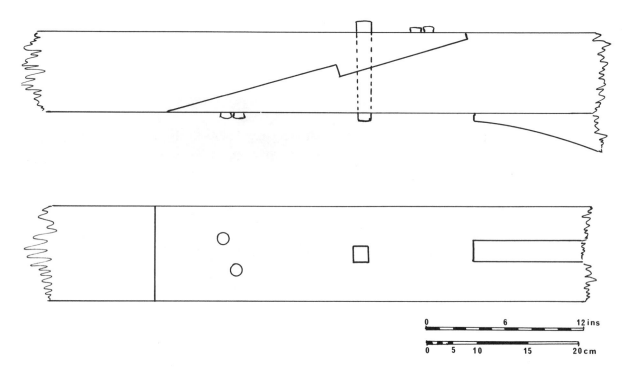

Fig. 52.   The inner and under side of the scarf joint.

the house. It is a tabled scarf, (Fig. 52) anciently known as a *Trait de Jupiter*, with a face key, and four staggered pegs which do not go right through the plate. It is similar to joints listed in Hewett (1969, 173. Hewett agrees that the Petham joint is '13th century or earlier.').

The main framework of the house can be easily visualised, for it is identical with a medieval three-bay barn, having two pairs of aisle posts supporting the roof. The arcade plates which sit on the posts run the length of the building, and are pegged to the hip rafters at each end. The cross beams, or tie beams, are straight, and not cambered, while the rafters of the roof above are paired in the shape of an A, that is, they have collars, or cross-pieces, and no connecting longitudinal timbers. Unfortunately, the joints between collar and rafter are hidden by plaster, but everything one can see appears to be consistent with the thirteenth century as suggested by the scarf joint.

THE PLASTER CHIMNEY

Little is known about plaster chimneys, except from the meagre evidence of those which remain. Apart from the Headcorn and Smarden examples, two were restored a few years ago at Thimbleby in Lincolnshire, in cottages which were thatched but not aisled. All are very similar, and appear to have been designed in the first place as a hood and tapering flue set over the old hearth, although one finds it difficult to comprehend how any could have survived centuries of wood-burning fires.

Each is based on a square frame around the fire, supported by four posts, above which the oak framework tapers up through the thatched roof. The infilling of this framework is of split

PLATE XLVII

Dormer Cottage from the south-west.

PLATE XLVIII

The timber fire frame, and later bread oven.

oak laths, plastered inside and out, with usually a colour wash on the outside. The Petham and Headcorn examples are capped with later brickwork, but at Smarden the original timber framing still protrudes a short distance above the ridge.

SUMMARY

Dormer Cottage is especially interesting in that it represents a rare and unusually complete example of the earlier type of aisled dwelling, in vogue say before 1350, a type whose chief features could be listed thus:

(a) Many of such buildings were thatched; the steeply pitched roofs were designed for this.

(b) Aisled houses in Kent were at that time hipped at both ends, with no upper rooms. Even Nurstead Court near Cobham, which dates from about 1320 and is probably the finest example of an aisled house of this type in the country, was so built, as early illustrations of it show (Parker 1882, 281), while Sole Street Cottage at Crundale, now removed for re-erection to the Museum of the Weald near Chichester, and Ratling Court near Wingham have evidence that they were constructed in like manner.

(c) The open hearth was usually in the centre of the hall, but was sometimes moved to one end, under a 'smoke bay' or a plaster chimney, to be replaced in due course by a brick fireplace and chimney. Curiously, the house called Tilden, near Headcorn, which is a continuous jetty house, built *c.* 1500, still has its wide timber-and-plaster chimney, almost identical to the one at Dormer Cottage, but with a brick fireplace and chimney built inside it.

(d) Some large aisled halls, such as Cogan House in Canterbury (Parkin 1970, 123) employed long, diagonal cross-bracing to give strength to the main framework. In smaller houses such as Dormer Cottage, the long curved braces between principal members appear to have been thought adequate.

(e) The tradition of barn-like, aisled dwellings appears to have been of Saxon origin, beginning some time before the Norman Conquest, and continuing in south-east England until at least 1400, but later further north, by which time the low hipped ends were being replaced by cross-wings, thus providing an additional upper room on each side of the central hall. Fairfield, at Eastry near Sandwich, is a good example of this later type. The house then had the same accommodation as the 'Wealden' hall-house, but with a much more complicated construction. This may well explain the demise of the aisled house in the early part of the fifteenth century, when the Wealden, with its attractive and more straight forward design ruled supreme for another century at least.

A NEW TYPE OF GEORGE NOBLE OF HENRY VIII

J.P.C. KENT

It is very unusual for a major new variety of a modern English coin to be discovered, and even more unusual for it to have been predicted. The coincidence would have appealed to Stuart Rigold, a former president of the British Numismatic Society, and this brief discussion is offered in memory of the man and his catholic interests in even the most unpromising branches of numismatics.

In a note published seventeen years ago (Kent 1964, 162), I drew attention to the fact that handbooks of coins published in the sixteenth century for the use of merchants in the Netherlands illustrated two varieties of Henry VIII's gold George noble, of which only one type was known to exist. The missing type has now appeared in a recent sale (Sotheby 1981, lot 14); it has been acquired by the British Museum, and may be described as follows:-

obv.: Rose (privy mark) hENRIC D G R AGL Z FRANC DNS hYBERNIE +, Tudor rose over ship with three cruciform masts.

rev.: Rose TALI DICATA SIGNO MENS FLVCTVARE NEQVIT +, St. George, on horseback, attacking a protrate dragon with his sword.

It differs from previously known specimens in many ways:-

the 'Ship' side:
1. the ship has a naturalistic hull and three cruciform masts with rigging;
2. there are no initials by the central mast;
3. the inscription is formed of mixed Roman and Lombardic letters.

the 'St. George' side:
1. the saint carries a sword instead of a lance;
2. the horse has a spike on the forehead of its head-armour, wears draped trappings with the royal arms on the crupper, and its tail waves in the air;
3. the dragon lies on its back, its tail in the air;
4. the inscription contains the full and unabbreviated version of Prudentius's hymn line, and is expressed entirely in Roman letters.

There is no doubt as to the order of the two varieties. The new type is certainly the earlier; the unabridged legend of the St. George side and the extensive use of Roman capital letters are decisive evidence. One may compare two other coins of this very date whose sequence is certain. The short-lived gold crown of the rose was proclaimed on 22 August, 1526 (Symonds, 139); its successor, the crown of the double rose is first mentioned (together with the George noble) in a document of 30 October of the same year. The former, of which two specimens are

PLATE XLIX

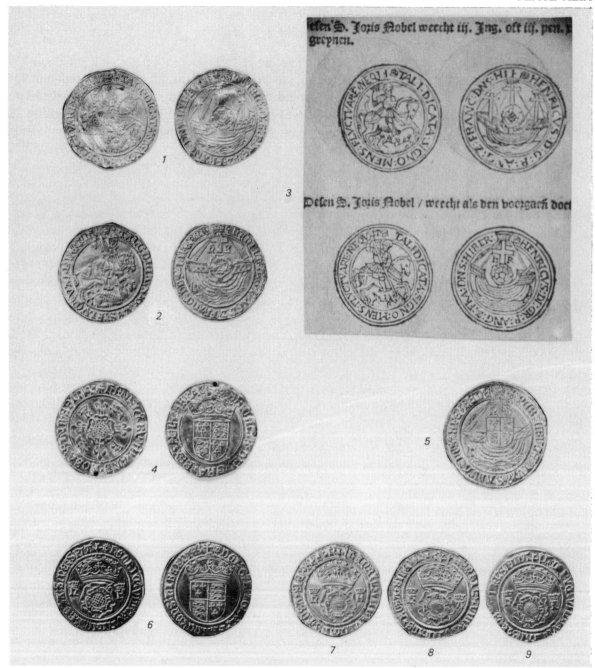

1. George noble: newly discovered type. 2. George noble: type previously known. 3. Both types of George noble: illustration from Anon., *Die figueren van alle Goude ende Silvere penninghen* etc., Antwerp 1580. 4. Crown of the Rose. 5. Angel, reverse only. 6. Crown of the Double Rose, *Rose* privy-mark.
Crowns of the Double Rose (obverses only), *Arrow* privy-mark: 7. Initial of Katherine of Aragon. 8. Initial of Anne Boleyn. 9. Initial of Jane Seymour.

known, has mostly Roman letters; the latter passes steadily from the use of a mixed fount of letters to one exclusively Lombardic. All George nobles of the type hitherto known are inscribed solely in Lombardic letters.

The type of the gold crown was altered because its standard had been changed from 54 grains weight, 23 carats fine (current for 4*s.* 6*d.*) to 57 grains weight, 22 carats fine (current for 5*s.* 0*d.*); it was important that the public should be able to distinguish them on sight. The George noble, however, during its brief life, was never anything else but a coin weighing 71 grains, 23 carats 3½ grains fine, current for 6*s.* 8*d.*, and the newly found piece conforms precisely to these specifications. There may have been some objection to the type. One might conjecture that the crosses of the two thieves had evoked ecclesiastical or royal criticism, or even ribald and pungent public comment on the probity of the administration. It is interesting to see how the type of the second issue was much simplified in detail. The royal arms on the horse-trappings, suggesting the identification of king and saint, were omitted, while the design of the ship was brought into line with that on the angel. Its entirely Lombardic letter-fount suggests that an appreciable time separated the two issues, long enough for the Roman founts to have gone completely out of use.

George nobles and half nobles figured in the Trial of the Pyx on 4 June, 1527 (Symonds, 143). Since this event covered coins struck since October 22 of the preceding year, it is clear that it must have included the earliest coins of the new type, and we shall see that considerable numbers must have been struck. The George noble and its half make their last certain appearance on 6 April, 1533, when the newly-appointed master-workers at the Tower mint were authorised to strike them (Symonds 1913, 146; Challis 1978, 311). Although small quantities of fine gold appear in the accounts for 1536-37 and 1543-44 (Challis 1978, 307), there is no likelihood that any George noble was struck so late. All bear the Rose privy mark, to the date-limits of which we now turn.

Successive Trials of the Pyx during the relevant period may be summarised as follows:-

Date	Coins tried										
	Fine gold				Crown gold				Silver		
	A	½A	G	½G	C	½C	G	½G	1*d.*	½*d.*	¼*d.*
4 June, 1527	x	x	x	x	x	x	x	x	x	x	x
21 November, 1527							x	x	x	x	x
20 May, 1530							x	x	x	x	x
1 March, 1533							x	x	x	x	x
30 October, 1534					x	x	x	x	x	x	x
8 May, 1537	nothing known										
16 June, 1540					x	x	x	x	x	x	x

The data are manifestly incomplete, but provide the basis for our investigation. The first two trials are probably to be closely associated — that of 1530 refers back only to that of June 1527. A fixed point seems to be furnished by the Arrow privy mark. Gold crowns so marked bear successively the initials of Katherine of Aragon (K), Anne Boleyn (A) and Jane Seymour (I) combined with that of the king. Katherine's marriage was pronounced null and void on 23 May, 1533, Anne's on 17 May, 1536, while Jane died on 24 October, 1537. Whether initials were promptly changed with the wife may be doubted, for the many 'mules' randomly pairing incompatible initials show that old dies were used without compunction. The issue certainly survived Jane's death, for its final stages are simply inscribed HR. The Arrow coinage presumably began with the indenture of 6 April, 1533 — one of the master-workers was Martin *Bowes* — and may have continued until the end of the account on 15 May, 1540 (pyxed 16 June), or even beyond. Half crowns were 'tried' in 1534 and 1540; known examples bear only the initials of Katherine and Jane. Perhaps the trial of 1537, for which no details are known, was essentially for the crowns with the initial of Anne. At all events, it is clear that the basic privy mark did not necessarily change with each pyx trial, as was the case later in the century.

Earlier than the Arrow-marked coins — the crowns bear Katherine's initial exclusively — are those coins marked with a Rose, a Lis or (rarely) a Sunburst. Rose, a mark which covers the very early crown of the rose and other coins with Roman letters, is certainly the first, and it has been convincingly argued (Whitton 1949, 60) that the Sunburst is but a brief interruption of the long period during which the Lis was in use. There are thus in effect two marks to cover the span of years in which there were (for silver, certainly) four pyx trials. During these years, the following amounts of silver were coined (Challis 1978, 305):-

22 October, 1526-4 June, 1527	13703 lbs.
4 June, 1527-20 May, 1530	94755 lbs.
20 May, 1530-1 March, 1533	20467 lbs.

The number of surviving specimens suggests an approximate equality of Rose- and Lis-marked coins. This is very hard to reconcile with the above figures, but it would be possible if one were to postulate that the pyx of 21 November, ignored by the trial of 1530, came at the end of the use of the Rose mark; there would then have been a very intense coinage of silver between June and November of 1527.

If this should prove to have been the case, both varieties of George noble would fall within 1526-27, and be no more than a few months apart. No less than £30 0s. 0d. of fine gold was pyxed on 4 June, 1527, implying a very large issue of the order of 700 lbs. in weight, and about £20,000 in face value. No Rose-marked angels or half angels are in fact known, though they figure in the pyx record along with the George noble and its half. Since the latter pair are themselves notable rarities, one must suppose an exceptionally low rate of survival. The appearance of the missing angels and half angels may, however, be anticipated. Other gold coins of Henry VIII remain to be discovered, though they seem not to have come to the notice of the Netherlands printers. An undated document (Symonds 1913, 148) — it perhaps relates to the detail of the pyx trial of 4 June, 1527 — records the trial together of ryals, angels, half angels, George nobles and half George nobles. The authenticity of the unique earlier ryal of Henry has been defended elsewhere (Kent 1964, 161), but later pieces are certainly provided for in the Mint indentures, and figure here in a pyx trial, which records the striking of no less than 746 lbs. weight of these very rare or non-existent coins. Clearly, we have much yet to learn, and happily, even modern numismatics can still provide the occasional surprise.

IMPORTED MOTTO TILES: A GROUP OF MID-SIXTEENTH-CENTURY SLIP-DECORATED DUTCH FLOOR TILES IN ENGLAND

M.C. HORTON

INTRODUCTION

A small group of slip-decorated floor tiles are to be found in Kent, as well as elsewhere in southern England; they are characterised by Dutch inscriptions (mottos) and floral decoration. Previously they have been variously dated to the fourteenth (Eames 1980, 666), fifteenth (Ward Perkins 1937, 443) and sixteenth centuries (Eames 1980, 274; Emden 1977, 871; Platt and Coleman Smith 1975, ii, 199). Some of the tile fragments are not so obviously foreign that they have in the past escaped recognition, whilst others have been only imperfectly drawn from very worn and broken examples. For these reasons this paper has attempted to publish all the known tile designs represented by this small group of imports (Figs. 55-56) as well as to list provisionally all the sites both in England and abroad where this group is known to come. Future discoveries may thus be more easily recognised and documented. The tiles in the Low Countries were all personally seen by the writer; he is very grateful for help on the location of the English sites from the late Dr A.B. Emden and Mr E.C. Norton.

The continental origins of these motto tiles can be clearly shown by the Dutch inscriptions, the technique of manufacture, and their frequent occurrence on the other side of the North Sea (Berendsen *et al*. 1967; Vis and de Geus 1926, 3). The fact that they must originate from a single source will be shown by the identity of fabric, size, designs and the techniques employed in manufacture. They are closely dated to within the life of a single enterprise, and this will be shown to lie between 1550 and 1560. The tiles themselves are perhaps of added interest as markers of a more widespread trade and contact between England and the Low Countries during the reign of Queen Mary; in particular, they provide some evidence for the development of cultural relations between the two areas in the middle of the sixteenth century.

This group of Dutch motto tiles today survives in only minute quantities; although they have been reported from over eighteen different sites in England (with a further four unprovenanced museum collections) the total numbers of tiles at each site is often less than a handful. In adition, the losses sustained during the nineteenth century were apparently substantial, as these motto tiles were not considered wholly 'medieval', and along with much other post-medieval material, discarded. We therefore have to rely on the records of antiquaries such as Streatfield (1878), Renaud (MSS in Society of Antiquaries), Lord Alwyn Compton (MSS in Society of Antiquaries), and Nichols (1845). On the Continent, the losses sustained have probably been much greater; certain numbers have remained in private collections, and fragments are occasionally found during archaeological excavations and building works.

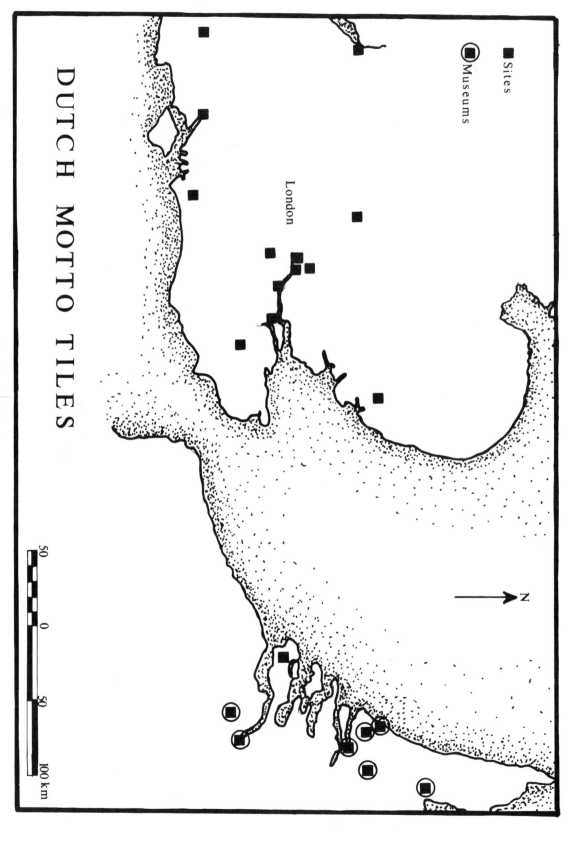

Fig. 58. Distribution map.

DUTCH MOTTO TILES

■ Sites

◉ Museums

London

N

50 0 50 100 km

DESCRIPTION

The tiles are fairly uniform: between 140 mm. and 148 mm. square, and between 18 mm. and 23 mm. thick. There is a pale orange pink medium hard fabric, with occasional streaks of creamy pink clay. The temper is well sorted, with sand, flint and small pieces of grog, all less than 1 mm. in size. The tiles are oxidised throughout, with small, well distributed air holes. The tiles have cut edges and a smooth non-sanded base. The sides have a medium bevel and the decoration is applied to the upper surface by the slip-over-impression method (Drury and Pratt 1975, 139-40), and then glazed with a yellow-orange or green lead glaze. Each tile has one nail-hole in each corner and, occasionally, a fifth hole in the centre.

Tile Designs (Figs. 54-55)

Nos. 1-4	Tiles forming continuous pattern, with a single inscription on each tile, surrounding a shield bearing a briquet (the badge of the Duke of Burgundy). The text of theinscription reads:

ALLE   DINC   HEEFT   SYNEN   TYT

	(Translation: There is time for all things). Tile no. 1 is probably the earliest in the series, and no. 2 often occurs with a crack across the stamp, together with no. 3 uncracked. No. 4 must be the last version.
No. 5	This tile has the same inscription as nos. 1-4 but is set in a roundel, with Roman rather than Gothic lettering. The briquet is also not included.
No. 6	The inscription is arranged on the tile in the same manner as nos. 1-4, but in Roman lettering with a different text (Rijken 1966):

(EEDRA)   CHT   HEEFT   GROOTE   (GRACHT)

	(Translation: Unity has great strength)
No. 7	Continuous pattern with date, 1556, set as central motif.
No. 8	Continuous floral motif, set within pattern of saltire crosses, and a shaded background of hatched lines.
No. 9	Simplified version of no. 8, without hatched lines.
Nos. 10, 11.	Four-tile design, forming repeated roundels, with an inscription in Gothic letters set on each. The complete text can be arrived at by considering the two different designs together:

Die tyt is cort
Die doot is snel
Wacht U va sonde
Soe doedi wel

	(Translation: Time is short, death is soon, beware of sin, act righteously).
No. 12	A variant of no. 11, but with the text in bolder figures. The tile that forms the other pair to this design has not yet been recorded.
Nos. 13, 14.	Border tiles, with a plaited decoration and a border.

CATALOGUE OF TILES

The Netherlands

Amsterdam, Rijksmuseum. Unprovenanced tiles from a private collection.

No. 2	5 tiles, 23 mm. thick, with green orange glaze (9218, 9219, 9220).

No. 11   2 tiles, 23 mm. thick, with green orange glaze.

Delft, Huis Lambert Van Meerten. A large tile collection now displayed in a special museum; most of the tiles were from Delft (Peelen 1922).

No. 1   1 tile fragment, 21 mm. thick, with orange yellow glaze (21 A 11).
No. 4   1 tile fragment, 24 mm. thick, with an orange yellow glaze (21 A 10).
No. 10   3 fragments, 24 mm. thick, with an orange yellow glaze (21 A 10).
No. 11   4 fragments, 24 mm. thick, with an orange yellow glaze (21 A 10).

Brussels, Musées Royaux d'Art et d'Histoire

No. 10   2 tiles, 22 mm. thick, with a brown yellow glaze.
No. 11   1 tile, 22 mm. thick, with a yellow green glaze.

St. Nickolas Museum. Found locally.

No. 10   1 tile, 24 mm. thick, with yellow glaze.

England

Boughton Malherbe Church, Kent.
Patch of tiles, relaid behind the altar and on the chancel step. (Streatfield 1878, f 17).
No. 1   1 tile, orange-green glaze.
No. 2   11 tiles, 18 mm. thick, orange-yellow glaze.

Boxgrove Priory, East Sussex
Tiles are relaid in the south aisle, at the east end, (Knapp 1956; Nairn and Pevsner 1965, 117)
No. 11   17 tiles, with brown-orange glaze.

Chalgrave Church, Bedfordshire.
Tiles were reported by Renaud (MSS ii, 263), and now appear to be lost (Ward and Perkins 1937).
No. 10   1 tile
No. 11   1 tile

Edmonton Church, Greater London
A collection of tiles from this site is in the Victoria and Albert Museum, South Kensington. No tiles remain in the church today, (Lane 1934, 34).
No. 10   2 tiles
No. 11   2 tiles

Eltham Palace, Greater London.
A single tile is loose, and on display in the Great Hall (Ward Perkins 1937).
No. 10   1 tile, 19 mm. thick, yellow-green glaze.

Exeter, Goldsmith Street, Paul Street and Rach Street Excavations.
At Goldsmith Street, one tile was found in a late sixteenth-century garden trench (G.S. F 38). Single fragments were found at each of the other sites, but in unstratified contexts (John Allen, personal communication).
No. 7   3 tiles, yellow glaze.

Gloucester, Blackfriars.
A single tile which now appears to be lost, was recorded by Renaud, (MSS iv, 475) and Lord

Alwyn Compton (MSS f 153 r).
No. 1   1 tile (probably lost).

Halnaker House, East Sussex.
A number of fragments have been reported from this site. One tile is in the British Museum (Eames 1980, Cat. 1360, no. 1433), a second identical fragment remains on the site. Another piece was illustrated by Nichols (1845, no. 58), (Ward Perkins 1937).
No. 11   2 tiles, 20 mm. thick, brown-orange glaze.

Ibberton Church, Dorset.
J. Hutchins noted tiles with an inscription 'Los de Wel' in the north aisle and in the south porch (Hutchins 1815, iv, 195). Today, however, only a single tile survives in the south porch (Emden 1977, 87, no. 231)
No. 11   1 tile, with a yellow glaze.

Ifield, Kent.
A single tile was found recently in a farmyard, and remains in the possession of Mr D.F. Allen.
No. 10   1 tile, 18 mm. thick, yellow glaze

Ipswich, St. Margaret's Church.
A tile remains in Ipswich Museum that came from this building. On the reverse is noted, 'a broken tile, similar in every respect has recently been found by Mr William Turner, in the roots of a tree in Mr Fournereau's Park', (Sherlock n.d. 38, no. 123; Drury and Norton forthcoming).
No. 8   1 tile, 18 mm. thick, with a clear yellow glaze.

London, Bank of England.
The tiles in the British Museum collection have recently been attributed to this provenance (Norton 1981; Eames 1980).
No. 10   1 tile, 20 mm. thick, orange-brown glaze (Eames 1980, Cat. 13558, no. 1432).
No. 11   1 tile, 20 mm. thick, brown-orange glaze (Eames 1980, Cat. 13559, no. 1433).
No. 14   1 tile, 18 mm. thick, orange-brown purple glaze (Eames 1980, Cat. 13560, no. 1276).

London, Unprovenanced.
A small group of tiles in the Museum of London (Ward Perkins 1937).
No. 3   1 tile.
No. 10   1 tile.
No. 11   1 tile.

Nonsuch Palace, Greater London
A number of tiles was recovered from destruction levels in the excavations directed by Martin Biddle.
No. 1   2 tiles, 22 mm. thick, with a yellow green glaze.
No. 2   1 tile, 20 mm. thick, with green yellow glaze.
No. 10   1 tile, 2 fragments, 23 mm. thick, with a yellow glaze.

Oxford, Rewley Abbey
P. Manning noted a tile from the site, and his drawing is preserved in the Bodleian Library,

Fig. 54.   Dutch tiles (¼).

Oxford (MSS top oxon d.194, f151).
No. 8   1 tile, (now lost).

Southampton, Winkle Street Excavations.
Traces of a floor were excavated at Winkle Street B, where a mortar bedding was exposed, with fragments of floor tiles in the rubble above. This floor rested on a layer dated archaeologically to *c.* 1550, (Platt and Coleman Smith 1975, i, 275, Pl. 51).
No. 8   5 fragments, 17 mm. thick, with yellow orange glaze (Platt and Coleman Smith 1975, ii, nos. 1468, 1469).

Fig. 55. Dutch tiles (¼).

No. 13   1 fragment, 20 mm. thick, with a yellow orange glaze (Platt and Coleman Smith 1975, ii, no. 1470).

Unprovenanced, British Museum, London.
No. 3   1 tile, 18 mm. thick, purple brown yellow glaze (Eames 1980, Cat. 11496, no. 1430).

Unprovenanced, Society of Antiquaries Museum, London
No. 10   1 tile, with a yellow glaze.

Unprovenanced, University Museum of Archaeology and Ethnology, Cambridge.
No. 10   1 tile, with a yellow glaze.

DISCUSSION

There are three possible ways in which the date of these tiles can be precisely established: by studying the tiles themselves, by comparing their designs with other products being made in the Low Countries at the same time; finally, by identifying the archaeological contexts of their discovery. At first sight, the tiles do not form, stylistically, a uniform group. A variety of scripts are used, both Gothic and Roman, and each is arranged in different ways. The some-what archaic designs (nos. 10, 11 and 12) occur with up-to-date Renaissance motifs (nos. 8 and 9). But there are good reasons for assuming the tiles are all the products of a single small industry, working only during a very limited period. The similarity in fabric and conditions of firing is reflected in the same dimensions of length, breadth and width being employed throughout. Furthermore, where the products occur as imports, different designs occur together, in several different orders. Thus at the Bank of England, nos. 10, 11 and 14 are found, but at Nonsuch Palace, nos. 1, 2 and 10 only occur. If we assume that the stamp that produced design no. 10 had a limited life, then all these tiles must have been approximately contemporary.

At each site, all the tiles of this group appear to have been made with the same nail board. This is a square template, with four or five nails hammered into the wood, onto which the clay can be firmly placed for trimming. This technique is found on many of the fifteenth-century and later tiles being produced in the Low Countries; it continues into the early production of Delft tiles (De Jonge 1971, 8-13; Eames 1980, 276), and was especially common in the production of plain Flemish tiles of the fifteenth and sixteenth centuries. The technique was apparently not employed on English tiles of this date, even with products from kilns in Essex, that were in direct imitation of the plain Flemish tiles (Drury and Norton, forthcoming).

The group of tiles at Huis Lambert Van Meerten is particularly important for our purposes. Tile designs nos. 2, 3, 6, 7, 10, and 11 all occur together. Although the precise provenance of these tiles is unknown, they form a closed group, because the same nail board has been employed in the making of each tile. The board had four nails each being randomly placed in each corner. The probability that two different nail boards would match up is therefore very small, and we can conclude that this whole group was made at the same time. The collection contains the dated tile, 1556 (no. 7). As it is. very unlikely that the stamp would have been cut before this date (although it could have continued in use for some time afterwards), it provides a firm *terminus post quem* date for the manufacture of these tiles. In this group, design no. 2 occurs, with a large crack across the stamp. The same crack can be observed in the tiles at Gouda and Rotterdam. Tile design no. 3 (a variant of no. 2) also occurs at Huis Lambert Van Meerten, uncracked, and is therefore presumably a replacement for design no. 2. On stylistic grounds, it is probable that no. 1 was the earlier prototype for the series, and that nos. 2, 3 and 4 are successive copies.

Turning to the English material, these conclusions are significant. No cracked version of no. 2 has yet been found in England, no examples of no. 4, and only two unprovenanced examples of no. 3. At Nonsuch Palace and Boughton Malherbe, nos. 1 and 2 occur together, with no examples of no. 7. The implication is that the Nonsuch and Boughton Malherbe groups are slightly earlier than the Huis Lambert Van Meerten tiles, around or slightly prior to 1556. The whole production, however, must have had a finite life, as design nos. 10 and 11 occur at virtually every site, and the stamps were employed from the very beginning. The life of an individual stamp is impossible to judge accurately, but if we assume that it lasts no longer than ten years, then it is reasonable to suggest that the whole series dates to between 1550 and 1560.

The stylistic dating is more difficult. Certain archaic features have already been noted. The two most up-to-date designs, nos. 8 and 9, appear to be direct copies of similar tin-glazed Majolica tiles. These were being produced throughout the early to mid-sixteenth century, and an import has recently been recovered on the Mint Yard Excavations at Canterbury (Horton, forthcoming). The polychrome is clearly being hinted at, by the use of shading in no. 8, within the limitations of the two-colour technique. The double lines on the tiles seem to be an imitation of mosaic tiles that were commonly employed in the Majolica Pavements, laid in the first half of the sixteenth century. Examples of this work can be seen from the Abbey of Heickenrode (Belgium), Nassau Castle, Breda (Netherlands), The Vine (Hampshire, England) and possibly at Halnaker House in East Sussex. They are generally attributed to the Italian tile maker, Guido Andries, who may have introduced the technique, and was operating in Antwerp between c. 1530 and c. 1540 (Rackham 1926; Lane 1960, 53; Nicaise 1935; Laurent 1922; Gronemann 1959). As is often the case, patterns introduced as mosaic arrangements are carried over to the more economical square tiles. A date somewhat later than the Antwerp products would seem reasonable, probably between 1540 and 1560.

The archaeological contexts of the tiles discovered in England go some way to confirm these dates. The Dutch motto tiles occur in England at three monastic sites, Boxgrove Priory, Gloucester Blackfriars and Rewley Abbey, Oxford, so it could be maintained that the tiles were imported before the Dissolution, 1536-1539. There are good reasons to doubt this, however. At both Rewley Abbey and Gloucester Blackfriars, the claustral ranges were partly demolished and turned into a private residence, in the mid-sixteenth century (Knowles 1932, 168). At Boxgrove Priory, although the priory church continued in use, some of the materials were built into Halnaker House, only one mile away. The Lord de Warr, the owner of Halnaker House took an interest in the church, even building himself a chantry chapel, in which he was never to be buried in, when he died in 1554 (Godfrey 1942). At Halnaker House, Dutch motto tiles of identical design have been found to those in the priory church. It seems likely that they were laid at the same time as they were being put down in the house (Lewis André 1900; Steen 1958; Turner 1863).

A similar relationship between 'house' and 'church' can be suggested at Ipswich. A tile of design no. 8 has been recorded from St. Margaret's Church, Ipswich. On the reverse of this piece, a label notes that an identical tile was also found in the roots of a tree, in Mr Fournereau's Park. In the nineteenth century, a Mr Fournereau owned land near to St. Margaret's Church, containing the site of Christchurch Mansions, the main buildings of which were erected in 1548-50, with a later wing added in 1564. It seems very likely that the tile from the roots of the tree in fact came from this building. At Boughton Malherbe, although no tiles have yet been reported from Boughton Place, set next to the church, it is significant that this building itself was being completely rebuilt in the mid 1550s by Sir Edward Wotton; there is a dated fireplace of 1553 on the first floor (Newman 1969). At Ibberton Church. Dorset, the north aisle, where according to Hutchins (1815, iv, 195) the tiles were originally laid, was completely rebuilt in the sixteenth century (R.C.H.M. 1970, 124).

Edmonton Church seems to have been rebuilt also in the sixteenth century, (personal observation).

At Nonsuch Palace, the tiles were all derived from destruction levels, there being none found *in situ*. The building of Nonsuch was started in 1538 (Summerson 1955, 8; Clapham and

Godfrey 1913; Nairn, Pevsner and Cherry 1971) but was not completed at the death of King Henry VIII. In 1556 the Earl of Arundel was granted the lease of Nonsuch and shortly afterwards was said to have completed the palace. It is possible that it was during these building works that the tiles were laid (Malden 1911, iii, 363-87). At Eltham Palace, there were also extensive sixteenth-century alterations (R.C.H.M. 1930, 103-8).

The excavations at Winkle Street, Southampton produced tiles of design nos. 8 and 13. Although no tiles were found *in situ*, the mortar bedding with the tile impressions was uncovered; fragments of the tiles themselves were found in the fill above (Platt and Coleman Smith 1975, i, 275). This floor rested on a layer that the excavators dated to *c*. 1550 on the basis of coin and pottery evidence. At Goldsmith Street, Exeter, one fragment was also excavated in a late sixteenth-century context.

To sum up: wherever Dutch motto tiles occur at monastic sites, in each case they could have been laid after the suppression, when the buildings were turned into private residences. At Nonsuch, in any case, the tiles must be later than 1538, and probably date to 1556-58. At Ipswich, a date shortly after 1548 is most likely; at Southampton Winkle Street, the pavement was laid a few years after *c*. 1550 and at Boughton Malherbe a date in the 1550s is acceptable. In addition, at most of the other sites, major sixteenth-century building works were being conducted where Dutch motto tiles have been found. The archaeological evidence very much confirms the date *c*. 1550 – *c*. 1560.

Figure 54 shows the distribution of Dutch motto tiles. Within England the group is wholly confined to the southern part of the country, reaching as far west as Exeter, and as far north as Oxford. The greatest concentration, however, lies in Kent and London, with a complete absence of tiles in Essex. In the Low Countries, the tiles are known mainly from the Gouda and Delft areas, with examples reaching Middelburg and Antwerp. It is significant that no tiles are recorded further west than Antwerp. The distribution is limited to the central part of the Netherlands, and in England, to sites that have access to either London or the ports along the English Channel. The absence of tiles (except at Ipswich) in the east coast ports, is as noteworthy as their occurence as far west as Exeter and Dorset. No kiln has yet been found, manufacturing the motto tiles. De Jonge (1971, 5) has suggested that they were made in Gouda, but the distribution suggests that they were in fact being produced near a sea port that had close links in the trade across the English Channel rather than the North Sea; perhaps Middelburg or Antwerp.

The absence of Dutch motto tiles in the southern Netherlands is more surprising. There is not a single example in the large collection of tiles in Bruges or Ghent, or in the French-speaking areas of modern Belgium. This could suggest that Antwerp or Middelburg were not the centres of production; a more likely explanation, however, lies in the content of the tiles themselves. The mottos are surprisingly 'Protestant' in spirit, exhorting the reader to be always righteous, and to be able to face death. Such sentiments would hardly have been popular in an area that remained Roman Catholic, and may well explain why no tiles are found. If this is the case, it is of great interest that the mottos were popular in the Roman Catholic England of Queen Mary. Either their meaning was not understood, or their content was considered inoffensive.

Imported Floor Tiles

The motto tiles were probably intended to be set on the floor. The tiles from Nonsuch were all very worn, and at Southampton in the Winkle Street Excavations, the traces of the original mortar bedding were identified. To find a context for this group of tiles, we should therefore perhaps look at the trade in floor tiles across the North Sea and English Channel in the late Middle Ages.

From the latter part of the fourteenth century, huge quantities of plain Flemish floor tiles were reaching the churches of southern England. The tiles themselves can be recognised by the presence of nail holes on the upper surface, and have been reported from a very large number of sites (Drury and Norton, forthcoming). They appear in the Custom books for the ports of the south-east (Knapp 1956), in wills and bequests (Ward Perkins 1937) and royal building accounts (Lane 1960, 34). Although most of the plain tiles are found in the south-east, these tiles do reach as far away as the Isles of Scilly (Miles and Saunders 1970, 27, 29,) and Edinburgh (Eames 1977).

The organisation of the importation of decorated floor tiles into England was on a totally different basis; almost insignificant quantities of tiles reached across the Channel from the Low Countries during the Middle Ages. Some decorated and *Vert et Manganese* tiles are reported from Hadleigh Castle that probably came from Flanders and date from the latter part of the fourteenth century. Two tiles now in Cheriton Church (Knapp 1956), with similar tiles known from London (Ward Perkins 1940), were probably being made in the Utrecht area, and are known from a number of Continental sites (Horton and Drury, forthcoming). Another small group of tiles again from Utrecht has recently been found in south-east Essex (Drury and Norton, forthcoming) and fifteenth-century tiles, perhaps from Flanders, have been discovered in Maldon Church. The decorated tiles, imported prior to the Reformation, from the Low Countries would just about fit into a shoe box.

The Dutch motto tiles do not readily fall into this category. There are rather more of them and there is a considerable gap between the last medieval imports and the suggested dates for these tiles. The distribution is different, and the demand lay with the large domestic houses and palaces, not with the parish churches. The context of the importation of these tiles lies not in ecclesiastical, but wholly secular contacts between the two areas.

Tile design no. 8, it has been pointed out, copies almost exactly early Majolica tiles, with tin glaze and painted decoration. The importation of Majolica tiles into the great houses of southern England from Antwerp has been discussed elsewhere (Rackham 1926; Lane 1960, 34). In addition to the imported pavement at The Vine, fragments have been found at Tichfield Abbey, Malling Abbey, Tunstall, Kent, Gorhambury, Herts., and Halnaker House. The distribution of these tiles is remarkably similar to that of the Dutch motto tiles. The two-colour, slip-decorated motto tiles may have been introduced as cheaper substitutes for the grander Majolica pavements.

Both in the Low Countries and in southern England, the cheap mass production of plain tiles undermined the decorated floor tile industry, and virtually no decorated tiles can be attributed to the fifteenth century. The introduction of Italian Majolica work, based in Antwerp in the early sixteenth century, appears to have rekindled an interest in 'decorated' floors. Soon they were laid in a number of important buildings (Gronemann 1959). By the middle part of the sixteenth century the products were no longer just floor tiles, but included wall tiles; an innovation that led to the development of the northern Dutch Delft tile industry. One result of the increased demand for decorated tiles, both floor and wall, in the middle part of the sixteenth century, seems therefore to have been the revival of two-colour techniques (Kok 1949), using white slips and lead glazes (Korf 1963). The motto tiles appear to be the first part of this revival, and a whole series of similar tiles, also carrying inscriptions is known from the Abbey of Duinen, from Tournai and Valenciennes. By the end of the sixteenth century a limited range of tiles was being made by the same technique, in order to decorate the surround to fireplaces (De Knock 1976). This industry even continued producing very similar tiles, near Turnhout, until the nineteenth century. But in England there was no such revival of interest in two-colour tiles, and the Dutch motto tiles were the last new tiles made by this technique, to be laid on either domestic or ecclesiastical floors.

Conclusions

This paper has reported a small group of Dutch motto tiles that are known from English and Continental sites. On typological, stylistic and archaeological grounds the production seems to have been limited to a period between about 1550 and 1560, and was probably centred around Middelburg or Antwerp. The demand for the tiles was mainly secular, where they often formed part of the furnishings of the important houses being built at the time. Their survival in parish churches is a result of these activities. The importation of motto tiles is probably linked to the introduction of Majolica floors from Antwerp; they were cheap substitutes copying some of the designs of their tin-glazed counterparts. Motto tiles were always more popular abroad, where they started a new post-medieval interest in slip-decorated, two-colour tiles that continued until the nineteenth century.

ACKNOWLEDGEMENTS

The fieldwork for this paper was conducted during 1977 and 1978, where it was partly funded by the Ridgeway Venn Fund, and my college, Peterhouse. The suggestion that I should do the work came from the late Dr. A.B. Emden. I am very grateful to the staff of all the museums and to the many people whom I visited as part of this survey in Belgium and the Netherlands.

Whilst in a 'foreign field' attempting to complete this paper, I am greatly endebted to Mr Christopher Norton, who resolved many of the problems and supplied much new information on the English sites. The errors that remain are all my own. I am also very grateful in being able to quote in advance of their own publications, the important discoveries of Paul Drury in Essex, of Christopher Norton at Ipswich and the Bank of England, of Martin Biddle at Nonsuch Palace, and of John Allen at Exeter. Mr Nicholas Rodgers advised on heraldic matters.

STONE FROM THE MEDIEVAL LIMESTONE QUARRIES OF SOUTH YORKSHIRE

ERIC GEE

This essay began as a study of the stone used in York Cathedral, but it was soon realised that the quarries of south Yorkshire had been used extensively for important structures elsewhere. The stone much favoured from the Conquest onwards was from Caen in Normandy, but when politics made it difficult to obtain, English magnesian limestone was discovered as a worthy substitute.

The magnesian limestone of the Tadcaster area has been used since the earliest times and the statement that "Tadcaster stone was not used for building or sculpture before the middle of the twelfth century" (Stone 1955, 75) is quite untrue. It was known in Roman times (Frere 1974, 335) and a Roman road near Hazelwood was found to be constructed over the infilling of a quarry. The walls of Roman York (Eboracum) were all faced with magnesian limestone and the well-known inscription stone of Trajan was made of it (R.C.H.M. 1962, 8, 10 and Pl. 41).

A few Saxon crosses, such as the tenth-century fragment found in Newgate (Hall 1976, Pl. 19) were made of limestone, though most were made of the Bramley Fall type of gritstone found north-west of Leeds. (Clifton-Taylor 1972, 135-6) The earliest Norman cathedral found at York, built in 1075-1100 for Archbishop Thomas of Bayeux, was of re-used Roman gritstone and magnesian limestone. Limestone was first quarried specifically for the cathedral after the fire of 1137; then the eastern arm, erected by Archbishop Roger Pont L'Eveque in 1160-75, used this excellent new stone. The Percy family did not give stone to the cathedral (Browne 1847, 13); although their gifts of wood are well documented there is no reference to stone amongst the Percy charters. (E.Y.C. 1963, *The Percy Fee*) Between 1225 and 1385 the only source of magnesian limestone for the cathedral was from the Thevesdale quarry at Hazelwood near Tadcaster, but in 1385 Huddleston near Sherburn-in-Elmet began supplying stone; Thevesdale stopped sending stone to the Minster in 1423, but Huddleston continued until 1543-44. From 1399 until 1403 stone from Stapleton near Pontefract was used with lesser quantities from Doncaster (1400-16), Bramham (1419-22) and Hampole near Doncaster (1512-30). In the detailed accounts which follow it should be understood that although the owner granted the use of a quarry, he still retained the ownership and often derived an income from it. All references to York Minster will be from my own transcription of the Fabric Roll for that year unless otherwise stated.

THEVESDALE QUARRY

In 1184-89 stone from a quarry at Hazlewood was granted by William le Vavasour to Salley Abbey (E.Y.C. 1963, no. 115, p. 131), but the first specific reference to Thevesdale is in a grant of *c.* 1225 by Robert le Vavasour (*d.* 1227) to St. Peter's church at York of the use of his quarry there with free passage over his land (E.Y.C. 1947, 169). The witnesses, all Minster officials, confirm the date. (Clay 1959, vol. 2) The upper part of the monument to Archbishop Walter de Grey (*d.* 1255), otherwise of Purbeck marble, is probably of Thevesdale stone which was also used at Beverley Minster (Cifton Taylor 23).

John le Vavasour (*d. c.* 1285), son of Robert le Vavasour, gave to St. Mary's Abbey, York, 10 acres and half a rood of his quarry in Thevesdale near to the quarry of the Blessed Peter of York, the head of which quarry abutted the new road which led from the quarry to the Vale of Thevesdale and extended to the quarry of Thevesdale eastward. (Browne 1847, 48) In 1246, John le Vavasour re-confirmed the grant of a quarry to the Prior of St. Mary at Marton (Browne 1847, 48; Deed 83). The church of St. Peter at Howden was made collegiate in 1267 and in 1277 half an acre of quarry in Thevesdale was assigned to it for eighteen years (Browne 1847, 48). In 1281, the canons of Howden complained that a nook of the King's quarry amounting to an acre, used for the repair of York Castle, was in the way so they could not remove their stone (VCH 1912, 376-7).

In 1283, John le Vavasour granted two acres of his quarry in Thevesdale to the Abbot and Convent of Thornton in Lincolnshire for forty years (Browne 1847, 48; Deed 88) and in the same year Archbishop Wickwane obtained permission from Thornton Abbey to use the same quarry for his building works (Browne 1847, 48). In 1300, Sir William le Vavasour granted a quarry in Thevesdale to the Abbot and Convent of Thornton for thirty years. (Browne 1847, 48, Deed 99). Selby Abbey had a quarry there (Browne 1847, 48; Deed 199) and in 1291 John de Lunda, Prior of Marton, granted the Abbot and Convent of Selby three acres of his quarry in Thevesdale, which abutted that of the Abbot and Convent of Thornton on the west side and that of the Prior and Convent of Drax on the north (Y.A.S. 1891, 317-8).

In 1302, Sir William le Vavasour received acknowledgment from the Dean and Chapter of York for stone to repair the Precentor's house (Browne 1847, 115), and in 1311 Archbishop Grenefeld was allowed stone to repair his manor houses (Browne 1847, 118). In 1322, the King gave protection for a party sent by the Mayor and Corporation of York with four carts to carry stone from Thevesdale to the Wharfe at Tadcaster to repair the city walls. (CPR, 1321-24, 233).

The fragmentary first York Minster fabric roll of *c.* 1360 recorded at least 23 'damlades' of stone (a damlade = 10 tons) carried by water from Tadcaster on the Wharfe to the Ouse at Cawood and thence to St. Leonard's Landing at York and dragged by sled to the masons' lodge in the cemetery south of the cathedral nave. In 1364, stone from Thevesdale, for York Castle, was bought at Tadcaster in three categories, 'werkstane rugh' (rough ashlar) 'werkstane scapeld' (trimmed ashlar) and 'mayilliom' (probably rubble), costing £70 10*s.* 8¾*d.* (Salzman 1952, 122). A fabric roll of 1371 had a full account for stone, 100 damlades coming from Thevesdale in the usual way; it included clearing the top of a new quarry, the purchase of mallets and iron wedges, and constant drinks. The roll for 1399 combined the quarry accounts, but six shiploads of stone came from Thevesdale and the master of the masons, Hugh de Hedon, visited the quarry with his warden, Lawrence de Broghton.

The fabric roll of *c.* 1400 contained a complete quarry account which showed clearly that Thevesdale stone was sold in 'damlades' and Stapleton stone in 'fothers'. At Thevesdale there was one quarrier full-time and 8 part-time (£15 17*s.* 4*d.*) and 34 damlades of stone came from the quarry by cart to Tadcaster and thence to York by boat and sled. (£18 7*s.*) In *c.* 1402 the

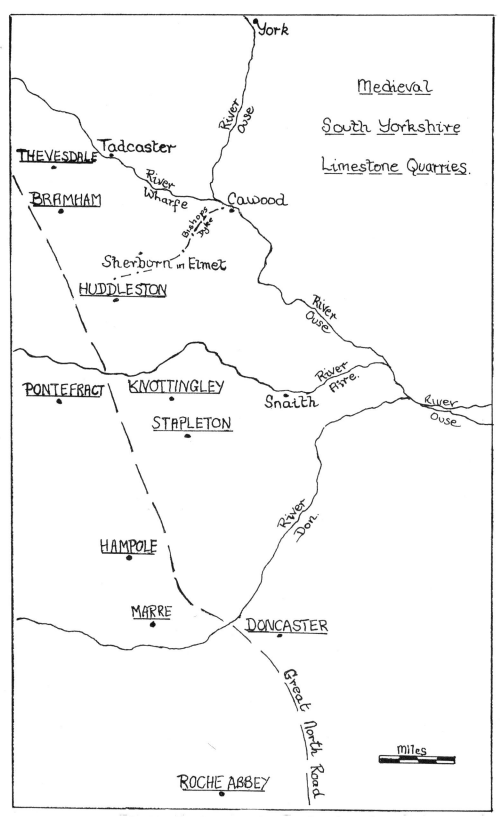

Fig. 56. Sketch map to show location of quarries.

quarry accounts were separated. At Thevesdale three quarriers worked over 46 weeks each (£12 8s. 4d.) and over 32 damlades of stone came to the cathedral (£15 13s. 10d.). Four quarriers in c. 1404 earned £11 15s. and 20 damlades of stone cost £10 5s. to be moved to York. The chief Minster masons, Hugh Hedon and Lawrence Broghton, visited the quarry. In a complete fabric roll for 1415-16 there were four quarriers, three of whom were given robes (£12 9s.) and 387 tuntights of stone were brought to York (£22 8s.) The stone measure was changed this year from a 'damlade' (10 tons) to a 'tuntight' (1 ton). In the combined account of 1418-19 the quarries can still be differentiated by the measures and methods of transport. Two quarriers worked for a full year at Thevesdale (£9 6s. 8d.) and 220 tuntights of stone were brought to York (£13 1s.). Another roll in 1419 had a separate entry for Thevesdale; two quarriers worked all year, receiving robes by agreement (£9 5s.) and 200 tuntights of stone arrived in York (£12).

In 1421-22, four quarriers worked spasmodically at Thevesdale (£13 4s.) and 120 tuntights (including 40 tuntights of Bramham stone) were carried to York (£6 6s. 8d.) Three loads of stone were carried overland by cart because of some trouble in the river, and the quarry was cleared. In 1422-23, three quarriers worked at Thevesdale, one full-time (£9 17s.), 240 tuntights of stone reached York (£10) and a robe cost 6s. 8d.

Thevesdale stone seems to have stopped coming to York after 1423. In 1447, the King obtained from Henry Vavasour the use of a quarry in Thevesdale in his lordship of Hazelwood near Tadcaster. The stone was to be carried to the river Wharfe and thence shipped to King's College, Cambridge (Colvin 1963, i, 274). Thevesdale supplied stone until arrangements were made in 1449 to use the neighbouring quarry at Huddleston. Henry Vavasour dined at King's College in 1451 (Willis and Clark 1886, i, 466 and note 2). It is interesting to see that masons' marks in the first two of the chapels on the north side of King's College, presumably built of Thevesdale stone in 1447-49, are those of York masons. (R.C.H.M. 1959, 114) After the deposition of Henry VI, King's College chapel started using oolitic limestone from Northamptonshire instead. (Willis and Clark 1886, i, 486) At York perhaps the last reference to this stone was in 1515-16 when John Robinson was paid for 60 cartloads of stone from Newton and Hazelwood (£2 10s.). After the eastern arm of York Minster was burnt in 1829, Sir Edward Marmaduke Vavasour, Bt., granted the use of Thevesdale quarry for the restoration (Browne 1847, 49).

HUDDLESTON QUARRY

There is no reference to Huddleston stone being used at York before 1385, but in 1361 Archbishop Thoresby granted the materials from his hall at Sherburn-in-Elmet for the fabric and that was almost certainly of the nearby Huddleston stone. The quarry was owned by the Langton family of Farnley near Leeds, and the stone was measured by the 'fother' (1 ton) as was that from Stapleton. In 1385 the Dean and Chapter of York took a lease of the quarry of Huddleston for eighty years.

The fabric roll of 1415-16 has a separate entry for Huddleston. 5 roods of quarry were bought from John Langton and John Newton, mason (£10 3s. 4d.). 2 roods of it were cleared and 160 fothers of stone were brought to York (£10 5s.); 285 fothers were moved by cart from Huddleston to Cawood and thence to the Minster by boat and sled (£21 13s. 4d.). There were also expenses for moving stone from the wharves at Cawood to the river; these wharves were probably on a basin, later represented by a mill pond, at the Cawood end of an artificial channel called the Bishop's Dyke (J. Miller. Y.A.J. forthcoming issue) still 16 ft. wide and 3 ft. deep, runs east from Sherburn-in-Elmet near Huddleston quarry and then north-east to the basin. These wharves were therefore some distance from the Ouse.

In 1415, both Huddleston and Stapleton stone were used in the royal house at Sheen in Surrey, and Stapleton stone 'worked for the main gate of Sheen' is mentioned in an inventory of 1419-20. (Colvin 1963, ii, 999) In 1418-19, the Minster quarry accounts were put together and although two men worked all year at Huddleston, it is not clear whether the 237 fothers of stone carried to Cawood (£11 10s. 10d.) were included in the 280 tuntights carried thence to the cemetery (£9 9s.). There was a separate account in 1419; three quarriers were working (£10 8s. 8d.), 220 fothers were moved to Cawood (£10 16s. 8d.) while an accumulation of 648 fothers was moved thence to the cathedral (£18 18s.) Various roads were repaired and dust was removed from the quarry.

In 1421-22, two quarriers worked full-time (£8 16s. 8d.), 375 fothers of stone came to Cawood (£16 13s. 4d.) and 480 tuntights from Cawood to York (£9), while 20 fothers were carted from Huddleston to York (£2) possibly because a new quay was being constructed at Cawood on the basin at the canal end. Sir John Langton was paid £10 for 5 roods of quarry; he gave a rood to the Minster fabric, and he and his wife were given wine (2s.). (Henceforth Thevesdale apparently ceased to supply stone for the Minster.)

In 1422-23, two quarriers each worked full-time (£8 16s. 8d.), 369 fothers of stone were carried from the quarry to Cawood (£15 7s. 6d.) and 732 tuntights shipped to York (£13 14s. 10½d.); dust was removed from the quarry. In 1432-33, only Huddleston was mentioned in the account; two quarriers were employed (£8 16s. 8d.). 71 plaustrata (cartloads) of stone were carried to Cawood (£2 19s. 2d.), 64 cartloads to Kentilbarnbrigg on the Wharfe (£2 13s. 4d.) 26 shiploads from the banks of the Ouse onto the boats at Cawood and 613 tuntights from Cawood to the cemetery (£22 7s. 5d.) Other methods of transport were tried and roads were repaired. Thomas Goldesburgh with three companions cleared 15 roods of quarry in 1433-34, and gravel was moved thence to the shore; removal of stone cost £28 9s. 8d., but not all stone that arrived at Cawood was sent straight to York.

There is only part of a fabric roll for 1434-35, including two quarriers working full-time (£9 6s. 8d.); movement of stone cost £6 15s. and of gravel £1. Between 1441 and 1443, Sir John Langton sold over seven roods of quarry to the Dean and Chapter, removing gravel and dust from the top (£22 2s. 8d.) Three quarriers worked yearly, receiving two robes each year between them, and dug over 650 loads of stone which was transported to the Minster (£37 16s. 7d.).

In 1442, Huddleston stone was used at Westminster (Salzman 1952, 132) and in 1443 John Langton supplied stone for St. Martin's Coney Street, York. Three quarriers, two robes, stone and transport to the Minster cost £34 13s. 6d. in 1444-45. Various men from Barkeston, Sherburn, Milford, Cawood and Wistow carried stone from Huddleston to Cawood; the men of Sherburn and Milford had received 50 cartloads for the church at Sherburn, probably to build the tower, some time before May 1445.

Meanwhile Eton College realised that Yorkshire magnesian limestone was a fine match for Caen stone. In 1445-46, the clerk of the works at Sion in Surrey sold 11 tons of Huddleston stone to the College for £3 6s. at 6s. a doliate in London (Willis and Clark, 1886, i, 395; Colvin 1963, i, 282) and in 1453 James Palden of Laughton in Yorkshire, mason, contracted to move 400 tonnetyght of Huddleston stone to London (Colvin 1963, i, 282, note 2).

The account in the York fabric roll for 1445-46 was very full and totalled £51 19s. Three men worked all year at the quarry (£13 6s.) and the tenants at Sherburn, Milford, Fenton, Newthorpe, Wistow and Cawood moved stone in carts to Cawood in three major operations at a cost of £31 6s. 8d.; transport thence to York cost £7 16s. A smith at Saxton worked on mallets and wedges (15s. 4d.) and the master of the masons, John Barton, went to the quarry and Cawood. The total in 1446-47 was £39. 15s. 8d. Three quarriers worked at Huddleston (£12 9s. 4d.) and also the master of the masons, John Barton, for 18 weeks (£2 16s.). Cartage to Cawood cost £16 19s. 8d. including 332 cartloads of stone, 2 'throghes' (through-stones or bonders) and 1 'lyntell'. Eight shiploads from Cawood to York Minster cost £5 4s. Gravel was removed from the quarry, the Saxton smith made four wedges and other ironwork, and the quay at Cawood was repaired by two carpenters with piles and faggots (12s. 10d.). A building was erected in the quarry (32s.).

By now Eton College and King's College Chapel were both using Huddleston stone. In 1448-49, John Denman, mason, was paid travelling expenses to Huddleston to arrange for a supply of stone. (Knoop and Jones 1967, 43) In the autumn Roger Keys, clerk of the works at Eton, went to Huddleston to negotiate with Sir John Langton for a grant of part of his quarry, 45 ells long by 21 ells broad, lying next to the part belonging to the Dean and Chapter of York. The king certainly had the right of quarrying there before, as not only was stone supplied from that quarry in 1446-47 but the accounts speak of making a fresh indenture between the king and John Langton. In December 1448, Roger Keys went to London to meet Nicholas Close and look over the accounts of John Welles, superintendent of the quarry. An account of Michaelmas 1450 to Michaelmas 1451 mentions eight quarrymen scappling stone, which was then moved rough-dressed to Cawood. The Eton authorities paid John Perrison, a Dutch shipman, £10 6s. 0½d. for carrying 47½ doliates of stone from Cawood to London. (Knoop and Jones 1967, 48) In 1450-51, the stone cost £34 15s. 5d. and carriage £38 0s. 7d., half the expenses being borne by King's College. (Willis and Clark 1886, i, 397) Stone for King's was taken by land to Cawood whence it was shipped to Lynn and then along the Fenland rivers to Cambridge. All the foundations of the chapel at King's were laid out, and work was begun at the east end and continued until the outbreak of the Civil War. Between 1448 and 1461, the only stone used at Eton was from Huddleston or Taynton (Colvin 1963, i, 289); it cost 12d. a load at the quarry and 6s. 6d. a load for transport. (Knoop and Jones 1967, 46).

In c. 1450, the Dean and Chapter of York were favouring Sir John Langton. His arms were painted above the door of the south transept by John Paynter of York, and he was given more than a pipe of red wine, a toothpick and half a pound of green ginger when he renewed the agreements about Huddleston quarry (73s. 4d.) Henry Thwaites, a lawyer, and the Chapter clerk measured the quarry and received possession for the Dean and Chapter (£4 15s. 9d.). Three quarriers were mentioned, one of whom brought a great iron mallet from the quarry and back. Sir John Langton of Farnley died in 1459 and was buried at Leeds.

The three fabric rolls between 1456 and 1458 allow for a yearly expenditure of over £30, with three quarriers producing about 200 loads of stone yearly, including 4 throughstones, all carried to York in the usual way. There are tool repairs by the smith at Saxton, removal of gravel and constant road repairs. In January 1465, stone was brought from Huddleston for the ground floor of St. William's College, York. (Dobson 1977, 97) In 1465 an eighty-years lease to the Dean and Chapter of certain quarries at Huddleston terminated; the lease was renewed for eighteen years, but henceforward annual payments were made to the owners for the stone that was required.

The bill for quarry work in 1469-70 was £18 2s. Thomas Langton, younger son of Sir John Langton, was paid £1 13s. 4d. for the use of the quarry where quarriers dug 200 cartloads of stone (£4 3s. 4d.). The men of Wistow, Cawood and Sherburn carried 130½ loads from Huddleston to Cawood, and 8 shiploads from Cawood to York cost £3 4s. Richard Smyth of Ulskelf made wedges for the quarry. In 1470-71 the bill was £18 15s. 2d. Thomas Langton was again paid £1 13s. 4d. Quarriers prepared 100 loads of stone (£4 3s. 4d.) 254 loads were carried from Huddleston to Cawood (£10 11s. 8d.) and gravel was cleared out of the quarry. The account for 1472 totalled £10 19s. 6d. Thomas Langton sold 60 loads of prepared stone and transport to the cathedral cost £6 3s. 10d. The quarry account was £24 18s. in 1475; Thomas Langton sold 204 loads of scappled stone (£8 10s.) and cartage from Huddleston to Cawood cost £8 10s.

In 1478-79, the total was £20 13s. 11d. Thomas Langton sold 160 loads of scappled stone (£6 13s. 4d.), carriage, including movement from the quarry to the wharf at Cawood cost £13 19s. 7d. and John Smyth of Sherburn looked after the tools for six years. The quarry account for 1481-82 was £11 2s. 1d. Thomas Langton sold 80 loads of scappled stone for £3 6s. 8d. and the quarrymen received a bonus of 12d. Thomas Langton also supplied lime (a natural by-product) to the cathedral. Carriage on stone cost £5 4s. 5d. and the cemetery stoneyard was cleaned. The lease of Huddleston quarry should have been renewed in 1484 but there is no reference to this. The stone bill was £15 2s. 1d. Thomas Langton sold 120 loads of scappled stone (£5); transport to York cost £9 6s. 9d. and 'cross-shafts' and 'mantiltres' were shipped from Cawood to York. In 1497-98, Huddleston stone cost £14 8s. 4d. Thomas Langton sold 120 loads of prepared stone for £5 and transport cost £9 3s. 4d. Richard Farechild sledded 160 loads of stone from the wharf at Cawood to the boat (6s. 8d.); by this date therefore stone was again brought by barge on the Bishop's Dyke to the wharf at Cawood and then sledged to the boat on the river Ouse. The cost of stone was £33 19s. 1d. in 1498-99. Thomas Langton sold 260 loads of scappled stone (£10 16s. 8d.) and the quarrymen received 2s. reward. Movement to the cathedral cost £23 0s. 5d. Henry VII's chapel at Westminster Abbey, begun in 1503, used some Huddleston stone in the springers of the flying buttresses (Lethaby 1925, 156-7). At York cathedral in 1504 the total was £18 18s. 4d. Thomas Langton sold 160 loads which the quarriers scappled and received a reward of 3s. 4d. The stone was moved from the quarry to Cawood (£56 14s. 4d.), from the 'stagnum' (basin) to the boat (14s. 4d.), shipped up river and sledded to the cemetery (£1 13s.). Thomas Langton apparently had given up the production of lime.

The stone bill was £30 14s. 2d. in 1507-8; Thomas Langton sold 260 loads of scappled stone (£10 16s. 8d.) which was transported as before (£19 17s.) No stone was provided in the 1509-10 fabric roll. In 1515-16, the stone bill was £19 15s. 1d., but for the first time it included stone from Newton and Hazelwood (£5); Mr. Langton senior provided 100 loads (£2 10s.) and wine was given to him. John Atkynson, quarrier, prepared stone and received bonuses of 4s. 4d. Movement of 170 'doliates' (1 doliate was equivalent to the weight of a tun of wine, or a tontyght) from Cawood to York cost £9 12s. 1d. In 1518-19, the bill was £23 0s. 4d., but it included stone from other quarries. Thomas Langton provided 120 loads of scappled stone (£5 16s. 8d.), 20 loads were brought from the quarry at Huddleston (16s. 8d.); 160 loads travelled by canal and river as usual (£12.10s.)

The total in 1525-26 was £42 16s. 8d. but again included other stone. Thomas Langton supplied 200 loads, properly scappled (£10) and gave 40 loads to the cathedral. Transport cost £26 13s. 4d. The cost in 1527-28 was very high (£65 12s.) but included a lot of other stone besides Huddleston. Thomas Langton sold 240 loads (£40) and transport cost £19 10s. The rise in demand was due to the erection of St. Michael-le-Belfrey at York.

Thomas Langton was not mentioned in 1529-30, but 80 dolia of Huddleston stone were provided by William ffentyman and Anthony Hawmand. Transport was by the usual route. In 1530-31, John Forman, master of the masons, bought 100 dolia of stone at Huddleston and Mr. George Ireland of Huddleston sold 60 dolia, which were brought in the usual way. Stone also came from Tadcaster and Hampole. The fabric roll of 1531-32 records a stone bill of £43 6s. 8d. including some from Hampole; Mr. Anthony Ireland sold 128 dolia of scappled Huddleston stone. There was no stone account at all in 1535-36 and in 1537-38 the total was only £3 13s. 9d. comprising 30 dolia of stone (£1 5s.) and carriage (£2 8s. 9d.)

The last reference to Huddleston stone in the fabric rolls was in 1543-44 when 60 tons cost £2 10s. and movement to the cathedral cost £1 0s. 4d.

In 1834, when Westminster Hall was being restored by Sir Robert Smirke, who was also restoring the eastern arm of York cathedral, the inside was being fitted by Robert Johnson, mason, with a 'beautiful ashlaring of Huddleston stone.' (Colvin 1973, vi, 503)

STAPLETON QUARRY

The quarry at Stapleton was being worked c. 1300 and in 1344-45 William of Wighthill received £7 10s. for 67 pieces shipped in 20 loads to London for Windsor Castle, (Hope 1913, i, 125) where it continued in use until 1377 (Colvin 1963, ii, 881). Henry Yevele supplied 13 tons to Windsor Castle in 1368 (Knoop and Jones 1967, 21) and more in 1373 (Salzman 1952, 31). In 1385 Robert Gamulston supplied 40 tons of Stapleton stone for a flying buttress on the east side of Westminster Hall, at 10s. a ton with carriage from Yorkshire (Salzman 1952, 31). An account of 1390-91 by Geoffrey Chaucer for work at Windsor Castle included 101 doliates of Stapleton stone to repair St. George's Chapel (Hope 1913, i, 221, 225). In 1393-94, 64 tontyt of 'northern stone' was bought for Westminster Abbey nave (Rackham 1909 iv, 11) and from 1394-96 a royal house at Henley was using Stapleton stone originally bought for St. George's, Windsor (Colvin 1963, II, 962). At this time there was work on a royal manor at Windsor (not the castle) which also used stone bought for St. George's Chapel (Colvin, 1963, ii, 1008).

In 1398, John Skargull, lord of the manor, received £10 from the Dean and Chapter of York, probably to recognise a legal agreement, and Stapleton quarry was first mentioned in the rolls in 1399. The stone was assessed by the 'fother' (ton). The account included stone from Thevesdale and Stapleton, but the latter was shipped on the Aire to Snaith, then the Ouse to York. Seven quarriers were mentioned; 142 fothers were carried to Snaythland, and 340 fothers thence to York. A list of equipment mentioned 19 iron wedges, 2 iron mallets and 4 'gavelokes' (crow-bars). Hugh de Hedon, master of the masons, and Lawrence de Broughton visited the quarry and on July 17th, 1400, Henry VI allowed the Dean and Chapter to carry stone from Stapleton, toll free. The accounts were again merged in 1400, but 110 fothers of stone cost £4 18s. 8d. to be moved from Snaythland to York, and the clerk of the works visited the quarry.

Stapleton stone was used for door jambs at the Tower of London in 1400 (Salzman 1952 131). In 1403, John Clerk worked at Stapleton (£1 12s. 6d.), and 69 fothers were carried to Wrelland by cart or sled (£3 2s. 3d.), 116 fothers were shipped to York and sledged to the cemetery (£5 8s.); tools were repaired and sharpened, and Lawrence de Broughton visited the quarry. This is the last mention of Stapleton stone in the fabric rolls.

477 doliates of Stapleton stone were used in the nave at Westminster Abbey from 1413-16 (Rackham 1909, 15), a royal house at Sheen in Surrey used it c. 1414 (Colvin 1963 ii, 999) and in 1417 ships were sent to fetch stone for Sion Abbey (Salzman 1952, 131). In 1448, Stapleton stone was being used at Eton College (Colvin 1963, i, 281).

MISCELLANEOUS QUARRIES

These references are in chronological order and there may be cross-correlations.

100 fothers of stone were bought in c. 1400 from William Barbour of DONCASTER (£9 3s. 4d.); it was carried by boat and then sled to the Minster (£6 3s. 4d.). The quarry had a separate heading in the fabric roll for 1415-16 when 40 fothers were bought from John Wyrsop; transport cost £2 6s. 8d. These could be early references to Hampole, but there is no proof.

Five roods of quarry were bought from Thomas Yhonge of KNOTTINGLEY (8s.) to repair the mill at Brotherton in 1415-16.

In 1419, John del Grene worked at BRAMHAM quarry for 19 weeks (£1 11s. 8d.), the stone being moved by cart to Tadcaster, boat to York and sled to the cemetery (£10 13s. 4d.); and 6 stones called 'thurges' were bought (18s.) 40 tuntyghts of pendants were carried in 1421-22 via Tadcaster to York (£2 6s. 8d.) and Robert Hardy was rewarded (6s. 8d.) Although Bramham stone was not valued highly, it produced special forms at the time.

Early in the sixteenth century HAMPOLE quarry near Doncaster appears in the records. In 1512-13, the porches at King's College Chapel, Cambridge, were vaulted in Hampole stone (Willis and Clark 1886, i, 613; Colvin 1975, iii, pt. i, 192), and it was used there again in 1513 (Salzman 1952, 132). In 1527-28, John Anderson was paid £5 for 120 loads of Hampole stone for York Cathedral which were carried to Doncaster and thence to York (£16 10s.). Between 1529 and 1532 he sold 360 tons of stone which reached York the same way.

The Cistercian Abbey of Roche in Yorkshire was completed by 1170 in a local stone which continued to be quarried commercialy. ROCHE ABBEY stone was used at Windsor Castle in 1350-77. In 1360-65, Richard de Thwayt sold 80 'pond.dol.' (ton weight) at 10s. a pond. dol. with carriage. In 1367-68, 28 pond. dol. of Roche stone cost £8 11s. including carriage (Hope 1913, i, 186, 187, 199, 206, 207). Stone from Roche was used at Sheffield Castle in 1446-47. (Knoop and Jones 1967, 46).

Freestone from the quarries at MARRE, near Doncaster, was used in 1393 for the rebuilding of Westminster Hall where two Gloucestershire masons, Swallow and Washbourne, were to make 26 corbels of Marre stone to take the roof principals at 20s. each (Colvin 1963, i, 529).

Dressings of PONTEFRACT stone were used in 1342-43 at St. Stephen's chapel at Westminster to complete the west end and porch owing to the difficulty of obtaining Caen stone from what was then enemy territory (Colvin 1963, i, 517).

ENGLISH MONUMENTAL BRASSES BEFORE THE BLACK DEATH

JOHN BLAIR

INTRODUCTION

One of the innumerable byways of medieval archaeology which attracted Stuart Rigold's attention was the study of monumental brasses. His work, which took him to so many monastic ruins, familiarised him with despoiled slabs preserving the indent outlines of brasses now lost. Thus he was one of the first scholars to appreciate fully the extent to which indents supplement the evidence of surviving brasses, especially in the early period from which so few brasses remain. Over the years he collected substantial notes on the style and epigraphy of fourteenth-century indents, though nothing except three short articles ever reached print (Rigold 1967 a, b and c). Some ten years ago, when I had recently become interested in the subject, he passed all his material to me. As one of the many younger medievalists who owe much to his great knowledge and unfailing readiness to share it, I gladly dedicate this paper to his memory.

The few surviving figure-brasses of the early fourteenth century are magnificent and famous; it is easy to forget that they represent a tiny and probably biased sample. Before c. 1340 brasses were not riveted but were held merely by their own weight and the adhesive strength of pitch. Designs were often composed of narrow strips and foliations, and inscriptions of separately-inlaid brass letters, all of which were light and easily detached. Hence these brasses were exceptionally vulnerable to theft and accidental loss, and a fair proportion may already have perished by the end of the Middle Ages. The abundance of early indents now demonstrates how wrong it is to deduce a small workshop output from the paucity of surviving brasses. Luckily, indents of this period are more than usually informative. Their delicate components leave informative outlines, and the technique of inlaying each letter separately enables the inscriptions on despoiled slabs to be read and classified (Badham, Blair and Emmerson 1976). A few full-size figures have survived by virtue of their sheer weight; a wider range of types, more modest but iconographically more varied, can only be studied from indents.

Indents, unlike brasses, have never been recorded systematically, and it will be long before a full corpus is available. Nonetheless, outlines and letter-forms can now be used to identify the main products of the London workshops and some smaller provincial groups. The present paper is an interim summary of this work. I have avoided stylistic comments on the major surviving brasses; it will be time enough to reappraise them when all the indent evidence is available for comparison.

BRASS PRODUCTION IN ENGLAND BEFORE 1300

By 1280 monumental brasses were becoming known throughout northern Europe, and workshops had existed in France and the Low Countries for some decades (cf. Norris 1977, 1-3, 25-34). While the almost total loss of their products makes foreign prototypes for the English material hard to find, it seems likely in the case of separate-letter inscriptions that such prototypes once existed. The technique occurs on a late thirteenth-century incised slab at Santarém (Portugal), probably of French or Flemish origin (Greenhill 1952), and a French nobleman's tomb ordered in 1313 was to include brass letters made at Dinant (Dehaisnes 1886, 196-8). Salzburg marble slabs at Wilhering and Baumgartenberg in Austria, and a fine series of brasses at Lubiaz in Poland (Norris 1977, 4-8), all early fourteenth-century, have separate-letter inscriptions. Probably these isolated Continental examples and their more numerous English counterparts have a common origin in the lost work of the northern French *tombiers*.

Discounting a small dedication-plate of 1241 at Ashbourne (Derbys.) (Norris 1977, Fig. 13), the first English brasses were plain separate-inlay inscriptions with little or no embellishment. The earliest known example is not strictly monumental. The presbytery pavement of Westminster Abbey, in the characteristic style of the Cosmati family, was laid in 1268 by masons from Rome (Wander 1978). Around the perimeter, and interweaving between the porphyry roundels and their mosaic background, are long inscriptions in separate brass letters (Plate L *a*). The letters (Fig. 57*a*) are uniform, regular and cast to an even thickness of 3 mm. These inscriptions were almost certainly not made by the Italian craftsmen. No other Cosmatesque work has such lettering, and at Westminster it is set not in imported material but partly in Purbeck marble and partly in a hard wax-based composition. Two simple cross-brasses in Purbeck slabs, probably executed in the 1270s and set in the Cosmatesque floor of Edward the Confessor's chapel, have identical lettering (Lethaby 1906, 317-9). This letter-series must therefore have been used by London craftsmen closely associated with the royal works. At present there is no evidence that these men made monumental brasses on a wider basis, but some continuity between their work and London products of *c.* 1300 onwards seems *prima facie* likely. A Purbeck slab at North Stoke (Oxon.) has a marginal inscription in letter-indents of aberrant form (Fig. 57*b*) to Robert de Esthall (*ob.* 1274), while four loose letters from the Oxford Blackfriars (Fig. 57*c*) are of a different but equally unparalleled type. These seem best interpreted as isolated products of small London workshops preceding the era of rapid output and standardised lettering.

In the manufacture of brass-lettered slabs London was closely followed by Lincoln, probably a consequence of trading contacts between the Low Countries and the east coast. In Lincoln Cathedral Dean William de Lessington (*ob.* 1272) and Archdeacon Simon de Barton (*ob.* 1280) are commemorated by small slabs with lineated inscriptions in a small, rather crude alphabet (Fig. 57*d*). Barton's has a trefoiled outline and was originally set at the 'head' end of a plain coffin-shaped slab. Closely related are a fragment of similar form at Navenby (Plate L *b*), once embellished with brass inlays of the sun and moon, and a cross-indent of 1279 formerly in Lichfield Cathedral (Fig. 58*a*). Plain marginal inscriptions in this distinctive 'Lincolnshire style A' alphabet are common in and near Lincolnshire; the handful of surviving letter-inlays are all cast to a uniform thickness of 3 mm. Thus the epigraphic evidence for at least one workshop at Lincoln from the 1270s is virtually conclusive; the slabs, usually of Purbeck marble, must have been freighted from Corfe in an unworked state. By the same date the production of simple brasses had probably begun in York (below, 265), the capital of the North and a very

PLATE L

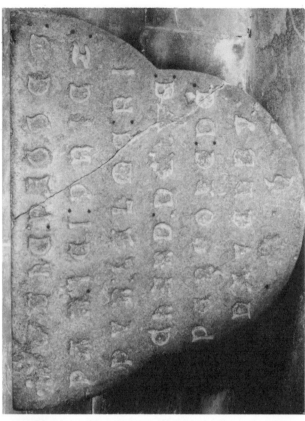

a (Photo. C. Blair).

Westminster Abbey, detail of presbytery pavement.

b (Photo. C. Blair).

Navenby, Lincs, inscription indent.

✠ LES:CORS:IRE:RICHARD:DELINDONE:
✠ CDAME:IVECE:SA:FEME:CISENT:CI:PRIES:
✠ PVRLES:AMES:RE:DEVS:EN:EIE:MERCI:

(Photo. R.C.H.M.; Crown copyright reserved).

c

Easton-on-the-Hill, Northants., inscription indent.

predictable centre for demand.

A major development was the adoption by workshops of a standardised alphabet (the 'Main Group' series, Fig. 57*e-g*), destined to remain in widespread use for half a century. With minor variants, these letters are strikingly consistent both in shape and in manufacturing technique. They occur in three standard sizes to suit brasses of different scale, and the only perceptible change over time is a heightening of the serif on letter L after *c.* 1330. Letter-inlays, cast in open moulds, are generally 2 mm. thick and edge-filed on a slight bevel; some bear traces of gilding. This uniformity suggests that 'Main Group' letters were mass-produced in a single specialist workshop. In the fourteenth century they occur on indents of different styles made in London and at least two regional centres (below, 265) and occasional mixture of sizes suggests that even the London workshops sometimes ran out of particular founts.

'Main Group' letters are ubiquitous on the prolific London-made indents of *c.* 1300-50, but there is also evidence for earlier use. They occur at Hook Norton (Oxon.) in a crudely set marginal inscription for Isabel de Pleci (*ob.* 1272-8) (Hemp 1949). A lineated inscription in oolite at Easton-on-the-Hill (Northants.) for Sir Richard de Lindone (*ob. c.* 1255) and his wife has well-cut indents for 'Main Group size II' letters (Plate L *c*); since the manor had passed into royal hands before 1290 a date of manufacture later than this seems unlikely. Evidently these letters were available for use some years before the main London workshops opened. Who, then, was making them, and where? The answer to this may lie outside England. Dinant in the Low Countries, where brass letters were being made in 1313 (above 257), was a noted centre of metal-working from which latten pots and similar small objects were imported into England (Unwin 1918, 31). Possibly a Flemish manufacturer had been casting letters for the *tombiers* of Tournai and Paris from the 1270s and supplied a regular English market through the first half of the fourteenth century, though until foreign indents with matching letters are found this remains pure hypothesis.

The mere setting of pre-cast letters in marble slabs need not imply a capacity to engrave brasses. Nothing more ambitious than a simple cross is attributable to any English workshop of the 1270s, and since the re-dating of the military brasses at Stoke D'Abernon and Trumpington (Norris 1977, 9-13) evidence for figure engraving in England before 1300 has become rather tenuous. On the other hand, St. Thomas Cantilupe's Purbeck marble indent at Hereford (Fig. 58*b*) has now been shown on near-conclusive evidence to date from 1287 (Emmerson 1980). This proves that at least one English workshop could, when occasion demanded, produce a sophisticated composition of full-length figure, canopy and border fillet, a monument which in the absence of written evidence might easily have been dated fifty years later.

THE LONDON WORKSHOPS, 1300-1350

Most early English indents are concentrated in the south-east and East Anglia and show a marked consistency of execution. They also prove, when identifiable, to commemorate people who died after 1300, though their chronological spread over the period 1300-50 seems fairly even. Around the turn of the century at least one major workshop must have opened in London to satisfy the new vogue. Slabs attributable to this source are always of Purbeck marble. Separate-letter inscriptions are invariably 'Main Group', usually marginal, and set between border fillets on the larger brasses. Inscriptions engraved on continuous strips occur occasionally from the beginning (e.g. Fig. 58*b*) and became popular after 1320, though separate letters remained a common alternative until *c.* 1350. Enough indents are extant to permit

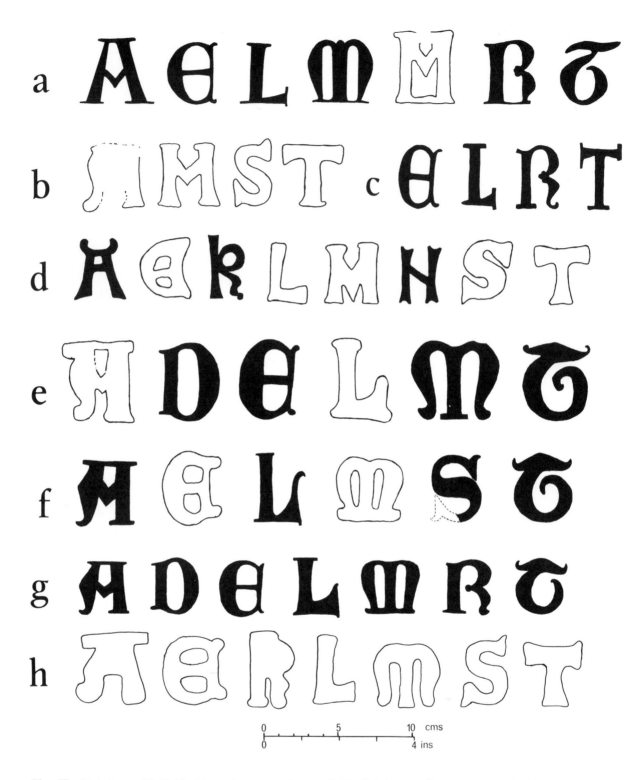

Fig. 57. Alphabets of individual brass letters used on early English brasses (for sources see Badham, Blair and Emmerson 1976). (*a*) Westminster Abbey series; (*b*) Non-standard letter-indents from slab at North Stoke, Oxon.; (*c*) Non-standard letters from Oxford Blackfriars site; (*d*) Lincolnshire style A; (*e*) 'Main Group size I'; (*f*) 'Main Group size II'; (*g*) 'Main Group size III'; (*h*) Lincolnshire style B.

Fig. 58. (*a*) Lichfield Cathedral (sketch by T. Martin, 1724, in Bodleian MS Top. Gen. e.85 p.97. *Not to scale*); (*b*) Hereford Cathedral (after *MBS Transactions* 8. vii (1949). opp. 324); (*c*) Ely Cathedral (after *MBS Portfolio* 7 (1976) Pl.31); (*d*) Letheringham, Suffolk (after *Proc. Suffolk Inst. Arch.* 33.ii (1974), 176); (*e*) Exeter Cathedral (after *MBS Bulletin* 27 (1981), 8).

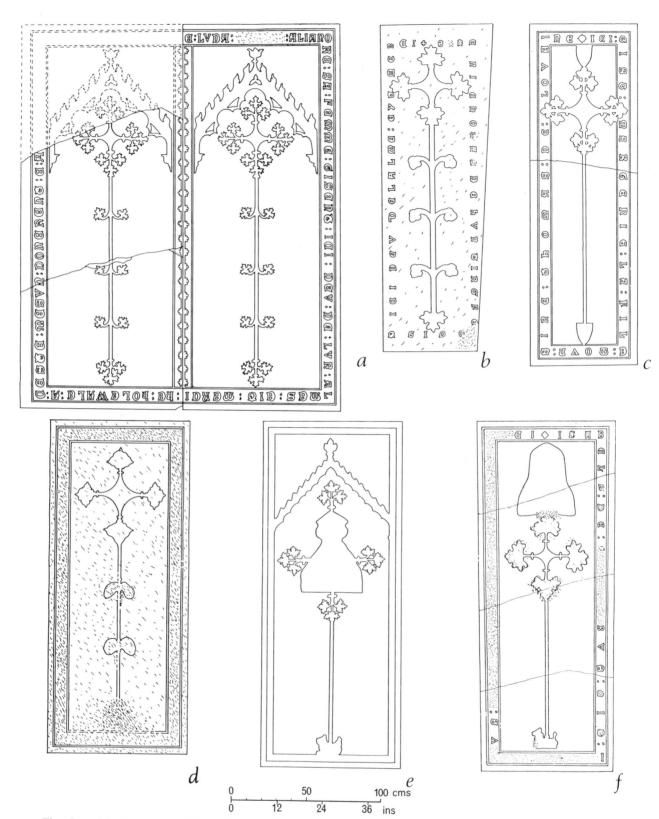

Fig. 59. *(a)* Abbotsbury Abbey, Dorset (after *MBS Transactions* 8.iii (1945), opp. 82): *(b)* Rampton Cambs;
(c) Little Easton, Essex (after *Trans. Essex Arch. Soc.* n.s., xii (1913), 231); *(d)* Clare, Suffolk; *(e)* St. Albans
Cathedral (after *Home Counties Magazine*, i (1899), 247); *(f)* Garsington, Oxon.

systematic classification, which reveals some well-defined groups.

Large brasses are often the least original. The 'set pattern' of full-length figure and gabled canopy, with ancillary details such as censing angels and heraldic shields, was imported ready-made from Europe (cf. Adhémar 1974, *passim*). It is fully developed on the earliest of the main English series, such as Bishop de Luda (*ob.* 1298) at Ely (Fig. 58c), and it holds the field thereafter (e.g. Fig. 58d). A common simplification, as on the famous brass at Stoke D'Abernon, omits the canopy but leaves two shields flanking the head. Occasional major indents of *c.* 1300-20, notably Bishop's Bitton at Exeter (Fig. 58e) and Haselshaw at Wells (Connor 1970, Pl. XXXIX), are more ambitious and include tabernacles and tiers of saints. By the 1330s and 1340s the rich, fluid 'court style' is reflected in the lavish brasses of Bishop Beaumont at Durham and Laurence Seymour at Higham Ferrers (Page-Phillips 1972, 18, 30); above all, it finds expression in that most magnificent of English brasses, Sir Hugh Hastings's at Elsing (Plate L).

More modest arrangements, in which the dominant motif is usually a long-stemmed cross, are wholly English. The close link between London brass workshops and the Purbeck marble trade is emphasised by prototypes such as the Purbeck incised slab for Prior William de Basynge (*ob.* 1295) in Winchester Cathedral, where a bust surmounts a shafted cross bottony (Edleston 1935, Pl. VII). The typical middle-range London brass of *c.* 1310-35 was a foliated cross with or without a head-and-shoulders bust above it. In either case the commonest type of cross was a highly standardised pattern with ivy-leaf foliations (Fig. 59a-f). Among so many indents only one precious survivor, at Chinnor (Oxon.), retains its brass inlay (Fig. 60); the small face in the centre of this crosshead may well have been a normal embellishment. Variant arrangements all display the characteristic foliations, the 'trademark' of the main workshop. This reduplication of standard components, sometimes producing a certain awkwardness of layout (e.g. Fig. 59b-c), suggests a highly organised pre-farication of elements which could be assembled on the slab to suit the patron's needs.

Close variations on the main ivy-leaf pattern (e.g. Fig. 61a-c) may have been late developments or imitations, while crosses with fleur-de-lis and bottony terminals (e.g. Fig. 61d-e) form distinct though less prolific series. The late 1330s and 1340s saw a new fashion for crosses with open octofoil heads enclosing small figures. After some early examples (e.g. Fig. 61 f) the main workshop settled down to a stereotyped crosshead formed of elegant ogee cusps, with trefoiled terminals and engraved ring-and-dot ornament. The substantially complete example at Oxford (Fig. 62) is matched by several indents (e.g. Fig. 61g). Comparison of a stray excavated fragment from Canterbury with the relevant portion of the Oxford brass Fig. 63) emphasises the degree of standardisation.

A few patrons preferred more original designs. At Wotton-under-Edge (Glos.) the deceased kneels to the Virgin and Child enclosed in a crosshand (*MBS Portfolio*, i, Pl. 6). Abbot Sutton's brass at Dorchester-on-Thames showed an arm grasping a crozier, a type of abbatial monument long known in France (e.g. Adhémar 1974, nos. 644, 909). The simplest brasses, those with inscriptions only, may account for nearly half the pre-1350 total. Their contrast of gilt letters against dark polished marble produced an effect more pleasing than that of mere incised inscriptions; easy and probably cheap to make, they were popular monuments for parish clergy, minor gentry, and even freeholders and yeoman farmers.

Although London probably contained two or three brass workshops, responsible for the different crosshead patterns, one major workshop seems to have dominated the trade with an

Fig. 60.   Chinnor, Oxon.; overall width 66 cm. (from Norris 1977, Pl. 24).

output justifying routine mass-production. For this early period written evidence is still lacking, but in the late fourteenth and fifteenth centuries London brasses were made by marblers (Blair 1980; Emmerson 1978, 65-8). In a craft involving specialised skills, valuable equipment and heavy materials, workshop continuity is to be expected: we should probably look to the marblers in the early fourteenth century also. Foremost among them was Adam of Corfe, who emerges as the main purveyor of Purbeck marble with a tenement near the Dorset quarries and a London base in St. Paul's churchyard (for published information see Leach 1978, 84). With a working career in London from before 1305 until his death in 1331, Adam seems the most promising candidate for master of the main brass workshop during these years.

PROVINCIAL SCHOOLS, 1300-1350

Epigraphic analysis reveals several regional workshops. Their output must have been far less than that of the London producers, and the available sample is consequently small. Nonetheless, it gives some idea of their distribution and range.

The Lincoln craftsmen adopted in the early fourteenth century a new but equally distinctive alphabet ('Lincolnshire style B'; Fig. 57h); the localised distribution of slabs bearing it proves the continuance of the school. Of its extant products the most interesting are one full-length figure, a miniature figure on a bracket and a bust surmounting a shield (Fig. 64a-c; cf. Blair 1978). An oddly-proportioned episcopal indent at Lincoln (Fig. 63d) lacks the joining-bar recesses characteristic of London work and is perhaps also local. At Sleaford, a large cross between two priests standing on corbels (Fig. 64e) may be another product of the Lincoln workshop, though no parallels are known for its big lettering and odd design. Towards the mid-century 'Main Group' letters were sometimes substituted for the ungainly 'Lincolnshire B' alphabet, though some such indents can be distinguished from London work by the large, single lozenge-shaped stops which are peculiar to the Lincoln school (e.g. Fig. 64f; cf. Blair 1978). This provincial use of 'Main Group' letters may point the origin of a few East Midland indents which resemble London work epigraphically but differ in other ways from standard London patterns (e.g. Fig. 64g).

As Miss S. Badham has shown, brasses were probably being produced in York from the 1270s with lettering similar though not identical to the 'Lincolnshire B' alphabet (Badham 1979, 2-4; Badham 1980). A handful of simple indents show full-face heads in isolation, in one case flanked by a pair of shields (Fig. 65a). The type may have originated as imitations of the Flemish incised slabs, common imports to north-eastern England, on which faces and hands were emphasised by the use of brass or marble inlays. Indents of probable York origin, in a variety of different stones, continue through the fourteenth century.

Another northern workshop, perhaps based in Newcastle or Durham, is suggested by the large, florid letters found on two Northumberland indents and on a fragment in Durham Cathedral, both the former having isolated full-face heads in the York manner (*History of Northumberland 4*, 130, 394). An episcopal brass in Durham Cathedral with a strange, ungainly canopy (Fig. 65b) may be a more ambitious product of the same school. These brasses were set in various, probably local, limestones and in one case in the distinctive 'Frosterley marble'.

Four Shropshire indents (three at Haughmond Abbey and one in St. Julian's, Shrewsbury) employ standard 'Main Group size II' lettering but are made of the local 'Shropshire marble', a heavy, fossiliferous limestone from Wenlock Edge. Two of the Haughmond slabs bore long-shafted crosses bottony rising from large shields (Fig. 65c), a type otherwise unknown. A fifth slab of this stone at Buildwas Abbey is inscribed in elegant, spindly letters, and a letter-inlay of unusual shape and exceptionally thin metal has recently been found at Wenlock Priory. Few though these examples are, they justify postulating a small workshop in Shrewsbury which obtained some of its brass letters from the central supplier.

In Wells Cathedral are three Blue Lias slabs with indents for slender, elegant brass crosses

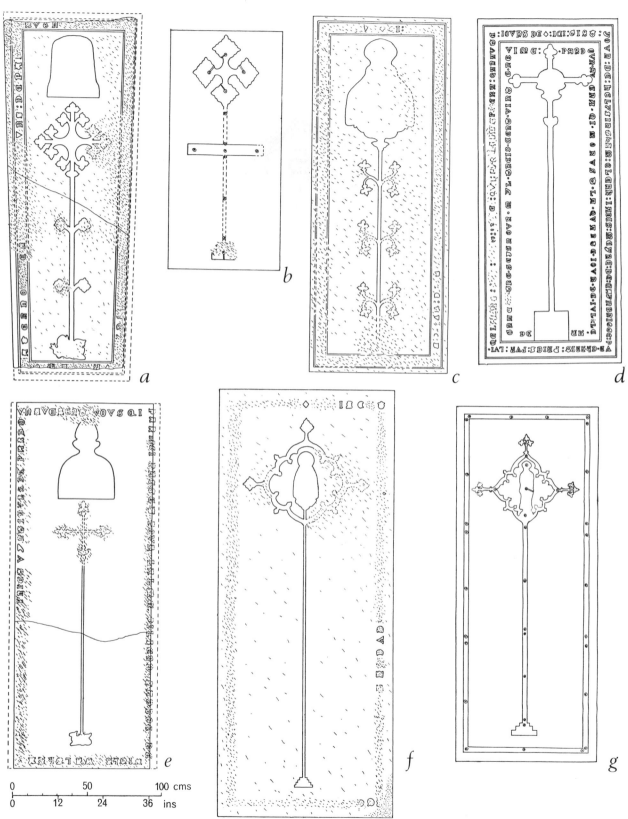

0   50   100 cms

0   12   24   36 ins

Fig. 61. (*a*) Dorchester Abbey, Oxon.; (*b*) St. Mary the Virgin, Oxford; (*c*) Stevenage, Herts; (*d*) St. Clement, Cambridge (after sketch by S. Lysons, British Library Add. MS 9461 f.4*v*); (*e*) White Waltham, Berks; (*f*) St. Mary the Virgin, Oxford; (*g*) Anstey, Herts.

Fig. 62. Merton College Chapel, Oxford; overall width 72 cm. (after A. Bott, *Monuments in Merton College Chapel*, Oxford, 1964, Pl. III).

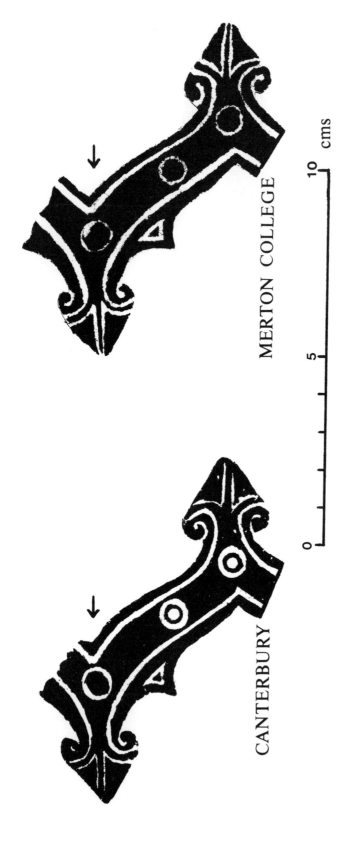

MERTON COLLEGE

CANTERBURY

0   5   10

cms

Fig. 63. Comparison of a detail from Fig. 62 with a fragment found on the site of St. Augustine's Abbey, Canterbury, and now in the Victoria and Albert Museum. Arrows indicate rivet positions.

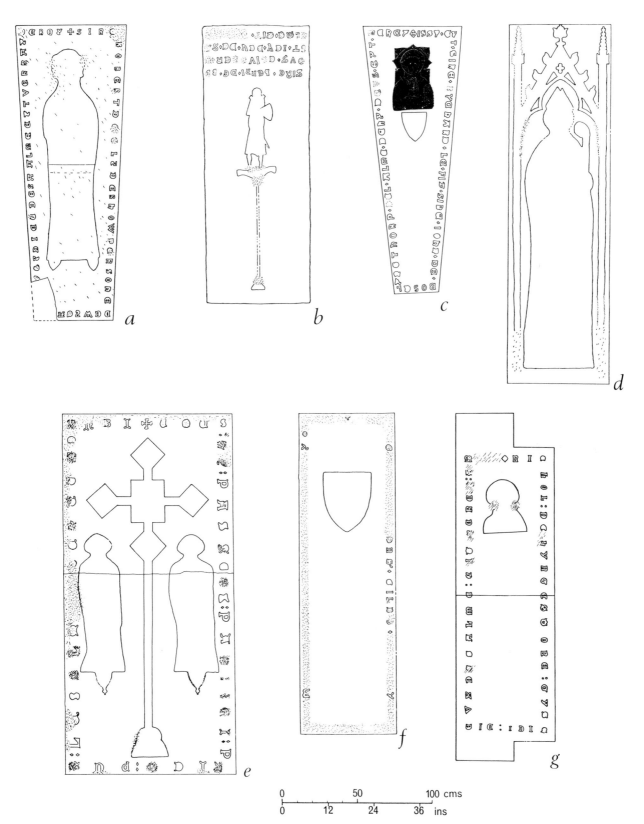

Fig. 64.   *(a)* Sawley Abbey, Yorks.; *(b)* Linwood, Lincs.;   *(c)* Buslingthorpe, Lincs.;   *(d)* Lincoln Cathedral; *(e)* and *(f)* Sleaford, Lincs.;   *(g)* Stretham, Cambs.

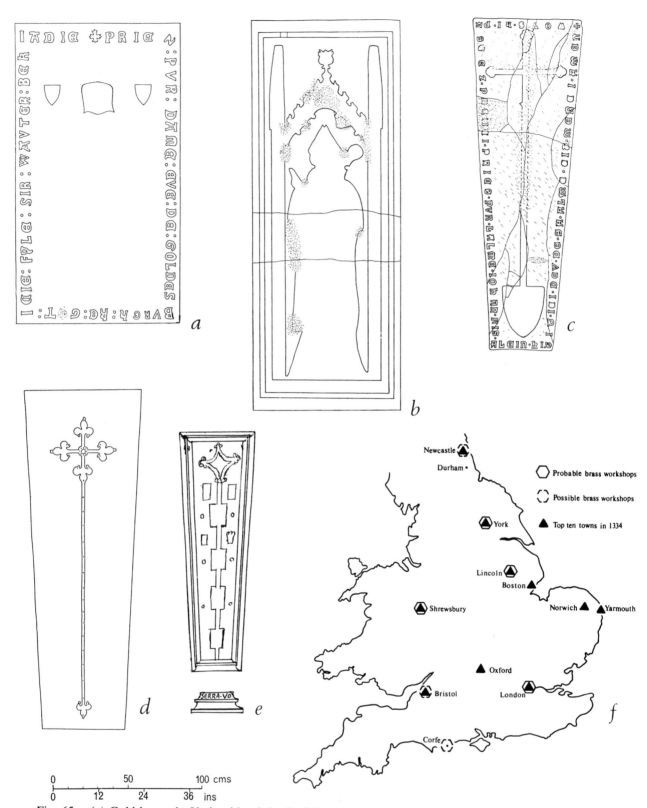

Fig. 65. *(a)* Goldsborough, Yorks. (sketch by B. Gittos. *Not to scale*); *(b)* Durham Cathedral; *(c)* Haughmond Abbey, Salop; *(d)* Wells Cathedral; *(e)* Kingswear, Devon (sketch by J. Milles in Bodleian MS Top. Devon c.10 f.67. *Not to scale*); *(f)* Map of suggested centres of brass production.

PLATE LI

Elsing, Norfolk, brass of Sir Hugh Hastings. (From
Archaeologia, lx (1906), opp. 27).

(Fig. 65d; Connor 1970, Pl. XXXIV). Possibly related to these is a fragmentary Lias slab from Plympton Priory (Devon) on which a rectangular brass inscription-plate was enclosed within an incised cross (Sadler 1980, 25-6). At Kingswear (Devon) was a slab of Beer freestone with an incised Lombardic inscription in the edge moulding and indents for an unusual brass cross flanked by rectangular inlays (Fig. 65e). Once again, the evidence is sparse but a local origin can scarcely be disputed. Bristol, already notable for its school of monumental effigies, seems the most likely source.

CONCLUSION

The speed with which brass-engraving was introduced and regional workshops established is truly remarkable. Within forty years of their first appearance monumental brasses had become easily the most popular type of medium-priced monument in southern and eastern England, and could probably be bought in at least half the main provincial towns (Fig. 65f). When all the evidence is collected, the total of recorded English brasses from before the Black Death seems likely to fall not far short of a thousand, and this can only be a fraction of the original total. The study of indents has well justified itself in establishing these unexpected facts; explaining them must be left to a wider enquiry into monumental fashions and the religious and social motives in commemoration.

ACKNOWLEDGEMENTS

Several figures are based on illustrations in Monumental Brass Society publications. Plate Lc, an R.C.H.M. photograph, is reproduced by permission of Her Majesty's Stationery Office; Plate LI by permission of the Society of Antiquaries of London; and Figs. 58a and 65e by permission of the Curators of the Bodleian Library. For material on which other illustrations are based I am grateful to Claude Blair (Plate La-b), Dr John Blatchly (Fig. 58d), Alan Bott (Fig. 62), The British Library (Figs. 58e, 61d), F. Fowler (Fig. 64a), Brian Gittos (Fig. 65a), Stuart Naunton (Fig. 61g), Malcolm Norris (Fig. 60) and Hugh Richmond (Plate Lc). Drawings are my own except where stated otherwise in the captions. For comments on the text, I am grateful to Sally Badham, Claude Blair, Robin Emmerson, Roger Greenwood and John Page-Phillips.

MEDWAY HOUSE, CHATHAM DOCKYARD

J.G. COAD

Within the southern area of Chatham Naval Base there still survive most of the buildings needed to construct and equip wooden warships of the sailing navy. Many of these buildings have been little altered externally or internally, and this end of the yard has hardly changed since Pocock painted it with such masterly detail soon after 1800[1]. Its architectural completeness makes Chatham unique; an irreplaceable survivor of a Georgian dockyard from the time of Cape St. Vincent and Trafalgar.

The river Medway first began to be used on a regular basis by the navy in the 1540s when its sheltered waters below Rochester bridge were found to be ideal for laying up the fleet during winter. In 1547,[2] a storehouse was rented ashore and this marks the real beginning of Chatham dockyard. From then on, shore facilities expanded with few interruptions. In the seventeenth century Chatham, strategically well-placed for the North Sea, grew to be the country's premier naval base, eclipsing the Thames yards and Portsmouth. By modern standards it was still small, but in the agricultural England of the time, the royal dockyards were among the country's largest industrial communities, each one containing a wide variety of crafts and skills.

In overall charge were the Navy Board Commissioners in London. By the seventeenth century it was accepted practice for the senior officials in each dockyard, men such as the Master Shipwright and Master Attendant, to be provided with houses within the yard boundaries, and by 1700 the major dockyards of Chatham, Portsmouth and the fledgling Plymouth each had an outstationed Navy Board Commissioner in overall charge of their day-to-day activities. These men, too, were provided with official residences commensurate with their status. Medway House is the most recent name for the Commissioner's House built at Chatham in 1703 and now the oldest intact naval building in the country[3]. Medway House owes its existence to the ambitions of one man: Captain George St. Loe, appointed as commissioner to the dockyard in 1703. From what is known of his career, St. Loe comes over as a forceful and possibly overbearing man possessed with strong feelings of his own importance[4]. In April 1695, he had been appointed commissioner in succession to Captain Henry Greenhill at the brand-new dockyard at Plymouth[5]. Although small compared to the established yards,

---

1. The painting is now in the National Maritime Museum.
2. VCH Kent, ii, 'Maritime History.'
3. Part of the Officers' Terrace of the 1690s remains at Devonport, but eleven out of the thirteen houses were destroyed in the last war.
4. Pool 1966, 72, has brief details of some of his actions.
5. Collinge 1978, 136.

Plymouth Dock[6] had been conceived on a generous scale, nowhere more apparent than in the accommodation provided for the twelve senior officials and the commissioner. This was a spacious terrace of thirteen houses overlooking the heart of the dockyard and most probably designed by Edward Dummer surveyor of the Navy Board[7]. St. Loe remained at Plymouth for eight years during which time he tried to have additions made to the terrace. Unlike his predecessor, his architectural ambitions were thwarted by the Navy Board in London, but the spacious residence for the commissioner undoubtedly gave him a taste for gracious living, so it was probably with mixed feelings that he viewed his appointment to Chatham[8].

In 1703, a posting as commissioner at Chatham was a prestige appointment for the dockyard was still at the height of its seventeenth-century importance. It stretched along the southern bank of the Medway with the long buildings of the ropeyard at the south-western end and the new mast ponds to the north-east. In the centre, forming the heart of the Tudor and Stuart dockyard was an irregular three-sided range of buildings open to the river and focussing on the great double dock and building slips. These buildings formed a mixture of stores, workshops, offices and houses. They had been constructed at various dates in the seventeenth century, the heavy mullioned windows and pronounced dormers typical of the period and giving a rather domestic scale to the dockyard, belying its central importance to the country's defence effort. The only architectural pretension was a clock tower over the central gateway arch.

At the western end of the southern range was the commissioner's house. Like the rest, it was brick built and, in 1698, had been valued at £653 13s. 1d., a sum considerably in excess of the other residences but one which reflected its superior facilities which included a 'banqueting house' and a fountain[9]. Compared to the commissioner's house at Plymouth though, it was undoubtedly cramped, a fact which must have been known to St. Loe and one which prompted him to demand a new house even before he had arrived at Chatham[10].

Not until the appointment in 1795 of Brigadier General Sir Samuel Bentham as Inspector General of Naval Works and the establishment of his small staff did the Royal Navy possess a permanent professional architect. Before then, the design of individual buildings was largely the responsibility of the master shipwrights, but in the days before the rise of the architectural profession senior officers felt qualified to join in the fun, as we know that both Greenhill and St. Loe did at Plymouth. The designs had to be submitted to the Navy Board where the Surveyor was responsible for vetting them, but this seems to have been a fairly flexible arrangement well into the eighteenth century, probably no more so than when a commissioner was seeking accommodation for himself. Only in exceptional circumstances did the Navy Board commission an outside architect, although we know that they had connections with leading London architects of the day who may well have been consulted informally on designs submitted to the Board.

Unfortunately, Medway House has few documentary references to its construction, but from what we know of St. Loe it seems improbable that he left the design entirely to the master

6.   Renamed Devonport in 1823.
7.   National Maritime Museum, Unindexed MSS 1695-1832, 6/2/1695.
8.   *Ibid.*, 9/7/1695
9.   British Library, Kings MS 43.
10. P.R.O. ADM/1/3596 10/7/1703.

PLATE LII

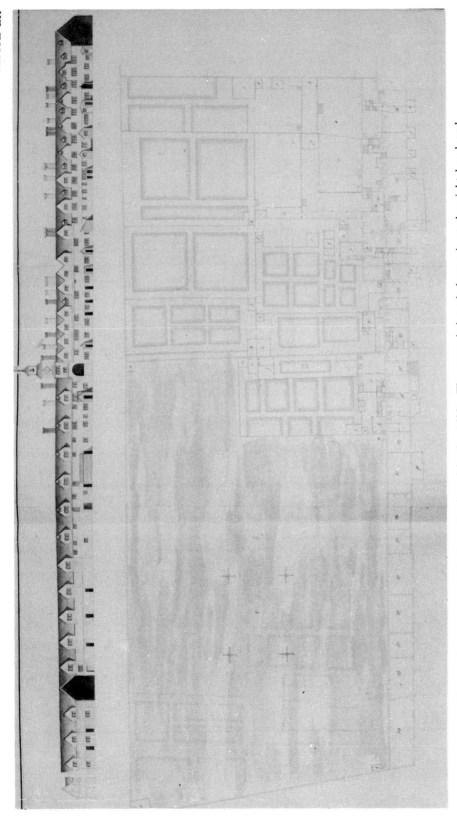

The southern range of Chatham Dockyard in the 1690s. The commissioner's house is at the right hand end. (British Library, Kings MS 43, fol 106).

PLATE LIII

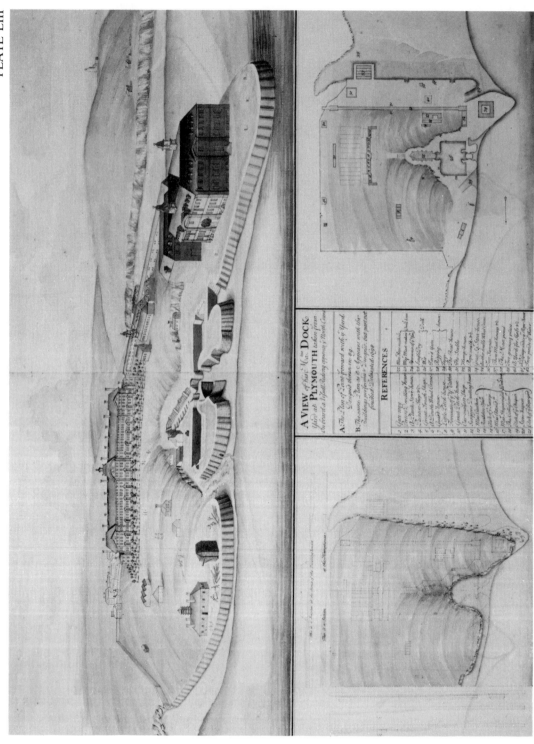

Plymouth Dockyard in 1698. The commissioner occupied the imposing house in the centre of the terrace.
Note the roof balcony. (British Library Kings MS 43 101, 129-30).

PLATE LIV

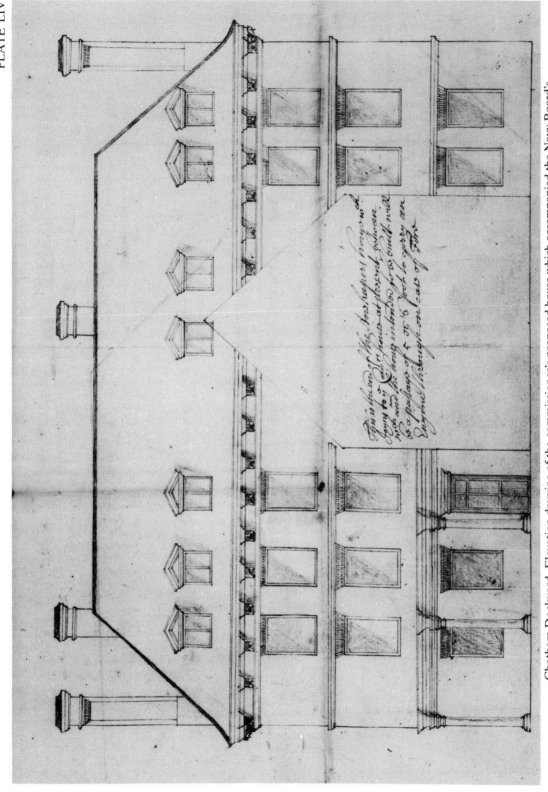

Chatham Dockyard. Elevation drawing of the commissioner's proposed house which accompanied the Navy Board's
letter of 10 July, 1703.

PLATE LV

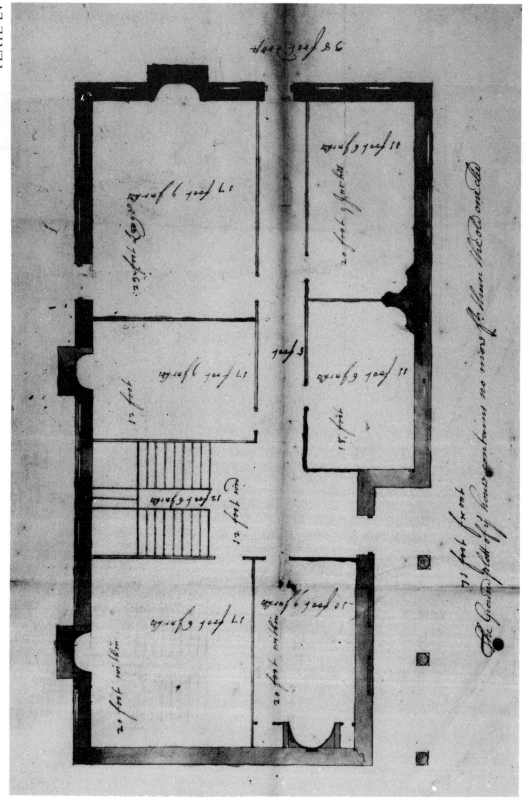

Chatham Dockyard. The ground-floor plan of the proposed house which was sent with the elevation drawing on 10
July, 1703.

PLATE LVI

ADMIRALTY HOUSE.
The residence of the Admiral Superintendent.

(Army and Navy Illustrated).

Chatham Dockyard. The commissioner's house in the late nineteenth century. Since then, the porch has been altered and the windows replaced with plate glass.

PLATE LVII

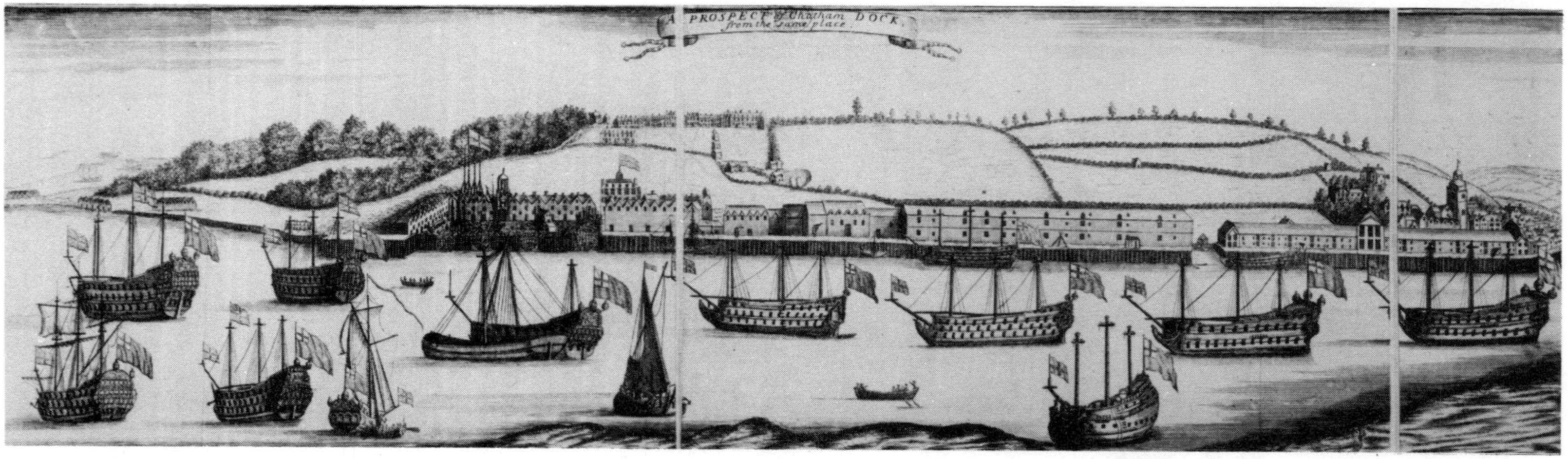

A PROSPECT of Chatham DOCK from the Same Place

(British Library)

Chatham Dockyard in 1708. One of the earliest illustrations to show the commissioner's new house in the centre flying the union flag. Note the cupola and roof balcony.

PLATE LVIII

The commissioner's house in 1774. A contemporary model in the National Museum. By this time, the roof had assumed its present form. In the background to the left is one end of the officers' terrace built in the 1720s and, like Medway House, little altered.

PLATE LIX

Medway House in 1981

shipwright. In July 1703, the Navy Board, clearly wearied by his importunate demands and perhaps anxious to protect themselves from charges of favouritism, wrote to the Admiralty Board saying 'Captain St. Loe, not only before he came to Chatham but since having desired to have the house the commissioner lived in pulled down and a new one built in its place. . . we send you the same in form, together with a plan of the new house desiring you to lay them before his Royal Highness[11] that in case his Highness shall think fit to have the said work gone in hand with, they may be confirmed to be sent to us. . .'[12]. If the Navy Board had hoped that the project would be quashed at this stage, they were disappointed: four days later, the Admiralty signified approval and agreed to the estimated cost of £912 10*s*. 0*d*.[13]

11.   Prince George of Denmark, Lord High Admiral May 1702-October 1708.
12.   ADM/1/3596 10/7/1703
13.   ADM/A/1906 14/7/1703

Plate LIV shows the elevation and Plate LV the ground floor plan which were sent with the Navy Board's letter of 10 July, 1703. The cramped nature of the site is at once apparent in the inscription written in the gabled outline on the elevation drawing: 'This is the end of the storekeeper's house w$^{ch.}$ joyns to y^e Com$^{rs.}$ house at present between w$^{ch.}$ and the house intended to be built will be a passage of 5 or 6 foot to carry an Engine through on case of Fire.' This lack of space probably also accounts for the decision to recess the northern three bays to provide room for a porch for the front door. Medway House owes much to these plans, but they were clearly early versions of the final scheme. As built (Plate LVI) the house has been raised by the incorporation of a basement, proportions and spacing of the windows have been refined, the northern recess has been omitted and the front door located in the centre of the elevation.

What is perhaps surprising is that as late as 1703 the Navy Board was prepared to allow a purely domestic building to be constructed in a part of the yard where working space was at a premium. It would have been quite possible to have sited the house to the south-east, using part of the commissioner's large garden, in anticipation of replanning the central area. Fifteen years later when just such a replanning and expansion were begun and the rest of the officers were rehoused in the present terrace, the commissioner's house was too new to justify demolition and had to be left in the comparative isolation that it enjoys today.

Construction of the house seems to have begun soon after Admiralty approval was forthcoming and it was probably completed in 1704. When first built, the flat top to the roof apparently had a central cupola and a balcony (Plate LVII), an idea clearly derived from similar features on the commissioner's house at Plymouth[14], but these had been removed by the 1770s[15]. There are few documentary references to the subsequent history of the house. In 1740, Commissioner Matthews was complaining that the position of the kitchens in the basement was offensive, and the Navy Board sympathetically agreed to the construction of a new kitchen 'and a small room over it to be taken out of the back yard.'[16] Three years before, Matthews had had a Dutch barn erected in the south-east corner of the yard for his hay crop, an instance of how agriculture intruded into the lives of most people in the country then[17]. The only major extension is the two-storey wing to the south, perhaps to be identified with a laundry and other domestic facilities proposed and approved in 1801[18].

In 1737, the commissioner was provided with a handsome coach house, a harness room and stabling for five horses sited against the dockyard wall where the buildings remain a pleasant enclave[19]. These were clearly too ambitious for one subsequent commissioner who noted on a plan of them: 'This is larger than I require, but as I find it a great convenience to my large family to keep cows, a portion of it is required to keep two cows during winter.' This large family probably accounts for a note in the same hand on another part of the plan: 'This place is absolutely requisite as there is no spot in the house where a cask of wine can be stowed

14. B.L. Kings MS 43, fol 129-130.
15. See the contemporary model of the dockyard in 1774 in the National Maritime Museum.
16. CHA/E/5 18/2/1740
17. CHA/E/4 17/6/1737, 22/6/1737
18. P.R.O. ADM/140/76 31/3/1801.
19. CHA/E/4 8/4/1737

away'[20], a space problem which probably comes as a surprise to his late twentieth-century successors.

The interior of Medway House forms a gracious and charming residence. Over the years successive occupants have altered the interior and modernised facilities, but the principal staircase is original as is much of the panelling here and in the hall. It seems probable that the main living rooms were always on the first floor above the noise and bustle of the dockyard and overlooking the big walled garden to the rear. On the ground floor is a modest ball room, while off it is a cloakroom containing an extensive collection of English Delftware tiles[21].

The most remarkable feature of the house is the great painted ceiling at the head of the main staircase (Plate LX). It depicts an assembly of the gods with Mars in the centre receiving a shell crown from Neptune. In the foreground recline Peace and Plenty, flanked on the left by Pity helping up the deserving and on the right by Justice putting down the undeserving. In the background, Minerva advises Mars. Around this painting, which is in oils on wood, is an elaborately carved and gilded frame of crabs and other marine life. Outside the frame, and not part of the original composition, are subsidiary panels painted with birds, perhaps the work of a nineteenth-century Admiral Superintendent's wife.

The origin of this painting is shrouded in a certain amount of mystery. Traditionally, it is said to have been painted by Sir James Thornhill for the Great Cabin of the *Royal Sovereign*, launched at Woolwich in 1701. In his sketchbook in the British Library are preliminary drawings which could be for this ceiling and a note referring to the *Royal Sovereign*, but the late Edward Croft-Murray felt that the final work was not by Thornhill himself, who would still have been a servant at this date, but was more likely to be by his master, Thomas Highmore, serjeant-painter to William III[22].

Thus, whether by Thornhill or Highmore, there seems no strong reason to doubt the tradition. But two further problems need consideration: was the painting ever on board the warship? And when was it installed in Medway House? There are no references to this ceiling in the eighteenth-century Chatham dockyard records, but this need not surprise us if it was not painted specially for the commissioner's house. Its somewhat awkward fit at the head of the stairs is sufficient proof that it was not originally intended for this position. Lacking direct evidence at Chatham, the only other possible source of information are references to the ship herself.

The *Royal Sovereign* was the earliest of the eighteenth-century warships to be launched, but her elaborate decoration marked the peak of a trend which had flourished in the latter part of the seventeenth century. The excess and expense of carving and gilding on board caused something of a scandal even before the ship was completed and led the Admiralty to order that henceforth carving was to be confined to the beakhead and stern galleries, and any further decoration was to be carried out in paint (Archibald 1968, 36).

---

20. ADM/140/76 pt. 4
21. These have probably been in the house since manufacture, but have almost certainly been resited here. In October 1814, the Navy Board sent one 'Bramah's spring water closet, complete' for Commissioner Sir Robert Barlow (CHA/E/113 4/10/1814), a no doubt welcome present but one which shows the Navy Board's reluctance to be in the van of innovation. Bramah's patent had been taken out in 1778 (Wright 1960, 107). The present fixture came from the Judge's Lodgings in King's Lynn.
22. Personal communication from the late E. Croft-Murray. The reference to the *Royal Sovereign* is on fol.15v.

PLATE LX

Medway House. The painted ceiling at the head of the main staircase. For description, see main text.

The Admiralty minutes for 5 February, 1700-01, record that 'A letter was read from the Master Shipwright about sealing the *Sovereign's* cabin. Resolved that he be acquainted we would rather have the same sealed between the beams because it will be an advantage to the height of the cabin, but if that cannot be conveniently done, he must do it as he proposes.'[23]

A few days later Fisher Harding, the Master Shipwright, wrote to the Navy Board: 'According to your directions of ye 19th December last I having prepared draughts of my design as to ye accommodations and ornaments for the *Royal Sovereign* laid the same before the Right Hon. the Lords of ye Admiralty ye 1st instance; and their Lordships after having taken a view thereof, bid me proceed accordingly (*ye ceiling of the Great Cabbin under ye beams only excepted*)'(author's italics)[24].

In August 1701, the Navy Board wrote to the Admiralty: 'Mr Harding. . . having applied to us for directions in surveying and putting a valuation on the extraordinary carving and painting works on. . . the *Royal Sovereign* which have been performed to her and are out of contract. . . . . .we are at a loss to give any directions about the surveying and valuing the said works in as much as by a standing order of the Board in November last, all carved works in ye cabbins, coaches and other improper places in His Majesty's ships was positively forbidd, and an established charge settled for the several rates and rankes of ship wherein a first rate was not to exceed £500. . .'[25]

It is very clear from these letters and minutes that the *Royal Sovereign's* decoration had become something of a political embarrassment to the Navy, while the two specific references to the ceiling of the Great Cabin would suggest that no painting was placed in position. However, if the painting had been completed by the time of the correspondence, there would have been considerable temptation for Woolwich to fit it and ignore the fuss upriver in London. Master Shipwrights were powerful men, and Fisher Harding may well have felt that his professional reputation was at stake. This can only be surmise, but if correct, there could have been three occasions in the ship's career when the ceiling could most conveniently have been brought ashore at Chatham.

The *Royal Sovereign* was overhauled at Chatham in 1723, 1728 and 1755 before being broken up at Portsmouth in 1768. The 1723 refit was probably the most extensive, lasting at least two years. In September 1725 the Navy Board wrote to the Admiralty informing them that the Master Shipwright at Chatham wished to know if the ship was to be 'carved and ornamented as she was formerly, or as the *Royal George, Britannia* and *Royal William* are now.'[26] A note in a different hand at the bottom of the letter reads: 'as the *Royal George* and other ships are.' If the painted ceiling was on board, this would have been the most likely time for it to find its way to the commissioner's house when the rest of the ship's decorations were being considerably scaled down.

However, there is another and perhaps more probable explanation. If the painting was completed by 1701 and was not installed in the *Royal Sovereign*, its presence unused in a royal dockyard would have been an embarrassment to the Navy Board, a constant reminder to its

23. P.R.O. ADM/3/16 5/2/1700-1.
24. P.R.O. ADM/1/3590 11/2/1700-1.
25. ADM/1/3591 14/8/1701
26. ADM/1/3638 24/9/1725.

political enemies of extravagance, incompetence and lack of financial control. The Board could hardly use the painting in London, and it was too fine for an ordinary dockyard house. But two years later, St. Loe's desire for a new residence could well have given everyone the opportunity to find a reasonably worthy use for the painting in a commissioner's house sufficiently removed from the capital not to excite comment. Quietly shipped round from Woolwich in a naval transport with the minimum of fuss and documentation, the painting could have been installed as soon as the house was completed. Such a hypothesis may remain incapable of proof, but Medway House and the Navy are fortunate indeed to possess this unusual and intriguing work of art.

ACKNOWLEDGEMENTS

I am very grateful to Rear-Admiral G.M.K. Brewer, Flag Officer Medway, and his staff at Chatham for their help and interest. The late E. Croft-Murray kindly made available to me his research notes on the decoration of the *Royal Sovereign*.

A CHILD OF HIS TIME: CANON ARTHUR ST. LEGER

C.R. COUNCER

Of all the religious in the monasteries of Kent at the time of the Dissolution, few indeed afford much material for the biographer. In many cases a name subscribed to the Oath of Supremacy or to the instrument of surrender of the house is the sum total of our knowledge of a particular person. Arthur St. Leger, however, emerges from the records as a somewhat less shadowy figure than many of his contemporaries, and enough evidence exists to enable us not only to attempt a sketch of his life but to form some estimate of his character.

The family of St. Leger of Ulcombe holds a notable place in Kentish history. Generation after generation, sometimes as knights but more often as country squires, they had taken a full part in the life of the county and had served in Parliament. At the end of the fifteenth century the reigning squire of Ulcombe was Ralph St. Leger, afterwards J.P. for Kent and Sheriff; and to him and his wife Isabel, daughter of Sir Edward Haute, Arthur, a younger son, was born at a date which cannot be precisely determined. From the pedigree in Wykeham Martin's *History of Leeds Castle* (1869) one would assume a date of birth *c.* 1500. But Arthur became Prior of Bilsington in 1521, which would make him very young for such office even in that corrupt age and assuming that "influence" was used. A more likely date would be *c.* 1495. His elder brother was Anthony (*b.* 1494) who was destined to go far in the King's service and to carry the name of St. Leger into Ireland.

Within a short distance of the Ulcombe estates was the great Priory of Leeds, and here, probably, Arthur was professed as an Augustinian canon: at any rate he was a member of the convent before 1521 (Neilson 1928, 141). At that time life in the Priory, whatever it may have been like later on, would appear to have been no bed of roses. At Archbishop Warham's visitation in 1511 (Bateson 1891) Prior Richard Chetham was accused of withholding stipends and fees which should have been distributed to the canons, and there were complaints about his temper and even personal violence: instead of dealing with erring brethren in accordance with the Rule he sometimes beat and kicked them.

One reason for Prior Chetham's bad temper may have been his involvement in the affairs of the small Priory of Bilsington in east Kent. This house had got into chronic financial difficulties, and the prior, William Tilman, persuaded Prior Chetham, in the best Trollopian manner, to back some bills for him. As might have been anticipated, Prior Chetham had been let in, and on appeal to Archbishop Warham in 1510 the income of Bilsington was sequestrated and Leeds allowed to farm the estate until the debt was paid off. (VCH Kent, 1932). In 1511 a canon of Leeds, John Goldstone, was serving Bilsington parish church.

It was perhaps this close association with Bilsington which led to Arthur St. Leger's transfer there as prior in 1521, though, anticipating his later record, it may be doubted whether the financial affairs of the priory prospered under his administration. He was not, however, there for very long, for in 1528 he resigned (Cal., iv, 4557), to return as Head of his old house.

Recent excavations on the site of Leeds Priory have shown that the presbytery of the church was rebuilt — or that rebuilding was begun — at a late, but uncertain, date, and if the works were still going on in 1528 this might account, at least in part, for the parlous financial situation which Arthur left behind when he resigned the priorate in 1536. His everyday life during his eight years as prior was enlivened by hunting, and although details are lacking the impression one gets is of a more relaxed and certainly more indulgent atmosphere than that which had prevailed under Prior Chetham. Arthur's signature, with those of other members of the convent, to the declaration of Royal Supremacy on 22nd December, 1534, still exists (Cal., vii, 1594 (4)).

The egregious Dr. Richard Leyton's royally empowered visitation of the monasteries in Kent in the autumn of 1535, and the injunctions which he issued, must have come upon this easy-going community as a considerable shock: back doors to be blocked up and the main gateway only used; no religious to leave the monastery; women to be strictly excluded, etc. Arthur's reaction to being "gated" was to appeal to his elder brother Anthony, now in the king's service, persuading him to write to Cromwell sending a gift of pheasants and asking permission for the prior to continue to ride to hounds, as it was for the benefit of his health (Cal., ix, 713).

Apart from loss of amenities, other pressures must have made a reappraisal of his career uppermost in Arthur's mind in 1535-36. Although Leeds could escape the Act of 1536 for the suppression of the lesser monasteries, its future, in the light of what was going on all over the country, was obviously open to question; but even more urgent was a financial problem of the most serious kind. The *deus ex machina* in this situation was Archbishop Cranmer, whose acquaintance Arthur must have made at about this time. Cranmer made him his chaplain, and in 1537, soon after Arthur's resignation as prior (on a pension of £16) presented him to the rich sinecure rectory of Hollingbourne, worth £28 in the King's Books, with accommodation in the Manor House. Much of the parish of Hollingbourne, including the church and manor, was and had been for many years Christ Church property.

The financial scandal to which allusion has already been made appears to have come into the open only after Arthur's departure from Leeds, where the newly elected prior, Thomas Day, was faced with debts, incurred by Arthur, amounting to the enormous sum of £1400, the creditors being named as the king, the late prior's brothers, brother-in-law (one Wheler, husband of his sister Dorothy), and others in London and Kent (Cal., xii, pt. 1, 867). It is not clear that these debts were discharged before the dissolution of Leeds in 1539, when Sir Anthony at least was presumably recompensed by gaining possession of the site of the priory.

In 1541 when, following the dissolution of the Cathedral Priory, the new collegiate arrangements were inaugurated at Christ Church, Canterbury, Arthur St. Leger is named in the Foundation Charter as prebendary of the Second Stall, at a stipend of £40 a year. Nominally, of course, the appointments were made by the king, but Cranmer, who disapproved of the collegiate system, must have made the best of what he would have considered a bad job and contrived to have some say in the nominations. "The sect of pre-bendaries," he wrote to Cromwell, "spend their time in much idleness and their substance in superfluous belly cheer."

At Canterbury the new prebendaries were given temporary quarters in the monastic buildings while permanent houses, adapting as far as possible existing buildings, were being planned. Arthur's lodging appears to have been the 'long hall' (in 1545 ordered by the Chapter to be demolished) and adjoining buildings near the Deanery afterwards occupied by Robert Steward, Bishop of Caithness, of the eleventh stall. (Willis 1868, 196). Arthur was now reasonably well-off, his pension from Leeds, still being paid, the proceeds of Hollingbourne rectory, and the Canterbury stipend, totalling the respectable figure of £84. And there were perquisites: when, for example, the monks' great dormitory was demolished each prebendary received one foder of lead from the roof. "Mr. Deane" had two! A curious entry, dated 1550, in the Treasurer's book in the Cathedral archives headed "For overweyght off loade," refers, Miss Oakley tells me, in all probability to extra corn shared out among the Dean and canons from the corn rents. Arthur paid 3s. for half a hundredweight and 40 pounds.

Hardly, however, was Arthur in possession of his new preferment when he proceeded to bite the hand which had fed him. Cranmer's "reforming" tendencies were widely disliked, and some of the prebendaries, including Arthur, and "certayn gentilmen of Kente" joined in a plot to ruin him by concocting "articles" accusing him of heresy. The archbishop must have got wind of what was going on. We hear of a conversation at Faversham about a Palm Sunday procession at Christ Church of which he had disapproved. Arthur said he had not been present at it as he was at his benefice. The archbishop was not satisfied, and rejoined that they were in a conspiracy against him which he would break. 'Oh, Mr. Sentleger,' he exclaimed, 'I had in you and Mr. Parkhurst [another prebendary] a good judgment, and especially in you, but ye will not yield your old *mumpsimus*.' Arthur replied that he hoped they used no *mumpsimus's* but those that were consonant with the laws of God and the prince (Cal., xviii, 378).

When the conspiracy finally burst with the delivery of the "articles" to the king it was a complete fiasco. The king sided with Cranmer, imprisoned some of the conspirators, and appointed the archbishop as judge in his own cause. The interrogation of the victims and their depositions which fill many pages of the *Calendar* can only have been exceeded in tedium by the actual proceedings. Arthur's testimony is included, and gives nothing away: in sum it is a protestation of ignorance of what had been going on. (Cal., xviii, 363-4). The outcome was indecisive, but Arthur kept his stall.

The atmosphere in the precincts after this affair can hardly have been very agreeable. As with Leeds, so now with Canterbury, a change seemed desirable. A new career opened in Ireland, where Arthur's brother Sir Anthony, still rising in the king's service, had been appointed Lord Deputy in 1540. Arthur obtained a licence of non-residence for two years from 8th July, 1544 (Cal., xix, pt. 1, 619), and on 8th November, 1546, the licence was renewed for as long as Sir Anthony remained Lord Deputy (Cal., xix, pt. 2, 235). The latter's first term of office ended with the death of Henry VIII, but he was reappointed in 1550, finally retiring in 1555, four years before his death. Arthur must have accompanied him on his second term of duty, for a further licence for as long as Sir Anthony should retain his post was obtained on 11th August, 1550. Somewhere in the ashes of the Four Courts in Dublin, destroyed in 1922, any records of Arthur's career in Ireland must finally have perished.

Arthur's renewed licence of 1546 is almost exactly coeval with a decree of the Chapter of Canterbury assigning him and the other prebendaries permanent homes in the Precincts (25th-29th November, 1546). Professor Willis (1868, 193) quotes a document by Somner in which these arrangements are detailed: "Mr Sentlegers Lodging. First, he to have ye North side or Isle of ye ffermary chapell, wth ye garden on ye North side; the old table Hall with ye kitchin, buttery, ye chamber called Gonnissons chamber, and ye Lodging at ye upper end of ye hall, the little garden there, and ye stable next Mr Deanes stable with ye little barne.''

Arthur's life after his final return from Ireland seems to have been uneventful, and any records of his participation in the deliberations of the Chapter have been lost with the Canterbury Act books of the period. His time was doubtless divided between Canterbury and Hollingbourne. Like the Vicar of Bray, he retained his preferments through all the religious changes of the times and incurred, with the rest of the prebendaries whom he found in office on his appointment, Archbishop Parker's censure for scandalous non-residence and neglect of hospitality. Still he lived on, well into the reign of Queen Elizabeth, finally dying in 1569 at Hollingbourne, where the burial register records his interment on 22nd May. He has no monument, and the precise place of his burial, whether in the church or churchyard is, I believe, unknown.

A SHOEMAKER'S NOTES ON A GEORGIAN TOWN

LESLEY LEWIS

Among Stuart Rigold's endearing talents was his memory for the detail of old buildings, old methods, old appliances, old things generally, and how often have I heard him bring light and sense to a theoretic discussion by some reference to an obscure fact from his inexhaustible store. I hope that the modest contribution I am making to his memorial volume would have been to his taste in that it assembles practical details from a little-known contemporary source, the notebooks of Robert Hird 1768-1841, shoemaker of Bedale in North Yorkshire (now in the Beresford-Peirse Archive, County Record Office, Northallerton). These have been summarised in three articles in *Country Life*, 4, 11, and 18 March 1971, and published in full as Hird's *Annals of Bedale* by the North Yorkshire County Record Office. The four volumes of this publication are page-numbered consecutively and references here are identified simply by one page number. Hird wrote the history of his birthplace in 3000 naive rhymed quatrains which have few passages of literary merit and went on annotating them until just before his death. Starting in about 1808 he recorded what his elders told him about times he could not have remembered, his own boyhood reminiscences and contemporary observations, all mixed up, with no firm chronology between the starting point of his own birth and his last setpiece on the celebrations in Bedale for Queen Victoria's coronation.

An unfinished drawing by Samuel Buck of about 1716 (BM Landsdowne MSS 914 184) shows Bedale much as Hird himself visualised it in earlier times. The noble tower of St. Gregory's church with its conspicuous clock-face, which still dominates the scene, rises above a motley collection of houses, many of them single-storeyed as Hird described them. A group of more substantial buildings left of the church must represent the old manor house which was the core of the present Bedale Hall. Buck's interest in this obscure little town was probably sparked off by imminent building developments there. A Yorkshire gentleman, Henry Peirse, having inherited considerable estates, adopted Bedale as his seat from about 1716 and, although Buck may have been disappointed by his delay, did in about 1730 insert between the wings of his old house a spectacular stuccoed saloon. During the long minority of Henry's heir, born in 1754, Hird as a boy knew the old hall with its once-fashionable garden adorned with pools and statues. Then as a young man he saw Henry junior landscape the park in the modish naturalistic way and enlarge the house by incorporating into it an inn which joined it to other houses in the market place. (Plates LXI and LXII).

Buck's drawing does not show a house of some consequence built north of the church, in brick with moulded dressings, by a rector, Francis Pemberton, in about 1700. He belonged to what must have been the leading family before the Peirses settled in Bedale and Hird thought James I slept at their house, Cowling Hall, on his way to or from Scotland (548, 549); his

PLATE LXI

Bedale in 1716. From a drawing by Samuel Buck (B.M. Lansdowne MSS 914 184).

bedstead was said to be in the Old Crown Inn at Leeming. This was not the only historic bed in the place however. When Lord Exeter dismantled much of Snape Castle in 1738 one Firby bought a bedstead which he kept in his house as a showpiece and "entail" (502, 503):

It is made of the finest oak,
Old age has made it black!
It's now entire, and carved work,
Made near three cent'ries back!

The tester is made of the same,
As also is the head!
Date, and initials of their name!
For whom the same was made!
[1587, William and Charles Cecil]

Good furniture, outside the grander houses, was evidently rare. Hird mentions as a great treasure (578) an oak dresser which had descended to him from his great-grandfather, a joiner, who had made it for his daughter on her marriage, apparently about 1727 (578). In his youth many houses only had seats against the walls as the chimneys let hail, rain and sometimes coping stones fall on those who unwisely sat too near the fire. They were built straight to the top, of timber plastered with mud and straw, crowned by two slates. One old woman had her leg broken but, failing to take the warning, was burnt to death in 1789 (358, 359). As Hird said, perhaps thirty years later:

The open chimneys in the town,
I think are done away,
And now here's greater comforts known,
All near the fire may stay

They then at a great distance sit,
And quite against the wall,
Both form and settle, some had fit,
Sofa, they'd none at all!   (357)

Hird does not mention the smoke which must have plagued these humble dwellings but one grander householder at least was having none of it. When Lord Darlington made a large addition to Newton House in about 1812 he had to get "cure-all", the chimney-doctor from East Retford, to prescribe. This was disastrous because one of the huge funnels he fitted fell through the roof in a gale and killed a charming young woman whom Hird had only recently fitted for white satin shoes (528-30).

East of Bedale was the twin township of Aiskew of which Hird usually spoke in somewhat superior tones although it was only separated from Bedale by the beck and to all intents and purposes was the same place. Here, however, were the stocks;

Near t'bakehouse hill, there stood the stocks
A punnishing machine!
A bugbear was to Aiskew folks,
They dar'd not one get in.

There was iron Hackles for your wrests!
And great holes for your legs,
No matter which you put through first,
If Wags threw rotten eggs!

If you got there you were lock'd in,
I say both hands and feet!
And thus a man they fast did pin!
Beside he had no seat,

Except a friend brought him a chair,
And this a friend indeed!
And there he sat at public stare,
And disgrace did suceed!!! (183)

Hird also took a poor view of Aiskew's well from which people used first to dip out water. Then they built it up like a pit and let all kinds of vessels down into it by ropes; tiring of this, they got a new bucket and fixed up a post with lever and chain to lower it but this did not succeed for long either. Finally, they installed a pump which was uncommonly hard to prime, says Hird with glee, and then they had to sink another well altogether (184).

Wherever the water was drawn from it must often have been heavily polluted, and a main theme of Hird's narrative is the improvement of Bedale in his lifetime. The lively and evidently delightful beck which powered the mills, giving the town its early eighteenth-century prosperity, was also its main drain. The sewage ran above ground downhill from the market place, "then filth it ran above", said Hird (303), and the first conduit he saw made was one near the bridge in about 1773. What he says about it conveys some idea of the foul bog on which some houses stood:
"The Drain not only made the houses more dry, but it had another effect which was of great benefit in allaying the fears of the inhabitants, whose platters danced in the delf rails, and their whole dwelling shook around them upon their Quagmire foundation, on the passing by of every loaded cart or waggon, as if under the tremmer of an Earthquake" (27). Particularly noisome was the bakehouse yard in which stood three unseemly "jakes" and across which the new bread was precariously and not always safely carried:

In the same yard, on the south side,
The gutter it was deep,
When I a boy, it was so wide,
We scarce could overleap! (303)

The bridge between Bedale and Aiskew was the focal point for both and usually the scene of the mild excitements which occasionally diversified the normal routine. Hird indeed chose it for his only pictorial effort, a primitive captioned and illustrated map which shows the constable, a horse and a boy bathing, someone fishing in a top hat and the old bridge itself. (Plate LXIII). This was the first ridge for wheel traffic, built in 1740. It had five stone-and-brick arches carried on angular piers which cut the water so that whatever the floods the bridge remained steady. Its single planked and metalled track was fenced with strong oak rails, angled out over the piers for the protection of foot passengers, but in fact the latter were only in danger at times of flood. Normally, carts and carriages used the fords and the bridge was barred to them by two upright posts at each end. One of the pair was fixed but the other could be let down by a hinge, unlocked by a key kept at the nearest houses at both ends for a modest annual fee paid by the constable. Inevitably, the drivers of heavy loads, with horses liable to founder on the steep and slippery bank, got into the habit of tipping the custodians of the keys to let them across when there was no flood. The old bridge must have been suffering from much wear and tear before it was replaced in 1828, but Hird thought the original rails were never renewed. The pleasant refuges over the piers were, however, done away with in his lifetime, to the regret of fishermen (26, 32 etc.).

The river banks and the garths, which ran down to them, bore witness to the industries which depended on the water-driven mills along the beck, tanning, fulling, weaving, dying. The latter gave its name to the Dyers' Garth, near the bridge, where Hird and his little friends

PLATE LXII

(*Country Life*, 1971).

The Market Place, Bedale.

PLATE LXIII

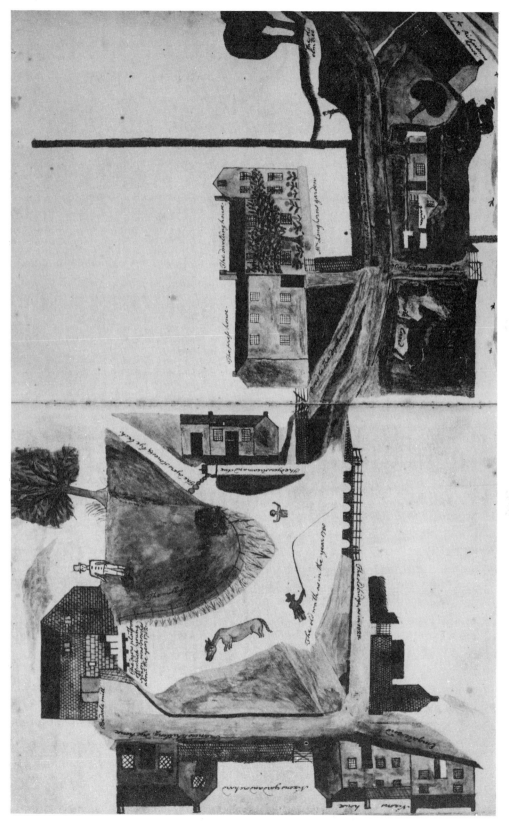

Hird's Drawing of the Bridge between Bedale and Aiskew as in 1828. (Hird's Notebook No. 1, Beresford-Peirse Archive).

used to gather gaily coloured strips of cloth to decorate their hats. There were what he described as "streets" of tenter rails where "webs" were stretched by means of windlass and roller. His own father was a tanner and dried his lambskins in the millyard by the waterside where the ground was also covered by homespun cloth and tow-wicks set out for bleaching (369, 486).

All this industry enriched the inhabitants of Bedale and Aiskew but increased the squalor and overtaxed the roads. In addition to farm produce from the dales, lead came into the town and lay around in backyards until it could be transported in waggons which also brought in from outside the foreign woods used in building and joinery (488). An ambitious scheme for making the Swale navigable and joining it to the Ouse at Boroughbridge seemed to offer an opportunity for Bedale to acquire its own cheap water transport, all that was required being a harbour at Bedale and a lock at Leeming, a short distance to the east. These were indeed completed, but the parent scheme failed shortly before Hird was born in 1768 and they were never used. He knew well however the magnificent remains of the spacious harbour where the boats would be loaded and he noted the solid mooring-rings, one of which can be seen in the accompanying photograph (Plate LXIV). The fine cascade he describes is still a striking feature:

> They made the harbour very wide,
> Safe for the craft to moor,
> High battlement on the West side,
> The North cascade to roar!
>
> The water there comes rolling down,
> You hear its thunder far!
> A stranger coming to the town,
> At night it would him scare. (488-491)

Despite the failure of the navigation scheme and the decline of its industries, Bedale with its important market remained a flourishing place and, as the eighteenth century advanced, began to think of tidying itself up a bit. Or at least some leading characters did, like the beloved Dr. Campbell. Apprenticed to a Dr. Moor whom he succeeded unexpectedly early in 1801, he laid about him at the filth and those who caused it. Bedale was anything but a Sweet Auburn — it stank to high heaven. (472-475). There were hardly any cottage gardens and the fairly ample plots were used as latrines, rubbish dumps or what Hird graphically called "golgothas" (12). The stripping off of turf or topsoil precluded improvement and the few rooms of a miserable hovel might be flanked by the ruins of a former abandoned dwelling. The substance of some of the old houses was so flimsy that boys could knock them down in an afternoon, as when a clearance was made round the Tolbooth to form the wide market place: "These being old houses were soon leveled to the ground by the boys, who were encouraged to it by Mr. Prest, and other adjacent gentlemen of the town" (29). In about 1780 Joseph Ward, a horsedealer with much money passing through his hands on fairdays, had one of the worst: "They were seven in family and had but one room in a state of great delapse, as also was one beyond; and between was laid the ruins of one that had fallen down. Below these mean hovels was a large unwholesome waste of ground with the soil taken off, and the remains of dead dogs and horses lying about!" (243). John Gibson too, with a large family weaving at home while he conducted a carrier's business to Richmond, was content to live as follows: (367)

> He kept his pig, likewise his horse,
> All under the same roof,
> At stable door, his dunghill worse!

The mire above the hoof!

Eight persons they, in family,
And only one fireside!
'Twas on the hearth, no range had he!
The fam'ly had no pride.

Improvements, when they came, were not particularly the work of landlords and landowners but the latter, belatedly, made them possible by granting leases secure enough to make rebuilding and refurbishing worth while to tenants. The standard working-class dwelling of Hird's youth seems to have been of mud and plaster, timber-framed, or "post and pan" as he called it. Rubble or "common stone", apparently so plentiful, was little used at this level and brick, first used in Bedale in about 1700 (see 292, above) did not become common till at least the middle of the century. Hird well understood the principles of timber-framing: (217, 218)

Houses were built a ready way,
They ceils or centres set
Of strongest oak, or ash some may,
But oak when they could get.

Some times it was, they slit the tree,
According to its size,
But all for strength as we may see,
They used no disguise.

The centre was the main support
On which the roof was laid!
Thus they did set a house throughout,
And thus division made.

The walls they were of little aid,
The side ribs were made strong,
And all the spars of oak were made,
Kept dry, they then stand long.

If a house had two storeys the lower one was below ground level, and the upper one was lit by windows in the roof: "No sash windows in them days; the principal glazing was diamond squares"(7). Roofs were either of thatch or Harnby slate, and Hird thought the first person who made tiles in the district was a Jonathan Sowler who died towards the close of the eighteenth century. He often mentions "cones" and these were evidently a type of dormer, designed to give maximum light. Extremely vulnerable to wind and weather, as he suggests, it is doubtful if any now remain in England. I did however once glimpse from a bus in Edinburgh New Town something which seemed to answer the description. A glazed wall, almost full circle, was built out round a window in a sloping roof and covered with a conical slate hat, considerably enlarging the space in the room as well as admitting much light. Although Hird says there were many in Bedale none can be seen in Buck's drawing of 1716 and the last was taken down in 1840 (49), so their life was short and the building of better houses with adequate upper rooms must have made them unnecessary.

Hird describes the improvement of several of the gentry's houses and the landscaping of their grounds but he did not admire Thomas Coore's at Firby. By some murky deal he managed to annex the back garden of the almshouses where six old men once lived in single-room dwellings with cupboard beds, of which I must have seen one of the last, with its chamber-pot still under the bed. Nothing that Tom Coore did was ever quite right, even in his mother's eyes. He was an unlucky professional soldier and she did not think his return from

PLATE LXIV

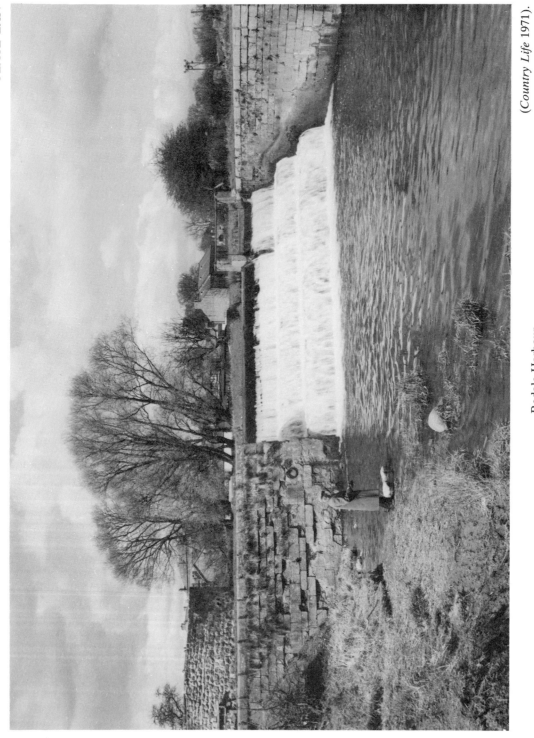

Bedale Harbour

(*Country Life* 1971).

the War of Independence warranted a salute from the cannons she kept for use on great occasions: (71)

> He was made pris'ner in the field,
> Fighting in a bad cause!
> The Americans would not yield
> To England's inforc'd laws!
>
> When he came home no cannon roar'd,
> As he'd unlucky been!
> To him it did no joy afford,
> Though he sav'd ev'ry limb.

Another set of cannons was to be found at the Rapers' house, the best one on the west side of the market place close to the Hall. They were firing them to salute George III's accession, but a ropemaker's apprentice, rashly running past on his way to dinner, was killed by a wad: (183)

> The cannon ceas'd, no more to roar,
> So long as Rapers liv'd!
> They laid them by with the old store,
> A many was not griev'd.

Hird describes a happy childhood in what must have been a very old-fashioned place: "When I was learning to walk I was bandaged about the head with a roller made of black silk and stuffed with wool, black ribband went across the head to each side and two strings tyed it fast to my head. My head thus secured, I was let go, my nurse behind me having hold of two long and broad strings which were sowed fast to my stays. Sometimes those strings were fastened to a sliding frame which was secured to the chamber joist. Thus secured I had my little walk, which I daresay was oft unpleasant" (11). He learned to read from the hornbook: "There I was taught the alphabet, in the hornbook which is now totally laid aside, but it was the most durable of all others. The back was made of a thin piece of board about the size of a common playing card. In the centre of one end was a short handle which the teacher held with his finger and thumb. The book contained the alphabet, small and great, the double letters, vowels, consonants and the Lord's prayer. The letters were secured from the fingers of the schollar by a transparent horn light such as is used in lanterns, which was laid over the print, and its edges was secured by tin or thin brass shreds, which was nailed fast to the board" (13).

Hird swam in the beck, larked about with other boys in the woods and as yet unenclosed commons, plagued his elders, earned an honest penny when the cry of "hey! boys hey!" went up for help in carrying leather on the eve of the leather fair (344), played around the graves in the churchyard adjacent to the school, but made the most of his education under the two excellent masters he described. When his apprenticeship as a shoemaker ended, he no doubt burned his "old wife" in effigy in one of the hilarious celebrations which traditionally marked this important stage in a man's life (352, 353). Ordinary as his life was, however, he had a strain of lyricism which sometimes emerges in charming descriptions of nature, and a truly antiquarian bent which made him store up both what he saw and what his elders told him of times past. We may well end by a long look back to a packhorse train: "At this time the roads were very bad and all that merchandise was convey'd upon Packhorses, which had a large wooden packsaddle, shelved before and behind so that the load could not go either backward or forward, beside, was fastened under the horse belly; the foremost horse had a large ball and tuft upon his head, likewise a quantity of Bells at his breast by which his approach was known, either on the road or upon his entrance into any Town. In June 1780, being then twelve years old, and at Brough in Westmoreland, I there had the pleasure of seeing a set of these Horses which I believe carried goods upon the Moor roads. The appearance of which I was much delighted. It is said of the Bell Horse that he suffers none of his train to pass by him on the road. They were attended by two men in case of accident" (3).

GENERAL INDEX

GENERAL INDEX

306